Programming Mobile
Objects with Java™

Jeff Nelson

Programming Mobile Objects with Java™

Jeff Nelson

WILEY COMPUTER PUBLISHING

John Wiley & Sons, Inc.
New York • Chichester • Weinheim • Brisbane • Singapore • Toronto

Publisher: Robert Ipsen
Editor: Theresa Hudson
Assistant Editor: Kathryn A. Malm
Managing Editor: Micheline Frederick
Text Design & Composition: Benchmark Productions, Inc.

Designations used by companies to distinguish their products are often claimed as trademarks. In all instances where John Wiley & Sons, Inc., is aware of a claim, the product names appear in initial capital or ALL CAPITAL LETTERS. Readers, however, should contact the appropriate companies for more complete information regarding trademarks and registration.

This book is printed on acid-free paper. ∞

This publication is designed to provide accurate and authoritative information in regard to the subject matter covered. It is sold with the understanding that the publisher is not engaged in professional services. If professional advice or other expert assistance is required, the services of a competent professional person should be sought.

Library of Congress Cataloging-in-Publication Data:
Nelson, Jeff, 1971–
    Programming mobile objects with Java / Jeff Nelson.
      p. cm.
    Includes index.
    "Wiley Computer Publishing."
    ISBN 0-471-25406-1 (pbk./CD-ROM : alk. paper)
    1. Object-oriented programming (Computer science)   2. Java
    (Computer programming language) I. Title.
QA76.64.N43 1999
005.13'3--dc21   98-50956
                                         CIP

Printed in the United States of America.
10 9 8 7 6 5 4 3 2 1

To my niece and nephew for reminding me that there's more to life than bits and bytes.

Author Biography

Jeff Nelson has developed Java software with mobile objects for the last three years and is currently working to draw attention to the importance of this new software development technology. He has worked in the field of distributed computing on the Internet since 1990. His articles on topics in object technology and distributed computing have appeared in several magazines. He holds a Masters Degree in Applied Mathematics and industry certifications from Sun, Microsoft, and IBM. He can be found on the Web at http://www.DistributedObjects.com and reached through email at jnelson@DistributedObjects.com.

Contents

Acknowledgements   xv

Introduction   xvii

Chapter 1   A Look at Distributed Objects   1
  What's an Object?   1
    Elements that Contain Meaning   2
    Encapsulation: Hiding Complexity   4
    Reusability   5
  Client/Server 101   6
    Packets   7
    The Limits to Object Interaction   9
  Distributed Object Computing   9
    Using Object Request Brokers   10
    Defining and Implementing an Interface   12
    Tower of Babel   14
  CORBA: Interoperability with a Capital "I"   14
    Standardized IDL   15
    Standardized API   15
    Stubs   16
    Object Adapters   17
    Skeletons   17
    Standardized Streams and Packets   19
    Hardware Independence   20
    Language Independence   20
  CORBA as an Object Bus   21
    Pluggable Software   22
  Limitations to CORBA   22
    Least Common Denominator   22
    Objects-By-Value   24
    No Mobile Code   24

Contents

Client-Side Installation 25
Broadcast 25
Broken Encapsulation 26
Components 27
Static Systems 27
What's Next 29

Chapter 2 Taxonomy of a Mobile Object **31**
Mobile Objects Defined 31
Ramifications 36
Object State 40
Class Loading 47
Object Identify 51
Security 53
Object Sharing 57
Concurrency 58
Mobile Objects Versus Mobile Agents 70
What's a Mobile Agent? 70
Building Agent Software 72
How Do Mobile Objects Differ? 75
What's Next 77

Chapter 3 Building Mobile Objects with Caffeine **79**
Caffeine 79
More on Stubs 81
More on Skeletons 83
Mobility Features 84
Mobile Components 88
The Argument for Components 89
Distributed Components 90
Mobile Objects Versus Mobile Components 92
JavaBeans 94
What's Next 107

Chapter 4 COM/DCOM and Java **109**
COM 109
Using COM In Java 110
Building COM with Java 119
DCOM 122
Using COM Components with DCOM 122
Feasibility of Mobile Objects with DCOM 125
Enhancements for COM 128
Transactions 128
Messaging 134
Security 136
What's Next 138

Chapter 5   Building Mobile Objects with Voyager   **139**
    What Does Agent-Enhanced Mean?   139
    Mobility Features   141
        State Preservation   143
        ClassLoading   144
        Security   148
        Object Identity   151
        Object Sharing   153
        Concurrency   154
        Other Goodies   156
    Mobile Objects for Mobs   158
        Using Spaces to Simultaneously Communicate
        with Groups of Objects   159
        The Problem   161
        Traditional Approaches   161
        Voting with Mobile Objects   165
    What's Next   188

Chapter 6   RMI   **189**
    Brief Introduction to RMI   189
    Building Distributed Applications with RMI   192
        Identify the Problem   192
        Choose the Objects   192
        Implement the Objects   196
        Write a Server   198
        Write a Client   201
        Run the Example   204
        Work through the Kinks   205
    RMI and Other Java Tools   206
        JavaSoft's JDK   206
        Symantec's Visual Cafe   207
        Borland's JBuilder   207
        Microsoft's Visual J++   207
    RMI and Web Browsers   209
        Netscape's Navigator   209
        Microsoft's Internet Explorer   209
    Developing Mobile Objects   210
        Mobility Features   211
        Building a Mobile Stream   214
        Implementing the Mobile Stream   214
    What's Next   215

Chapter 7   Dabbling in Groupware   **217**
    Looking at the Old Approach   217
        Saving Files   218
        Sharing Files   218

Executing Software   219
Collaboration with Mobile Objects   219
  Choosing What Should Be Mobile   220
  Choosing a Common Base Type   220
  Not Choosing a Common Base Type   221
Building Mobile Groupware with RMI   221
  Implementing the Root Interface   221
  A Generic Server   222
  A Generic Client   227
  Where Do Tasks Come From?   228
Implementing Tasks   231
  TrivialTask   231
  AppletTask   233
  SerializableAppletTask   236
Parallel Computing   241
What's Next   245

Chapter 8   Building the Dynamically Upgradable Text Editor   247
The Application   247
  Architecture   249
  Stumbling Blocks   259
  Supporting Mobile Objects?   260
Mobilizing the mpEDIT Application   263
So What Is the Big Deal?   291
  Adding the SendTo Action   291
What's Next   304

Chapter 9   Clustering   305
Fundamentals   306
  Failover   306
  Restarting   306
  Replication   307
What's Next   319

Chapter 10   Securing Mobile Objects   321
Risks   321
  Who Is at Risk   321
  What's at Stake   323
Technology   323
  Cryptography   323
  Trust Models   327
  Java   328
What's Next   341

Chapter 11   Trends in Mobile Objects   343
Protocol Interoperability   344
Implementation Interoperability   346

Object Web   348
Pass-By-Value   350
    Versioning   351
Object Groups   354
Replication   356
Messaging   357
Shippable Places   359
Sea of Objects   360
Ad hoc Collaboration   362
What's Next   362

Chapter 12   Overview of Design Patterns   **363**
What Are Design Patterns?   364
Using Patterns   366
Pattern Format   366
Why Mobility?   371
What's Next   372

Chapter 13   MVC [Krasner88]   **373**
Intent   373
Structure   374
Motivation   374
Applicability   375
Participants   375
Collaborations   376
Consequences   376
Implementation   377
Sample Code   378
Related Patterns   388

Chapter 14   Remote Proxy [GoF95]   **389**
Intent   389
Motivation   389
Applicability   390
Structure   391
Participants   391
Collaborations   392
Consequences   392
Implementation   393
Sample Code   394
Related Patterns   398

Chapter 15   Smart Proxy [Meszaros94]   **399**
Intent   399
Motivation   399
Applicability   400
Structure   401

Participants   401
Collaborations   401
Consequences   402
Implementation   402
Sample Code   403
Related Patterns   406

Chapter 16   Actor [GoF95]   **407**
Intent   407
Motivation   408
Applicability   408
Structure   409
Participants   409
Collaborations   409
Consequences   410
Implementation   410
Sample Code   411
Related Patterns   414

Chapter 17   Object Group [Maffeis 96]   **415**
Intent   415
Motivation   416
Applicability   416
Structure   417
Participants   417
Collaborations   417
Consequences   418
Implementation   419
Sample Code   420
Related Patterns   432

Chapter 18   Replication [Nelson98]   **433**
Intent   433
Motivation   434
Applicability   435
Structure   435
Participants   435
Collaborations   436
Consequences   436
Implementation   437
Sample Code   439
Related Patterns   446

Chapter 19   Command [GoF95]   **447**
Intent   447
Motivation   448
Applicability   448

Participants   448
Structure   449
Collaborations   450
Consequences   450
Implementation   451
Sample Code   453
Related Patterns   463

Chapter 20   Predicate [GoF95]   **465**
Intent   465
Motivation   465
Applicability   466
Structure   466
Participants   467
Collaborations   468
Consequences   468
Implementation   469
Sample Code   470
Related Patterns   478

Chapter 21   Composable Views [Krasner88]   **479**
Intent   479
Motivation   479
Applicability   481
Structure   482
Participants   482
Collaborations   483
Consequences   483
Implementation   484
Sample Code   485
Related Patterns   509

Chapter 22   Extension [Nelson98]   **511**
Intent   511
Motivation   511
Applicability   513
Structure   513
Participants   513
Collaborations   514
Consequences   514
Implementation   515
Sample Code   517
Related Patterns   523

Chapter 23   Smorgasbord [Mowbray97]   **525**
Intent   525
Motivation   525

Contents

Applicability   526
Participants   526
Structure   527
Collaborations   528
Consequences   528
Implementation   529
Sample Code   531
Related Patterns   538

Chapter 24   Interpreter [GoF95]   **539**
Intent   539
Motivation   540
Applicability   541
Structure   541
Participants   542
Collaborations   542
Consequences   542
Implementation   543
Sample Code   544
Related Patterns   560

Chapter 25   Federation [Nelson98]   **561**
Intent   561
Motivation   561
Applicability   562
Structure   563
Participants   563
Collaborations   563
Consequences   564
Implementation   565
Sample Code   572
Related Patterns   581

Bibliography   583

Appendix   What's On the CD-ROM?   585

Index   589

End User License Agreements   603

Acknowledgments

The concept of this book germinated back in 1995 while exploring visionary work by Hirano Satoshi in the development of a Java distributed object tool called HORB. Hirano had a vision for Java distributed objects that was far ahead of it's time.

Robert Orfali proved to be an excellent collaborator on our past projects and started me down the road to authorship. As the top writer in the field of distributed objects, I could not ask for a better mentor. I'd like to thank the reviewers of this book, Silvano Maffeis, Ronald Resnick, and Joseph C. Williams, for their valuable work looking over this book. Andreas Vogel and Keith Duddy have been valuable collaborators with me in our Java Report column, CorbaTalk. Finally, a big thanks to Christopher Stone for providing me with an opportunity to bounce ideas off him and the excellent staff of Novell's Java Technology Group. I am fortunate to have had the insight of these, some of the top minds in the field of distributed computing, during the creation of this book.

This book is not just the work of one author, but indirectly the work of thousands of software developers who have put together the powerful tools described in this book. I'd like to the brilliant folks at ObjectSpace for producing one-of-a-kind products of unparalleled quality like Voyager and the

Java Generic Library. VisiBroker was created as a result of the combined vision for a Java-based future of the people at Post Modern Computing, Visigenic, and Inprise. John Jensen gave us the wonderful mpEDIT text editor, which can only really be appreciated by a software developer who understands the concept of beauty in source code. John had the help of other voluntary contributors including John Johannsen, Artur Biesiadowski, and Steve Lawson.

I'd like to thank my management at DiaLogos Incorporated, Joseph C. Williams, Thomas Wagner, and Lydia Bennett, who were incredibly understanding during the creation of this book and tremendously flexible in the scheduling of my work on this book. I'd also like to thank my coworkers, Thomas Erdevig in particular, for fostering a working environment that encouraged innovation and excitement about the technology.

My editors at Wiley, Terri Hudson, Kathryn Malm, Gerrie Cho, and Sandra Bontemps, deserve a huge thanks for putting up with the sometimes difficult to work with author of this book. This project could not have been completed without their almost daily encouragement.

Finally, I'd like to thank my friends and family for providing tremendous encouragement to continue work on this project while at the same time they were asked to understand the sacrifices I had to make to finish this project: Jenny, Jessica, Jordan, Ardy, and Bob Nelson, Trevor Woodford, Heather Diaz, Kelly Asselin, Carol Webb, Seraphim Leemon, and Tanja Fitzgerald. I couldn't have completed this project without their support, and I am grateful for how they have all touched my life.

Introduction

This book explores an emerging new software development technology, *mobile objects*. This new technology goes well beyond simply facilitating communication, the role traditionally played by distributed objects. Mobile objects enable separate applications, even separate computers, to exchange objects at runtime. When an object moves, the state of the object made up by the value of it's member variables moves to a new computer, but that's not the whole story. Even the implementation code of objects, including graphical user interface, file and database access, network protocols, and other features that traditionally are completely static in applications, can be moved along with the object. This capability permits an incredible amount of flexibility that was never available until now.

Most applications have new capabilities added to them on a continuous basis. Mobile objects facilitate this. For example, a traditional word processing application is a static composition of hundreds or even thousands of different interacting objects. Using traditional approaches to software development, the word processor is written and delivered to the customer as one shrink-wrapped product. If additional functionality, such as email and Web capabilities, or bug fixes are to be added to the word processor, an updated copy of the shrink-wrapped application must be obtained and manually installed by the customer.

A mobile object approach to software development fundamentally changes all aspects of software development and delivery. The product is no longer a static collection of thousands of objects The objects initially in the program can be replaced, and new objects that implement new functionality, such as email and Web support, can be added over time. The objects may introduce new graphical user interfaces to the software application and even add entirely new windows. In addition, all of the replacements and upgrades of mobile objects are done behind the scenes, from servers running on the Internet or Web sites adapted for this purpose, requiring little user interaction. This means the days of manually installing software upgrades are over.

Once an application obtains a new object, the new object becomes part of the permanent running code of the application. The possibility of replacing objects in an application after the shipping date is a powerful capability. How many of us have wished we could tweak a few different details of our product after the delivery? With mobile objects, it's not only possible, it's easy.

Another common reason to upgrade software is to eliminate bugs in an old program. Bugs are generally the result of an unexpected, complex interaction of several objects in an application under rare circumstances. Bugs are hard to detect prior to shipping a software application due to the very complexity afforded when thousands of objects interact with each other. Bug fixes are often identified on a continuous basis after a product is shipped; however, the difficulty of distributing product upgrades to all customers and asking the customer to install revision after revision is a daunting task.

Mobile object software approaches can solve this problem by introducing replaceable objects. When a software vendor discovers that a bug exists in the program, the relevant objects can be immediately rewritten and instantly distributed to a testing group. The software testers have no need to manually upgrade the software; instead, the new objects can be incorporated into the software at runtime, replacing the buggy objects. Once suitable verification that the new objects eliminate the bug, the software developer broadcasts the new objects across the Internet, fixing thousands and potentially millions of buggy copies of the software.

In addition, mobile objects lend themselves to emerging technologies in software development, such as clustering and fault tolerance. When a mobile object can be broadcast arbitrarily to one of a thousand host computers, the possibility that even a large fraction of them might unexpectedly crash is inconsequential. The rest of the system can continue even after a large fraction of the hosts have crashed. Further, an individual application can effectively command each of these host computers to complete tasks concurrently, transforming a network of cheap personal computers into a powerful multiprocessing super computer. We'll see that using mobile objects, this is not only possible, it's easy.

Who Should Read This Book

The modern software organization is more than just a group of heads-down programmers developing spreadsheets and word processors. Today applications are developed by well-organized armies of decision makers, managers, technical architects, and developers. Decision makers must be aware of what kinds of software are possible and how it may be delivered. Managers must be aware of the tools available to perform a task and know roughly how long each task will take to accomplish. Technical architects must have broad awareness of many technologies and how they can work together efficiently. Developers must be able to use the tools effectively to build applications.

Participants in each role must have an understanding of the software development tools in order to successfully perform their role. Mobile objects has broad effects on what kind of software is possible, how it is delivered, and how quickly initial tasks may be completed before the product is ready for delivery. With this in mind, this book was written to benefit each type of reader.

How This Book is Organized

The early chapters of this book set the context and describe mobile objects at a high level for all types of readers. Next, this book examines how different technologies, such as CORBA, DCOM, and RMI, can be used to implement mobile objects, a concern of great importance mainly to architects and developers. Then, the book goes into more to consider a few coding examples that will mainly be of interest to developers. The book closes with a set of design patterns both for developing and managing the development of mobile object software projects.

Fundamentals of Mobile Objects.

The first part of this book explores the features of mobile objects as well as comparing mobile objects with traditional technologies, such as distributed objects. The tools with support for building mobile object software are examined in detail. Many different examples are included along with an analysis of how mobile objects impact some of the key issues for building robust software such as clustering and security.

> **Chapter 1: A Look At Distributed Objects.** Distributed objects are a powerful software development tool that solve many of the problems of writing distributed software. Distributed object tools automate and standardize many of the tasks which had to be done by hand. This chapter takes a look at distributed object

tools and the benefits they offer and answers the question about when to use distributed objects, when to use mobile objects, and when to use both.

Chapter 2: Taxonomy of a Mobile Object. Here we look at the concepts behind mobile objects and how they work. This chapter also describes what kind of tools are used to build mobile object software.

Chapter 3: Building Mobile Objects with Caffeine. This chapter introduces Visigenic's Caffeine tool, which provides everything required to make mobile objects software. This chapter serves as a quick introduction to how to use the tool to write software.

Chapter 4: COM/DCOM with Java. Microsoft's COM/DCOM architectures are perhaps the most well known development tools. This chapter looks at how COM/DCOM can be used to write mobile object software.

Chapter 5: Building Mobile Objects with Voyager. Voyager is one of the few tools which was designed to support mobile objects from the start. Voyager is one of the most advanced tools and has capabilities that Caffeine and RMI do not, such as multicasting requests to multiple objects and remotely constructing objects on remote hosts. This chapter briefly introduces these features and provides a quick tutorial on Voyager applications.

Chapter 6: RMI. This chapter introduces the Remote Method Invocation package of Java. RMI provides fair support for mobile objects and can be used to implement many of the examples in this book. This chapter rapidly covers the features of RMI and how it can be used to write mobile object software.

Chapter 7: Dabbling in Groupware. Next we look at a simple example of mobile objects, an application which initially does nothing more than display a "Panic" button. Since mobile objects are used to build the application, we then look at several interesting extensions to the original simple application.

Chapter 8: Building the Dynamically Upgradable Text Editor. Thus far, this book has referred to the ability to dynamically upgrade applications. At this point, an actual example can be written. This chapter examines how a text editor can be converted into an email reader using mobile object techniques, without installing new software.

Chapter 9: Clustering. Clustering is an interesting area of high performance computing in which many computers work cooperatively. Normally, this cooperation is an administrative nightmare since every system must be configured with all the software used for clustering. With mobile objects, the software can be dynamically delivered and used on demand. This makes it easy to actually delve into some powerful examples of clustering using only fairly simple mobile objects.

Chapter 10: Securing Mobile Objects. This chapter introduces some of the security problems to watch out for when dealing with mobile objects. Mobile objects have basically the same security vulnerabilities as Java applets in that software written by someone potentially intending to do harm is being loaded on to your system and run. Java's SecurityManager remains the best tool for protecting yourself.

Chapter 11: Trends in Mobile Objects. This chapter serves to more or less conclude the portions of the book not dedicated to design patterns. I chose to do this by introducing a few of the radical concepts that academic researchers are discussing for the future of this area. I think that developers will find them outright fascinating if not a little wild.

Design Patterns.

Design patterns are recipes that software developers can use to write software. The design pattern approach is an outgrowth of traditional architecture suggested by Christopher Alexander in the early 80s. He observed that veteran architects used many common structures to create a building that was both functional and pleasing to the occupant. Design patterns cover not just the successful design, but also the successful management of a project. Today software developers are re-examining his work in a new light, tackling the problem of codifying the design patterns that make successful software and successful software management.

Chapter 12: Overview of Design Patterns. This chapter introduces design patterns for the novice reader. The role of design patterns in the software development process is compared to the traditional design process. A standard, concise format is used to represent design patterns.

Chapter 13: MVC. This chapter looks at how to use the MVC pattern to Implement models, views, and controllers (hereafter referred to as components) as mobile objects that can be replaced and extended at runtime.

Chapter 14: Remote Proxy. Here, we look at how to use the Remote Proxy pattern to encapsulate the location of a target object inside a mobile object that delegates to the target object. This enables location and implementation transparency at runtime when the mobile object is dynamically loaded into a new address space.

Chapter 15: Smart Proxy. This chapter explores how to extend Remote Proxies to perform caching, load balancing, and local request processing in order to optimize the efficient use of system resources.

Chapter 16: Actor. Actor pattern encapsulates a thread within a mobile object and moves this thread with the object to enable the object to react to its environment without depending on other threads.

Chapter 17: Object Group. This chapter shows how the Object Group pattern defines a single abstraction around several objects that react to the same events or messages.

Chapter 18: Replication. This chapter explores how to implement fault tolerance and load balancing by cloning several copies of the same mobile object with the Replication pattern.

Chapter 19: Command. This chapter demonstrates how to build a mobile object representing a Command that can be sent to other nodes.

Chapter 20: Predicate. This chapter demonstrates how to use the Predicate pattern to perform a test on a remote node, define a mobile object representing the test, and send it to the appropriate destination for execution.

Chapter 21: Composable Views. This chapter shows how the composable views pattern implements the view for each object as a composite of many views of member objects implemented as mobile objects to enable reuse in disparate applications.

Chapter 22: Extension. This chapter shows how the Extension pattern is used to create a set of associated mobile objects that adds functionality to a mobile object, then distribute these mobile objects to appropriate hosts.

Chapter 23: Smorgasbord. Using the Smorgasbord pattern, this chapter shows how to provide a pick list of available mobile objects representing additional or optional capabilities that may be added to an application at runtime.

Chapter 24: Interpreter. This chapter shows how to use the Interpreter pattern to implement network protocols and other interpreters as mobile objects in order to dynamically replace and extend these at runtime.

Chapter 25: Federation. When a large task is too much for a single server, share the work across objects on multiple servers according to some mutual relationship between the servers. This chapter shows how the Federation pattern is used to do this.

The design patterns that address software development (as opposed to software project management) have been implemented in Java and are included on the enclosed CD.

What's On The CD-ROM

This book includes a CD-ROM that contains tons of great third-party software designed to make your exploration of mobile object more exciting.

Examples. Nearly every chapter in this book contains a substantial example to demonstrate the concepts under discussion. By running these examples, exploring their source code, and even modifying and extending them to suit your own needs, you will get much more out of this book.

Design Patterns. The second half of this book is dedicated to documenting some design patterns for mobile objects. Every single design pattern includes a running example of the design pattern implemented in Java. These examples can teach you how to implement the design patterns in source code.

Trial Edition of VisiBroker for Java, version 3.2. The leading Java distributed object tool also supports mobile objects. VisiBroker, a product of Inprise, is an implementation of the CORBA standard developed by the OMG. One of the VisiBroker tools, Caffeine, makes writing CORBA applications extremely easy and also has the essential support for mobile objects that is critical to it's use in this book. Many of the examples of this book are written with VisiBroker.

Voyager versions 1.01 and 2.0. An innovative pure Java distributed object product by the makers of the Java Generic Libraries. ObjectSpace continues to produce winners with this ORB toolkit. In addition to supporting mobile objects, Voyager has support for CORBA, transactions, and basic security.

JDK version 1.1.7. The Java Developer's Kit is the standard for Java development. In order to insure maximum interoperability across multiple platforms and development environments, the JDK was used to build all of the examples in this book. However, you can also import these examples into another development environment of your choice with ease.

BDK version 1.2. JavaBeans are the component standard for Java development. The Bean Developer's Kit, while not absolutely required to develop Beans, contains a useful set of examples and tools for testing your JavaBeans.

MpEDIT version 1.13. A great text editor put together by a group of software developers collaborating over the Internet. While mpEDIT has roughly the same functionality as Notepad, mpEDIT excels at the source code level. The elegant design of mpEDIT makes it an excellent starting point for use as an example of mobile objects in this book.

TogetherJ/Whiteboard Edition. TogetherJ is one of the leading object-oriented analysis and design tools with support for UML. Each of the design patterns used in this book are diagrammed with UML. Diagramming your work like this can help you organize your thoughts and spot elements of your design that you might otherwise miss without a formal design. This tool can help you create and analyze the designs of your own projects.

iBus Java Software Bus version 0.5. iBus is a unique toolkit from Softwired AG of Zurich for writing robust group-based distributed systems using objects. It may be an invaluable tool to you if you decide to further explore the use of object groups and replication in your own software.

Trial Edition of JBuilder 2. Inprise, the developer of one of the best development environments in the market, now owns one of the best Java ORBs. Both products come together in the latest version of JBuilder. The trial copy on this product can be used to run the examples throughout the book.

System Requirements

All of the examples in this book are written with pure Java, so all you need is the following system requirements to use these examples:

♦ Any computer with a JVM

♦ Any development environment that supports JDK 1.1 or better

♦ TCP/IP Networking

Sample Code

Many different examples are used throughout this book to demonstrate the powerful capabilities of mobile objects. All of these examples are available on the CD, ready for installation. You can import them into your favorite Java development environment in order to try them out. All the examples are written in pure Java using the Sun Microsystems' JDK 1.1, so you'll be able to use them in on any operating system or hardware that has a JVM!

Design Patterns

The design patterns described cover not just the development of mobile object software but also the management of the development process and software lifecycle. However, many of the design patterns can be implemented as source code. These are all provided for you on the CD. You are free to use them in any of your own software projects free of charge.

The Next Step

You've seen briefly how mobile objects will change the way you write and deploy software. They permit deployed applications to be extended without manual upgrade, facilitate the creation of fault tolerant applications, and leverage the power of computer networks into multiprocessing computers.

Now you are ready to begin exploring how you can use mobile objects in your own projects. In the next chapter, we'll examine the basic of how distributed object technology differs from mobile object technology.

A Look at
Distributed Objects

The last five years have seen a spectacular push toward object software due to the benefits of long-term productivity and software reuse. Most software development has transitioned into the use of object-oriented programming languages such as C++ and Java. Traditional, non-object-oriented programming languages like COBOL have been redesigned to support objects. Some of the older, traditional programming languages now claim to support objects even if they don't. Some calculators even claim to support an "object-based" programming language.

Distributed objects, or objects that are used across computer networks, are a natural outgrowth of these new object software projects. Software developers that employ distributed objects enjoy many benefits of compatibility but also suffer from some of the same limitations found in traditional software development.

Isaac Newton once said that he was successful because he "stood on the shoulders of giants." Before diving into a discussion of how to build software with mobile objects, let's take a look at some of the giants that led up to this new technology by examining the principles of object software and the capabilities and limitations of related distributed technology.

What's an Object?

To the uninitiated, the term *object* may seem a little out of place in software development. In the real world, almost any physical thing is an object. This book is an object. Every other book in the bookstore is also an object. The bookstore itself can be viewed as an object, albeit a very large one.

In addition, each object has a certain set of properties that describe it. For a book, these properties include size, shape, color, price, number of pages, and whether or not a CD-ROM is enclosed.

How do you interact with these physical objects? You can buy a book from a bookstore. The bookstore then removes the book from its inventory and orders another copy. You read the book. Perhaps, if you are feeling particularly offended by the idea of mobile objects, you burn the book. You perform actions on many objects throughout the course of a day.

Software objects are the same as physical objects. An application developed with an object-oriented programming language is composed of many different software objects that interact with each other. Often, software objects are little more than placeholders for physical objects. For example, if you develop an information system to track inventory in a bookstore, you would probably program software objects that represent both a book and a bookstore. The actions you perform on these software objects include many of the same actions you perform on the physical objects, such as purchasing the book, ordering more books from the distributor, and tracking the inventory of your books. In software lingo, these actions that are applied to an object are often called *methods*.

Traditional software development differs substantially from this object-oriented approach to software development. Until about 10 years ago, most computer software was written as a list of mathematical commands. The software developer first considered the problem and then phrased it in such a way that each step in the problem was represented as a small, mathematical function. All of these functions were grouped into lists called *procedures*. Popular languages that use such an approach include FORTRAN, BASIC, and C. Objects represent a significant breakthrough over the traditional, software-development approach. Software objects have several desirable elements. Software objects contain meaning, have the ability to encapsulate details, and are reusable. Let's look at these properties in more detail.

Elements that Contain Meaning

Software objects are *meaningful* elements of a problem. Different from variables and functions, software objects provide a higher level of abstraction. Bookstore software may be broken down into books and customers rather than ones and zeros. As previously mentioned, a software object may be simply a placeholder for a physical object.

The value derived from writing software with meaningful elements cannot be understated. End users demand software that makes their lives easier by solving increasingly complex problems. As a result, software applications themselves are becoming increasingly complex and expensive to develop. Today's software applications are usually developed by large, well-organized teams with hundreds or thousands of people. Each team member is responsible for completing a portion of the application and then preparing this piece of the application for integration with the rest of the project. The task of integrating the work of hundreds of team members is often daunting. In order to complete an assigned task accurately, a team member must understand how to properly use the work of many other team members.

Traditional software applications are implemented as a list of variables—any piece of data, such as number or a name—and operations. Variables may or may not have meaningful names. Some traditional programmers who pride themselves on writing source code that is compact and yet virtually impossible to read may choose names such as "t," "p," and "index." More careful developers choose names such as "tax," "title," and "price." However, a software developer who attempts to reuse this software must often read the source code line by line in order to understand the meaning of each variable. Even a variable that at first glance appears to be relatively well named, such as "price," may not be precise enough. For example, does "price" refer to the unit price of a book or the entire price of a sale? Is it the price before taxes? Was a discount already determined? Is the price represented as the number of cents or as a decimal value of dollars? The software developer must spend some time to determine the variable's precise meaning by examining the source code of the original developer.

Other programming methodologies call for the use of prefixes in variable names to identify their data type. Rather than naming a variable "title," these methodologies name the variable "strTitle." Although these additional notations make it easier to determine what a variable means, they do make variable name a little harder to read.

To complicate the problem of determining the meaning of a variable further is that variables that describe similar concepts may not be grouped. For example, the title, name, and discount for an individual book may be located in entirely different parts of a program. The title may be listed as part of the inventory. The price may be found in a separate operation for purchasing. Any applicable discounts may very well be applied as a separate step. Thus, writing new software that integrates this hypothetical bookstore purchasing software requires a detailed examination of many different portions of the program.

Compounding the problem, the operations in a program may be equally meaningless. Operations are simply lists of actions performed on the variables.
Operations can have meaningless names and be placed anywhere in a program.
Often, programs are divided into separate files. The software developer is free to
decide how to place operations in each file. When a particular operation is used in
a program, the developer who tries to understand the code is faced with the problem of locating the operation that may be in any one of many different files.

Software objects greatly simplify the problem of understanding other people's
software by grouping variables and operations in a meaningful way. An implementation of the bookstore software that uses objects would have a book object with
properties such as "title," "price," and "discount." Since the properties are for the
book object, the developer knows immediately that the "price" property is the price
for this individual book. The other properties related to the book are located in
exactly the same place. In addition, the operations for the book are also found in
the same location. Since software objects often correspond closely to physical
objects, developers can usually understand what an object means in the context of
the real world. Your past experience with books helps you understand the meaning
of a program about books.

Encapsulation: Hiding Complexity

Although objects are more meaningful than the traditional approach to software
development, the modern application is so complex that a developer who attempts
to reuse code still has to understand the meaning for potentially hundreds of different objects. The properties and methods available on an object may not relate to
the many other properties and methods that exist on an object. For example, the
customer purchasing a book doesn't want to know how the bookstore tracks inventory, maintains its ledgers, or works with distributors. Each of these details is essential to the transaction, but the customer doesn't need that level of detail when
conducting the purchase. Imagine how annoyed you would be if you walked into a
bookstore to purchase a book and the cashier asked you to name the distributor of
the book. You don't care; you just want to buy the book.

The same can be said of a developer working with a software object. The Book
object may hide many of the internal details of how a book purchase is conducted.
A software developer who writes software to purchase a book can simply invoke
the purchase method without spending a great deal of time understanding what
goes on under the covers. Often, developers accomplish this hiding by indicating

that certain properties and methods on an object are private and should not be available to anyone. For example, the information about the distributor of a book might be considered private in a bookstore program. The Book object provides an abstraction that allows books to be purchased without requiring the purchaser to understand what happens with distributors and inventory systems. The details of the software object are all *encapsulated* in one little bundle, and the complexity is hidden from view.

Hiding is perhaps too strong a term here. Hiding has an unfortunate connotation of malevolent concealment. Here, hiding complexity simply means that software objects make sense at first glance, without the need for users to examine their guts. That doesn't necessarily mean that the guts themselves are not available for examination. Sometimes, though not very often, teams of software developers do share their code for informational purposes.

Reusability

Objects encourage code *reuse* in several ways. First, as we've already discussed, objects are generally meaningful and hide much of the complexity of a problem. A software developer has an easier time learning how to use an object than a traditional piece of code. Thus, software developers considering the options of reusing software written by another developer or implementing their own software to perform the same task are more often inclined to reuse the existing objects.

Furthermore, because all the properties and methods of an object are grouped, the task of reusing an object is easier to tackle. This re-use helps in both the task of understanding the object and the task of copying the object into other programs.

Object-oriented programming languages have two special types of reuse: inheritance and polymorphism.

Inheritance

Physical objects often have similar characteristics. For example, a bookstore object may contain several types of books, all of which have basically the same properties, such as "title," and methods, such as "purchase."

However, some books may be special. For example, some books in the store may be priced differently depending on the day or whether a coupon is presented at the time of purchase. All books may have certain common properties and methods, but some books may have a set of individual properties and methods.

In this case, a relationship called *inheritance* may be established. Inheritance between software objects works in much the same way as inheritance does in bloodlines. In software objects, a child object has the same characteristics as its parent objects. If a parent object has a certain property, the child object also has that property.

Through the establishment of an inheritance tree, different objects can share common properties and methods with other objects. In the case of the hypothetical bookstore, a Book object that contains the common properties and methods of "title" and "price" is created. Then a new DiscountedBook object is created that adds more properties and methods for those books that are discounted under certain circumstances.

Polymorphism

Don't let the word polymorphism intimidate you. *Polymorphism* is a difficult term that has a very simple meaning. Suppose a parent object, called Book, has two child objects DiscountedBook and TwoForOneBook, and each child has a slightly different purchase method. The DiscountedBook applies a certain discount during the purchase, and the TwoForOneBook determines when some of the books are free.

The developer who uses the purchase method doesn't want to know about the details of how the two children differ from each other. The developer wants to simply purchase a book no matter what sort of child it happens to be, letting the child object itself determine what is appropriate inside its own purchase method. *Polymorphism* is the name for this capability. Through polymorphism, the developer can use the methods on different child objects without concern for exactly how the child objects differ from each other. Thus, in our example, the developer has to understand only that a purchase method exists on every Book object without knowing all the actions that different child objects take in order to perform the method.

Client/Server 101

Companies are joining the Internet as fast as you can say "DNS." In addition, every company wants to adapt its software for use on the Internet. This move to the Internet is only natural. However, adapting software to run over the Internet is not as easy as you may think. It's not a simple matter of giving your customer a copy of the software you already developed for in-house use. Customers have a variety of systems to choose from—Windows 3.1, Windows95, Windows NT, Macintosh, and many flavors of Unix. It's highly unlikely that all of your customers will use the same system. If your software works on only Windows95, you'll lose a segment of the market. The solution is Java. Its Virtual Machine model allows software to run on any system in the world with only a little care during the software development process.

A second consideration is ease of use. You won't have access to your customers for training purposes, so your automated point-of-sale system used directly by the customer must be extremely easy to use and directed only at the task of selling your products and services. Your software may need to be rewritten before it's appropriate for customers. If you used object principles to write your software, restructuring to support customers is probably not an insurmountable task.

Finally, you need to make the software you give to the customer communicate with your information systems to track sales, accounts, shipping, and billing. The exchange of packets is a way to make these two software applications communicate.

Packets

Traditional technologies for communicating between different software applications require a great deal of effort by the software developer and are often error prone. Applications communicate with each other by sending sets of raw data back and forth between different computers. When two computers communicate in this matter, the application that requests a certain service is called the *client*. The application that provides that service is called a *server*. *Packets* are the sets of raw data that both the client and the server understand.

In order for an object in a client to utilize an object in a server using the traditional methods of software communication, the client must be able to convert the request into a chunk of raw data and send this data as a packet. The client must include identifying information about the object in the server that is the target, the method on the object that is used, and all the parameters for the method. Note that because all the parameters must be communicated to the server, the software developer has to be able to convert each and every type of the parameters into raw data for storage inside a packet. This process is called *externalization*; all the internals of the objects are written out to raw data as shown in Figure 1.1.

The task of implementing a server to accept these kinds of network requests and pass them on to objects is not simple. Server-receiving requests from clients must be capable of interpreting all the data that is received in order to invoke the right method on the target object. The software developer must write all the code

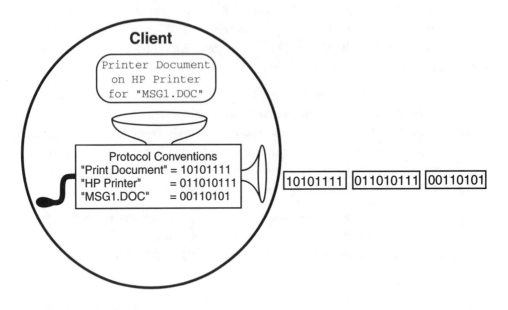

Figure 1.1 Client to 110011.

required to make the server read whatever the client wrote, including all the variables in the parameter list. (See Figure 1.2.)

This situation is analogous to a company tracking information about customer accounts by writing down a straight list of numbers on a piece of paper for each customer. For example, the sales force carefully creates this list of numbers based on a table for how to convert the customer information into this list of numbers. Then, billing translates this list of numbers back into customer information using a similar table.

This approach requires agreement by both the client and the server about the content of packets. If the two parties lose their synchronization by even a single byte of data, they cannot communicate. Obviously, this requires a great deal of care by the software developer to confirm that the client and server correctly interpret the data sent between them. Much of the content of the communication between them is dedicated to maintaining this synchronization by communicating values such as the length, order, and checksum of packets. These values are provided from the software developer. The task of using packets can make up a large fraction of the code for an application.

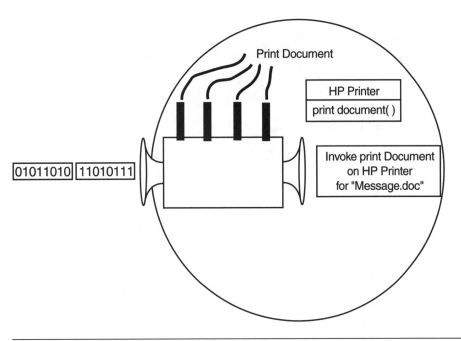

Figure 1.2 110011 to server.

The Limits to Object Interaction

Objects interact with each other, often by initiating an action on another object. As in the physical world when you purchase a book, you (a Person object) are causing a purchase action to occur on a particular Book object. This interaction of objects is commonplace and is the basis for object software. The shortcoming occurs when two objects in different applications need to interact. One object cannot cause an action on another object unless both objects are in the same application. The software developer can make an action on an object in a different application happen manually by communicating between the different applications. In traditional software this requires the use of packets, as shown in Figure 1.3.

Distributed Object Computing

Bridging the gap between objects in different programs is a technology called *distributed object computing*. Distributed object computing enables objects in different applications to access each other. Objects themselves can act as servers on a net-

Programming Mobile Objects with Java

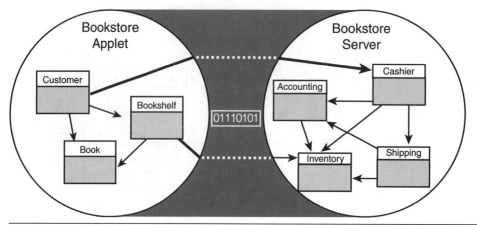

Figure 1.3 Objects in separate processes.

work, responding to requests by invoking methods in the same way that Web servers respond to requests by serving up Web pages. Distributed object computing makes certain key observations about how objects and their actions—methods— relate to streams and packets.

The first observation is that each object can itself act as an entity to communicate on a network, as seen in Figure 1.4. The object is viewed as something that independently listens on the network, even the Internet, for information that is sent to it.

Second, when two entities on a computer network interact, it's generally to perform some action, analogous to the actions on an object, as shown in Figure 1.5. These actions may be as trivial as an exchange of information, but they are actions nonetheless.

These two key observations facilitate distributed object technology because they provide a way for any object in a program to effectively communicate on a computer network and act upon the information that is sent to it.

Using Object Request Brokers

The tools that allow objects to communicate on a computer network are called *object request brokers (ORBs)*. The word broker comes from the fact that these tools perform a service on behalf of objects to facilitate their communication with other objects on the computer network. Objects communicate with other objects by sending requests and getting back some response, thus the name object request broker.

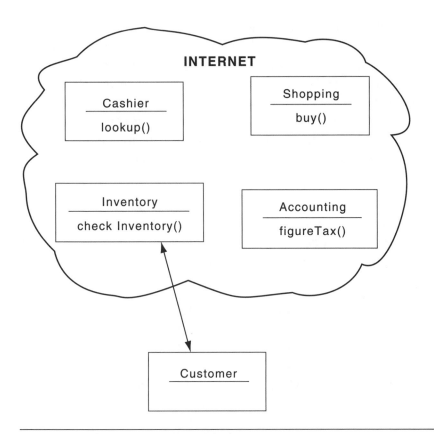

Figure 1.4 Objects on a network.

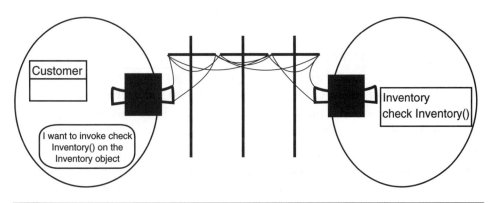

Figure 1.5 Object invocations to 100110.

Developing for ORBs is much easier than using packets and streams. For instance, an old project, developed over the Internet by a team of several people, required nearly 10,000 lines of source code to work with the packets and streams in the application. This is not uncommon. Because the Internet itself is so unpredictable, software that communicates over it must anticipate many of the possible problems and deal with them. For example, on the Internet, a network connection may unexpectedly stall or even break. When this happens, a well-built Internet application uses several different techniques for proactively trying to restore the connection.

Amazing as it sounds, rewriting the original project would take only about 400 lines of source code developed through use of an ORB toolkit and require less than four hours for one person to develop, as opposed to several weeks for a team of three people. The deliverable program would also be more reliable than the original application because the vendors of the ORB toolkit would have built-in solutions to several unanticipated problems, such as computer crashing.

Defining and Implementing an Interface

The first step for making an object communicate using an ORB is to create an interface for that object. An interface in an ORB is similar to an interface in Java—the interface defines what actions the object is capable of performing. For example, if a Book object has a purchase method, the interface for the Book object will have this purchase method.

An interface is a sort of contract between the object and anyone that communicates with it. Since the interface to the Book object has a purchase method, the Book object essentially promises to anyone communicating with it that the Book object knows how to perform the purchase action.

One rule of object-oriented software development is that each object has an interface, whether it is written in C++ or Java. This interface is used by the ORB to allow interaction between objects written in different languages. From a technical perspective, interfaces are defined in different ORBs that use a separate language called *Interface Definition Language (IDL)*. Even if an object were itself implemented in a language like C++, a separate file containing IDL must be created to define the interface for each object. This sounds much harder than it really is. IDL is an extremely simple language that usually requires only a few minutes to create for an entire project. Even an extensive project generally has fairly simple IDL.

N O T E : Modern ORB tools have come a long way. It's now possible to use ORBs in most languages without ever writing IDL for each object. For example, Borland's JBuilder Client/Server "reverse compiles" Java objects into IDL. IBM's VisualAge products allow C++ developers to define a CORBA interface by adding special keywords, called pragmas, into the C++ source code.

"Implementing an interface" is common object-oriented lingo. It just means that you create an object that contains the methods and properties declared in the interface. For example, if a Book object with a purchase method had already been created, a developer implementing the interface would need to write an object with a purchase method. Other programs that need to purchase a Book object can perform this operation through the interface.

The ORB uses the information in the interface to establish the methods supported by a particular object. This information is used to determine what packets the object can and cannot receive on the computer network. The ORB actually handles all of these concerns under the covers. The software developer doesn't need to ever touch packets or streams when using an ORB. Because the software developer doesn't need to use packets and streams, the encapsulation of the objects doesn't have to be broken apart in order to communicate all the data in each object. The details of the packets and streams are themselves encapsulated within the ORB, so any changes to the networking software that might be required for switching between network architectures or hardware platforms is isolated from the program. The object request broker completely automates the interaction of objects, even if they are not located in the same program.

Since the ORB takes care of all the details of communication, it is possible to write object-oriented software that employs a mixture of local and remote objects. The usage of the remote objects in source code appears identical to that of local objects, but the remote objects may actually be located across the computer network, inside of a server perhaps. Distributed object professionals call this *location transparency*. Location transparency is one of the main benefits of an ORB, permitting an application to use objects that might be located in vastly different places on a computer network without real concern about their location.

Tower of Babel

By the late 1980s, several ORB tools had surfaced from vendors including Sun Microsystems, Digital, and IBM. These ORBs were developed with virtually no consultation among vendors and were incompatible. Each ORB had its own interface definition language (IDL) syntax that slightly differed from those of the others. While most ORBs used an IDL that was fairly similar to the others, some ORBs didn't use IDL at all. Instead, these ORBs relied on the software developer to use a special API within the source code of a program to define the interface. The result of all of these different approaches and syntaxes for IDL was that an interface created for an ORB written by one vendor could not be shared without substantial redevelopment.

Each ORB also had its own unique programming API. The result of these API differences was that software moving from one ORB vendor to another ORB vendor had to be slightly rewritten. With some amount of forward planning, the cost of this rewriting was minimized, but software developers under the pressure of deadlines may be reticent to perform this amount of preparation for future possibilities. As a result, a user of a particular ORB quickly became married to that ORB vendor by the expanding base of code developed exclusively for that vendor's product.

Worst of all, each ORB defined a slightly different way to translate packets on a computer network to actions on the objects in a program. In computer lingo, each product defined its own network protocol, and none of the products worked with other protocols. This means that in order for two objects to communicate, they must be designed and built with an ORB from the same vendor. If your business writes its software with one ORB and your supplier writes its software with another ORB, you cannot communicate with each other.

CORBA: Interoperability with a Capital "I"

CORBA (common object request broker architecture) came on the scene with the goal of changing the problems caused by incompatibility. It represents a common standard that allows ORBs to interoperate. The standardization of CORBA was so important that a standards body was formed by ORB vendors to create and manage the emerging CORBA standard. This standards body, the Object Management Group (OMG), has been one of the great successes in the open standards community, with more than 700 companies as members.

Standardized IDL

The first goal of CORBA was to provide a standard IDL syntax. This allowed an object developed with one ORB to interact with an object developed with another ORB simply by copying an IDL file from one computer to another. The CORBA standard frees the developer from the need to rewrite vendor-specific IDLs. CORBA IDL specifies what operations and properties are available on a particular distributed object. It is not tied to any specific programming language or development environment. CORBA IDL doesn't use C++ or Java-specific data types, but it defines its own small set of basic data types, like short, long, float, and double. Other CORBA IDL constructs, such as the syntax for declaring an interface, are also slightly different from the constructs of other programming languages, though CORBA IDL may have more similarities with than differences from a Java interface.

Any language can work with CORBA IDL by providing a suitable mapping between its own constructs and the CORBA IDL constructs. Some of the existing CORBA language mappings are shown in Listing 1.1. When each of these languages is mapped to CORBA, client and server applications can be written in entirely different languages without additional effort on the part of the developer. CORBA can be used as a powerful tool for integrating different languages in a manner similar to JNI's integration of Java and C. A small sample of CORBA IDL is shown below.

```
module com {
  module javasoft {
    interface DancingDuke {
      void dance();
    };
  };
};
```

Listing 1.1 CORBA IDL compiles into many languages.

Standardized API

The second goal of the CORBA standard was to propose a standard API for most of the tasks that are performed by an ORB, such as initializing ORB, invoking methods on remote objects, and mapping data types between programming languages. In the initial CORBA specifications, only a portion of the API was standardized. After several revisions of the standard, CORBA has come to include the entire API.

By standardizing the API, the source code for applications written with one ORB are moved to another ORB without change. Vendors of development tools and libraries also have an easier time supporting many different CORBA products because they all use the same API. In practice, minor differences in how the ORB vendors interpreted the standard still require that minor source code changes occur, but these differences in interpretation will eventually be worked out.

Stubs

One of the goals of distributed object software, including tools that conform to the CORBA standard, is to make distributed object use as simple and transparent as possible. When a method is invoked on a distributed object, these tools strive to make them as simple as when a method is invoked on a local object. From the perspective of a client, whether the object is local or distributed should not be important.

However, in the real world of object-oriented programming languages, only local objects—those that are part of the local address space and referred to by some local reference or pointer—can be the target of a method invocation. In order for the distributed object to, first, exist only in a remote address space and, second, provide the illusion that the object is invoked like a local object, a new object must take the place of the distributed object in the local address space. This new object should support all the methods that the remote object supports, providing the illusion that these methods on the remote object can be invoked locally. In practice, IDL is used to specify exactly which methods are available on the remote object. Often, not every method is available for remote invocation.

This new object that provides the illusion that the remote object may be invoked within the local address space is called a *stub*. The stub is essentially an object written in the target programming language and residing in the address space of the client. In practice, the distributed object toolkit automatically generates the stub by compiling the IDL file. The stub accepts invocations on the methods defined in the IDL and forwards these requests to the remote object. The stub accomplishes this task by performing many of the tasks regular objects cannot. Since the stub is automatically generated, software developers do not have to worry about completing these tasks themselves!

CORBA loosely standardizes what each ORB should place in the stubs and what API should be exposed to the CORBA developer for manipulating the stubs. In this way, stubs generated with one CORBA product are at least loosely compatible with other CORBA products.

Object Adapters

A distributed object tool, including those that conform with the CORBA standard, must have some way of exposing the objects that are remotely accessible to the rest of the network. Since the object will be receiving requests that originated in other address spaces, some mechanism must also be devised for providing a universal address for the object. Not all objects should be available for remote invocation, even in a server that is built with distributed object tools, so some registration must be performed for objects that are remotely accessible. The tool that performs these tasks is called an *object adapter.*

The earliest versions of the CORBA standard specified the API for the Basic Object Adapter (BOA), which all CORBA products must implement in order to be CORBA compatible. The API requirements of BOA included operations to register and unregister objects as available for remote invocation as well as other operations required for the housekeeping operations of exposing an object as a target for remote invocation.

However, BOA was specified very loosely in these early versions of CORBA, perhaps to simplify the task of making the existing distributed object products CORBA compatible. Several portions of the BOA specification were represented only as empty interfaces, such as the InterfaceDef object. For these objects, the vendors of different CORBA products were free to use their own discretion in determining how to implement these objects without regard to what any other vendor might use in their own product. Many software developers will immediately recognize the poor value of such a loose specification. In the time since the original specification of BOA was released, the vendors and consumers of CORBA have come to the same conclusion.

In order to solve the lack of specification for BOA, a new object adapter standard called Portable Object Adapter (POA) was recently adopted into the CORBA standard. POA is specified in a much tighter manner. At the time of this writing, the specification is so new that it is unclear whether it will successfully accomplish its goal of providing source code portability between different CORBA products.

Skeletons

Software developers who create servers face the challenges of designing these servers to accept requests from across the network and to invoke the appropriate methods. Network communication is always through the exchange of raw data, in the form of an array of bytes or packets between the client and server applications. The stub in the client is designed to write the request out as a packet and send the packet to the server. The work is just starting for the server; it has to read this packet and invoke the appropriate request.

In order to free the software developer from having to manually read the packet and invoke the method, some code is automatically generated for the server for converting the raw data into an actual method invocation. This code, called a *skeleton*, acts as part of a framework for invoking the remote object. As long as the developer of the server application associates the objects that are available for remote invocation with a skeleton, the skeleton can interpret the raw data and invoke the appropriate methods automatically. In CORBA, several different methods, such as inheritance, are available for accomplishing this association. The skeleton in this case may be a common base class from which the distributed object inherits as shown in Figure 1.6.

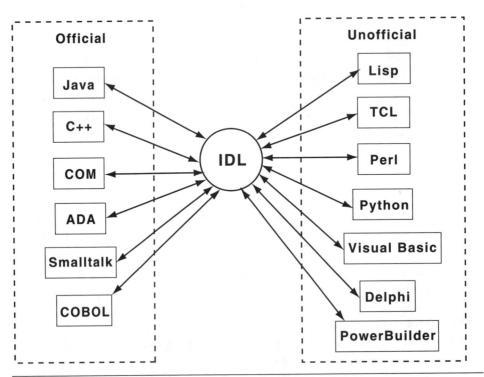

Figure 1.6 Object adapters, stubs, and skeletons.

Standardized Streams and Packets

The final key to offering complete interoperability of different ORB products is the standardization of the way ORBs translate actions on the object into packets on the computer network. The CORBA standard defines down to the bits and bytes exactly how this should look. Thus, any software that conforms to this standard can communicate with any other software product that conforms to the standard. In fact, two applications that communicate across the wires of a computer network aren't even aware of what ORB vendor was used to create the software on the other end of the wire.

Common Packet Format

Distributed objects tools that are not CORBA compliant utilize disparate packet formats. When the client and server are built with different distributed object tools, one tool must agree with the other on the packet format, or they cannot communicate with each other. Traditionally, distributed object tools used different packet formats and therefore could not communicate. CORBA changed this problem by providing a common standard for packet format, called General Interoperable Protocol (GIOP).

GIOP is not a protocol like TCP/IP. GIOP is just a standard format for packets. GIOP defines this standard format, and protocols using CORBA employ this standard format.

Common Protocol

Packets are exchanged on computer networks in many different ways, depending on network hardware, operating system, and other factors. When two software applications communicate with each other, they must agree on a common protocol with which to communicate. Some of the most common protocols include TCP/IP, UDP/IP, IPX, and NETBEUI, but many other protocols are available.

The Internet is a massive network of computers supporting both TCP/IP and UDP/IP. The growth of the Internet has propelled these protocols to the forefront. Any software that communicates using the TCP/IP protocol can access millions of other computers over the Internet.

CORBA takes advantage of this access by standardizing the way TCP/IP is used to communicate between clients and servers, called Internet Interoperable Protocol (IIOP). Standardizing TCP/IP as a common protocol facilitates the use of existing

TCP/IP tools, such as firewalls, routers, network hardware, and operating system drivers to support CORBA.

Hardware Independence

Another benefit to creating a rigid standard for ORBs' intercommunication is that different hardware platforms can now communicate without difficulty. Normally, when different hardware systems try to communicate, several problems occur related to how variables are represented on one computer as opposed to on the other computer.

One example of this type of difference is byte ordering. Each hardware platform chooses a particular ordering for its bytes, called upper endian or lower endian. The difference has to do with the simple convention for what order bits are written for variables that have more than 8 bits. It's difficult to justify one way or the other which should be the standard, thus different chip manufacturers choose different orderings. In particular, in this age of Unix-based Web servers and PC clients, the largest problem is that Unix machines are little endian while personal computers are big endian.

Historically, software developers worked around this problem by taking precautions of their own, such as manipulating the bits in the data to provide a specific byte ordering. Such bit manipulation software is necessarily not easy to implement or relevant to the problem a specific program is solving. However, the CORBA standard eliminates the need for even this much concern. By defining a rigid standard for representing variables by bits, different hardware platforms will no longer be unable to communicate with hardware that has a different byte ordering. As a result, software developers don't need to be concerned about writing special software to deal with the byte ordering issues on hardware platforms. Instead, the software can be written once for all hardware platforms with the guarantee that the ORB will solve byte ordering problems.

Language Independence

Software developers employ many programming languages in order to develop distributed objects. One company might employ C++ while another employs Java. Occasionally, different groups within the same company may be required to support different languages, such as legacy Visual Basic or COBOL software. CORBA attempts to address the needs of all of these groups by defining a separate standard for CORBA development in each programming language.

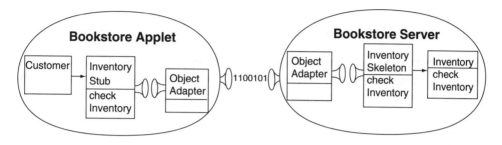

Figure 1.7 Java client, C++ server.

Indicating how CORBA constructs are mapped into language constructs is called *language mapping*. An example is a standard that addresses how exception handling in CORBA is mapped to languages that may not support the object-oriented exception handling familiar to many Java developers. Another important point addressed by these language mappings is how data types in different languages are converted from one to the other and the standard CORBA data types. For example, language mapping would create a standard for the way a 32-bit unsigned integer in C++ is converted into a 32-bit unsigned integer in Java (see Figure 1.7). The details of programming distributed objects using CORBA in different languages is beyond the scope of this book. These topics are covered well in books such as *Client/Server Programming with Java and CORBA*, 2E by Robert Orfali and Dan Harkey (Wiley, 1998) and *CORBA: Fundamentals and Programming* by Jon Siegel (Wiley, 1996).

IDL specifies the interface of each object in a language-neutral way. The interface may then be implemented in a server written in any programming language with a CORBA language mapping.

One of the benefits of language independence is that the client may be written in a different programming language and still use the remote object. The client and server communicate using a network protocol, so the programming languages used by client and server don't have to match.

CORBA as an Object Bus

Bus architectures are popular in digital hardware. Nearly any digital device you purchase, whether it's a computer or a Walkman, has a bus. The *bus* may be thought of as a computer network entirely enclosed within a single electronic device. The components of the device communicate with each other over this internal computer network.

Hardware busses follow standards just as software follows standards. The hardware bus serves as a common communication standard used by the components of a digital system to communicate with each other. A manufacturer of components for digital systems has to be sure only that the component plugs into the appropriate bus to know that the component can be used with the rest of the system.

Pluggable Software

Past software has lacked such a bus architecture. Whenever two software systems worked with each other, a proprietary protocol or API was developed to connect the individual pieces of software. All the major Internet software packages are examples of this approach. Web, e-mail, ftp, and news services all use specific protocols that are not compatible with each other. You cannot send e-mail through ftp or use news to browse the Web. Software systems have not been able to plug together in any useful way. Rather, when two software systems had to work together, often one system or the other had to be completely rewritten. For example, adding e-mail support to a Web browser requires the expensive development of what amounts to a complete e-mail program inside the Web browser.

By creating a standard in which objects can communicate with other objects, independent of concerns about hardware, programming language, vendor, and location, the CORBA standard still serves as the best bus architecture available in the software industry. When two applications use CORBA objects, they interoperate simply by exchanging IDL files. At that point, applications can immediately share objects.

Limitations to CORBA

No software is the magic solution to all problems. Distributed object software is no different. CORBA provides almost magical interoperability where there was none, but it does so by making certain assumptions about the underlying technologies.

Least Common Denominator

Many experts would quickly point out that CORBA can provide only a least-common-denominator solution to distributed objects in different programming languages. They argue that since CORBA works with many different programming languages, including Java, C, C++, COBOL, ADA, and Smalltalk, CORBA can have only the minimal toolset common to these widely different languages. They would point out features such as the lack of garbage collection in C++, the inability to serialize objects in COBOL, and the primitive meta-class support in Java as examples of features that cannot possibly be found in a least-common-denominator solution such as CORBA. Because CORBA must work in all of these languages, it cannot provide all the best features of every language, such as garbage collection, serialization, and meta-class capabilities. Instead, it must aim at a limited subset present in every language.

It is not wise to rush to judgment on this accusation. CORBA has successfully provided powerful capabilities in every language in which it is implemented. As the OMG experts consider how to work with CORBA in any particular language, they consider how the features CORBA can be mapped in a custom way to that particular language.

Examples of how CORBA can take advantage of the special features of a particular language, without suffering as a least common denominator, are easy to find. When developing CORBA distributed systems with Java, CORBA takes advantage of Java's garbage collection in order to control the cleanup of stubs on the client side. Java interfaces may be used as an alternative to CORBA IDL for the specification of the interface of distributed objects. Finally, because Java supports object serialization, some CORBA ORBs support the passing of serialized Java objects between two CORBA applications. The Java language mapping in the CORBA standard also places additional responsibilities on ORB tool vendors that their byte code be compatible with one another, permitting Java classes compiled with different tools to work together as byte code. Thus. CORBA is not limited in its feature set to what Java and COBOL have in common. Instead, many of the best features of Java work with CORBA to facilitate the development of CORBA applications.

The story is much the same for C++. Constructors and destructors are used to manage resources in a technique popular among C++ developers called Construction Is Initialization. C++ CORBA products also take advantage of the availability of pointers and references in C++. C++ CORBA ORBs can take advantage of inheritance in C++ to simplify the application development process, even mapping inheritance in CORBA interfaces into inheritance of C++ objects.

In an interpreted language like Smalltalk, CORBA objects may be invoked through the interpreter, not just after compilation, as in compiled languages. Writing small interpreted scripts is useful for testing distributed servers without having to compile an entire application. If CORBA were a least-common-denominator solution, you wouldn't expect to have the freedom to choose between compiled and interpreted languages.

These differences in how CORBA is used, customized to take advantage of the good features of each language, make it doubtful that CORBA is in any way a least-common-denominator solution. CORBA has seen remarkable success at taking advantage of all of the features of each programming language and not working as a least common denominator.

Objects-By-Value

In the CORBA standard, objects interact with each other from across the network. Generally, this is more than enough capability to build powerful software.

It's worth noting that the Object Management Group is working on a solution to this problem. The OMG is working on an extension to the CORBA standard called Objects-By-Value, which promises to provide much of the capability that is desired.

No Mobile Code

An application written with CORBA may simultaneously take advantage of objects written in several languages. Objects written in Java may utilize objects written in C++ or COBOL. These different objects always interact through an agreed-upon interface, often written in IDL.

However, modern software is gradually beginning to take advantage of a new capability, mobile code. With mobile code, the software that describes an object can be moved from one computer to another on demand.

Mobile code can be viewed as an extension of Objects-By-Value, the new CORBA extension. When objects are passed by value, the data inside the object is copied from one computer to another computer with the assumption that the implementation of the objects will already be present on the two participating computers. This assumption requires that the software for each object be installed on every computer that uses the objects passed by value. For example, if you have written a Book object in your bookstore information system, any software that expects to properly interact with your Book object must have some software installed on it that represents the instructions about a Book object. For a large client base with traditional applications installed by hand, this can be a significant task. Of course, applets have greatly simplified this problem in Java.

Mobile code solves this problem entirely because the software that supports each object may be copied from computer to computer on demand. In the case of the bookstore example, the source code that implements the Book object may be copied whenever the Book object is needed.

CORBA, supporting several languages simultaneously, cannot pervasively support mobile code for all objects. Further, using mobile code in some programming languages, such as C++, is exceedingly difficult.

The Object Management Group has issued a request for proposal (RFP), inviting vendor companies to suggest a solution for a mobile agent framework. Such a framework would naturally have to address the problem of mobile code, so the responses to this RFP will have a significant impact on the future of mobile code support in the CORBA standard.

Client-Side Installation

Distributed systems designed to support corporate information systems often have just a small number of servers that are kept under close supervision. The software on these servers may be customized and modified on a continuous basis as the project requirements change and additional requirements are identified.

However, those same distributed systems often have many clients. One Fortune 500 company recently deployed 11,000 CORBA clients to desktops worldwide. Such a large number of clients makes the process of installing and upgrading new revisions of client-side software an extremely daunting task. Distributed object tools offer no solution to this problem.

Broadcast

Many people may not be aware that while most communication on the Internet is through point-to-point protocols such as TCP/IP, the Internet also has some support for a broadcast, one-to-many protocol, Multicast UDP. This protocol allows not just two parties to communicate with each other, but many. Through Multicast UDP, one party can broadcast a message to potentially thousands of recipients.

The support of broadcast communications in distributed objects is still relatively primitive. The CORBA standard does not yet specify how broadcast protocols may be used for communication between different parties, though some of the CORBA specifications are flexible enough to allow different CORBA product vendors to employ it.

Distributed objects software is an approach for invoking a remote object and receiving a response. The object issuing the request is a client, and the target object resides in a server connected by a point-to-point protocol. Broadcasting requests adds a great deal to this. Broadcasting a single request to multiple servers has some value. Suppose a request is broadcast to ten servers. If nine of those servers crash for some reason while trying to answer the request and only one server manages to respond to the request, the client making the request can happily continue on its way. Thus, broadcasting requests can add fault-tolerance to an application. In addition, broadcasting a request to multiple servers gives the servers an opportunity to perform load balancing so that only one server might use the processing time required to answer the request.

All of these benefits are common to both distributed object and mobile object software. However, we will see in the coming chapters that mobile object software can take greater advantage of broadcast communications because objects themselves, not just requests on objects, may be broadcast.

Broken Encapsulation

Objects provide a nice abstraction for the pieces of a problem, breaking it up into parts that make sense individually. Objects encapsulate the data and implementation within themselves regarding the implementation of the methods on the objects.

However, different kinds of method implementations may be difficult to encapsulate and nearly impossible to expose from across a computer network. Drawing a graphical user interface is a good example of broken encapsulation.

When an object is implemented in a local program, often a set of objects, called "views," are also provided that give a graphical representation of the object. The use of object views often promotes reuse of graphical user interface elements because the view for a particular object may be used over and over again whenever a particular object must be drawn. Views of composite objects may reuse the views of their contained objects. This whole approach to creating what amounts to an object-oriented user interface results in easily maintainable code; the graphical representation for an object can always be found and modified in its views and nowhere else.

In distributed object software, the remote object is represented by only a stub. No views are provided with the stub. Indeed, the original object and its associated views may have been implemented in an entirely different programming language.

This lack of reusable views means that often graphical user interface code must be sprinkled throughout the clients and servers in a distributed system. The encapsulation of the graphical user interface within a set of reusable view objects must be broken. Each client and server must provide its own graphical representation of the object. Obviously, this can result in a significant code maintenance problem as the user interfaces for the same object are created in slightly different ways on different platforms.

Components

Some proponents of component software have claimed that developers achieve a 30- to 200-fold productivity increase by utilizing components rather than developing with traditional source code tools. Whether or not this claim is true, most of us realize that we can build applications faster by dragging and dropping icons onto a form than by typing source code.

From a technical perspective, a component is little more than one or more objects that implement a certain API. The different objects in a component provide things like the graphical user interface of the component, tools for customizing the component, and extensive information about the capabilities of the component.

The area of intersection between distributed objects and components is an area of intense research. Several possibilities exist for ways clients and servers in distributed systems may be encapsulated within components. Distributed object servers, for example, provide everything required to create a component that exposes certain services to the network. Dragging and dropping such a server component on a form would be like implementing a Web server with only a few clicks of the mouse.

However, distributed object tools do not allow objects to move from place to place across the network. Because components are bundles of one or more objects, components themselves are also restricted to the applications they were "born to." This locality restriction is extremely unfortunate because components provide a natural abstraction for documents, business objects, and other high-level programming constructs migrating across the network, participating in transactions, and conglomerating in fault tolerant groups.

Static Systems

Distributed object systems are composed of objects located on computers that are interacting with each other over a computer network. The participants in this interaction cause actions to be performed on other objects on the computer network. A software application written for distributed objects may utilize objects from many different host computers. The application might use these objects to accomplish certain tasks, from routing e-mail to looking up telephone numbers.

However, one key observation about the system is that the objects are essentially static. An application that uses some distributed objects can only continue to use those same distributed objects or distributed objects that have exactly the same interface.

Once a client or server that performs a particular task is deployed, that client or server remains essentially unchanged until new software is deployed. This response often results in distributed object systems in which each object in the system performs some well-defined task; to replace the objects in the system requires the introduction of a completely new system. This might not mean that all the clients and servers in the system have to be immediately reinstalled, but over time, each portion of the system must be reinstalled to use the latest modifications.

Are Distributed Objects Extinct?

Distributed objects, and the CORBA standard in particular, provide extremely powerful capabilities, especially with regard to the interoperability of disparate hardware, software, and programming languages. The interoperability of hetergeneous systems remains a significant requirement to many software projects.

Whatever comes up today, whatever comes up tomorrow, you can be fairly certain that it will be compatible with the CORBA standard for distributed objects. In an environment that requires the best solutions to each problem, CORBA can act as the glue between technologies solving different problems.

Finally, it's important to remember that more than 700 companies are working on expanding the CORBA standard to meet their business needs. Even if someone proclaimed the CORBA standard unsuitable, the very act of enumerating any shortcomings of CORBA provides the fuel for the ongoing effort of the OMG and its contributing companies to develop new products to solve those shortcomings.

What's Next

♦ Now that we've seen what distributed objects can and cannot do for us, the stage is set for mobile objects. The next chapter looks at what mobile objects are, how they can be programmed today, and what they can do for you.

2

Taxonomy of a
Mobile Object

O bject-oriented software development has led to several advances in the way applications interact with each other. Previously, objects located in different applications communicated with each other by exchanging raw data in the form of packets to distributed objects—they communicated through direct method invocation. Today, we are starting to see the benefits of applications exchanging complete objects, including state and implementation, with each other.

A mobile object application is characterized by an object moving from one application to another. Although this sounds simple in principle, the ramifications are startling. The objects involved may implement network protocols, database access, user interfaces, and other features. They may replace old versions of objects to implement bug fixes or feature upgrades. Objects may broadcast copies of themselves to multiple listeners to provide state replication and fault tolerance. Mobile objects provide a framework for changing the capabilities of an application at run time without restarting the application, recompiling the code, or reinstalling any software. This list just scratches the surface.

Mobile Objects Defined

Mobile objects are objects that move between two or more applications. Both the state and the code of the object move from one application to another. Conceptually, this is similar to an application breaking off a piece of itself and giving it to another application. For example, in a mobile object setting, a word processor might break off a mobile object providing the capabilities of a spell checker and send the spell checker object to a text editor. The text editor would then include all the capabilities of spell checker mobile object.

In a Java setting, moving the state of the object is easy because of a facility built into Java called *Object Serialization*. Object Serialization provides a default, automatic mechanism for reading and writing the state of an object to a data stream. Moving the code for an object is somewhat trickier, but Java *ClassLoaders* fill this role. A ClassLoader is responsible for locating and loading the bytecode for a Java class, even across the network. ClassLoaders literally load classes. In this manner a network-enabled ClassLoader can actually move the implementation of a Java object across a network to a new computer. For example, AppletClassLoader downloads classes for applets used within a Web document. The protocol it uses for downloading classes is simple HTTP, the same used for almost any Web document. The HTTP protocol also proves an admirable solution to the problem of how to download a class from across the network.

The following code (Listing 2.1) is a small example of a mobile object. This object represents a contact inside a contact database. Contacts like this are common within tools such as mail readers, help desk applications, and marketing support software. Here, each contact has a name, phone number, and e-mail address. The implementation of the object performs tasks such as e-mailing the contact a message.

```
public class Contact
implements java.io.Serializable
{
    public String name;
    public String ph;
    public String email;

    public Contact() {}

    // These methods aren't shown for brevity
    public void mail(String message) { ... }
    public void paint(Graphics g) { ... }
    public boolean mouseDown(Event evt, int x, int y) { ... }
    public boolean keyDown(Event evt, int key) { ... }
};
```

Listing 2.1 A simple mobile object.

Notice that Listing 2.1 not only has state and code, it also paints a user interface as shown by the presence of the paint operation. As this object moves from one application to another, the user interface is made available to other applications at run time. The object also processes its own user input. The user input for this object is rather simple—just a form, as shown in Figure 2.1. The object uses this form to modify the values of its member variables. It also pops up a new Web browser window when the return key is pressed. The mobile object has total control over its own user interface and user input, so it can do anything at all with these.

The example object has the look and feel of any object you might implement in a Java application. Indeed, your own Java code probably has many objects like the preceding one. So what makes this example a mobile object? With the help of a mobile object tool, such as Caffeine, Voyager, or RMI, we can move this object to another application. When we do, its state, code, user interface, and user input all move with it. The state of the object isn't restricted to the application in which it was created. When the state moves, an exact duplicate of the current member variables of the object moves across the network. The application at the receiving end can then use this object, invoking operations on it and accessing its member variables, checking the current balance of the Contact, for example.

The actual bytecode implementation of the Java object is also transmitted across the network and is loaded by the receiving application. The mobile object includes all the methods for the object with their code. When you invoke the charge method on the object, the code for the charge method is invoked in the local application. In the case of this application, a dialog box, shown in Figure 2.2, is popped up to confirm the charge. This dialog box appears on the application that just obtained the mobile object, not the application that originally instantiated the mobile object. Mobile code allows the object to perform any Java operations within the restric-

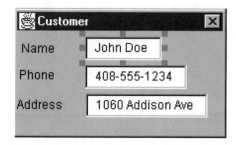

Figure 2.1 User input form.

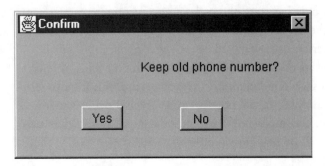

Figure 2.2 Dialog box.

tions of the current SecurityManager. Popping up a dialog box is just one example of this type of action. Other examples include writing to a file, implementing a TCP/IP client or server, accessing a database, or performing any other actions of a Java application.

As previously mentioned, the mobile object in Listing 2.1 paints its own user interface. This is just another example of a feature of mobile code. When the object is moved into a new application, the user interface of the object becomes available in that application, as shown in Figure 2.3. Moving the user interface of an object from place to place provides a powerful tool for properly factoring an object model

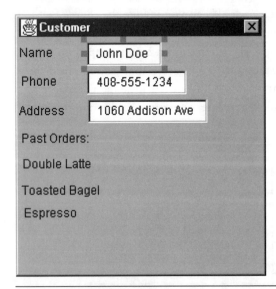

Figure 2.3 User interface in a new application.

or breaking a particular problem down into a natural set of objects. When you develop a new object, the object may be distributed to already deployed clients without having to replace the clients. Because the new user interface moves along with the object to the clients, it isn't necessary to rewrite and redeploy your entire client base when you want to update the user interface of some of the objects. Of course, many object-oriented developers are familiar with the pitfalls of closely coupling a user interface with an object, following the Model-View-Controller pattern of software development.

Code that heavily mixes user interface code, also called a View, with application logic, also called a Document, quickly becomes difficult to enhance and maintain. The mobile object approach to moving user interface objects across the network does not imply that the Document and View must be merged. When the View is extracted from the client, the implementation of the View becomes easier to modify and deploy because both the View and Document may be maintained on the server side. This does not imply that they must be closely coupled—just that they may evolve together. For example, there's no reason you can't split the user interface of the preceding object into an additional ContactView object as well. The Views of an object may be available as mobile objects!

Mobile code allows mobile objects to accept their own user input. The example object accepts both mouse and keyboard events to allow the end-user to fill out a form to change the values of the mobile object. If you press the return key, this mobile object also pops up a Web page—just another example of mobile code at work.

Listing 2.1 is simple, but not trivial. Mobile objects don't necessarily have to paint a user interface, process user input, or even have state. The following is another example of a mobile object that neither has state or any user interface nor implements any operations at all:

```
public class Trivial
{
};
```

This object is so trivial that many experts might challenge its status as a mobile object. Even though the size of the state of this object is zero, it can still be a mobile object. A mobile object isn't required to have state, though the fact that state is preserved is one of the main benefits of object mobility. This object doesn't do anything at all, yet it can still be treated as a mobile object.

The preceding mobile object doesn't implement java.io.Serializable. Implementing this interface is not required for this object to be mobile. The requirement that a mobile object implement java.io.Serializable is imposed by many, but not all, mobile object tools. Object Serialization is used by these tools to copy objects to low-level data streams, but other tools, such as HORB, can convert an object into a mobile object without Object Serialization. Instead, tools such as HORB rely on their own processing of Java objects to serialize them. In such cases, these other tools have their own rules about how objects are serialized and which parts of each object are not serialized. However, because they do not use Object Serialization, the rule in Object Serialization that serializable objects implement java.io.Serializable is no longer mandated.

The most trivial Java object can be treated as a mobile object in some settings as shown by the preceding Trivial class. No specific requirements force mobile objects to utilize any particular API, though Object Serialization is often used. Existing objects may be converted to mobile objects with minimal source code changes. Often, existing code can be used in a mobile object setting with no changes at all. Software developers have very little additional learning required of them when they develop mobile objects because few or no changes to their traditional approach to software development are necessary.

Ramifications

When objects can move between applications, entirely new ways of approaching application design quickly become apparent. First and foremost, deployed applications suddenly become flexible. *Flexible* applications evolve easily and may change the way they utilize resources and paint user interfaces. Flexible applications are easier to expand and enhance with new capabilities. Mobile objects enable applications to be flexible by providing the essential mechanism for moving new objects to and from applications, replacing or upgrading any existing objects in an application, or simply adding to the existing set of objects.

To understand what this flexibility implies for a developer, consider some of the object-oriented applications you have written. Now, imagine being able to arbitrarily replace or add objects, including new classes, to the application at run time. Some of the objects in your application implemented a graphical user interface, which is a good example of an application feature that is normally static. In a mobile object application, the user interface object could simply be replaced with a new user interface at run time.

The inability to change the user interface of already deployed client applications in the traditional approach to client/server software development is just one indication of a large problem with the traditional approach. Local objects are normally given direct access to operating system resources, including painting user interfaces, manipulating files, invoking operating systems commands, accessing threads, communicating over sockets, performing computations on the CPU, and participating in a shared memory. All of these are examples of local resources that are available only to local applications in popular operating systems. In order to expand the capabilities of distributed software, we want to make these resources available to all the objects in a distributed system, not just the objects that are part of deployed client software. Mobile objects provide one approach to consuming these resources in a distributed system. An object that wants these resources can simply move or be sent to the target computer and begin consuming the desired resources. Of course, the object may be subject to limitations imposed by SecurityManagers, quotas, and the like.

Resource consumption is only one side of the coin. Resource management is another. *Resource management* addresses a broad problem of monitoring, managing, and administrating the ways resources such as memory, hard disk space, threads, and processor are consumed by objects. Normally, any process capable of consuming a resource will also have at least a limited ability to monitor the status of that resource. The traditional approach to distributed object systems addresses only the way objects in different applications may communicate with each other. This approach helps to simplify the ways applications responsible for managing resources communicate with each other. But distributed objects systems don't address the ways the applications that monitor resources may be implemented and installed on the many computers on which resource management might be required. Mobile objects can help address the issue of resource management by moving to the host computer that owns the resources and taking the steps required to monitor and manage the resource. In practice, the design of the Java Virtual Machine makes consuming resources a great deal easier than monitoring their status. For example, the Virtual Machine can create and write data to new files, but it doesn't provide a means of querying for information about available disk space.

However, the benefits of object mobility are not restricted to resource consumption and management. Replacability concepts are not entirely applicable across the board. For example, in any distributed system, applications communicate with a protocol. Web browsers and server communicate using the HTTP protocol. E-mail readers and servers communicate using the SMTP protocol. Normally, the protocol is compiled into an application and is incapable of changing at run time. The protocol is not capable of changing without the reinstallation of a new executable supporting the code for the new protocol. In an object-oriented environment, the protocol may be implemented as a set of objects, often called *protocol objects*. When mobile objects enter the equation, the next natural step is to replace the protocol objects themselves with new objects sent across the network. This replacement provides a facility for changing the protocol of an application at run time, perhaps to optimize the protocol or to provide an entirely new communication mechanism. Your mail reader probably understands only SMTP and POP3 protocols, but if you swap in a few mobile objects, you might be exchanging real-time audio and video.

Rather than all clients issuing remote invocations on a server, each client may receive its own copy of the object, then issue more efficient local invocations on its copy. Different benchmarks have found local invocations hundreds of times faster than distributed invocations because of network latency, and once an object is local to the client, network failure does not result in the automatic failure of the object.

Why send e-mail in the form of a simple text message when you can forward a complete object, implementing the behavior of an application such as meeting scheduling or workflow processing? If you exchange spreadsheets with the accounting department or slide presentations with a group of students, don't worry about whether you are using the same version of MS Office on a Windows 32 platform. In a mobile object environment, the software in the form of class files may be loaded by the receiver of the object if required. In Java, anything is an object, so the capability of sending objects to other computers makes anything possible.

Generalizing on the concepts of mobile objects leads to a discussion of mobile components. *Components* represent a software development approach that defines a common API for reusing software within a simple drag-and-drop framework. Component software development is extremely productive as a result of the simplicity of building applications from simple drag-and-drop operations, without the complexity of correct source code syntax. The component palette in a component software development environment normally shows all the available components that can be used within an application. These components are normally stored on the hard disk as part of the development environment. Adding new components means running an installation process and registering the component inside the development environment. When two developers collaborate on a project, they must manually exchange components periodically through the normal mechanisms of floppy disks, ftp, and installation procedures. Mobile components provide a framework that enables components to move across the network.

Component software development is much like object software development in that a typical application may be built up of many different components interacting. The traditional software development approach requires a component software application to be completed, implemented, and then deployed to the target audience. With mobile components, portions of the application may be expanded by the addition of components or an exchange of existing components. For example, a startup software company could ship an early version of a component application with a relatively primitive Web browser component, then later transmit upgraded versions of the same component to existing customers, automatically upgrading their applications.

Mobile components are useful not just in deploying components to the enduser; they can also be useful for deploying components to other members of an application development team, enabling more effective collaboration. The current approach to collaboration used by many development teams is a source code repository, either on a network hard disk or in a source control system that is shared by all the developers of an application. Mobile components can move themselves as a whole to a common repository. An appropriate mobile component framework might then download these components on demand. Developers could discover new components as they become available inside the repository, and a version history of components rather than a low-level source code tracking system might be available. New versions of components could be automatically pushed to both developers and end users of the mobile component software, eliminating the need for manual installation to improve the capabilities of an application. This style of mobile component development is the next generation of the development process that developers use in building software. See Chapter 8: Building the Dynamically Upgradeable Text Editor for an example of this kind of dynamic upgrading with mobile objects.

The new capabilities of mobile objects also introduce new concerns, such as how well mobile objects interact with multithreading and concurrency. For example, many software developers build active objects, which encapsulate their own threads. An active object is a powerful way of creating objects that automatically respond to their environment. However, Java does not provide a mechanism for serializing a thread as it does for serializing an object. Without developer intervention, a thread cannot move from application to application.

Security is yet another concern. In a distributed object environment, objects are simply communicating with each other by remotely invoking methods. The security of a distributed object environment is generally limited to concerns about the privacy, authentication, and integrity of the arguments and return values of the remote invocation. In a mobile object environment, an object moves from one application to another. Unrestricted, the object might be able to do anything on reaching its destination, even reformat the hard drive. Hosts must have ways of protecting themselves against malicious mobile objects. The reverse is also true. Mobile objects should have ways of protecting themselves from malicious hosts. For example, a mobile object might contain sensitive information such as a customer credit card number. A hostile computer could try to dissect the mobile object in order to obtain unauthorized access to this credit card. Mobile objects need some way of protecting this kind of sensitive information. Chapter 10: Securing Mobile Objects looks at the state of the art in mobile object security.

Version and dependency resolution also becomes increasingly important in an environment in which objects are mobile. Applications deployed utilizing mobile objects might come into contact with copies of out-of-date software or may become out-of-date themselves over the life of the object. In the typical, static application deployment process, a software application is developed, tested, and deployed entirely by a single team of developers. When new features are added, the team goes through the iteration of develop-test-deploy over again. A mobile object approach radically changes the way software deployment is viewed. No longer is a single monolithic application shipped; instead a small groups of objects may be incrementally deployed to upgrade the capabilities of the application. In such an environment, one set of upgrades may be dependent on another in the same way that software releases and patches are dependent on each other in modern software deployment. A robust mobile object application should be capable of determining if all required components of the system are present and loading those that are not.

Object State

State is where the action for mobile objects begins. The state of an object is a snapshot of the current values of all the member variables of the object. As the object is moving across a process boundary, the state of the object must be copied from one address space to another address space. The state of an object does not include source code in Java, though source code can be part of the state of an object in some weakly typed, interpreted languages. Although mixing state and source code has interesting and complex implications for the way software is developed, a simpler way to view software development is to separate the source code and state of an object. In this book, we differentiate between the source code and state of the object, saying that the source code is included in the implementation of the object because this is true in Java and other strongly typed languages.

Object Serialization provides a nice, automatic facility for copying the state of an object in Java. During the process of serializing a Java object, Object Serialization looks at all the member variables of the Java object and writes these out in turn to a stream. When the same object is read back in from the stream, each of the member variables is read from the stream in the same order. In this manner, Object Serialization can automatically read and write Java objects to a stream without requiring the developer to provide custom code to read and write the object, as required in other programming languages when objects are serialized.

That Object Serialization is such an effective, automated tool for serializing Java objects has led to its having a central role in several mobile object tools, including all those described in this book. The design of Object Serialization thus turns out to be central to the construction of mobile objects. In fact, for nearly all the mobile object tools examined here, with the possible exception of Voyager, Object Serialization perhaps plays a larger role in the implementation of mobile objects than the tool itself. That's because Object Serialization is responsible for providing the magic of copying the object to a stream. The mobile object tools just have to write and read the stream, doing very little else to provide additional mobile object functionality. Object Serialization was designed and built by the same team at JavaSoft that implemented Remote Method Invocation (RMI), discussed in Chapter 6: RMI. The implementation of RMI probably suggested the power of automatic object serialization to the JavaSoft team.

Providing a complete reference for Object Serialization is beyond the scope of this book. However, developers of mobile objects should have a basic awareness of how to create Java objects compatible with Object Serialization. With all the tools examined in this book, Object Serialization is always used to copy a mobile object to a remote application on a computer network, though this may not be the case for some mobile object tools, such as HORB. Mobile objects and Object Serialization are not synonymous; the pervasive use of Object Serialization by the mobile objects tools used in this book is merely a detail of the way these tools are currently implemented.

Serialization and Externalization

Object Serialization requires that the serializable object implement one of two special base interfaces: java.io.Serializable or java.io.Externalizable. Object Serialization will attempt to serialize only objects that implement one of these two interfaces. Objects that don't implement one of these two interfaces cannot be used as mobile objects with the tools used in this book. If a software developer incorrectly attempts to use a nonserializable object in a mobile object setting, the object cannot be written and read from the low-level network data stream that is used to communicate between two applications, and an exception is thrown, indicating that the object is not serializable.

Objects that extend java.io.Serializable are automatically serialized to a stream using a set of rules defining how the members of the object should be serialized. An example of such a serializable object is shown in Listing 2.2. This simple serializable object could be used as a mobile object in some software applications. This example demonstrates how easy it is to create a mobile object; very little, if any, additional work is required to convert an existing object into a mobile object.

```
public class FullName
extends java.io.Serializable
{
    public FullName() {}
    public String firstName;
    public String lastName;
    public char middleInitial;
};
```

Listing 2.2 A serializable mobile object.

Objects that implement java.io.Externalizable must provide their own readExternal and writeExternal methods that are responsible for specifying how an object is written to or read from a stream. Although this task requires much more work from the developer, flexibility is gained in the tradeoff. An Externalizable class can contain any custom code required to sufficiently write and read instances of itself from a stream. For example, in Listing 2.3, an ExternalizableImage class is defined. The built-in Java Image class is not serializable, so a child class responsible for external- izing itself and Image must be developed by hand. The Image object is critical to the development of many Java applications because the Image object is used to repre- sent images and icons present in any kind of user interface.

```java
public class ExternalizableImage
extends java.awt.Image
implements java.io.Externalizable
{
  public ExternalizableImage() {}
  public writeExternal(ObjectOutput o)
  {
    o.writeInt(this.getHeight());
    o.writeInt(this.getWidth());
    // ...
  }

  public readExternal(ObjectInput o)
  {
    this.setHeight(o.readInt());
    this.setWidth(o.readInt());
    // ...
  }
};
```

Listing 2.3 An externalizable mobile object.

When externalization routines for the ExternalizableImage object that write out the required member of the Image object are hand coded, a way is established for using Image objects in a mobile object system.

The rules for Object Serialization control how an object implementing java.io .Serializable is serialized. These rules control which member variables are automati- cally copied into the stream and which are ignored. For example, the static and transient member variables of a class are ignored during automatic serialization. As a developer of mobile object software, you must be aware of these kind of rules so that you don't depend on the static state of an object moving with the rest of the object. However, the developer can force Object Serialization to behave in different ways.

First, the static state of a class is normally associated with the class and not the individual object. In some languages, these are called *class variables* because the variables may be considered stored in the class rather than the instance. Consider that static variables normally have *process scope*, meaning that all the static variables in a single process are bundled together. Changing the value of a static variable in one place in a process affects the value of the static variable in any other location in the application. Any object of the appropriate class may access the static variables in the process. Since the static variables are not associated with a particular instance and have process scope, it would appear no easy solution exists regarding what to do with the static variables of an object during serialization. One way of forcing the serialization of the static state of an object is to make the object implement java.io.Externalizable and define readExternal and writeExternal operations that read and write the static state for the object. However, the developer of such an application has to provide all the code required to do this rather than take advantage of the more automatic features of Object Serialization.

In addition, automatic serialization ignores *transient variables* by design. Transient variables are intended to represent those variables that should not be copied with the state of an object. Transient variables might include constructs like circular references, references to the short-lived Applet object, and the like that should not be serialized with the object. The transient keyword was introduced in the Java language specifically for this purpose.

Other Approaches to Serialization

Is Object Serialization required for any conceivable mobile object software? Absolutely not. By building an object serialization service directly into the core Java Virtual Machine, JavaSoft has provided a useful tool that many developers have opted to use in their own products, including all the tools examined in this book. However, the same functionality can be implemented in other tools without Object Serialization.

The bytecode contains all the information about how an object is implemented, including all of its member variables and implementation code. Some ORB tools—

HORB, notably—have opted to ignore Object Serialization and implement similar capabilities on their own.

However, HORB has its own set of rules for serializing objects. One of the trade-offs is that HORB ignores private member variables during serialization. Private member variables of serializable objects that are not static or transient are copied to the target stream by Object Serialization along with all the other nonstatic and non-transient variables. This treatment of private variables is somewhat controversial. Some tools, such as HORB, which implement their own mechanism for copying the state of variables, might make other choices about how to treat private variables.

Member variables may be declared private, protected, or public in Java, representing the access permissions for the member variable. *Public* means that anyone can access the member. *Protected* means that only classes in the same package or derived classes may access the member. *Private* means that only the methods in the object may access the member—not even methods implemented in derived classes are given access to private members.

Declaring member variables private is therefore one of the most effective ways to encapsulate the implementation of an object, hiding the details of how the member variable was implemented. This encapsulation is a very desirable property in an object-oriented system; indeed, the ability to encapsulate and hide the complexity of an object is one of the key benefits of object-oriented software. Therefore, this declaration of member variables as private is a common technique among object-oriented software developers.

Unfortunately, another way of viewing private variables is as a security measure. That only the object has access to the variables might be construed as a way of protecting the encapsulated data from a hostile outside world. In order to avoid violating this kind of security architecture, tools supporting this view of private member variables as sensitive data may not serialize private variables with the rest of the state of the object. This is extremely unfortunate because many developers declare variables private out of hand to encapsulate the complexity of the object, not to protect the state. This practice throws a significant monkey wrench into the process of converting existing objects into mobile objects. That private variables are not serialized means that many objects must be rewritten to be serializable with tools that have this restriction. None of the tools reviewed in this book suffers from this problem, however.

Does "private" mean "secure"?

The practice of making member variables private is viewed by some as a security measure for protecting variables inside an object. Because only the object has access to private member variables, it's argued that this is an effective security measure for preventing other objects from tampering with the internal state of the object. This approach is misguided. A great deal of research has gone into the partitioning of data into "secure" and "public" segments. The conclusions reached are quite damning when it comes to variables and their state. Most objects leak the state of their member variables and provide mechanisms for modifying this state. The restriction of these mechanisms to the methods available on the object is generally not an effective security model. The types of algorithms that correctly protect the "secure" state have been well studied in security literature, and the conclusion that may be drawn from this research is that most objects do not actually protect their private state in a secure manner. Encapsulate? Yes. Secure? No.

Why implement your own custom code for serializing objects when this facility is automatically provided by Object Serialization, a facility built into the Java core Virtual Machine? One benefit of opting out of Object Serialization is that many of the restrictions and tradeoffs of Object Serialization can be eliminated in preferences for choices that are more appropriate for the mobile object environment. In the case of HORB, the need to inherit from a particular class, java.io.Serializable, was eliminated and private member variables were not transmitted along with the rest of the state of an object. Many might argue that this makes it much easier to serialize existing objects without having to rewrite them to make them compatible with Object Serialization.

Another consideration is speed. Object Serialization is a very flexible tool that examines Java objects at run time to determine how to serialize them. Examining an object at run time is not a cheap operation, however. Looking at all the different member variables of an object requires a great deal of run-time processing, slowing down the application. This approach is powerful because any object can be serialized as long as it implements either java.io.Serializable or java.io.Externalizable without the overhead of a great deal of generated code that performs the serialization of the object at the expense of run-time efficiency. HORB uses the alternative approach of manually generating all the steps required to serialize an object at compile time, minimizing the amount of run-time logic that has to be performed to serialize an object. As a result, the serialization of objects by HORB is demonstrably faster than Java's Object Serialization.

Will other tools explore alternatives to Object Serialization? This is likely as the tradeoffs of Object Serialization in a mobile object environment become better understood.

Class Loading

The state of an object does not an object make. The state of the object is simply a snapshot of the values of the member variables according to the rules briefly described in the preceding section. No code is associated with these values.

This state with no code is analogous to a *structure* in languages like C. A structure is a data type that lists the elements of other data types. The structure can be passed around as a single entity, acting as a bundle of all the elements inside the structure. However, no methods are associated with a structure in C. An instance of a structure is therefore considerably different from a Java object in that a structure is only data with no code.

In simple tools that pass objects by value across a network without supporting mobile code, the values of the object are passed in a manner similar to that for structures. The member variables are serialized without associating any code with them. The code is expected to be preinstalled in each of the address spaces. For example, in C++, this means that the object is compiled into the application along with all of its other objects. Then, when this "data with no code" is received during communication, the object may be constructed through a match-up of the data with appropriate code already available in the application. This type of approach is common in several tools for building distributed systems and object databases.

However, much more flexibility may be achieved when the code (or implementation) for an object moves across the network along with the values (or state) of the object. Requiring that the code be precompiled restricts each application to using only the objects that were compiled into it. In building mobile object systems, we want the flexibility to send arbitrary new objects to a particular application.

In Java, class loading comes to the rescue. Class loading is the process by which the class for a Java object may be dynamically loaded from a source. One of the founding observations of the Java language is that the source of these classes should be flexible, even network extensible. In other languages, classes can be loaded only from disk, often in the form of object code compiled into executables or shared libraries. Java classes may be loaded from a file, Web server, database, other source code, arbitrary byte array, newsgroup, ftp site, or nearly any other means. Software developers may even provide a custom class loader that loads classes from any source they can dream up.

In building mobile objects, the flexibility of Java class loading is critical. As the state of an object moves from one place to another, the class for the object must also move with the object. Once the object arrives in a new address space, the required class for the object should be located, and an instance should be created with the serialized state.

Object Serialization again plays an important role, in not just automatically serializing the state of an object, but also in automatically loading the class for an object on-demand. Object Serialization accomplishes this mission through the use of a ClassDescriptor. This object describes the class for a particular object. In the writing of a serialized object, the first element that is written to the underlying data stream is not the first nonprivate, nonstatic, nontransient member variable. Instead, a ClassDescriptor is written to identify the class of the object stored in the stream. The reader of the stream can use this information to determine which class must be instantiated. In practice, if the class is not already available within the local virtual machine, the class must be loaded.

By default, Object Serialization attempts to load the class by first locating the ClassLoader for the caller invoking Object Serialization. To be precise, one loads a new class by invoking the resolveClass method on the ObjectInputStream object. The resolveClass method invokes the ClassLoader.

In the case of an applet, the default ClassLoader is AppletClassLoader, which transfers classes as Web documents. The classes from the serialized objects can then be loaded from the same Web server that provided the applet. Such Web server-based class loading has significant disadvantages, though. Chief among them is that the Web server is the only source of new classes for the applet. In a flexible distributed system, we should be able to use objects from almost any source.

Fortunately, the behavior of class loading with Object Serialization is not limited by the default behavior for ObjectInputStream and AppletClassLoader. The JavaSoft team in charge of architecting this service had the foresight to provide an extensible architecture for adding derived classes of ObjectInputStream to use custom ClassLoaders with Object Serialization. Developers can leverage this architecture by implementing custom ObjectInputStreams that provide their own resolveClass method, locating and loading the appropriate classes from any desirable source.

For example, we can build a custom ClassLoader called NetworkClassLoader, as shown in Listing 2.4, that downloads classes over a TCP/IP network connection. The classes themselves for this simple example reside on a server someplace on the Internet, perhaps in another country. When the loadClass method is invoked on this ClassLoader, the bytecode for the class is transferred, and an instance of the Class object is created.

```java
class NetworkClassLoader {
 String host;
 int port;
 Hashtable cache = new Hashtable();
  private byte loadClassData(String name)[]
  {
    // load the class data from the connection
    // . . .
  }
  public synchronized Class loadClass(String name,
           boolean resolve)
  {
    Class c = cache.get(name);
    if (c == null)
      {
        byte data[] = loadClassData(name);
        c = defineClass(data, 0, data.length);
        cache.put(name, c);
      }
    if (resolve)
      resolveClass(c);

    return c;
  }
}
```

Listing 2.4 A custom ClassLoader.

This feature provides an important part of the flexibility for loading the class for an object. In practice, such advanced approaches to class loading, combining multiple sources of classes, provides an important component for the implementation of mobile object systems that might include objects from multiple sources. With ObjectInputStream and ClassLoader subclassed, mobile object tools can implement new mechanisms for loading classes for serialized objects. Such problems as dependency checking, version control, caching, and database class storage could be addressed through this subclassing.

However, class storage and loading concerns in a mobile object system are quite different from those in a static system. Participants in a mobile object system may be passing on objects from application to application in a manner similar to the one used by modern systems to pass on data from application to application. We should not let ourselves be trapped by the normal mindset of class loading as coming from a fixed set of sources. Class loading itself should be flexible. Indeed, class loading is just another type of protocol, so the preceding discussion regarding protocol objects applies equally to class loaders.

An alternative way to view class loading is as a form of gossip. As data and messages are passed from participant to participant, so too should classes be passed from participant to participant on demand. Rather than consulting some central repository of class information, a mechanism might be implemented for classes to be passed between participants in the distributed system, just as data is passed. When a Java applet discovers it needs a new class, it communicates with the Web server. In a more complex system, serialized objects should move from a Web server to an applet to an application to a second Web server to another applet, yet still maintain the appropriate information about loading the correct class. Much as a town full of gossips spreads a story, enough information should be communicated about the classes involved, and the class loader should be smart enough to instantiate all the objects, even though you might receive the object from a friend of a friend of a friend. As we will see, mobile object tools like Voyager are starting to make progress in this area.

A simpler solution to this problem of loading the classes for objects that may have come from an unknown source is to simply embed the bytecode in with the serialized data. ObjectOutputStream and ObjectInputStream may be overridden in Object Serialization, so a developer can do just this. The ClassDescriptor object, also a part of Object Serialization, is responsible for writing such identifying information into the ObjectInputStream and reading it back out of an ObjectOutputStream.

Such identifying information could be the actual bytecode. Therefore, you are guaranteed that both the state and the class are always available in the stream without having to figure out the source of the class. However, this method would be terribly inefficient because the bytecode for an object would be communicated even if the participants in the distributed system already had a copy of the class. The bytecode for an object really must be loaded on demand, whether from a centralized server or a more open, gossip-based approach as discussed.

NOTE: A gossip approach to building a distributed system may sound sloppy, but recent successes have occurred in research relating to the design of gossip protocols for communicating in a large-scale distributed system. Reliably distributing messages to a large number of listeners has always been a problem in distributed computing. IP Multicast addresses the ways a message may be sent to a large number of listeners, but IP Multicast is unreliable. Some recipients may not receive some messages. Various algorithms have been studied for building a system in which messages are delivered to a large number of systems with a guarantee that the message will be received by every recipient. However, most of these protocols do not scale well to thousands of participants. Gossip protocols approach this problem in a different manner. Rather than trying to build a system that guarantees message delivery to every recipient, why not build a system in which the message is passed to only a small group of the intended recipients? Each recipient in turn forwards the message to yet another randomly chosen small number of recipients. In technical lingo, gossip protocols work well because they actually become more reliable when a large number of participants are involved, yet the number of messages increases only linearly with the number of recipients as each recipient passes on the message. At the same time, it can be shown that eventually, all recipients receive the message with a probability that can be made arbitrarily close to 1.

Object Identify

When an object is moved across the network effectively, the object is cloned inside a remote address space. Conceptually, you might think of the object as having moved to the destination host, but how well is this illusion preserved?

An object never really moves from one address space to another in the same way an automobile moves from San Francisco to Dallas. The object is not a physical thing that can be moved as a cohesive whole when a force is applied to it. The process of moving the object from one point to another is more complex. As discussed earlier, the object is actually first serialized to a stream. The stream writes to a TCP/IP socket or some other communication mechanism, then a new instance of the object is constructed in the remote application through the process of deserialization. At this point, two copies of the object exist: One in the local address space and one in the remote address space. The object isn't moved so much as it is cloned.

To provide the illusion that the original object moved to the remote address space, the local copy of the object should be destroyed. Java doesn't provide a means of forcing an object to be destroyed because that would violate the basic premises of a garbage-collecting language. To force the local copy to be destroyed, all the Java references to the local copy must be removed. If any references are available to the local object, the Java garbage collector will not clean up the local copy of the object. Modifying all the references would be a difficult task in a complex Java application. Few Java developers go through the trouble of keeping track of all the references to their objects. Indeed, the Java garbage collector is supposed to be responsible for performing these kinds of tasks.

One approach to this problem is placing each object under the management of the mobile object tool, prohibiting any other object from having a direct reference to the underlying Java object. The mobile object tool can then discard its reference to the local copy of the object with confidence that that is the only reference in the Java Virtual Machine.

Although direct references to the object may not be allowed, indirect references, those that first consult the mobile object tool, are still required. Otherwise, a means of manipulating the object would not be available. Naturally, we should be concerned about what happens to these indirect references when an object moves to a remote address space. To preserve the notion of object identity, indirect references should not suddenly become invalid. A better solution would be to automatically redirect the reference to the new location of the mobile object. Thus, whenever a message is sent to the mobile object in the form of a method invocation or an event, the correct instance of the object in the remote address space may be invoked.

The cloning of objects is again implemented through Object Serialization. An object serialized to a stream and then read back from the stream may not have exactly the same state. As mentioned earlier, private, transient, and static variables are not copied during the automatic process of serialization. This situation is analogous to cloning a human but getting the blood type wrong.

Do we still have the same object if some of these values have changed? Maybe, maybe not. Of course, the developer may choose to carefully hand-code a procedure for resetting any values that might have been lost during serialization.

The reality of how well object identity is preserved varies from tool to tool. Many of the tools discussed in this book are adapted for use with mobile objects and were not explicitly designed to support them. Thus, a notion of object identity is often not built into these tools.

The lowest common denominator is simply copying an object from one address space to another through Object Serialization. This approach provides almost no illusion of object identity; the original copy of the object may still exist in the original address space, the values might have changed, and no redirection to the new location of the object occurs. However, simply copying an object from one place to another is common.

Security

The world is racing onto the Internet. Virtually every computer has at least limited access to Internet services like e-mail. Although only a few years ago many people hadn't heard of e-mail, it is a critical part of lives and businesses today. As a result, security is a large and growing concern.

Product research, customer accounts, and even monetary transfers occur on the Internet. One story following the Gulf War was that a Danish hacker organization solicited Iraq for $1 million to temporarily disable the infrastructure used by the U.S. Department of Defense to exchange tactical battlefield data on the Internet. Closer to home, telecommunications companies lose billions of dollars a year due to breaches in the security of the cellular telephone network. Industry observers expect that financial institutions suffer similar losses but may be unwilling to disclose their true losses to the public because of the significant loss of face—and business—that might result. Sadly, few organizations take security seriously. Most are aware that it's a concern but fail to set aside a portion of their overall budget to adequately address it.

Mobile objects are no different. In a world where objects, rather than documents, are exchanged, clearly some security concerns exist. Flexibility is both a benefit and a curse. Java, as one of the first programming languages customized to work well on the Internet, has pioneered some of the techniques for providing security in a mobile object environment.

In a very limited sense, applets might be considered a form of mobile object with no state. The applet is made available on a Web server for anyone to download. Once the class files, the code for the object, are downloaded into the Web browser, an instance of the object is constructed there. Effectively, the applet moved from the Web server to the Web browser, although only in the roughest possible sense.

However, some of the same issues that were explored in the context of building applets apply equally to mobile objects. Security is one such issue. Once the applet moves into the Web browser and is instantiated, the Web browser and the system resources available on the destination machine must be protected from a potentially hostile applet. The applet should not be able to reformat the hard disk or do other malicious acts unless it has permission to do them. The applet should not be able to overconsume resources like the CPU, disk space, or memory. Applets shouldn't be able to do things like send e-mail on behalf of the owner of the machine or otherwise masquerade themselves.

There is another security requirement of applets. Not only should hosts be protected from malicious applets, applets should be protected from malicious hosts. A malicious host—that is, a host that is intent on doing harm—can attempt to manipulate an applet to force it to perform tasks that are beyond the original intent of the applet. For example, many software companies are now deploying a significant part of their software in Java. This software might be designed and sold for specific purposes. However, on a malicious host, applets might be subject to unauthorized modification or a theft of intellectual property, but some means of protecting the applet should be available. Some might argue that this is a problem for a licensing service, but when the applet itself can be tampered with, the licensing service can be amputated out of the applet, demonstrating the serious threat represented by tampering. The bytecode obfuscation industry was born out of this concern, but it provides only very limited protection.

A more direct monetary loss might result from an applet that is part of a mission-critical process. An applet might be a component of the accounting system in a particular business. Tampering with such an applet could provide a means of corrupting the accounting system for that company. Many organizations do not think through these risks when deploying any client/server system; this applet scenario is just one example of such a system.

Java protects hosts through a sand-box security model. The term *sandbox* is used to indicate restrictions on the scope of an applet's capabilities. A full-fledged Java application can do anything on a computer, such as creating and deleting files on the hard disk, invoking operating system commands such as "format," and listening to any TCP/IP network socket, as well as plenty of other capabilities useful to a software application. It's not unusual for an application to have these capabilities. However, the average Web surfer does not want to let the average Java applet downloaded from a Web page have such free rein with the hard disk. An object called a *SecurityManager* establishes the policy for the resources the applet is permitted to access. When an applet wants to read a file with a particular name on the local host, it checks with the SecurityManager to determine whether this access should be permitted by invoking the checkRead method. The SecurityManager would normally allow the vast majority of Java operations and prevent those that can cause harm.

The SecurityManager object is somewhat misnamed in Java because it doesn't actually enforce security. Instead, the SecurityManager provides the policy of for allowing actions; SecurityPolicy might be a more accurate name. In any case, Java's SecurityManager provides an effective technique for protecting the host computer from abuse by explicitly restricting the scope of activities performed by an applet.

Very similar concerns exist with mobile objects. Hosts should be prevented from attack by malicious objects. The Java sandbox-security model, through the use of a SecurityManager, is an effective way of protecting a host. Many people think of SecurityManagers as tools used only by Web browsers to protect themselves from applets, but any Java applet or even application can create and use its own SecurityManager. The Java run-time environment, through the System object, provides an API for setting the SecurityManager that should be effective at any one time. Whenever a resource is accessed within the Java program, the current SecurityManager is consulted to determine whether that access should be allowed or denied. In a mobile object application, a SecurityManager should be used to protect the host from malicious attacks by mobile objects that might try to perform abusive actions.

Developers building applications or applets with mobile objects should keep this in mind. To adequately protect yourself from a hostile object, you must write a good SecurityManager. You can do this by subclassing the SecurityManager class and providing your own implementation for methods like checkRead. However, developing a SecurityManager is not an easy process, and if you make a mistake, you might be open to attack.

Some mobile object tools, such as RMI and Voyager, have recognized the need for an appropriate SecurityManager and provide a SecurityManager of their own to protect a host from malicious objects. RMI provides a class called RMISecurityManager that is intended to protect the host; Voyager provides the VoyagerSecurityManager. With other tools, a SecurityManager may not be provided. Even where you do have a SecurityManager provided by your mobile object tool, you must be aware of how to use it correctly and what it will protect you against. SecurityManagers provided by RMI and Voyager vary in the kinds of attacks they protect you from and the kinds of attacks that might still be possible even with the SecurityManager.

SecurityManagers do not tell the entire story, though. A SecurityManager defines a sandbox only for what a particular object can and cannot do. In a mobile object setting, you might want to have certain other guarantees. For example, you might want to restrict the objects that you use in your application to certain sources. You need a means of authenticating the source of the mobile object and verifying that it has not been tampered with by third parties. You may also want privacy guarantees.

Protecting the mobile object from a malicious host is a much more difficult problem. In the example cited earlier for Java, the development of a mobile object is an expensive process. An organization deploying a mobile object on the Internet may not intend to allow just anyone to use the mobile object in arbitrary ways. A mobile object might represent your medical records, for example. When you approach a doctor for a simple exam and turn over your medical records object, should the doctor be able to change this object in arbitrary ways? If not, how can the medical records object protect itself?

This is a specific case of a more general problem: The need for objects to protect themselves from malicious or accidental abuse. This turns out to be a very difficult problem to solve. An object might be restricted to a sandbox to protect the machine from the object, but how do you protect the object from the machine?

The area of protection is subject to ongoing research that has not yet been satisfactorily addressed in either Java or any of the mobile object tools. Each of them relies on Object Serialization, which itself leaves the serialized object open to attack. A secure system is only as strong as the weakest link, and the use of Object Serialization in this case is a very weak link when it comes to protecting the mobile object.

Tools vary in how and whether they address each of these security concerns. The chapters in this book dedicated to specific products describe what is available in specific tools. Chapter 10: Securing Mobile Objects also takes a much closer look at these issues and what you can do to protect yourself.

Object Sharing

Every child knows the rule: Share your toys. Application developers also should share. In an object-oriented application, many applications want to share their objects rather than move them from place to place. That is, in many types of problems, the same object should be available across multiple applications. You don't have to look far to find an example of an application in which you want to share an object. Document sharing, in which many people want to view or revise the same document at the same time, is a problem that many application developers have to tackle.

A common way to share an object is to take the traditional distributed object approach. In this approach, a distributed object server is available to multiple clients to invoke simultaneously. Each client holds an object reference to a single, shared object. In distributed object terminology, this situation describes a shared server. However, as with other uses of distributed objects, this approach is limited to communication with a shared remote object. The clients cannot paint a common user interface based on the shared object or interact with it as if it were a local object.

How do you solve this problem? The document object needs to be shared across multiple running applications. If you can share the document, it is simple and easy to implement a method for allowing multiple people to view and change it.

Here is a very simple example of a document to share among multiple viewers.

```
public class Document
    implements java.io.Serializable
{
    public String body;
    public void paint(Graphics g)
    {
```

```
    g.drawString( body, 12, 12 );
  }
}
```

A simple approach to sharing this document is to simply copy an instance of it to multiple viewers. All viewers, with their own copy of the object, can use the document object, including displaying it with the paint method. However, this approach is overly simplistic. If any of the viewers modifies the document, that person's copy immediately becomes out of synch with everyone else's copy of the document. We need a mechanism for keeping the body of the document synchronized across multiple applications.

State synchronization is a problem that has been well studied by the research community. Tools such as HORUS implement algorithms for synchronizing state information in a distributed system. Such approaches are not always easy to implement, however.

Object sharing is slightly beyond the scope of mobile objects. A tool that moves an object from one place to another does not necessarily have to support the sharing of objects by multiple applications, though this capability is clearly useful and a significant problem in a distributed environment. However, as we will see, some mobile object tools have begun to take a few hesitant steps in the direction of object sharing. Chapter 9: Clustering looks into how to build a more robust framework for object sharing using mobile object techniques.

Concurrency

Java provides a fairly intuitive facility for the manipulation of threads and concurrent access to objects. This facility is popular with Java developers, who frequently find it convenient to use multithreading even for simple applications. Mobile objects should have ways of dealing with threading and concurrency.

The importance of threading in Java applications is demonstrated by a particular programming technique called Actors. An actor is an object that owns its own threads. Objects that own their own threads may automatically respond to their environment and perform time-consuming operation invocations without blocking. For this reason and as a result of the easy-to-use integration of Java with threads, actors are common in Java. One way to build an actor is to subclass the Thread object itself.

In Java, threads are objects. The Thread class is the parent of all threads in Java. In order to perform some operations within a new thread, a derived class of the Thread class is created. Listing 2.5 demonstrates how a thread is implemented in Java by inheriting from the parent Thread class. We then look at how this thread can work as a mobile object.

```java
public class BunnyThread
    extends Thread
    implements java.io.Serializable
{
    public String message = "";   // Count number of "going" messages
    public MessageThread() {}
    public MessageThread(String m)
    {
        message = m;
        System.err.println( "It keeps going" );
    }

    public void run()
    {
        int counter = 1;
        while( true )      // aka. forever()
            {
                System.err.println( message + " [" + counter + "]"); counter++;
            }
    }
};
```

Listing 2.5 Implementing a thread in Java.

To start an instance of this new thread of control, an instance of the Thread object is simply created and started through the start method on the Thread class as shown in the following lines of code.

```java
BunnyThread pink = new BunnyThread();
pink.start();
```

The thread object may be treated in a manner similar to that for other Java objects. The Thread object may be a member variable of a Java object, and the thread may be controlled when methods are invoked on the instance of the Thread object.

The BunnyThread might even be a part of a large battery advertisement class, called BatteryAd, as shown in Listing 2.6.

```
public class BatteryAd
  implements java.io.Serializable
{
  public BunnyThread pink = new BunnyThread();
  public BatteryAd()
  {
    pink.start();
    pink.setName( "Bunny" );
    pink.setPriority( Thread.MIN_PRIORITY ); pink.setDaemon( true );
  }
};
```

Listing 2.6 A Java object with a member thread.

Note that both the BunnyThread and BatteryAd classes implemented java.io .Serializable, as required by Java's Object Serialization facility. Because most mobile object tools employ Object Serialization to move objects around on the network, any object that might be used in a mobile setting should implement java.io.Serializable.

However, a thread is a special type of object. Threads represent a computation, a flow of control that is currently under way in the Java application. In most Java Virtual Machines, Java threads are mapped directly onto operating system threads. That means that whenever a new Java thread is started, the Virtual Machine accesses the operating system API to create a new thread that continues to interpret the Java bytecode in parallel with any other threads already running the bytecode.

For these reasons, Object Serialization does not behave in the same way for Thread objects. A thread may not simply be serialized to a stream and recreated when it is read in Java. This is unfortunate because such a threading model provides a natural, powerful abstraction where it is available in other programming languages, such as Scheme. In such a language, a thread can be treated as any other serializable object; an active thread may be written out to a file, saved for a period of time, and eventually restarted after an extended period of time. The Thread object in Java is simply not serializable; an exception is thrown if you attempt to serialize a thread or if an object containing a thread as a nontransient, nonstatic member.

The BunnyThread shown in the preceding example is serializable because that class implements the java.io.Serializable interface. The parent Thread class is not serializable. The result of attempting to serialize the BunnyThread is quite simple: The member variables, the message, of BunnyThread are serialized. None of the member variables of the Thread object are serialized. For example, the name assigned to the BunnyThread using the setName method on the Thread class is lost. Worse, no underlying thread has been tied to the BunnyThread object.

This lack of serialization has particularly negative consequences for the Actor technique discussed earlier. An object that contains a live thread may not behave properly after it has been serialized and reinstantiated. The thread itself may lose its name and internal member variables, and the Thread object no longer references a running thread of control in the operation.

One approach the developer of a mobile object can take to tackle this problem is externalization rather than serialization of the object. Externalization is a second approach available in Java to writing an object out to a stream. Externalization differs from serialization in that externalization is not automatic. Instead, the developer has to manually implement code to write the object to a stream. The code that performs the externalization of an object can perform operations such as writing out all the visible states of the thread to the stream, reading these states back in when the object is read back in from the stream, and giving the thread a kick-start in the new object. In this manner, an Actor can maintain its live threads even after serialization.

The BatteryAd class in Listing 2.6 is an example of such an Actor. To properly externalize the BatteryAd object along with its thread, we need to make several changes. First, BatteryAd must extend java.io.Externalizable rather than java.io .Serializable. An example of a BatteryAd that does this is shown in Listing 2.7. The changes to the previous version of BatteryAd are shown in bold.

```
public class BatteryAd
    implements java.io.Externalizable
{
    public BunnyThread pink = new BunnyThread();
    public BatteryAd()
    {
```

Continues

```
    pink.start();
    pink.setName( "Bunny" );
    pink.setPriority( Thread.MIN_PRIORITY ); pink.setDaemon( true );
}


  public writeExternal(ObjectOutput o)
    throws java.io.IOException
  {
    pink.suspend();
    o.writeString(pink.message);
    o.writeString(pink.getName());
    o.writeInt(pink.getPriority());

    o.writeBoolean(pink.isAlive());
    o.writeBoolean(pink.isDaemon());
    pink.resume();
  }


  public readExternal(ObjectInput o)
    throws java.io.IOException
  {
    pink.message = o.readString();
    pink.setName(o.readString());
    pink.setPriority(o.readInt());

    boolean alive = o.readBoolean();
    pink.setDaemon(o.readBoolean());

    if (alive)
      pink.start();
  }
};
```

Listing 2.7 Adapting BatteryAd for externalization.

The BatteryAd object in this example externalizes the current state of the thread along with the object. Because the Thread class itself isn't serializable, the

BatteryAd does the best job it can to serialize its state. It writes out the name and priority of the thread along with information on whether the thread is alive or a daemon thread. A thread is alive if it is currently executing code. The definition of daemon threads is somewhat more obscure. A daemon thread performs maintenance tasks. When a Java program contains only daemon threads, the program automatically exits.

Testing whether the thread is alive by calling the isAlive method of the Thread object provides a simplified view of the thread. This view is perhaps oversimplified because the complete state of the thread includes information about the current instruction being executed, the state of any stack variables, and the like. Unfortunately, Java doesn't provide any way to access these stack variables, so we must do our best without them. The BunnyThread object has the counter as a stack variable. We can't externalize this stack variable. Instead, we need to rewrite the BunnyThread to move the counter variable off the stack and into the state of the object.

An approach that might be preferable is making the BunnyThread itself externalizable. Doing so makes for a more natural object model because the code related to externalizing the BunnyThread is bundled more tightly with the BunnyThread itself rather than stuck in the BatteryAd object. This approach would also let us work with the original, serializable BatteryAd class rather than make BatteryAd externalizable when the real problem is the thread. The code in Listing 2.8 is a first crack at making BunnyThread externalizable. The changes to this class are shown in bold.

```
public class BunnyThread
  extends Thread
  implements java.io.Externalizable
{
  public String message = ""and going";  // Count number of "going" messages
  public BunnyThread() {}
  public BunnyThread(String m)
  {
    message = m;
    System.err.println( "It keeps going" );
  }

  public void run()                                          Continues
```

```
    {
      int counter = 1;

      while( true )     // aka. forever()
        {
          System.err.println( message + " [" + counter + "]");
          counter++;
        }
    }


    public void writeExternal(ObjectOutput o)
      throws java.io.IOException
    {
      this.suspend();
      o.writeUTF(this.message);
      o.writeUTF(this.getName());
      o.writeInt(this.getPriority());

      o.writeBoolean(this.isAlive());
      o.writeBoolean(this.isDaemon());
      this.resume();
    }


    public void readExternal(ObjectInput o)
      throws java.io.IOException
    {
      this.message = o.readUTF();
      this.setName(o.readUTF());
      this.setPriority(o.readInt());
      boolean alive = o.readBoolean();
      this.setDaemon(o.readBoolean());

      this.resume();
      this.start();
    }
};
```

Listing 2.8 More changes to BunnyThread.

Now that BunnyThread is externalizable and captures its own state, classes that use BunnyThread, such as BatteryAd, don't have to worry about externalizing this object manually. BatteryAd can remain serializable and rely on BunnyThread's externalization.

Does BunnyThread do a good job of externalizing itself? No, not any better than BatteryAd does. The current point of execution of the thread is still not properly represented and restored. This is just as impossible to do in BunnyThread as it was to do in BatteryAd. Also, the stack variable, counter, is still not properly handled! We can fix the problem with the counter variable by rewriting the way BunnyThread deals with the counter, making it part of the object's state. A new BunnyThread with the counter in the object's state is shown in Listing 2.9. The changes are in bold.

```
public class BunnyThread
    extends Thread
    implements java.io.Externalizable
{
    public String message = "and going";  // Count number of "going" messages
    public BunnyThread() {}
    public BunnyThread(String m)
    {
        message = m;
        System.err.println( "It keeps going" );
    }

    public int counter = 1;
    public void run()
    {
        while( true )    // aka. forever()
        {
            System.err.println( message + " [" + counter + "]");
            counter++;
        }
    }

    public void writeExternal(ObjectOutput o)
```

Continues

```
      throws java.io.IOException
  {
    this.suspend();
    o.writeInt(this.counter);
    o.writeUTF(this.message);
    o.writeUTF(this.getName());
    o.writeInt(this.getPriority());

    o.writeBoolean(this.isAlive());
    o.writeBoolean(this.isDaemon());
    this.resume();
  }


  public void readExternal(ObjectInput o)
      throws java.io.IOException
  {
    this.counter = o.readInt();
    this.message = o.readUTF();
    this.setName(o.readUTF());
    this.setPriority(o.readInt());
    boolean alive = o.readBoolean();
    this.setDaemon(o.readBoolean());

    this.resume();
    this.start();
  }
};
```

Listing 2.9 BunnyThread with the object in the counter's state.

Finally, BunnyThread properly captures the information stored in the counter and works with the serializable version of BatteryAd. This solution is still not perfect, though, because we still fail to capture the current point of execution of the thread. For some types of threads, this might not be a serious problem. In the case of BunnyThread, not capturing the current point of execution can have an effect on the object.

BunnyThread executes the following two lines of code over and over again.

```
System.err.println( message + " [" + counter + "]");
counter++;
```

This code prints out a message over and over again with a counter. If it's working properly, we would expect to see only one message for each number and the number incremented after every message.

When the BunnyThread is externalized, the thread is suspended. That is, the execution of BunnyThread temporarily freezes at its current point. This gives the externalization code a chance to fully externalize the object without having it change in the middle of externalization, assuming no concurrency problems exist in the program using this object.

Suppose that the first line is executed, then the thread is suspended. At this point, the message has been displayed, but the counter has not been incremented. When an instance of BunnyThread is externalized, moved across the network, and then read into a new application, the message is printed out a second time with the same counter number. This violates the intention that the counter increment after every message is displayed, so we still have a bug in the mobile object—a minor bug, perhaps, but still a bug.

A Java language guru might suggest that a quick source code change could solve this problem: Combine the two lines of code into one. That way, if the thread is suspended, it can't be suspended between the point where the message was printed and the counter was incremented. The code for this follows:

```
System.err.println( message + " [" + counter++ + "]");
```

Sadly, this is a false hope because bytecodes, not lines of source code, form the unit of execution for the Java Virtual Machine. This single line of source code is broken up into several bytecodes for the Java Virtual Machine. In fact, the bytecode for this one line of Java source code is identical to the bytecode for the original two lines of code. When the Java Virtual Machine starts executing this bytecode and the thread is suspended, the same problem continues to arise.

Do we give up and say that multithreading is impossible with mobile objects? Although developers can try to tackle these problems on their own, a good mobile object tool should address the ways threading can be made to work with the mobile object environment.

The mobile object tools examined in this book take several different approaches to handling this threading problem. Some leave it up to the developer entirely. Others manage thread inside the tool itself. That way, the tool can entirely manage the way threads are used and make sure that they can be externalized properly.

One alternative to externalizing threads with their current point of execution is to view each method invocation as a single unit of computation. Although this method doesn't allow the fine granularity normally present in multithreading, individual method invocations provide a convenient, well-defined unit of computation. Before and after each method invocation, the object is in a state that is entirely defined by its member variables. The object can then be externalized and moved to another address space and restored with confidence that none of the state of executing threads and their stack variables was lost. This view of method invocations as a unit of computation turns out to be an extremely successful approach. As a result, this approach is available in several distributed and mobile computing products.

One immediate consequence of treating method invocations as the unit of computation is figuring out what to do when a new method invocation occurs while another method invocation is already executing. The answer is fairly obvious. You can either save the method invocation until the original invocation is done or execute the new method invocation on a different thread.

Both approaches have interesting benefits. Saving method invocations begs the question of how and where to save them. One common approach is to keep a queue of all the pending method invocations. As each invocation is made, it is saved at the end of the queue. As a thread becomes available to execute a particular method invocation, the next invocation is removed from the front of the queue.

Creating a new thread to invoke each new invocation is expensive. Often Java threads are made of a thin layer over operating system threads, which incur a substantial overhead during construction. Reusing existing threads reduces the number of new threads that must be constructed. A fixed-size pool of threads that are available for this purpose reduces this cost to the bare minimum. If the pool of threads is large enough to provide an adequate level of concurrency for the application, no new threads ever have to be created after the threads in the pool.

What should you do when an object moves from place to place? First, any executing method invocations should complete. That way, no active threads are running on the object with their potential to complicate the current state of the object with stack variables and their current point of execution. Any pending method invocations can wait until after the object reaches its new destination. The thread pool at the destination can then begin work on the queue of method invocations associated with the mobile object.

Multithreading has another consequence: concurrency. When two threads access the same object or resource, they might step on each other and cause unexpected errors. Java has built-in support for concurrency through the synchronized keyword. Any method or code segment marked synchronized can be accessed only by a single thread at a time.

Synchronized objects have only process scope, however. When a particular object is synchronized, only one thread *per process* is allowed to access the object. If the object is shared between applications as part of a mobile object, the synchronized keyword no longer applies. Two threads in two different processes may individually access the resource or code at the same time, even though that may not have been the intent.

Two separate problems result. First, in a mobile object environment, a mobile object tool is required to support only the moving of object. It is not required to share the same objects, along with the object's state, across multiple applications. This points us back to the problem of object sharing.

Second, we may want to be able to make certain guarantees about this shared variable. For example, we might want to be able to restrict multiple threads in different applications from accessing the shared variable at the same time. In the document sharing example, the document is shared across several viewers. If viewers are making changes to the document at the same time, concurrency control should protect the document from simultaneous, incompatible changes.

In addition, concurrency is often cited as an example of how distributed systems inherently differ from monolithic systems. In a distributed system, you can't avoid the fact that several different flows of control are running at the same time. These may be simultaneously accessing network resources that are non-reentrant or simultaneously making incompatible modifications to shared objects.

Again, some mechanism for protecting the network resource from concurrent access is required. Some mobile object tools can help us solve these problems by providing some notion of a distributed semaphore. In the absence of such help, we'll look at alternatives that can be implemented by the developer.

Mobile Objects Versus Mobile Agents

Mobile agents constitute another technology that has gained the spotlight in recent years. Mobile agents are based on a similar architecture in which code moves across the network. A natural question is how mobile objects relate to mobile agents. To answer this question, we must first have a good idea what mobile agent technology is all about and develop a working definition.

What's a Mobile Agent?

Although it is difficult to define a mobile agent, all the possible definitions agree that mobile agents are autonomous. An *agent* is an entity that performs some task on its own. A mobile agent is much like a complete program that moves across a computer network in order to complete its calculation.

One common example of an application area for mobile agents is remote computation on large data. An often-used example is that of a weather database that contains gigabytes of real-time atmospheric data and resides on a server machine run by a meteorological organization. Other organizations want to be able to make computations on the data in the database, but it's impractical to move the data across the network; it's just too large.

The solution to this problem is to move the computation to the database rather than move the database to the computation. The researchers involved in this project devised a way to send a particular atmospheric computation to the remote site, where the computation may be executed and the result sent back to the requester. The computation is a mobile agent, moving across the network to gather the data it needs to solve a particular problem.

Another often cited example of an application for agents is online shopping. Shopping, by its very nature, is a long process of comparing products and prices to find the best deal. Online users perform this task themselves right now, navigating from Web site to Web site.

An agent could perform this task for you. By creating an agent that is programmed to examine multiple Web sites based on a set of criteria for what makes a good deal, the agent takes the burden off the user to perform an exhaustive search for the best deal. Upon finding the best deal, the agent would presumably make the purchase and arrange to have the product shipped directly to the customer.

Mobile Agent's Patent

MagicCap's patent on mobile agent technology has several serious repurcusions on this technology. If MagicCap enforces its patent, any technology vendor using mobile agent technology may be required to pay a royalty to MagicCap in exchange for the rights to sell its patented technology.

So far, MagicCap has not attempted to enforce its patent against any of the companies producing mobile agent software. Because of the intracies of patent law, MagicCap may lose its patent if it does not attempt to enforce it. Thus, the company may change its policy with regard to enforcing this patent soon.

Will mobile objects be patented eventually? Mobile objects cannot be patented at this point. Several tools for building mobile objects have been publicly available for more than two years at the time of this writing. No one can apply for a patent if the technology is already publicly available.

Other examples of agent applications include searching the Web, forwarding communications to a traveling customer, and looking for and utilizing surplus computing resources on a cluster. The architecture for all of these is basically the same: An agent autonomously moves about the network to accomplish the specified task.

According to most definitions of agents, two components are involved in the implementation of a mobile agent architecture. First, the mobile agent itself moves around the network performing the appropriate task. Second, but no less important, each machine on the network participating in the agent system must have a place for agents to live. As an agent moves to a new node on the network, the agent becomes a part of the execution context of this place. In order to distinguish the two different but important parts of an agent architecture, the agent is often referred to as an agent process. The place is referred to as a place process. Again, a place process must be running on every machine participating in the agent architecture. Agent processes can move back and forth in any of the place processes on a network.

Mobile agents are patented technology. The company that owns the patent, MagicCap, an early innovator in this area, was granted the patent under U.S. law.

The patent includes a description of mobile agents as an essential part of the patent. According to MagicCap, a mobile agent is defined as the following:

> *A distributed computing environment in which agent processes direct their own movement through a computer network. Place processes provide a computing context within which agent processes are interpreted.*

Again, you see the recurring theme of the agent autonomously moving around the network to perform some task.

Building Agent Software

Agents must be written just like any other software. An agent may be autonomous, but that intelligence has to come from somewhere.

Scripting languages are most frequently used for building agents. The agent processes are scripts that are sent from place to place on a network.

Mobile agents can roughly be described as programs that exist within certain frameworks. These programs have the capability of moving themselves from place to place and performing actions within the framework. Therefore, an agent is forced to support a certain API for doing tasks such as starting, stopping, and moving.

When an agent arrives at a place, the place invokes a particular method on the agent to start the agent process within the place process. For example, this method might be called start. The invocation of the start method is what gives the agent a thread of control. This thread then interprets the code in the script in order to perform the actions of the agent process, such as searching a local document or implementing some other computation.

Another common operation in an agent API is a move operation to cause the agent to move to another node on the network. The move operation would normally perform whatever actions are required to cause an agent to package itself up and transmit itself to the new node. The entire process starts over again at the new node.

These two are by no means the only operations defined for an agent API. Many agent systems define a substantial set of operations that an agent must implement in order to coordinate with place processes. Agents often implement all the operations normally found in a thread, such as suspend, resume, and sleep. Methods to create, clone, and destroy agents also must be provided.

Mobile agents' architectures are often inflexible in this API. Any capabilities that aren't present in the API aren't available to the mobile agent as it moves to different place processes. Place processes are not extensible. Once a place process is created and available on the network, no additional capabilities can be added to it.

An analysis and design task for a mobile agent's systems is more difficult. The first task for writing mobile agent software is to decompose the problem into a set of agents that move about the network to solve the problem. Once these agents are defined, they may be implemented and set loose to tackle the problem.

As an example, consider the problem of searching for a particular document known to exist on one of a possible 1000 different Web sites. The process for conducting this search without agents would be to perform an operation such as the following, written in pseudocode:

```
FOR EACH WEBSITE
  FOR EACH DOCUMENT ON THIS WEB SITE
    DOWNLOAD DOCUMENT
    SEARCH DOCUMENT FOR CRITERION
    IF FOUND, STOP AND INFORM USER
```

This problem might be insurmountable without agents. In the process of searching for the right document, a large portion of the documents stored on each of the 1000 Web sites would need to be downloaded and searched on your computer. For large Web sites, this could be nearly impossible, no matter how fast an Internet connection is used to perform the download.

Instead, we can build an agent that performs the search on a specific Web site by first moving to the Web site, then looking at each of the local documents. In building this agent system, we need to simply send an agent to each of the 1000 Web sites. The agent can then search the Web site it arrives at and send back the first document that matches the search criteria. Let's give the name SEARCHIT to each of the agents that searches a Web site. Instantiating and communicating 1000 SEARCHIT agents is much easier than downloading and searching 1000 Web sites.

The implementation for the SEARCHIT agent can be something like the following:

```
MOVE AGENT TO TARGET WEB SITE
FOR EACH DOCUMENT
```

```
SEARCH DOCUMENT FOR CRITERION
  IF FOUND, STOP AND INFORM USER
INFORM USER WE ARE DONE SEARCHING
```

That is the code for just one agent. We also need something simple to dispatch the agents to their destination. The following is a simple program designed to dispatch the agents to their destination.

```
FOR EACH WEB SITE
  CREATE SEARCHIT AGENT FOR WEB SITE
WAIT FOR RESPONSES
```

This architecture does a good job of searching for a Web document. The agents are likely to find any documents that match the search criterion, if such documents exist, even if each of the Web sites is composed of several gigabytes of data. This agent architecture does assume that each of the Web sites supports a place process hospitable to our agent process. This is a reasonable assumption for a thought experiment, though it might be difficult to convince 1000 Web site administrators to cooperate in a trial.

This first example was a typical agent problem that is frequently cited in applications of agents. Most examples of agent technology are similar to this one, in which an agent goes to a resource to solve some problem for the user. Clearly, this class of problems is not entirely representative of the real world.

It's not as obvious how to use agents to solve most of the problems tackled by software developers. For example, in an applet that implements a point-of-sale for a business, what role do agents play?

Let's consider this point of sale as a second example of mobile agents. The user interface for this point of sale should display information about each product. By default, a simple name, price, and description are displayed for each product, but a picture is available for some products and should be displayed where available. In some cases, product sizes and models must be specified.

When a product is purchased, a complex set of events occurs. The payment is verified, the product is shipped, inventory and accounting systems are updated, customer support is notified of the new customer, and any rebates or reward programs are applied to the purchase. In short, the point-of-sale system provides a great deal of functionality that a software developer must adequately represent.

Customers are equally variable. Some customers are individual consumers who purchase small quantities of products. Other customers are value added resellers who purchase batches of thousands of units at a time. They are treated differently as far as price, taxation, and warrantee. Different customer support staffs are responsible for the different types of customers. Naturally, the customer support staffs should utilize interfaces into the system that are customized for their responsibilities in dealing with their particular type of customer.

How can you decompose this complex problem into agents moving around the network? What portion of the agent system differentiates between products that do have pictures and products that don't have pictures? Should we represent the products as individual agents that "move" into the customer's shopping basket? Do we spawn off custom agents responsible for providing a rebate to individual customers? Should customer support, accounting, and inventory all be notified of the sale by an agent?

It quickly becomes difficult to see how a real-world application may be decomposed into agents. Most software projects aren't about sending autonomous units of computation across the network; they are about representing a complex process of collaboration among individuals and data. How do you hide the complexity of this application? With what do you provide customized views and logic for the customers, products, inventory, support, and account staff? A software developer familiar with object-oriented concepts would naturally answer "objects," not "agents."

This confusion over how to view the relationship between mobile agents and everyday software development has left developers groping for their own answers. A popular agent mailing list on the Internet is filled with topics like "Agents as pheromones" in which developers struggle with how to incorporate mobile agents in their own software. How exactly do you develop software with pheromones? The answer is not yet available.

How Do Mobile Objects Differ?

Unlike mobile agents, mobile objects do not move themselves and are not autonomous. A mobile object might be autonomous in some cases, but experience has shown that creating objects that move themselves around the network at will is generally not required in most applications. Instead, mobile objects are part of some larger application, as is any other object, and are moved as part of a normal remote invocation-style communication.

Many Java objects are automatically mobile objects because very little is required of a Java object to behave as a mobile object; no special API is required to build a mobile object. With most mobile object tools, any serializable Java object may be treated as a mobile object, so an object may be mobile as long as it implements the java.io.Serializable interface. Some mobile object tools, including HORB, don't even require that the object be serializable to be treated as a mobile object. Thus, mobile objects avoid having to implement any special agent API.

Mobile objects also become more flexible as a result of having no rigid API. For example, one object may implement a graphical panel that should be painted into a user interface, and another might be a customer account. Applications implementing a point of sale could exchange these objects in the course of conducting a transaction, enabling an object-oriented approach to the problem of constructing the complex point-of-sale system. Mobile objects just add more capabilities to the existing object-oriented software development process.

The focus of mobile objects is tackling specific application development problems. This approach differs from the mobile agent-based approach in which the problem must be broken down into a set of autonomous agents that solve the same complex problem rather than into an object model. For example, the point-of-sale application might create and release a mobile agent to conduct the purchase of the product. However, the same application logic used to conduct the purchase, track inventory, notify customer service, and the like still must be implemented by the mobile agent. No significant benefit is realized when this complex system is constructed with mobile agents as opposed to a set of objects.

Further, mobile objects don't require a framework, as do mobile agents. All the mobile object tools examined in this book place the same minimal requirements on objects for them to be mobile; such objects must work with Object Serialization. A serializable object may be mobilized through RMI at one time and through Voyager later on. Even the CORBA-compatible Caffeine could communicate the very same mobile object without having to rewrite the object to match any constraints imposed by any of the tools. Such simplicity and compatibility are not possible with mobile agents, which must implement a special API to become autonomous and meet the definition of a mobile agent. Whereas mobile agents are restricted to hopping back and forth between place processes, mobile objects live in normal, everyday applications.

Mobile agents also tend to be heavyweight and large grained. Mobile agents tend to be large pieces of code that solve an entire problem all at once. Most agent applications are tackled by only a small number of agents that move around the network to perform the task implemented in the agent by the developer. In contrast, mobile objects may be either lightweight or heavyweight. A mobile object application might contain thousands of mobile objects of different classes that may be active or deactive, perhaps saved to a database, for extended periods of time. Simple mobile objects may be little more than tiny objects with a couple of member variables all the way up to entire applications that are transmitted in one lump sum. Mobile objects may also implement components that move across the network, implementing a text entry field or customized clickbox, or a full-fledged Web browser complete with accompanying html parser.

What's Next

♦ The next chapter looks at ways to code up some mobile objects using Caffeine, an extension to a CORBA-compatible product called VisiBroker for Java. We explore the plusses and minuses of using this tool to build mobile objects and look at some specific examples of mobile objects built with Caffeine.

Building Mobile
Objects with Caffeine

F ormally, mobile objects cannot be developed in CORBA because the OMG does not have a specification for mobile objects. This restriction has not prevented some ORB vendors from implementing mobile object technology in their products. Caffeine, a tool in Borland's VisiBroker for Java, is an example of such a product. Caffeine is designed with one goal in mind: to make the job of writing CORBA applications as simple as possible for Java developers.

Caffeine

As we saw in Chapter 1, developing CORBA applications usually requires the software engineer to learn IDL and to work with special automatically generated files called stubs and skeletons. With Caffeine, however, a Java interface may be compiled directly into IDL. Any object that implements that Java interface may be used as a CORBA server without requiring a special stub or skeleton. The CORBA stubs and skeletons still exist, even with the Caffeine tool, but are hidden from the developer under a layer of pure Java software development. Again, the developer has to worry only about writing software that matches the original Java interface—simplicity itself.

Converting a Java interface into a CORBA interface is more difficult than it sounds. CORBA defines a limited set of data types, such as characters, long, structures, and arrays. Java, on the other hand, has an extensive set of classes, including objects such as Image, Hashtable, Button, and File. How can a Java interface that includes these data types map into a CORBA interface? The solution comes in the form of a feature introduced in JDK 1.1,

Object Serialization. Many Java objects can automatically be converted into an array of bytes through Object Serialization. Any of these serializable objects can be written to an output stream or even transferred over a TCP/IP socket. Objects that are not serializable cannot be easily written to an output stream or TCP/IP socket. (For more information, see Chapter 6: RMI.)

The Future of Caffeine

CORBA and RMI are rapidly merging. The OMG recently approved a Java Reverse Language Mapping that specified how an RMI application could be compiled into a CORBA application. The specification was written largely by Visigenic, the company that originally developed Caffeine. Further, the RMI development team at JavaSoft announced the intention to support the CORBA standard IIOP protocol in its product for future releases. (These products may be available by the time this book is published.) Therefore, the future of Caffeine is somewhat in doubt. Caffeine and RMI provide much of the same functionality. If Visigenic or Borland does move toward building a product that is source code compatible with RMI, would it continue to support Caffeine? No hard plans had been hammered out at the time this book was written.

Caffeine takes advantage of Object Serialization to support the transfer of native Java objects during a remote invocation. For example, the following Java interface uses the data type Hashtable:

```
public interface AddressBook
{
  Hashtable allContents();
};
```

At first glance, it might appear impossible to create a CORBA interface that is compatible with this Java interface because Hashtable is a native Java data type that is not available in CORBA.

The trick Caffeine uses is that Java Object Serialization can be used to communicate a native Java object. Object Serialization allows Hashtable to be written to the output stream from the TCP/IP socket. Then the Java ORB on the other side can read in the object and instantiate it. In other words, the state of a native Java object can be communicated between different Java applications developed with Caffeine.

This is only half of the magic. While the state of the object moves from one place to another, something else occurs under the cover that is both more subtle and more powerful. The name of the class for the native Java object moving across the TCP/IP socket is also communicated by Java Object Serialization. This gives the application reading the socket the opportunity to determine if the class for the new object is already available in the Java Virtual Machine (JVM) or must be loaded from a ClassLoader.

When a ClassLoader must be used, the ClassLoader for the CORBA stub object is used to load the class. This ClassLoader may download the class from a network source, as in the case of a CORBA client downloaded from a Web server. The actual bytecode for the object moves from one of the participants in the distributed system to the other. In other words, code mobility is employed to transfer not just the state of the object, but also the implementation for the object. This method meets the definition for a mobile object!

More on Stubs

On the client side of a distributed application, invocations on a distributed object look exactly like those on the server object. A problem occurs when the client needs some object to look like the distributed object. Recall from Chapter 1: A Look at Distributed Objects that stubs are placeholder objects that live on the client side of a distributed object application. The stub has all of the operations defined on the IDL interface for the server object. To the client application, a stub looks and feels exactly like the remote server object. That the stub defines all the same operations as the remote server object is the secret behind the way distributed object tools provide the illusion that remote invocations are no different from local invocations; the object that provides this service looks exactly like a local object with all the operations of the remote object. In Caffeine, the stub is responsible for providing the mechanism for moving native Java objects across the network.

Based on the above AddressBook.java interface, the stub in Listing 3.1 is generated:

```
public class _st_AddressBook
   extends org.omg.CORBA.portable.ObjectImpl
   implements AddressBook
{
   public java.util.Hashtable allContents()                    Continues
```

```
        {
          try
            {
                org.omg.CORBA.portable.OutputStream _output =
                    this._request("allContents", true);
                org.omg.CORBA.portable.InputStream _input =
                    this._invoke(_output, null);
                java.util.Hashtable _result;
                _result = java.util.HashtableHelper.read(_input);
                return _result;
            }
          catch(org.omg.CORBA.TRANSIENT _exception)
            {
                return allContents();
            }
        }
      // ...
}
```

Listing 3.1 Stub generated from AddressBook.java interface.

The key invocation is the HashtableHelper.read(). This invocation provides the implementation for the way the distributed application will read the Hashtable. In more detailed view, HashtableHelper.read() is implemented as follows:

```
public static java.util.Hashtable
    read(org.omg.CORBA.portable.InputStream _input)
{
    return (java.util.Hashtable)
_input.read_estruct("java.util.Hashtable");
}
```

This code takes advantage of yet another layer of indirection provided by the org.omg.CORBA.portable.InputStream class through the read_estruct() operation. This class is a standardized interface for reading and writing all CORBA data types to an OutputStream. The ORB encapsulates the actual implementation of the org.omg.CORBA.portable.InputStream in order to provide some ORB independence to the source code. At least in theory, ORB independence enables this source code to work with any other ORB, even though it was originally generated by Caffeine.

In order to implement org.omg.CORBA.portable.InputStream, Caffeine provides a com.visigenic.vbroker.orb.CaffeineInputStream object. This object is part of the proprietary Caffeine implementation of the CORBA standard, so the org.omg.CORBA .portable.InputStream class will never be named explicitly in the source code of a CORBA application. Instead, you have to dig into the Caffeine class library in order to find this class.

The actual implementation of the read_estruct() method is hidden inside the bytecode for this object, so at this point, the trail goes somewhat cold. The implementation of the way Caffeine moves objects across the network cannot be investigated further than the API of read_estruct(). Based on experiments with the Caffeine product, it is apparent that the implementation of this operation is something like the following:

```
ObjectInputStream in = new ObjectInputStream(stream);
Object o = in.readObject();
return o;
```

This is a standard usage of Java Object Serialization. The object was originally written to the stream for the TCP/IP socket with a similar invocation. Now the object can be read by the code above.

More on Skeletons

On the server side, the server application may have a set of hundreds of different Java objects. The developer of the distributed system may have intended that only a handful of these objects act as servers in a distributed object environment. The problem: First, how to specify which objects are servers and which are just normal objects. Second, how to take data read from the network and convert it into an invocation on these objects.

In a traditional CORBA-based distributed system, the skeleton may be responsible for both tasks. The skeleton is often a base class that provides the behavior common to all distributed objects, such as solving the problems mentioned above.

In Caffeine, the skeleton is also responsible for providing the receiving mechanism for reading native Java object transferred as IN parameters in a remote invocation and for providing the writing mechanism for native Java objects used as OUT parameters in a CORBA system. The code in Listing 3.2 that implements this is similar to Listing 3.1 shown in the preceding section for stubs:

```
public static boolean _execute(AddressBook _self,
          int _method_id, org.omg.CORBA.portable.InputStream _input,
          org.omg.CORBA.portable.OutputStream _output)
  {
    switch(_method_id) {
    case 0: {
       java.util.Hashtable _result = _self.allContents();
       java.util.HashtableHelper.write(_output, _result);
       return false;
    }
    }
    throw new org.omg.CORBA.MARSHAL();
  }
```

Listing 3.2 Skeleton.

The differences lie in how skeletons integrate with Caffeine, through a generic method called _execute(). Any method invoked on the server object causes an invocation of the _execute() method. The implementation of the _execute() method then reads any IN parameters from the InputStream object called input and invokes the implementation of the target method on the server object by calling self.allContents(). The result is then written to the OutputStream through use of the HashtableHelper class.

Mobility Features

That Caffeine provides the features required to implement object mobility appears to be more or less accidental. The documentation for this tool mentions the moving of native Java objects in this manner as an example of *pass-by-value*. Pass-by-value is a common feature in distributed system in which the values for an object move from one place to another. Indeed, Caffeine does provide the capabilities of pass-by-value, but the actual tool goes well beyond that simple basis to implement full object mobility, including not just the state of the object, but the implementation of the object as well. The documentation does not mention any of the terminology of object mobility or the potential of this technology.

As a result, the Caffeine product does not support many of the features common in a full-scale mobile object utility, including moving threads, customized class loading, and other issues common to mobile objects. Of course, in defense of the very capable VisiBroker development team members, they simply did not intend to build a mobile object tool; that appears to have been more or less accidental. Their original goals were undoubtedly to create a simple, easy-to-use tool for reverse engineering Java.

Chapter 2: Taxonomy of a Mobile Object examined the basic feature set of a mobile object tool, including state preservation, class loading, security, object identity, and concurrency. The next sections look at each of the common features of a mobile object tool and the way Caffeine implements these features.

State Preservation

The state of the mobile object in a Caffeine-based implementation is copied into an OutputStream by Object Serialization in the process of communicating it to a distributed application over a TCP/IP socket.

The design of Object Serialization specifies how objects may be made serializable. Recall from Chapter 2: Taxonomy of a Mobile Object that objects must implement either the java.io.Serializable or the java.io.Externalizable interface to indicate that they are compatible with Object Serialization. Any Serializable or Externalizable object may therefore act as a mobile object with Caffeine. Unfortunately, this means that not every object can be used as a mobile object with Caffeine.

In addition, Object Serialization has a fairly extensive set of rules regarding what members of the object it will and will not serialize. For example, the member variables are serialized, but the static member variables are not. The bottom line is that the developer of a mobile object using Caffeine must carefully design with Object Serialization in mind. This is particularly unfortunate because of the vast amount of Java software that has been written without the ability to support Object Serialization. Since many mobile object tools rely on Object Serialization, these same limitations surface over and over with several of the products discussed in this book and not just with Caffeine.

Class Loading

Class loading is provided by the Object Serialization layer and is not addressed at all by the Caffeine tool. As a result, the default class loader for the stub or skeleton is used to load the class for the mobile object. No API is provided to register a new Class Loader other than the one used by the stub or skeleton. This is unfortunate because a large-scale mobile object system may load classes from multiple sources rather than always one source, such as a simple Web server.

Security

The Caffeine tool provides very limited support for Security. Caffeine is compatible with the popular SSL protocol for protecting the contents of TCP/IP sockets from prying eyes and unauthorized modification. This protection can ensure a basic level of confidence that the state of the mobile objects is not tampered with by a third party when mobile objects are used in a distributed system.

Some limitations do exist. The SSL protocol is used only to protect the IIOP communication in the distributed system. Often, class loading is conducted over some other protocol, such as simple HTTP with a Web server. This practice poses a real security risk; although the state of the objects is secure, the code may not be secure. In other words, the values of the mobile object may be reliable, but a malicious third party could change what the object does in the first place!

To protect yourself from this risk, you must use some other tool to ensure that class loading is also secure. For example, if the classes are downloaded from a Web server, a secure Web server should be deployed that uses SSL to distributed Java classes. In order to provide yet another layer of protection, use signed JAR files to guarantee that the classes stored on the Web server itself have not been tampered with. However, again, Caffeine doesn't provide this infrastructure, so the developer of an application would be required to build all of it by hand.

Chapter 10: Securing Mobile Objects discusses a number of other security issues surrounding the use of mobile objects. Sadly, the remaining security concerns are addressed by none of the mobile object tools, including Caffeine.

Object Identity

When an object is passed through a remote invocation, the object is always copied by Caffeine through the use of Object Serialization. When the serialized object is read and reinstantiated, a new instance is created by the receiver. The instance of the native Java object that was serialized by the sender continues to exist and potentially may still be in use within one of the Java Virtual Machines in a distributed system. At the same time, the receiver may start using the new clone of this object provided by Object Serialization in its own Java Virtual Machine. Thus, the original instance and a clone may exist and continue to be used simultaneously. Once different invocations are made on the separate instances of this object, it quickly becomes impossible to assign any notion of object identity in the distributed system. You have the original object as well as all sorts of modified clones all over the network.

What's needed is the capability to move an object from one place to another, without leaving extra instances of the object around in the original JVM. However, Caffeine does not provide this. Developers may be able to provide their own code to simulate object identity under Caffeine. However, doing so is no easy task.

In order to simulate object identity using Caffeine, the first hurdle is to provide some way of cleaning up after an object once it has moved to a new location. In particular, the old instance of the object in the original Java Virtual Machine should not be left around to potentially cause problems. The original instance of the object should be garbage collected. The Java garbage collector automatically cleans up any Java object that has no more strong references to it, but Java doesn't provide any clean and easy way of forcing an object to be garbage collected. If Java did provide such a mechanism of forcing an object to be garbage collected, invalid references to an object could easily result. The only way to force the garbage collection of a particular object is to ensure that all the strong references to the original object have been destroyed or updated to point to a new object reference.

A second hurdle is that any requests sent to the original instance should not be satisfied by the original instance. If they were simply satisfied by the original instance of the object, the illusion that the object was now located in the remote process would be destroyed, and potential problems would arise with regard to synchronizing the two different states of the separate instances of the object. Instead, either requests should be prevented from being sent to the original instance of the object, by throwing an exception or some other means, or they should be forwarded to the new instance of the object.

One can accomplish both of these tasks by providing a wrapper and forwarder for the object. The wrapper should be the only mechanism for accessing the instance of the object. No other objects should hold a strong reference to the original instance of the object; only the wrapper should hold the reference. This way, if the object moves to a new location and the original instance must be garbage collected, the wrapper is in full control of all the references to the underlying original instance of the object, and when those references are modified, the original instance may be safely garbage collected.

Another benefit of a wrapper object is that it serves as a natural encapsulation for a forwarding mechanism. Once the object moves, the wrapper object can contain a mechanism to forward requests to the remote instance of the object.

Alternatively, the wrapper object could throw an exception when the object moves to a new location, depending on the preferences of the developer.

The design, development, and use of a wrapper object with a forwarding mechanism are not simple tasks, however. Developers contemplating this approach to preserving object identity under Caffeine are in for a considerable amount of work.

Concurrency

Caffeine is a tool within a multithreaded ORB, and the developers utilizing Caffeine are probably developing multithreaded applications with active objects. However, Caffeine relies primarily on Java for all of the thread management issues, as perhaps it should. For object mobility, the issue of how to read and write an active object is still a concern that is not adequately addressed by either Java or Caffeine. This means that Caffeine is also no help to you when you are trying to figure out how to use mobile, active objects.

Threads are not addressed by Java's Object Serialization, so active objects, those objects that own their own threads, may require special handling on the part of the developer to properly serialize the object. In general, a developer using active object techniques should carefully implement code to save and restore the state of threads. For example, this type of code might be in custom readObject() and writeObject() methods inside the serializable object.

Mobile Components

Until now we've looked at the benefits and complexity of writing software with mobile objects. However, a large and growing force in the software development industry is crying out that objects themselves are too complex and low level. For developing object-oriented software, a substantial amount of source code must be provided that is precise and correct or the overall software will fail to work properly. But what possible substitute exists for source code development with objects?

Components are small bundles of programming functionality that can be easily incorporated into a program with only a simple drag-and-drop operation. Need to add a new window to your application? Click and drag a Window component into the application. What about adding a text editor into your application? Click and drag a TextEditor component into the appropriate window of your application. The productivity differences between these two approaches to software development are considerable because of the elimination of many of the complex steps via the component approach to software development.

The trouble with component software is that components normally are tightly integrated with a single application. This situation is analogous to that in Chapter 1: A Look at Distributed Objects regarding how objects are chained into a single application in the object-oriented software development approach. Once again, we can try to overcome this limitation through the use of mobility, resulting in mobile components.

This section examines the issues involved in constructing mobile components using Caffeine. We could implement yet another example of building mobile objects, but these are covered in fair detail in other chapters of this book.

The Argument for Components

Source code has formed the basis of software development since the first computers were designed. However, source code is complex. A misplaced character or a number off by one can result in complete failure of the program. Source code developers may require months to learn all the ins and outs of a particular programming language.

In a perfect world, developers would design software by taking pieces of functionality for an application and rearranging them in arbitrary ways. Components accomplish this goal by defining a *component integration framework*. Such an integration framework defines the API for allowing components developed by independent developers to work together in the same program without additional overhead for the user of the component. In the case of Java, the component integration framework is the JavaBeans specification and toolkit. Want to add Web browser capabilities to an e-mail program? Simply include a Web component. Want to communicate with the back-end database? Drag and drop a database component. Rather than complex source code development, many applications can be developed with a few mouse clicks. In this manner, components are radically different from objects. Developers can add components to applications with only a few mouse operations rather than writing complex source code. Inexperienced developers can often use an unfamiliar component after examining the component for a minute or two. Objects are not nearly so easy to use; they require substantial API documentation and complex source code manipulation.

In some ways, components are more restrictive than source code development. The resulting component-based software can have only a combination of the capabilities of its components. If a component doesn't make a desired feature available to the software developer, that feature may still have to be developed in source code. However, for simple applications that reuse the components over and over again, components represent a substantial productivity improvement over source code.

Developing software with components is easier than developing it with objects, which generally requires complex source code. Many industry observers believe that only highly skilled professionals can design and develop object-oriented software. This same argument applies just as well to mobile objects, which are extensions of object-oriented software. Component frameworks are often easy to use, requiring simple drag-and-drop operations to develop complex user interfaces and complete applications. More complex component-based software might require the writing of relatively simple scripts to combine the behavior of several components into an application. Many people who have no formal training find it easy to pick up a component software tool, such as Visual Basic, and begin writing software. A successful software development framework must take advantage of the gigantic potential of tapping this pool of relatively unskilled developers.

Distributed Components

Although component programming is a well-established tool that has been available for a number of years, *distributed component programming* just reached the mainstream over the last couple of years. Distributed component programming is the powerful capability of writing component-based software applications in which components can communicate across a computer network. This capability provides a natural extension to the old distributed objects architecture in which objects communicate with each other across a computer network. Distributed components enable one group to develop a component that solves a particular problem, implementing a customer tracking system for a particular company, for example, then publishing this component for other developers in the organization to include this functionality within their own applications.

The requirements for a good distributed component architecture are still not well understood. Some of the concerns of component software development are different from the concerns of object-oriented development. For example, one of the most fundamental features of a component integration framework is a technology called *run-time introspection*. This enables a component to be examined at runtime to determine its capabilities. Run-time introspection is one of the technologies that leads to the general conclusion about component software that what makes a good component architecture is the flexibility with which new applications can be quickly designed from pieces of existing software. In a distributed setting, such pieces of software may be scattered around the network. This scattering introduces new challenges into the design of a component-based system.

First, because the components are no longer installed on a local hard disk, some mechanism must be used to locate the components available on the network. The well-tried solution of a *naming service* solves this problem well. A naming service locates different servers on a network by assigning a well-known name to each server and enabling anyone to look them up by providing the appropriate name. This approach to naming a server is common to many distributed computing technologies, including RPC and CORBA.

Once a component is located on the network, the component framework should be able to examine the component for its capabilities. In other words, run-time introspection should be possible even on remote components. This is a challenging problem. Approaches such as DCOM require a stub to be installed on the local machine. If a stub has to be installed on the local machine for any component that may be used, the component integration framework does not truly allow completely unrelated components to find and examine each other at run time. In other words, this architecture is not flexible. The DCOM architecture cannot arbitrarily find a component on the network and use it at run time. Additional steps are necessary; the stub must be installed on the local computer. This is the challenge of distributed run-time introspection, enabling distributed components to examine and interact without special knowledge of each other. The DCOM approach has not yet adequately addressed this problem.

Another challenge is that a user interface does not map well into the distributed environment. That is, when a client object communicates with a server object, the client object cannot present some of the user interface for the server. The client may have a user interface of its own that has been designed into it, but it cannot obtain a new user interface from the server. In a distributed component environment, this means that the user interface of a particular component used as a server in the distributed component environment will not be available to its clients. This limitation is present in all distributed component environments to date, including DCOM and the early CORBA Component submissions.

Can mobile components solve the challenges of distributed components? Distributed run-time introspection is easy with mobile components because the component object may move directly to the target machine. In some mobile component architectures, such as the approach called Mobile Beans, which is discussed in the section of this chapter titled Building Mobile Components with Mobile Object Tools, a transparency exists in which a mobile component is indistinguishable from a local component. Thus, once a mobile component has moved to the target computer, the normal run-time introspection tools may be applied to the component to determine its capabilities.

Through the same technique, the mobile component once present on the target computer may also make its own user interface available. We've already seen how a mobile object may paint its own user interface once it reaches the destination computer. That the actual bytecode implementing a user interface moves to the destination computer allows both mobile objects and mobile components to create their own user interfaces. This technique illustrates a key fundamental difference between mobile component architectures and distributed component architectures. Mobile components provide a more natural extension of the normal component model, including both user interface and run-time introspection.

Mobile Objects Versus Mobile Components

Mobile objects are extraordinary tools for building flexible distributed systems, but they do have limitations. These limitations can be addressed through the use of mobile components. Mobile components are more productive to use and accessible to inexpert developers. They also provide a natural mechanism for integrating pieces of functional software developed by independent software developers.

A significant limitation for mobile objects is in the way they consume resources. Nearly any real-world application requires access to at least some resources, such as images, html pages, and other types of data. These resources may solve problems such as providing a button image for a user interface, acting as online help documentation, or implementing other data useful within a particular application. Some of these resources may be large and infeasible to move around the network, but other resources may have a smaller grain, such as button images, that are most naturally bundled with the object.

Mobile objects that solve such real-world problems need to have access to these resources as well. The traditional approach to making resources available to a mobile object requires that the resources and classes for the mobile object live on the same centralized Web server. When the mobile object is free to move around among many hosts, locating these resources on a distributed network is not trivial. One approach is to load html and images through a URL. This URL approach, though common, makes code unstable, causing the code to crash if the Web document pointed to be the URL cannot be loaded for some reason.

In addition, when a mobile object needs to work with other objects, often these other objects must also be loaded separately from the original object. In this manner, objects related to a specific mobile object may themselves be viewed as a resource consumed by the original object. In short, objects may be resources for other objects.

Components help to address these problems as self-contained bundles of related objects with their resources. They may include all the objects required to solve a specific task along with the additional resources, such as html and images that might be used as resources for the component. The goal is that once the component is deployed to the target audience, little or nothing else is required to perform the tasks of the component.

When related objects are bundled with their resources, components often represent a convenient package for shipping pieces of functionality from place to place. For example, the implementation of a particular feature in a software application may require 20 related objects. If mobile objects were used in such a situation, each of these objects might have to be transferred individually with the associated development and performance overhead associated with managing 20 objects. In the same problem, a component might wrap the 20 objects into a nice tight bundle that can be transferred with much less overhead.

Yet another factor is versioning. Robust applications often face the problem that features evolve over time. Users constantly want new functionality. How do you build software for today that will still be compatible with the software of tomorrow? The answer is in versioning. One of the main goals of a versioning system is to track the dependencies of each element to determine which pieces of the application require which other pieces. For example, Object A v1.0 might have been developed with Object B v4.0. Object A v1.0 might fail entirely if an old version of Object B is present, say Object B v2.1. At the same time, Object A v1.0 might have been developed in JDK 1.2 and may be incompatible with old JMS and Web browsers.

As a software project becomes larger, failure to properly track and resolve versioning dependencies can cause more problems. Objects, as fine-grained entities in an application, place greater burdens on a versioning system. When objects are included in a versioning system, the relationships of hundreds, even thousands, of objects must be tracked, presenting a daunting task. Components, as larger-grained compositions of multiple objects, are fewer in number and make it easier to track dependency problems.

Components are often designed for run-time introspection. When a new component is added to a particular software application, the component can be examined to determine what it can do, such as what operations and variables are available for the component. In the context of building mobile software, the situation of a new component added to the application is common.

Imagine a development environment that would let developers share the components that they write at an organizational level, track the versions and dependencies of these components, and provide a framework for exploring the capabilities of a component at run time. Sounds like the perfect approach to software collaboration, doesn't it? This is just one application of mobile componentry.

JavaBeans

JavaBeans form the component standard for Java. JavaBeans are remarkably simple to develop; many Java objects are also simple JavaBeans without additional modification. However, most JavaBeans are composed of multiple objects that work together to solve a particular problem. What follows is a brief introduction to JavaBeans. For detailed information about how to create JavaBeans, refer to *Developing JavaBeans* by Robert Englander (O'Reilly).

The JavaBeans specification is remarkably simple. Each JavaBean is represented by an object with a set of associated objects. Each bean may have properties, methods, and events analogous to objects. The properties, methods, and events available for a particular JavaBean may be documented, including the assignment of a name, short description, and some basic access configuration, such as whether a particular feature is meant only for an expert developer.

Each bean may include its own user interface. Some beans, however, may implement application logic without requiring a user interface. For example, a Web server bean may implement all the capabilities of a simple Web server without the overhead of adding windows or dialog boxes.

Beans also differentiate between design time and run time. A bean used in design time may expose editors to allow the software developer to customize it when building an application with the component. Meanwhile, at run time, such additional complexity in the components might actually get in the way of the usability of the application as the end user struggles with configuration details that aren't necessary. JavaBeans separate design time and run time, making additional customization for the component available to the developer during the construction of an application but simplifying the use of the component for the end user. For example, a developer can set the text of a Label component embedded within a user interface. The end user doesn't particularly need to be able to customize this because it's just a label.

The package for Beans is a JAR file. This file is little more than a compressed ZIP archive and contains all the files relevant to the JavaBean within the archive. A *metadata file* is also enclosed in the ZIP archive to specify which classes in the archive are Beans and which are just associated classes or resource files. The meta data file contains only minimal information, such as the name of each Java class or image stored inside the JAR file. For example, the metadata file does not specify the operations, properties, and events of each Bean. The Bean must be instantiated and introspected to determine this information. JAR files also provide a class-signing mechanism that permits each class to be signed with a strong cryptographic signature and checksum. This signature provides a guarantee to the developer that the JavaBean was created by a particular JavaBean vendor and not someone with malicious intent.

The JAR file may contain Beans in two different formats: as a class or as a serialized object. In the first case, a JAR file may contain class files for the JavaBean. When the JavaBean must be instantiated, the default constructor on the JavaBean class is invoked to immediately instantiate this Bean. This approach is best for Beans that don't need to maintain any state of their own, so a new instance may be created whenever JavaBeans are needed.

The second approach is more interesting in a mobile component environment. A Bean, including its current state, may be pickled into the JAR file. The Bean does not need to lose all of its state between invocations. In a mobile component environment, this may prove an important tool because this approach allows the mobile components to be pickled back into a JAR file and cached locally.

Finally, and most important, Java component models such as Beans are designed to work with Object Serialization. A Beans component developer creates Beans that are serializable. Indeed, Object Serialization is required in the Beans specification.

From the standpoint of mobility, that means that virtually all components, even those already developed without mobility in mind, are compatible with Object Serialization, greatly simplifying the task of using them with mobility.

Mobile Beans

Is there a tool that lets the developer combine the power of mobility, components, Java, Write Once Run Anywhere, and JavaBeans all in one utopian development environment? No. None of the development environment vendors are thinking in this direction today.

The good news is that it's not too difficult to build your own mobile component framework based on distributed computing tools such as CORBA. Several approaches could be used to implement a mobile component architecture. Two approaches to mobile components are explored in this book. The first approach, working with mobile components in a mobile object toolkit, is examined here. The second approach, building a custom mobile component framework, is explored later in the book. We examine both the power of these approaches and the challenges that remain to be answered.

The first approach, working with mobile components in a mobile object toolkit, looks remarkably like a mobile object system. The objects implementing a particular component are transferred around the network as mobile objects, not as packages of components. This approach has the benefit of integrating well with many of the tools discussed in this book for implementing mobile object systems, such as Caffeine, RMI, and Voyager.

The second approach, building a custom mobile component framework, is somewhat simplistic, but it is powerful in its simplicity. In this approach, a JavaBean is communicated in the form of a stream representing the contents of a JAR file. The JAR file format is convenient for several reasons. First, JARs are the main tools for authentication in Java. Authenticating the source of a mobile Bean would represent a significant step up for the security of the mobile component framework. Although it is probably not the complete security story, authentication is a good start.

Building Mobile Components with Mobile Object Tools

JavaBeans integrates closely with the Java object model. Every Bean has a core Java class that is the "Bean class," along with some associated classes that provide additional services. So, a Java class may be a very simple Bean.

Mobile object tools are perfectly capable of transferring objects with their classes around a distributed system. For example, in Caffeine, an instance of the Bean class may be obtained from a server machine and introspected at run time to determine the capabilities of the Bean. This capability sounds an awful lot like what we need for mobile components!

During the process of introspection, the Bean introspection object, called Introspector, attempts to locate other classes associated with a Bean, such as the BeanInfo class. BeanInfo itself might use a variety of Descriptor objects, such as FeatureDescriptors, OperationDescriptors, and PropertyDescriptors, to name just a few.

The differences between a true mobile component approach and this approach is that the Bean class, its associated classes, and any resources that it uses must be transferred individually. This requirement may represent a significant performance hit over transferring these classes as part of a single component. In addition, versioning and dependency considerations may become more difficult to track.

Hello Bean

To demonstrate mobile components in more detail, we need a sample Bean. We can discuss the construction of mobile components only so much before looking at some sample code. For the first approach, let's look at a fairly simple sample Bean that performs the tried-and-true operation familiar to all software developers: It says "Hello, World!" The implementation for this Hello Bean is shown in Listing 3.3:

```
public class Hello
implements java.io.Serializable
{
public String msg;
  public Hello()
  {
  }
```
Continues

```
// Define a property called Message.
public void setMessage(String s)
{
  msg = s;
}

public String getMessage()
{
  return msg;
}

// Provide a simple method for printing out the property.
public void printMessage()
{
  System.err.println("The message is " + msg + ".");
}
};
```

Listing 3.3 Hello Bean.

The Bean in Listing 3.3 does not differ from other JavaBeans. No source code changes are required to make this JavaBean work as a mobile component. Notice that this JavaBean is serializable, a feature recommended in the JavaBeans specification and required to provide the implementation of a mobile component framework.

In order to demonstrate some of the issues of implementing mobile components with non-trivial Beans, this Bean should be a little more complex than a simple Java class. In the JavaBeans specification, a BeanInfo class is used to provide additional, customized information about a JavaBean. The developer adds the BeanInfo object to a Bean simply by taking the name of the Bean and appending "BeanInfo" to it. The JavaBeans Introspector will locate the BeanInfo object for a given Bean by trying to load the appropriate BeanInfo class. If it's not there, the Introspector will construct its own BeanInfo class by default.

The code in Listing 3.4 is the BeanInfo class for the Hello Bean:

```
import java.beans.*;
```

```
public class HelloBeanInfo
  extends SimpleBeanInfo
{
  public HelloBeanInfo()
  {
  }

  public PropertyDescriptor[] getPropertyDescriptors()
  {
    PropertyDescriptor[] pd = new PropertyDescriptor[1];
    try
      {
        Class c = Class.forName("Hello");
        pd[0] = new PropertyDescriptor("Message",c);
        pd[0].setExpert(false);
        pd[0].setHidden(false);
        pd[0].setShortDescription("The message to display.");
      }
    catch (Exception e)
      {
        System.err.println("HelloBeanInfo: " + e);
        e.printStackTrace();
      }

    return pd;
  }
};
```

Listing 3.4 BeanInfo class.

This BeanInfo class provides some self-documentation for the Message property of our Hello Bean. The BeanInfo adds a short description to the Message property, indicating that Message represents "The message to display." In a mobile component framework, this BeanInfo object should be communicated with the Bean along with the Bean class itself.

In order to move this Bean between processes, let's define a Caffeine interface called HelloCaster. This interface passes an instance of the Hello component between a client and server. The HelloCaster interface does not differ from a typical usage of Caffeine's pass-by-value feature, although we will be taking advantage of some of the code mobility supported by Caffeine to implement a mobile component. The HelloCaster interface is as follows:

```
public interface HelloCaster
   extends org.omg.CORBA.Object
{
   public void push(Hello h);
   public Hello pop();
};
```

Caffeine takes this Java interface and can compile it into a CORBA interface, stub, and skeleton. In a CORBA-based distributed system, the interface definition, as shown above, is separate from the interface implementation, which we still have to provide.

To implement the HelloCaster interface, let's provide a simple Stack-based storage of Hello components. A client should push or pop some Hello components onto the underlying Stack. The mobile component framework should take care of all the details, like figuring out which BeanInfo goes with which component. The implementation of the HelloCaster interface is called HelloCasterImpl (Listing 3.5):

```
import java.util.Stack;

public class HelloCasterImpl
   extends _HelloCasterImplBase
{
   private Stack theStack = new Stack();
   public HelloCasterImpl(String n)
   {
      super(n);
   }

   public void push(Hello h)
   {
      Object o = theStack.push(h);
      System.err.println("Pushed \"" + h.getMessage() + "\".");
   }
```

```
public Hello pop()
{
   Hello h = (Hello)theStack.pop();
   System.err.println("Popped \"" + h.getMessage() + "\".");      return h;
}
};
```

Listing 3.5 HelloCasterImpl.

CORBA objects running on the network must reside in some server process. So far, we don't have a server for this HelloCasterImpl. Listing 3.6 is a simple server, appropriately called Server, that simply instantiates the HelloCasterImpl object and makes it available on the network through the VisiBroker SmartAgent, a proprietary distributed object naming service bundled with VisiBroker:

```
public class Server
{
   public static void main(String args[])
   {
      org.omg.CORBA.ORB orb = org.omg.CORBA.ORB.init();
      org.omg.CORBA.BOA boa = orb.BOA_init();
      HelloCasterImpl h = new HelloCasterImpl("HelloCaster");
      boa.obj_is_ready(h);
      System.out.println("Server is ready.");
      boa.impl_is_ready();
   }
}
```

Listing 3.6 Server.

Finally, we need a client to communicate with this server. The client needs to be able to push and pop Hello components on the HelloCaster stack. In order to simplify this task, let's split the client up into two separate applications: one for pushing Hello components, called PushClient, and one for popping Hello components, called PopClient.

PushClient should simply instantiate a component and push the component on the HelloCaster stack by invoking HelloCaster's push() method. To make the implementation of this PushClient as flexible as possible, the name of the class of the

Bean to instantiate is passed in as a command line parameter. Later, when we are building new Beans to work with this same client, all we will have to do is change the value of the command line argument. The Hello component also has a Message property, which is a string. The value for this property on the new component is passed in as a second command line argument. Bringing it all together, Listing 3.7 is the implementation of the PushClient:

```
public class PushClient
{
  public static void main(String args[])
  {
    try
      {

          org.omg.CORBA.ORB orb = org.omg.CORBA.ORB.init();
          HelloCaster caster = HelloCasterHelper.bind(orb,
                                                "HelloCaster");
          Class c = Class.forName(args[0]);
          Hello h = (Hello)c.newInstance();
          h.setMessage(args[1]);

          caster.push(h);
          System.out.println("Pushed \"" + args[0] + "\"." );
      }
    catch (Exception e)
      {
          System.err.println("PushClient: " + e);
          e.printStackTrace();
      }
  }
}
```

Listing 3.7 PushClient implementation.

The PopClient should simply invoke the pop() method of HelloCaster to retrieve a Hello component. PopClient then examines the component through introspection. PopClient can determine what properties are available on the component and print these out, allowing us to confirm that the right component moved into the PopClient application, as follows (Listing 3.8):

```java
import java.beans.*;

public class PopClient
{
  public static void main(String args[])
  {
    org.omg.CORBA.ORB orb = org.omg.CORBA.ORB.init();
    HelloCaster caster = HelloCasterHelper.bind(orb, "HelloCaster");
    Hello h = caster.pop();
    Class helloClass = h.getClass();
    System.out.println("Bean name is \"" + helloClass.getName() + "\".");
    BeanInfo i;
    try
      {
        i = Introspector.getBeanInfo( helloClass );
        PropertyDescriptor[] pd = i.getPropertyDescriptors();
        for (int j = 0; j < pd.length; j++)
          {
            System.out.println("Property \""
                                + pd[j].getName()
                                + "\" is described as \""
                                + pd[j].getShortDescription()
                                + "\"." );
          }
      }
    catch (Exception e)
      {
        System.err.println("PopClient: " + e);
        e.printStackTrace();
      }
    System.out.println("Popped \"" + h.getMessage() + "\".");
  }
}
```

Listing 3.8 PopClient.

The example is ready for compilation in your favorite Java development environment. For the JDK, type something like the following:

Prompt> javac *.java

To run the example, perform the following steps.

1. Start SmartAgent if it is not already running.

2. Start the server. Recall that the server instantiates a HelloCasterImpl and makes it available for the clients. In Win32, just type something like the following in a DOS shell:

    Prompt> Java Server

3. Instantiate a Hello component and push it onto the HelloCaster using PushClient. In this mobile component system, the new component actually moves from the PushClient to the Server.

    Prompt> Java PushClient Hello "Hello, World!"

4. Retrieve the component from HelloCaster using PopClient. The Hello component now moves from the Server to the PopClient application. Next, the introspector comes into play.

    Prompt> Java PopClient

Observe that the value set for the Message property of the Hello component remains the same when the component lands in the PopClient application! The component has moved across three different applications, yet it remains intact.

The PopClient also displays the list of properties available for the Hello component. Only the Message property is available because that is the only property built into the simple Hello component we coded earlier. However, something subtle is occurring here. The short description of the Message property is "The message to display." That description was assigned to the component in HelloBeanInfo! This demonstrates an important point. Although the push and pop operations on the HelloCaster interface returned only instances of objects implementing the Hello interface, the other classes associated with the Bean are also located and retrieved by the Java run-time environment! How does this work?

When the Introspector is examining a JavaBean to determine its properties, the Introspector attempts to load the associate BeanInfo class, HelloBeanInfo, for this example, using the same class loader of the Hello class. Since the Hello and HelloBeanInfo objects are both available from the same server, the Introspector puts two and two together, so to speak, and uses HelloBeanInfo as a source of the meta-data for the Hello Bean.

Inheritance

Notice that all the components in the preceding example are stored as instances of the Hello interface. Any Bean that is a child of the Hello interface is supported by this framework. Let's briefly confirm that we can instantiate Beans that are children of the Hello object and have them behave correctly within this framework.

To demonstrate this point, we use a child class of the Hello class, called Rapport. This Rapport class implements an entirely new Bean that extends the same behavior as the Hello Bean. A new boolean property called Rapport is added, which just confirms for us that this is a Rapport Bean. This property is completely superfluous because the introspector can tell us whether this is a Rapport Bean or some other type of Bean, but the Rapport property provides a useful demonstration that the capabilities of the Hello Bean may be extended arbitrarily. The implementation for the Rapport Bean is shown in Listing 3.9:

```
public class Rapport
extends Hello
{
  public Rapport()
  {
  }

  public boolean isRapport()
  {
    return true;
  }

  // Do something cooler than Hello here!!
};
```

Listing 3.9 Rapport Bean implementation.

Next we can push some Rapport components onto the HelloCaster stack. The PushClient is suitable for doing this; just give it a first command line argument of "Rapport" to specify the Rapport class and then choose a second command line argument of the message to communicate. Be sure that SmartAgent and the Hello Server are running, then start the PushClient. In MS-DOS using JDK, here's how to run PushClient:

Prompt> Java PushClient Rapport "Try to do this with Visual Basic!"

The PopClient can be used to examine the component just pushed on the HelloCaster stack. PopClient is compatible with any Hello-derived component. Run PopClient with something like the following:

Prompt> Java PopClient

Looking at the output of the PopClient reveals the name of the class of the component obtained from the HelloCaster is Rapport. Although our interface declared only that an instance of the Hello class was pushed or popped with the HelloCaster interface, that Rapport extends Hello means that an instance of the Rapport class can be used whenever an instance of the Hello class is required. The Rapport component instantiated by PushClient also was not truncated back to a Hello component in the process of moving the component from PushClient, to Server, to PopClient. Object Serialization helped us out with this.

Notice that the introspection on the Rapport component also was successful. The additional boolean property, called Rapport, is shown by the Introspector, so the new Rapport method added to the Rapport Bean was properly detected as a boolean property by PopClient. The description of the Message property is also still correct, even though the Message property was described in HelloBeanInfo. The Java run-time environment was smart enough to look there for the description of the Message property inherited from the Hello class!

This example hasn't used any fancy user interface features yet, but there's no reason that it couldn't. For example, a GUIHello Bean could be built that extends the behavior of the Hello Bean to create a dialog box when someone invokes getMessage. Such a GUIHello Bean would even still be compatible with PushClient, PopClient, Server, and HelloCasterImpl! Implementing such a GUIHello Bean is left for you, the reader, to experiment with doing for yourself.

What's Next

♦ The world of distributed objects is dominated by two approaches: CORBA and DCOM. These two approaches don't necessarily compete with each other because they solve slightly different problems. CORBA provides integration across multiple operating systems while DCOM is widely bundled as part of recent Microsoft operating systems. Now that you've seen how to build mobile objects with a CORBA tool such as Caffeine, we'll move on to exploring how (and if) you can build mobile objects with Microsoft's DCOM.

4

COM/DCOM
and Java

Many software developers view Java and COM/DCOM as diametrically opposing technologies. Java swept through the industry with the force of its "Write Once, Run Anywhere" message. Software written in pure Java should be compatible with many different virtual machines, executable without any code changes or recompilation change on many different operating systems. COM/DCOM, on the other hand, has until recently been a proprietary technology controlled by Microsoft and available only on its Windows operating systems.

Both Java and COM/DCOM are important technologies; both have places as building blocks for much of the other software in the industry. Developers should not attempt to build software while considering them either/or alternatives because great benefits can be derived from selectively utilizing both technologies together. This chapter examines one of the mechanisms for integrating COM/DCOM, setting the stage for utilizing DCOM in the implementation of mobile objects.

COM

COM components integrate well with many development environments. As for any component model, the goal of COM is to enable the quick addition of components into new applications. Development environments available from Microsoft, including Visual C++, J++, and Visual Basic, all are designed with robust support for COM. Third-party development environments, such as Borland's Delphi and Powersoft's Powerbuilder, also enable the addition of COM components to software projects. COM components can even be individually packaged and sold to other software developers. A large market has sprung up for the resale of COM components that can then be used to build new applications. A company that needs to build an application with an extensive set of pie charts and graphs can purchase components for displaying them rather than create its own from scratch.

Many corporations, having depended on expensive, unfriendly mainframe systems for years, have realized the benefits of moving their information systems over to COM for use on inexpensive, easy-to-use PCs. Such a corporation redesigns the way that information is handled internally to focus on easily reusable COM components to perform mission-critical tasks such as tracking customers and inventory, providing help desk support, and automating the sales force. Other corporations have taken a more hesitant step forward by reimplementing just the presentation layer of their information systems using COM. These corporations still depend on mainframe back ends but have migrated their staff from having to use crusty green-screen terminals to more productive Windows-based user interfaces. Both types of corporations are sitting on a mountain of great COM software.

Enter the Web. Now customers want to enter orders and track shipping on their own. Some particularly demanding customers even want to be able to download their own account records over the Internet. The MIS department projects that millions could be saved if the company eliminated the existing private nationwide leased line system and replaced it with simple, cheap Internet connections for each office. Finally, a few engineers start making noise about the benefits of Java.

The existing base of COM components is incredibly valuable, but it is not compatible with the Write Once, Run Anywhere approach to software development. COM components don't extend well over the Internet and aren't compatible with many Web browsers. Corporations moving toward more Internet-intensive software are faced with the problem of dealing with a mountain of legacy COM components.

Using COM In Java

Microsoft is encouraging developers to use Windows-specific code in their Java software. This position, if accepted by developers, ensures Windows' place in a world dominated by Java software. However, Java software using Windows-specific code loses the benefits of Write Once, Run Anywhere and can be run only on the Windows operating system, often with only the latest versions of NT and 95.

Microsoft has made COM very easy to use within Java programs. COM components integrated very naturally and easily with Java since the earliest releases of the Microsoft Java SDK. Creating a COM component within a Java program requires nothing more than a constructor-like invocation. For example, a registered COM component with the name CHello and an operation called say(), may be used within a Java program with the following code:

```
CHello h = new CHello();
h.say();
```

Any Java developer will have to admit that this is extremely easy. This code looks like any other Java code; the COM constructor looks like a Java constructor. In fact, if we replaced the COM component with a Java object of the same name with the method say(), the Java program would not have to be changed.

Replacing COM components with Java objects without changing code is very powerful. A company with a large installed base of COM components can take advantage of this capability successfully. Java software that makes use of the existing COM components can be coded today. These components can be replaced by Java objects with the same name and interface without any need to recode the applications that utilized the COM components. This ease of replacement facilitates the gradual phase-out of COM components rather than requiring sudden, total replacement of the system. Gradual phase-out is a much more realistic migration path than total replacement for many corporations. Only the bytecode generated by the Microsoft Java compiler (called jvc) would require recompilation, which is much simpler than a code rewrite.

Limitations

Any COM component can be instantiated and invoked in this manner, but integrating COM and Java does have some limitations. First, COM components cannot accept Java objects as arguments. COM supports only a limited number of data types, which have been part of COM for many years. Java objects, a relatively recent development in the software industry, are not included among the COM data types. Worse, the data types that COM does support can be traced back to COM's legacy as an architecture for Visual Basic. As a result, many Visual Basic data types are easier to use with COM than are any of the Java data types. For example, Varient, a Visual Basic data type, is allowed in COM arguments, but

Vector, a common Java type, has to be translated, or mapped, into a pointer to a COM IDispatch interface, an IDispatch* in C notation. Each Java data type maps into one of the COM data types, though often the two are not very closely related, as shown in Table 4.1.

Integrating COM and Java is also limited by COM's integration with the Windows operating system. When a COM component is used within a Java program, the Microsoft virtual machine must use the Windows Registry to determine the location of the COM component. All COM components must be registered with the operating system before they can be used in a program because the

Table 4.1 Mapping COM and Java Data Types

COM Types	Java Types
boolean	boolean
char	char
double	double
int	int
int64	long
float	float
long	int
short	short
unsigned char	byte
BSTR	java.lang.String
DATE	double
HRESULT	int
VARIANT	com.ms.com.Variant
IUnknown*	interface com.ms.com.IUnknown
IDispatch*	java.lang.Object
void	void

In C and C++; pointers are represented by using a * right after the data type. This is true of COM also; because it was originally designed for C/C++.

Registry is consulted for the location of each COM component used within a program. This registration requires special steps during software installation. In contrast, other distributed object tools, such as Caffeine, Voyager, and RMI, written in pure Java are ready to use immediately after download without special installation procedures.

Overall, Microsoft deserves congratulations for building a rather ingenious mechanism for integrating COM and Java. Surprisingly, Microsoft no longer recommends this approach to interacting with COM components. A new, slightly harder-to-use method for integrating COM components with Java is available in the latest version of the Microsoft Java SDK. The reasoning behind this move is unclear. One possible explanation may be the different approaches to object typing in Java and COM. Unlike Java, which is a strongly typed language, COM is not strongly typed and is based on run-time examination of the capabilities of each COM component. Merging the two approaches may have proven too difficult.

The new approach maps every COM component into a generic Java class called ActiveXControl. This class represents a handle to any COM component. For example, an ActiveXControl could represent a fragment of an Excel document, a Calendar, or something else whipped up by a Visual Basic programmer. Because all COM components can be stored in this single Java object, the differences in typing between COM and Java are no longer relevant. All COM types map into exactly one Java type. The COM component can no longer be accessed as if it were a native Java object, so this new approach may seem less elegant to many Java developers.

What Will Be the Next Acronym?

COM has gone through many name changes over its lifetime. The technology came into fruition in Visual Basic as VBX controls. These controls were nothing more than a particular API that C developers could use to code widgets that could be dragged and dropped within the Visual Basic environment.

VBX technology was extended to 32-bit environments with Microsoft-developed OLE, which initially stood for object linking and embedding. Microsoft defined ways of cutting and pasting using OLE components so that portions of applications could be embedded or linked with portions of other applications.

Continues

What Will Be the Next Acronym? *(Continued)*

With some API changes, OLE evolved into OLE2. Microsoft began encouraging developers to forget that OLE was an acronym for object linking and embedding, claiming that OLE had "grown beyond linking and embedding." The OLE acronym was still used for some time, but it came to refer to a vaguely defined component technology.

COM, aka component object model, was arguably just a renaming of OLE2 to fit in the "component" buzzword. Some say that COM is the name of the framework while OLE2 is the name of the components developed within the framework. Other explanations extended over the years to justify this specific name change have been used mostly to market the product.

ActiveX came about just after Java hit the Net in 1995. ActiveX was no less than a positioning of COM to compete with Java. The experiment has largely failed because COM components, unlike Java applets, are used rarely on the Internet. However, the ActiveX name began to eclipse the COM name in other contexts in addition to the Web.

DNA, the distributed Internet applications, is another component architecture from Microsoft that is due to be released. Microsoft describes it as the "first application architecture to fully embrace and integrate both the Web and client/server models of application development."

Prerelease specifications for COM+ are currently available. These stress COM+ as a language-independent version of COM. It is unclear at this time how COM+ and COM differ because COM is also language independent, requiring the use of conventions only for loading and executing components. Microsoft has also stated that COM will be forward compatible with COM+, allowing existing COM components to work with COM+. Further claims indicate that COM+ will be backwards compatible with COM.

Constructing an instance of ActiveXControl is somewhat more difficult than constructing an instance of the CHello component. The constructor for ActiveXControl requires a globally unique identifier (GUID).

GUIDs may be familiar to COM developers or implementers of RPC/DCE systems. A GUID is a 128-bit value that uniquely identifies a component. The GUID combines the host name of the computer, the time at which the component was generated, and random numbers to generate a 128-bit value that is unique to a particular software application and anywhere in the world. The downside of developing with GUIDs is that a special tool called GUIDGEN must be used to create each one to ensure a unique combination of numbers. The software developer can't simply make up a number because two software developers might choose exactly the same 128-bit value.

N **O T E** : GUIDs were common in distributed computing toolkits such as DCE/RPC until most vendors moved toward implementing them below the source level. CORBA, RMI, and Voyager all have their own mechanisms for identifying objects that do not require the software developer to explicitly specify them in code.

Working with GUIDs in software confuses the source code because embedded 128-bit values in an application are not self-documenting. The following code constructs a handle to a calendar control:

```
ActiveXControl mscal = new ActiveXControl("{8E27C92B-1264-101C-8A2F-
040224009C02}");
```

Could you tell from the 128-bit value in the source code that this is a calendar?

It is also unnatural to use the new approach to accessing COM components through the ActiveXControl to work with properties and methods on COM components. Recall that in a JavaBean called calendar, one gets the value of a property called Date by calling the method getDate, following the JavaBeans naming convention for reading the value of properties:

```
Date d = calendar.getDate();
```

This property could return an instance of a Date object directly.

The new ActiveXControl object doesn't allow the developer to use these kinds of getter and setter methods on the object directly. A number of methods of ActiveXControl implement the same capabilities in a manner that is consistent with COM's weak typing. For example:

```
Variant variant = mscal.getProperty("Date");
```

Note that the name of the property is passed in as a string. Any property can be named at run time if a different property name is specified. In other words, this is an example of weak typing, because any name can be specified at runtime. The getProperty method always returns a COM Variant. The developer is then responsible for reading the appropriate values out of the Variant. The code that performs this operation typically looks something like this:

```
long time = variant.getLong();
```

The Variant doesn't support the Java Date object, thus you have to read in a long value from the variant representing the number of seconds since January 1, 1970. Then, as yet another step, you can create a new Date object:

```
Date d = new Date(time);
```

You set properties through a setProperty method. Just like the getProperty method, the setProperty method achieves weak typing by passing in the name of the property as a string:

```
long time = d.getTime();
mscal.setProperty("date",time);
```

The first line converts a Date object into a Java long. Again, COM doesn't support the Java Date object, so you must convert the object into another form before using it within COM. The Java Date.getTime() method returns the number of milliseconds in a well-known date. This can be used to obtain a representation of the Date object as a long. The ActiveXObject.setProperty() at least takes advantage of Java's function overloading to eliminate the extra step of converting the Java long back into a Variant.

Compare the code required to work with properties on JavaBeans shown in Listing 4.1 and the code required to work with properties on ActiveXControls, shown in Listing 4.2.

```
Variant variant = mscal.getProperty("Date");
long time = variant.getLong();
Date d = new Date(time);
time = d.getTime();
mscal.setProperty("date",time);
```

Listing 4.1 Obtaining a Date property in COM.

```
calendar.setDate(d);
Date d = calendar.getDate();
```

Listing 4.2 Obtaining a Date property in JavaBeans.

The most significant difference is the number of lines necessary for the two codes, especially given that getting and setting properties are among the most common actions performed by component software developers. It is also likely that the JavaBeans code is much easier to read and understand.

Let's not let this code cloud our judgment too much, though. Developers have manufactured thousands of COM components with many capabilities. Visual Basic is based entirely on the composition of many small COM components into large, complex forms. The ActiveXControl object gives Java developers access to these objects, not just to work with their properties and methods, but also to include them in user interfaces.

Adding a COM component into a user interface is fairly simple. Because the Active-XControl is a child of java.awt.Component, adding an instance of ActiveXControl to a Java user interface is as easy as adding a Java component, such as Button or CheckBox. Windows and dialog boxes in Java inherit from a common base class, java.awt.Container. This base class represents all the user interface objects that can hold other components. The add() method is used to add a new user interface component to a container. Invoke the following code to add the calendar COM component to a Java user interface:

```
ActiveXControl mscal = new ActiveXControl("{8E27C92B-1264-101C-8A2F-
040224009C02}");
frame.add("Center",mscal);
```

Implementing this code in a sample program displays the calendar control in a Java frame, which indicates that COM visual user interfaces can be reused in Java without substantial changes.

Unfortunately, the calendar component is not pure Java. It's a part of Microsoft Office 95 and requires the Windows95 or NT operating system, a Microsoft Java Virtual Machine such as Internet Explorer 4 or better, and Microsoft Office 95. All three software packages must be installed (and royalties duly paid to Bill Gates) for the component to run.

As mentioned earlier in this chapter, the initial approach Microsoft used for integrating Java and COM had a convenient benefit: The code for creating and using COM components was the same as that for Java objects, facilitating the eventual replacement of COM components with Java objects. Does this new approach to accessing COM components with the ActiveXControl provide many of the same benefits? An instance of the ActiveXControl object is used to refer to any control at all, whether the control is a button, calendar, or Excel spreadsheet. In Java, components are referred to with an explicit class name. The components are strongly typed. Here, the COM components are weakly typed.

You can replace COM components completely by using a coding technique that prepares you for the rotation away from the ActiveXControls and toward pure Java objects. One technique would be to define a child class for the appropriate object, such as calendar in Listing 4.3.

```
public class Calendar extends ActiveXControl
{
public Calendar()
  {
super("{8E27C92B-1264-101C-8A2F-040224009C02}");
  }
}
```

Listing 4.3 Calendar subclass.

The calendar object can be used in place of its ActiveXControl parent. The code snippet for instantiating and adding a calendar to a Java frame would read as follows:

```
Calendar c = new Calendar();
frame.add("Center",c);
```

The revised code is identical to normal Java code, including a nice clean constructor with a real class name and no GUID. This code, combined with the class definition in Listing 4.3, still works exactly the same as the original ActiveXControl code with one key difference: The Calendar component can be replaced with a pure Java object. Once this control is replaced, one would not need Microsoft Office 95 to be installed to use the program. Once all the controls are replaced by compatible pure Java versions, the program will run in non-Microsoft virtual machines and operating systems.

The bottom line is that COM components can be used with Java software. You don't have to throw away your investment in COM to begin moving to Java. With a little care and planning, COM components can be used in your software today with an eye toward a non-COM, non-Microsoft future.

Building COM with Java

Surprisingly, COM components can be written in Java. COM is widely used as the component architecture of several development environments, compatible with Visual Basic, Visual C++, Delphi, and PowerBuilder. This means that you can embed your Java objects inside these development environments.

This capability may appeal to corporations that have made heavy investments in Visual Basic expertise. Legacy COM programmers don't need to be downsized in the process of moving toward a Java future. Legacy applications don't need to be taken out of development and turned over to a code maintenance team. You can continue to extend your legacy applications using the power of Java.

COM components are also widely used in the Microsoft operating systems. As a result, you can even register a Java object as a Windows NT service, for example.

Developing a Java object compatible with COM could not be easier. In fact, any Java object can be registered as a COM component. Microsoft supplies a tool called javareg.exe that can register any Java object as a COM component. Write your object, compile it with Microsoft's Java compiler, and then register it as a COM component with javareg.exe. That's it.

The properties and methods of a COM-registered Java object automatically become properties and methods for the COM component. COM specifically uses the same naming conventions, or design patterns, used by JavaBeans to determine the properties and methods that should be made available on the object. For example, a property called Date should have a get method with the name getDate, just as with JavaBeans.

COM components written in Java may also paint a user interface. Java components included in a user interface need to extend the java.awt.Panel class in order to paint a user interface when it is used as a COM component. The Panel class implements the common behavior for any object that takes up screen real estate in Java. One of the beautiful decisions in Microsoft's COM/Java integration work was the preservation of exactly this pattern. Any Java object that extends Panel can paint a user interface and be used as a visual COM component, even in development environments like Visual Basic.

Putting it all together, we can implement a simple COM component in Java. This COM component, shown in Listing 4.4, draws a friendly Hello message to the user interface.

```
public class Hello extends Panel
{
  public Hello() {}
  private String s;
  public String getGreeting()
  {
    return this.s;
  }
  public void setGreeting(String s)
  {
    this.s = s;
  }
}
```

Listing 4.4 COM component written in Java.

Because the message is a property, it can be changed at run time if the property is set. Properties on COM components implemented in Java can also be modified through the same techniques used for other COM components, such as Visual Basic property sheets.

COM also supports the standard Java event model, allowing for mouse and keyboard events using familiar Java code. The Microsoft virtual machine handles the task of mapping Java events from Win32 events, even those coming from sources like the Visual Basic run-time environment.

Components that listen to user interface events must first register their interest in a particular set of events by invoking the enableEvents method. For example, an object that listens to the mouse events should register interest in the AWTEvent .MOUSE_EVENT_MASK. A good place to perform this operation is in the constructor of the object that listens to these events, as shown in the following constructor.

```
public Hello()
{
  enableEvents(AWTEvent.MOUSE_EVENT_MASK);
}
```

The events will be delivered to the object when the processMouseEvent method defined on the Panel class is invoked. The object must provide an implementation of this method that does something with the event. For example, the case of the greeting is changed when a mouse event occurs as in Listing 4.5:

```
protected void processMouseEvent(MouseEvent e)
{
  if((e.getID()) == MouseEvent.MOUSE_PRESSED)
    {
      setGreeting(getGreeting().toLowerCase());
    }
  else if((e.getID()) == MouseEvent.MOUSE_PRESSED)
    {
      setGreeting(getGreeting().toUpperCase());
    }
}
```

Listing 4.5 processMouseEvent method.

The COM component can also throw its own events. An event can be passed not just to other Java objects, but to components in other development environments that register themselves as listeners to this component. In order to add an event to your object, create a subclass of the java.util.EventListener class, as in standard Java development.

One great feature comes out of this design: JavaBeans written in pure Java automatically become fully functional COM components.

Any JavaBean can be imported and used as a COM component! This suggests that a natural approach to integrating Java and COM might be to write for JavaBeans, then use the JavaBeans when necessary in COM-compatible development environments. JavaBeans work with any Java Virtual Machine or operating system, and are now compatible subsets of COM on the Win32 operating systems and in Microsoft virtual machines. Therefore, JavaBeans probably offer the best route if you want to develop components that work with COM and still have the benefits of pure Java.

DCOM

Integrating COM components and Java is like loading a dynamically linked library in a program. The two pieces integrate, but in a book dedicated to distributed computing, it's difficult to see where the distributed comes in. DCOM introduces distributed computing to COM.

DCOM is much different from other approaches to distributed computing, including CORBA and RPC/DCE. Unlike most distributed computing toolkits, in which the toolkit is responsible for communicating among the applications that make up the distributed system, activating new distributed objects on demand, and providing security to the distributed objects, DCOM leaves everything up to the operating system.

Another difference between DCOM and other distributed computing toolkits is their use of stubs and skeletons. In CORBA, RMI, and Voyager, stubs and skeletons are compiled based on an interface definition. In DCOM, stubs and skeletons are not always required. Instead, DCOM uses the information compiled into the COM component to determine its interface at run time. DCOM does have an interface definition language called Microsoft Interface Definition Language (MIDL), but DCOM developers can often skip the step of writing this MIDL file.

The final difference is that any COM component can be used with DCOM. Even legacy COM components that were developed prior to the introduction of DCOM may be remotely invoked through DCOM. This is perhaps one of the most confusing points of DCOM programming. Many developers new to DCOM don't understand why there is so little documentation and no tutorial on writing DCOM. The reason is simple: COM components and DCOM components are the same.

Using COM Components with DCOM

Some system configuration is required to use your COM components with DCOM. The main tool used to perform this configuration is DCOMConf.exe, which is installed in recent builds of Windows NT 4.0 and Windows95. DCOMConf will be in the System32 or System directories respectively on these operating systems. The main window for DCOMConf is shown in Figure 4.1.

DCOMConf is used to configure the way a COM component should work in a distributed environment. For each COM component on the system, DCOMConf controls when and how the component will be created. The administrator can also use this tool to establish the security specifications of DCOM, setting its authentication level and delegation policy.

To work with DCOM using one of the COM objects you wrote written earlier in this chapter, you'll need a registered COM component. If you have not already registered one of your Java objects as a COM component, do so using the javareg command. If you would like to demonstrate a distributed system by running your DCOM component on a second computer, make a copy of the COM component and register it on the second computer as well.

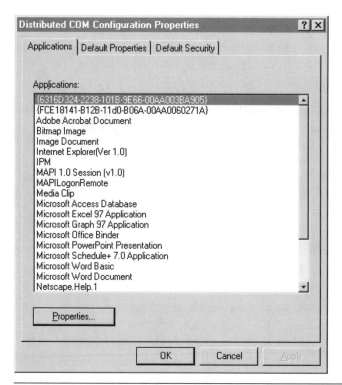

Figure 4.1 DCOMConf.

Next, find DCOMConf on your operating system. You obviously need one of the latest versions of Windows95 or NT for this. You should see a window similar to that in Figure 4.1 listing the registered COM components. The registered Java objects are included in this list beginning with the prefix "Java Class" followed by the class name. Select the Java class that you want to remotely invoke, then click the Properties button to view the configuration for the selected COM component. The DCOM Properties window for your COM component should appear with at least two tabs. The General tab shows information about your component such as the name and type of application. The type of application should read remote server, indicating that your COM component will be invoked as a remote server through DCOM. A space may be provided for the name of the remote computer on which your new DCOM component will run. This should initially be blank (Figure 4.2).

DCOM on Unix?

Much attention has been dedicated to the COM porting efforts by Software AG. Will COM and DCOM be available for use by Java developers in Unix any time soon? Unfortunately, the porting efforts have provided only the most basic interoperating between COM components and Unix. At this time, many of the value-added services of COM, such as Microsoft Transaction Service, do not integrate with Unix to any extent. The Microsoft Java SDK is also not available for Unix, so Java objects cannot be converted into COM components or vice versa on the Unix platform. Finally, it's not likely that COM components, which are often implemented as executables or dynamically linked libraries for the Intel processor, will ever be compatible with the Unix platform without Windows emulation.

The Location tab picks the host computer for the DCOM component. Three checkboxes are available for configuring this host information. The first checkbox asks whether to run the DCOM component on the computer where the data is located. This checkbox is used for persistent components, those that implement the IPersist interface. If you will not use COM persistence, which is probably a good idea anyway, do not click this checkbox The second checkbox asks whether to run the component on this computer. The third checkbox asks whether to run the component on a different computer. To demonstrate distributed computing, select the third and final checkbox, then click the Browse button to locate a machine on your

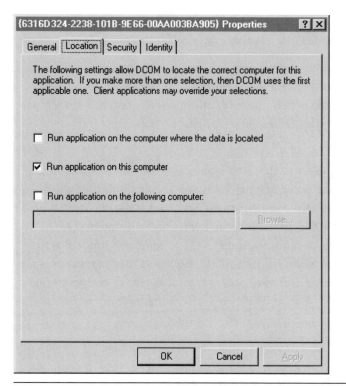

Figure 4.2 Configuring a DCOM component.

local domain to host the DCOM component. If you already copied your COM component onto a second computer (and registered it on that computer!), choose the second computer now. The COM object must be available and registered on the host computer before you will be able to use it remotely through DCOM.

Feasibility of Mobile Objects with DCOM

How do the integration of COM and Java and the ability of DCOM to remotely invoke COM components help to implement mobile objects? The answer lies in the core of the DCOM architecture. In DCOM, components are referred to through a pointer to a special COM interface called the *IDispatch interface*. The methods required to invoke the operations available on the component are made available through the IDispatch interface. Thus, in the previous section discussing the use of the DCOMConf tool to configure COM objects for distributed use, the IDispatch interface is used by the underlying system to represent the object reference that may be invoked.

This pointer to an IDispatch interface may be sent to other computers. The value of the pointer itself is not sent because of the different physical memory address spaces involved in a distributed system. Instead, information is passed between participants in the distributed system, allowing participants to construct their own copy of the IDispatch object.

The role of IDispatch is similar to that of a stub in any distributed object architecture. IDispatch provides the point of entry to invoke the methods on a distributed COM component. The COM component itself remains statically located on a single computer at all times while different computers access it through the IDispatch interface. Under no circumstances do COM components migrate across the network in the manner of mobile objects, partly because COM components are often installed as part of a larger software package, even as part of the operating system. Using a particular COM component on a new computer may require the installation of a new software package or even operating system.

In contrast, using a new Java class on a computer may require simply downloading some additional bytecode. In addition, DCOM doesn't lend itself to communicating instances of Java objects as the other distributed object architectures discussed previously do. Java objects used as arguments in a COM invocation are mapped into an IDispatch*. The Java object itself is not communicated between virtual machines; only an IDispatch is communicated. In effect, only the stub to a distributed object is sent between participants in the DCOM distributed system.

This lack of communication greatly limits our ability to implement a mobile object architecture on top of DCOM. It supports none of the flexibility of copying instances of Java objects that are required. The best solution to adding object mobility to DCOM boils down to building it from the ground up, implementing a new ORB alongside or on top of DCOM to add the capabilities of object mobility.

However, we may still utilize a second mobile object tool to enhance the capabilities of DCOM. Microsoft has provided Java developers with valuable Java/COM integration at an unprecedented level. Taking advantage of the capabilities of COM within mobile objects could prove extremely effective.

Mixing RMI and DCOM

Microsoft makes the only virtual machines that support DCOM. Microsoft also has taken a hard line against RMI in its virtual machines. Whether or not this issue is resolved, in or out of court, developers might see benefits in combining RMI and DCOM in some applications. In particular, mobile objects can be implemented with RMI while DCOM may be useful for remotely invoking COM components such as those found in Microsoft Office.

Although the outlook is grim, RMI and DCOM can be combined with a little creative joining of portions of the Microsoft Java SDK with portions of the standard Java Development Kit.

The RMI classes in the Java Development Kit are currently written in pure Java, which means that you can run RMI on top of any compatible Java Virtual Machine, even one that does not provide its own RMI classes. All you need to do is make sure that the RMI classes from the JDK are in your class path. Then the Microsoft virtual machine can actually load the RMI classes from the standard JDK! You are ready to run RMI applications on top of the Microsoft virtual machine and can mix DCOM code in with your RMI code.

Combining mobile objects and DCOM could have significant benefits. COM and DCOM components can be used within mobile objects. This access would permit mobile objects to access DCOM software such as Microsoft Office and Visual Basic. For example, a mobile object responsible for spell checking a document could be implemented in terms of the Microsoft Word spell checker through the appropriate COM component. Unfortunately, embedding DCOM components within mobile objects restricts the applicability of these mobile objects to the Windows operating system, Microsoft virtual machine, and computers that have the right COM components preinstalled.

The Microsoft virtual machine implements the Java standard to a point. Microsoft doesn't implement RMI or CORBA because it perceives these technologies as competitive with DCOM. However, the virtual machine does implement most of the rest of the Java standard.

Many distributed object tools are written in 100% Pure Java and are designed specifically for the broadest possible compatibility. Some distributed object tools can run with little or no limitations in older Java 1.0.2 Virtual Machines. These same tools are compatible with the Microsoft virtual machine and can be combined with DCOM.

Another approach that may make more sense is implementing COM and DCOM components in terms of mobile objects. Components developed with mobile objects can take advantage of all the flexibility described throughout this book, yet still integrate with Visual Basic and other popular COM compatible development environments. In addition, JavaBeans are automatically compatible with COM because of the close parallels to JavaBeans Microsoft chose when designing the Java/COM mapping. Any JavaBeans implemented with mobile objects automatically become compatible with COM.

Enhancements for COM

As a result of JavaBeans' compatibility with COM, Microsoft has deployed a number of services to enhance the capabilities of COM. The services provide added functionality that is not available in the basic COM environment, such as implementing transactions, messaging, and security. Java integrates with COM, allowing Java software to make use of these services.

Mobile objects written with other tools can still make use of the services of COM even though COM and DCOM don't specifically support the mobile object software approach. For example, a mobile object originating from another computer on a network may travel from node to node utilizing these COM services. Let's take a quick look at some of the services Microsoft has made available for COM.

Transactions

Suppose you walk into a pet store and after much consideration decide to purchase an armadillo. You pay the cashier, who happily drops your money into the register, then goes into the stockroom to get an armadillo. Suddenly, some prankster pulls the fire alarm. The cashier immediately runs for the front door, leaving you screaming, "Where's my armadillo?"

The pet store incident is an example of a transaction gone bad. You turned over your money expecting that you would get a armadillo in return. You implicitly assumed that the store would return your money if it couldn't produce an armadillo. The purchase was interrupted by the fire alarm, leaving you with neither money nor armadillo.

Transactions likes this are common in life, both real and virtual, particularly when it comes to commerce. Whenever you pay for goods or services, you expect that two things will happen. First, you will pay some money. Second, the goods or services will be delivered. You do not expect that only one or the other should ever occur. That is, you wouldn't expect to pay for the goods but not receive them. You also wouldn't expect to receive the goods and not pay for them.

However, software processes are normally the antithesis of transactions. A program executes a step-by-step algorithm, a list of commands. For example, if you were to write a program to ship products ordered from a pet store catalog, you might come up with the following algorithm:

1. Enter order.

2. Calculate total.

3. Charge customer.

4. Deliver products.

What happens if the computer crashes between Steps 3 and 4? The customer is billed for a product, but the product is never shipped. The customer will not be happy with this arrangement. As a result, you might try to revise your algorithm by swapping Steps 3 and 4. The algorithm would then look like this:

1. Enter order.

2. Calculate total.

3. Deliver products.

4. Charge customer.

Customers are not always great about paying their bills, though. Some credit cards are rejected and an occasional check is returned for insufficient funds. However, Step 4 happens after Step 3 in this program, so the merchandise has already shipped to a customer who never paid for it.

This scenario demonstrates the inherent trouble with implementing transactions with a list of commands. At this point, doing so seems impossible.

Years of studying this problem have resulted in a technique called two-phase commit. The general idea is that all the steps in a transaction are executed in a temporary memory where the actions don't actually have any lasting effect. If all of the steps in the transaction work properly, the temporary memory is saved and becomes part of the permanent record. If any of the steps fail, the temporary memory is simply thrown away, and it's as if the transaction never happened.

Two main commands, commit and abort, are used with a two-phase commit. Commit causes the current transaction to immediately become part of the permanent record. Abort causes the current transaction to immediately fail and be erased from the permanent record.

Successful transactional systems should be able to pass the ACID test. ACID is an acronym that stands for the four required properties of a transactional system as follows:

♦ *Atomic*. A transaction either happens or doesn't happen. A transaction should never partially occur and partially fail. (You either bought the armadillo or you didn't.)

♦ *Consistent*. A transaction should never result in an uncertain state of the system. (After attempting to purchase an armadillo, you would expect to either have your money and no armadillo or not have your money but have an armadillo. You would be in an inconsistent state if you found that you had both your money and the armadillo, or lacked money and armadillo.)

♦ *Isolated*. Transactions may be executed one after another. (You can buy an armadillo and then come back to buy another armadillo.)

♦ *Durable*. Once a transaction has been committed, the transaction cannot fail after the fact. The transaction becomes part of the permanent record. (After successfully purchasing an armadillo, no one forces you to return your armadillo.)

Transactions are a significant part of database technology. In a pet shop database, one table might correspond to the current inventory of armadillos and another table, to the known owners of armadillos in the area. Yet another table might contain the financial records for the store. For the purchase of an armadillo, all three of these tables have to be modified atomically.

Suppose that armadillos are moving so fast that the pet shop finds it has to add a second database just for armadillo records. A new challenge is faced: making two transactional databases work with each other. How can a transaction occur in both databases at the same time and yet remain atomic? That the two databases might be from different vendors and utilize different APIs adds to this problem.

The solution to this problem came with the introduction of a transaction standard called XA. Transactional software that implements the XA standard can participate in a two-phase commit with other software that implements the XA standard. The XA standard itself is remarkably simple. In a nutshell, the XA standard requires that XA-compliant software knows how to perform the commit and abort commands.

When COM components access XA-compliant databases, the COM components themselves become part of the transaction. In the design of a pet store application with COM, one COM component could represent the customer and another the armadillo. The armadillo component might have an ownership property, which changes when the armadillo is purchased. In a proper transaction, you would expect that the amount of money in the customer's wallet and the armadillo's ownership property would be updated atomically. However, in an everyday COM environment, the modification of COM components is nowhere near this reliable.

Suppose you were to write a Java program that manipulated the customer and armadillo COM components along with the financial and armadillo databases. The COM components must be part of the transaction somehow, or the system might end up in an inconsistent state. You might end up with a situation in which the armadillo component has already set its ownership property, but the databases have aborted the transaction.

Microsoft Transaction Server (MTS) provides the missing piece that links COM components with transactions. MTS implements an XA-compliant transactional framework for COM components. Even Java can be used to implement COM components that participate in a transaction.

COM components enhanced with MTS participate in a transaction in much the same way as other XA-compliant systems. COM components can invoke operations on MTS in order to commit or abort transactions. When a transaction is committed, all the XA-compliant systems participating in the transaction will commit the transaction. If the same transaction is aborted, all the XA-compliant systems will abort the transaction.

The operations available on MTS are closely associated with the XA standard itself. The main operations that a component that participates in a transaction employs are equivalent to the XA commit and abort commands. In order for a COM component written in Java to indicate that a transaction should abort once the method is completed, the component invokes Mtx.GetObjectContext().SetAbort(). Note that the transaction is not committed or aborted immediately. Rather, the current operation is completed and then the transaction is either committed or aborted. In order to indicate that a component is ready to commit a transaction, the component would invoke Mtx.GetObjectContext().SetCommit(). By invoking SetCommit, a component indicates only its own readiness to commit a transaction. The transaction won't be committed until every participant indicates that it can commit the transaction.

Let's go back to the armadillo pet shop software with the customer and armadillo COM components. The customer component has a spend() method that deducts funds from the customer wallet that participates in a transaction (Listing 4.6).

```
import com.ms.mtx.*;      // The MTS package in Java
public class Customer
implements ICustomer
    {
public void spend(double cash)
      {
boolean insufficientFunds;
// Deduct money and check for insufficient funds
if (insufficentFunds)
Mtx.GetObjectContext().SetAbort();
else
Mtx.GetObjectContext().SetCommit();
      }
    }
```

Listing 4.6 Transactions with MTS.

The armadillo component simply has to change its ownership. This change of ownership never fails to occur, so the armadillo component always calls SetCommit just before completion, as shown in Listing 4.7:

```
import com.ms.mtx.*;     // The MTS package in Java
public class Armadillo
implements IArmadillo
  {
public void setOwner(String name)
    {
// Set the new owner
Mtx.GetObjectContext().SetCommit();
    }
  }
```

Listing 4.7 SetCommit.

The pet shop software application written with these two COM components and two XA relational databases implements a transactional environment. If the Customer component has insufficient funds and invokes the SetAbort method, each of the participants in the transaction will be notified, and the transaction will abort. If both components and the two relational databases all indicate that they are ready to commit, the entire transaction can be safely committed.

One might finally ask exactly what part of the COM component is committed? Are the state or member variables of the component committed? Is the component saved in the transactional database? What exactly does it mean for a component to be transactional?

The answer is that it's entirely up to you, the developer. MTS does absolutely nothing for you when it comes to having your component participate in a transaction. If you want your component to save itself as part of a transaction, you must provide the code yourself. A common approach is to have a component save its state inside one of the relational databases participating in the transaction. That way, if the transaction is aborted, both the component and the database abort the transaction, and the state of the component is discarded.

Thus, it's important to realize that MTS is not magical in providing transactions to components. You, the developer, do all the real work of making your components work within transactions. MTS just provides some coordination among the participants in the transaction.

Messaging

Suppose you want to call the pet shop to order an armadillo. You pick up the phone, dial the shop's number, and wait for someone to answer the phone. If you are lucky, you are able to get a connect between the two telephones, and someone is waiting to answer the call. If all these things happen just right, you can place your order for an armadillo.

A phone call is an example of a synchronous system. Two parties are simultaneously interacting over a communication line. Both parties have to be present at the time of the interaction. If the telephone connection is lost, you have to pick up the phone and try your call again.

Many distributed systems are modeled after synchronous communication. For example, when you view a Web page, your Web browser first opens a TCP/IP connection to a remote Web server, sends the Web server a header containing the name of the document you wish to view, and the Web server responds by sending the document back to you over the TCP/IP connection. If the Web server "isn't home," you won't be able to view the document and will have to try again later.

Synchronous systems are sufficient for environments in which all the interacting parties are always available and the communication lines never fail. In the real world, people leave the house or office. Phone lines break. During Thanksgiving, the phone circuits are so overloaded that only a few calls trickle through the system. The same is true of Web servers. Software crashes, Internet lines go down, and popular Web sites are frequently overloaded.

In a system in which some of the components will not be available all the time, asynchronous communication may be superior. E-mail is an example of a very successful asynchronous distributed system. When you send e-mail, you don't have to wait to see if the recipient is home. You don't have to wait for the message to be read at all. You just send your message and forget about it. The e-mail system will quietly attempt to deliver the message in the background without your attention. If the computer to which you are sending the e-mail is not currently available, your mail server will make many attempts over several days to deliver the e-mail message. You have the guarantee that either the message will be delivered or you will eventually be notified if the message cannot get through for an extended period of time.

The recipient of your e-mail message can respond to you in kind. The recipient may be reading your message days later and respond to it when you are offline. However, when you check your e-mail, the message will be there waiting for you.

In a perfect world, the pet shop selling the armadillo would have so much Internet savvy that it would be shipping software to allow customers to order armadillos right over the Internet. A customer would have a client application that communicates with the server application at the armadillo pet shop. The customer picks an armadillo from a catalog of various colors and models, then submits an order with just a few mouse clicks.

With a synchronous communication approach, the client would immediately attempt to connect to the server. If the Internet connection were down or slow, if the server process had crashed, or if a power outage had affected the pet shop, the client might not be able to successfully communicate with the server, and the pet shop might unintentionally lose some business.

In a distributed system, asynchronous communication could have its advantages under these conditions. Objects in distributed object systems may benefit from being able to send messages to other objects even if those objects are not immediately available. That way, when the objects do become available, the message can still be properly handled. In the case of the pet shop, that means that the customer can submit an order to buy an armadillo even if the pet shop is experiencing a power outage, and the pet shop doesn't lose any business.

Microsoft Message Queue Server (MSMQ) provides messaging capabilities to software. Like many Microsoft software packages, MSMQ is invoked through COM, so the Java integration with COM allows you to use MSMQ within your own software.

When it comes to messaging in general, different software applications can send messages to each other in many ways. The primary way that distributed object software communicates with other distributed object software is by remote invocation of methods. For example, DCOM permits operations on remote COM components to be accessed as if they were local components. This same abstraction works well with messaging. A remote invocation can be delivered to a remote object through a messaging service, permitting the remote invocation to occur even if both parties are not simultaneously available.

Unfortunately, MSMQ messages are not quite that simple. MSMQ messages are sent through the manipulation of a set of COM components. The messages themselves may be either byte arrays, strings, or COM components that support the IPersist interface, a standard for externalizing COM components to a byte array. The developer who wants to utilize MSMQ with DCOM has to perform all the work of converting invocations into byte arrays. Since the whole goal of using DCOM is to eliminate the need to convert remote invocations into byte arrays, using MSMQ eliminates most of the benefits of DCOM. Perhaps in future versions of MSMQ, DCOM support will be added, increasing the value of combining MSMQ and DCOM substantially. Today, it's an either/or situation for all practical purposes.

Security

Computer networks are dark and scary places. They function much the same way as a den of thieves. A client can pretend to be another client. A server can pretend to be another server. Third parties can even pretend to be both servers to clients and clients to servers in order to eavesdrop and manipulate communications.

The core technology behind computer networks assumes that each computer can trust the other computers. For example, Internet routing tables are published with little or no verification. It's widely believed among security experts that a destructively inclined individual could bring the Internet to a screeching halt by simply broadcasting false information. In yet another example, people commonly live under the illusion that when their computer communicates with another computer on the Internet, only the two computers are involved. Actually, many computers are involved. The information you send is routed through as many as 30 different computers, much as a parcel is routed to several cities before reaching its destination. Ethernet communication is even broadcast to all the computers on a LAN, not a point-to-point connection privately held between your computer and another on the LAN.

In a distributed object setting, the lack of security on a computer network can cause real problems. In a financial application, the distributed objects may represent electronic commerce transactions. The ability of a possibly malicious third party to steal the information contained with the transaction could result in lost business, credit card fraud, loss of face, and more. Just use your imagination. Competing businesses could even quietly eavesdrop on each other and send competing bids to other businesses' customers based on what they learn. Such a bid could be made to appear coincidental, but it would have a devastating effect on the revenue flow of a victim business.

Distributed objects must protect themselves from such attacks. A distributed object must be confident that it is dealing with a legitimate party and not someone masquerading as that party. When a remote invocation is made, both client and server would like reasonable guarantees that the parameters in the invocation have not been interfered with by a third party. In many circumstances, sensitive information, such as credit card numbers, might be passed as part of an invocation. A mechanism must be available for protecting this information and providing the security guarantees required by a distributed system. Chapter 2: Taxonomy of a Mobile Object examined the issues surrounding distributed and mobile object security in more detail.

DCOM includes some limited support for security. The main intent of DCOM security is to provide simple access control. That means that only users who are allowed to use a particular DCOM component can. This access control integrates with the Windows security mechanism to actually check the user information and determine whether the user has sufficient privileges to invoke the object.

DCOM also provides higher levels of security, which include data integrity and privacy. Data integrity provides the guarantee that no one has modified the information sent between client and server. For example, in a bank setting, an attacker might modify the amount of a transaction from $10 to $10,000, then divert the extra funds to a second bank account. Data integrity prevents this kind of attack by providing a cryptographic signature on the data sent between the client and server. The signature can be checked before any trust is placed in the data.

Privacy is often referred to as the paranoid setting for DCOM. However, privacy is a basic component in our everyday lives. When you step into another room to make a telephone call, place a love letter to a sweetheart in an envelope, hold a private conference with your boss, or close the shower door, you are taking basic steps to ensure your own privacy.

DCOM can ensure the privacy of communication between client and server as well. When DCOM security is set to protect privacy, the information contained in the method invocations is not disclosed to third parties on the computer network.

Java objects implementing or using DCOM components can take advantage of DCOM security to protect the remote invocations they are sending across the network. Provided you can live with the inherent restriction of throwing out the window Java's Write Once, Run Anywhere capability by using DCOM within a Java application, DCOM security allows software developers to easily and cheaply achieve a fairly high level of security in distributed systems written in Java.

What's Next

♦ Now that we've seen how a mega-corporation like Microsoft is addressing the problem of mobile objects, let's go to the other extreme, looking at how an innovative startup called ObjectSpace is solving the same problems with their own technology, Voyager.

Building Mobile
Objects with Voyager

V oyager is probably the least-well-known tool of all those discussed in this book. It is a next-generation ORB developed by ObjectSpace, a small company best known for its work developing the Java Generic Libraries (JGLs) bundled as part of nearly every Java development environment today.

In developing Voyager, the ObjectSpace team made some visionary observations about the merging of distributed object and agent technology. The result is what the team members call an *agent-enhanced* ORB. This means that although Voyager has a superset of the capabilities found in most ORB products, even support for the CORBA standard, it also includes a number of features that would be more at home in an agent toolkit.

What Does Agent-Enhanced Mean?

Distributed systems built with ORB tools have several limitations that are part of nearly every ORB product available in the world today. First and foremost, the objects in a distributed system are not autonomous. That is, a distributed object is always under the control of some application that a developer has put together to host the distributed object. A distributed object cannot live in an ORB application without developer intervention.

Second, distributed objects are restricted to the application in which they were created. Voyager agents can move between different applications. Third, Voyager enables agents to be constructed in remote processes. Finally, Voyager supports a host of other features for supporting mobile agents, including security and persistence engines. That's why Voyager earns the name agent-enhanced ORB.

Voyager objects may be autonomous. That is, Voyager objects can move between different computers of their own volition. Voyager supports a notion of *place processes*, just as agent technology does. Place processes enable agents to become autonomous by providing a home for the agent on each host as the agent moves from host to host. Voyager agents that are moving around the network from host to host are actually moving in and out of place processes located on different computers connected to the network. The Voyager place process is the host application that contains any of the autonomous objects as they move around on the network. The place process, which is called *voyager* in the Voyager environment, contains no user code. To start it, the user simply invokes the voyager process. The server and the autonomous objects that it contains do all the rest.

N **O T E** : ObjectSpace has received a multimillion-dollar U.S. Department of Energy grant to further pursue Voyager development. Voyager, which has always been a free download on the Internet, now has commercial customer support packages available, and ObjectSpace has a list of Voyager customer testimonials a mile long.

Voyager objects may be constructed on different hosts through a remote invocation. Most distributed object tools don't allow objects to be remotely constructed. Voyager objects instantiated in this manner live within the voyager place process. A remote object reference, a *proxy* in Voyager terminology, is returned from the construction process so that the local process can begin using the newly constructed object right away.

Voyager supports *agents*, objects that can autonomously move around the network to accomplish a specific task. A Voyager agent actively hops between place processes and can utilize the resources made available to it at each node. The Voyager agent framework is naturally object oriented because an agent is an object that extends the com.objectspace.voyager.agent.Agent class. Default behavior for all the methods on Agent are provided by the Agent base class; all a developer has to do to create a Voyager agent is extend this base class. In order to move to a new place process, the application simply invokes the moveTo() operation on the agent object.

Voyager has a grab bag of other features with more on the way. These include an object persistence layer, CORBA integration, and a unique multicast invocation facility not found in other mobile object tools. Other features promised for upcoming releases include DCOM integration and transaction support.

By merging agent and distributed object technologies, Voyager has gone farther than any other tool toward supporting a number of the features of a mobile object tool.

Mobility Features

Voyager was built with mobile agents and distributed objects simultaneously in mind. This approach to developing the tool has resulted in some interesting features not available in other tools, making it perhaps the most advanced mobile object tool available to date.

Implementing mobility with Voyager can take several different forms. First, an object can be treated as an agent. Second, Voyager allows objects to be moved explicitly to a new location. Third, objects passed as part of a remote invocation are serialized and copied out the remote host as part of the process of making the remote invocation.

The agent approach to implementing a mobile object in Voyager treats the object as an entity that can move itself around the network. The implementation of such an object doesn't interact as part of a larger application, as we have stressed in this book. The agent is treated as a more or less autonomous entity that can move from application to application. Other applications can interact with this agent object through the agent's proxy, which may be listed in a Namespace. The agent in turn can interact with other objects by accessing their proxy interfaces, but the implementation of the agent does not move into a process and become a member object of the process. For agents, the voyager process is the host of the agent. The agent interacts with this voyager process only in a limited way defined by the Voyager runtime environment. As we've established in Chapter 2: Taxonomy of a Mobile Object, agents may apply to some specialized problems, but you probably won't find them as useful as mobile objects in general application development.

N **OTE:** Voyager supports a notion of facets for objects. Facets are value-added interfaces that Voyager supports for providing additional functionality to objects. Each facet represents a particular type of functionality that can be used to manipulate objects in Voyager. Many different types of facets are provided by default in the Voyager runtime environment. Agent and Mobility are examples of default facets, but the user can configure new facets for any object in Voyager.

Making an object into an agent in Voyager is a matter of accessing the Agent facet of an object. The Agent facet provides the AP for treating an object as an agent and for configuring agents within Voyager. By invoking the Agent facet of an object, an agent can be moved from place to place or can move itself from place to place. When an Agent moves, any pending requests for the Agent are temporarily queued. The Agent object and all of it's member objects are serialized using Java Object Serialization. The object is cloned in the destination process, and a forwarder is left to direct any future requests to the new host of the object. The old instance of the object is destroyed. Finally, the object begins processing queued requests in the destination process.

Moving objects explicitly in Voyager works much the same way. An object can be moved to a specific destination by obtaining access to the Mobility facet and invoking the moveTo() operation on that facet. When this happens, the object moves in much the same way as an agent, queuing pending requests and starting up a new instance on the remote server. Moving an object in this manner treats the object very much like an agent. The object, once moved to a new host application, is accessed through its proxy and is not part of the application in the sense of mobile objects as we've discussed them throughout this book. Therefore, the level of integration of the moved object with its destination application is limited, the destination application being just another *voyager* process. Still, one of the reasons to move an object is to minimize the impact of a system failure on the original host system. If the original host system is prone to failure, its failure may cause the object to become unavailable. Another reason may be to improve system performance. In system configurations in which the object is invoked repeatedly by objects on the destination system, system performance can be improved by moving the object from the originating host to the destination host in order to cause remote invocations to become local invocations. Remote invocations, involving network communication, are much more expensive to system resources than local invocations. Again, however, moving objects in this manner contributes little to the application development process itself. For example, you can't build a better user interface or provide an application with additional functionality by moving an object from one *voyager* process to another *voyager* process. At best, you are moving some application functionality around between hosts.

The simplest approach to mobile objects in Voyager is to use a serializable object as part of a distributed, or remote, invocation. Voyager automatically serializes any objects used as part of an invocation and passes them to the remote virtual machine. When the remote virtual machine reads the serialized object, the data is deserialized and converted back into an instance of the object. In order to move an object in this manner, it must be serializable. That is, the object must implement the java.io.serializable interface. The object can be incorporated into the running server process, taking advantage of the state and implementation of the mobile object. This simplest form of moving an object from application to application in Voyager provides the highest level of integration between the mobile object and its host application and corresponds to the notion of mobile objects stressed in this book.

In this approach, any serializable object may be treated as a mobile object and is completely under the control of the applications that are using it. These objects generally will not move to another location on their own. References to them are normal Java object references to a local instance of the object that lives within the application.

Substantial differences exist in these three different approaches to mobility in Voyager. As we look at the features of a mobile object tool present in Voyager, we focus on what we feel is the most valuable approach, the third approach to moving an object in Voyager.

State Preservation

As an object moves across the network, the state of the object moves along with it. However, the two approaches to mobility present in Voyager differ in usage. Both preserve the state of the mobile object, but the code provided in order to implement either of the two approaches is radically different.

Recall that a third approach to implementing mobile objects with Voyager simply requires that the mobile object is serializable and is passed as a parameter to a remote process. Listing 5.1 demonstrates a simple Hello object that is passed by value to the remote virtual machine:

```
public class Hello
implements java.io.Serializable
{
public String message;
public Hello() {}
public void say() { /* ... */ }
};
```

Listing 5.1 Source for Hello.

This approach of making a serializable object that is passed as an argument to a remote invocation is identical to that used with many of the ORB tools discussed in this book, such as RMI and Caffeine. In all of these approaches, the mobile object is created as a serializable object. Even better, the mobile objects written with these tools are compatible to some extent because you can take a serializable object taken from one mobile object tool and communicate it through another because the only requirement of most tools is serializability of the mobile object. Version 1.01 Voyager differed from Voyager 2.0.0, the latest version, and other mobile object tools in how previous versions of Voyager interacted with Object Serialization. Earlier versions implemented a layer of abstraction about Object Serialization, called VoyagerStream. However, in Voyager 2.0.0, Object Serialization is now used directly. The application developer no longer depends on a proprietary API defined by Voyager to interact with Object Serialization.

This means that all mobile objects, whether agents or simpler serializable objects, must implement the java.io.Serializable interface whether it is declared explicitly or indirectly through the Agent class. Voyager falls under the same rules of object state transmission of the other tools discussed in this book, such as that transient and static variables are not serialized with an object. In custom implementations of object serialization engines, these requirements may be eliminated.

ClassLoading

Voyager supports some very innovative approaches to class loading that are not available in other tools. For starters, Voyager implements a layer of abstraction over class loading in the class com.objectspace.voyager.loader.VoyagerClassLoader. Voyager uses a set of resource loaders to load classes and other resources from URLs or other resource sources. An application can register its own resource loaders. The set of resource loaders is examined when a resource is located. By default, when loading classes, the VoyagerClassLoader searches the directories specified in the CLASSPATH and any resource loaders that are configured in the application. A default resource loader is provided that loads Proxies for Java objects, but no other resource loaders are provided. In order to load resources such as classes remotely, the application developer has to construct and register resource loaders corresponding with these remote resources. Voyager provides a URLResourceLoader for loading resources from URL sources, but the user can implement and register their own custom resource loaders as well to meet specific class or resource loading requirements. For example, in an enterprise environment, classes might be stored within a database to provide a transactional client/server mechanism for collaborating among multiple developers and users. In other environments, more specific requirements of the ClassLoader might exist, such as looking in multiple locations or loading new versions of existing classes.

Second, in the case of an applet, VoyagerClassLoader examines any classes stored in the applet CODEBASE. This is the common place for classes to be stored when an applet is deployed along with a Web page. Here, the class is retrieved through an HTTP request by default. Custom resource loaders cannot be specified in the case of an applet due to the security restrictions of Java applets.

Third, Voyager implements a communication mechanism that enables different Voyager applications to send classes to one another directly. This last method is interesting because it is not available in most other mobile object tools. For example, RMI and Caffeine require that the classes in a particular application are stored either locally or within a particular Web server. Two distributed RMI applications cannot communicate directly with each other to send classes. With Voyager, two applications can communicate to exchange classes.

VoyagerClassLoader is a class that cannot be overridden in Voyager 2.0.0, unlike previous versions of Voyager. If developers want to implement their own class loader for use with Voyager applications, they should not attempt to override the default VoyagerClassLoader. Instead, they should define and register new ResourceLoaders within the existing VoyagerClassLoader. The implementation of the VoyagerClassLoader searches these newly registered ResourceLoaders for any resources, thus providing application developers with a mechanism for configuring new ways of accessing resources where required.

In order to implement a new ResourceLoader, a software developer must implement the interface com.objectspace.voyager.loader.IResourceLoader. The only operation on this interface is as follows:

```
public abstract InputStream getResourceAsStreamClassBytes(String name);
```

The getResourceAsStream method requests that the resource loader find the resource with the specified name and construct an InputStream for loading this resource. The default implementation of this examines the CLASSPATH or CODE-BASE in the case of an applet, but a user-defined class loader may implement any particular behavior specified by the developer.

Implementing your own ResourceLoader is simply a matter of providing an implementation for the IResourceLoader interface. Listing 5.2 shows how to implement a ResourceLoader that reads classes from the local hard disk. Any source of bytes could be used, however, including ftp, http, gopher, databases, and the like.

This example of a resource loader is very simple. More complex resource loaders can perform tasks like caching frequently loaded resources and storing several versions of the same resource where applicable. Tools like Supersede use intelligent class loaders to flush and reload new versioning of a class into a running Java program.

Most Java applications have only one class loader, but you can derive important benefits from having multiple class loaders in a single program. First and foremost, each class loader stubbornly refuses to use the classes already loaded by another class loader. Each class loader attempts to load its own copy of classes, even if a class of the same name has already been loaded by another class loader. As a result, individual class loaders can partition the set of all classes that are loaded into the virtual machine. This prevents conflicts between classes even if they happen to have the same name. Even static variables of different classes are not integrated when loaded with different class loader.

In Voyager 2.0.0, it's no longer possible to override the default VoyagerClassLoader, however. This restricts Voyager applications from taking advantage of the benefits of having multiple class loaders for the Voyager objects. The software developer can still instantiate and use their own custom ClassLoaders within a Voyager application, provided the current SecurityManager allows this. However, the resources loaded by Voyager cannot benefit from having multiple class loaders, making versioning and partitioning the static memory of the application difficult to implement with Voyager.

Because the actual bytecode of an object can move across the network, the object may paint a new user interface at its destination application. The two different approaches to building mobile objects with Voyager lead to difference in how such a user interface may be integrated with the application. In the first approach, a mobile object is just any serializable object that is passed as part of an invocation. The object, which is under the control of a host application, may include user interface elements that are painted seamlessly as part of the user interface of the host application (see the Composable Views pattern in Chapter 21). An example of such an application is given later in the Voting with Mobile Objects section.

```java
import java.io.*;
public class FileResourceLoader
  implements IResourceLoader
{
  public String directoryName = null;
  public FileResourceLoader(String n)
  {
    directoryName = n;
  }

  public InputStream getResourceAsStream(String name)
{
    try
      {
        RandomAccessFile in = new RandomAccessFile(
          directoryName + "/" + name + ".class", "r" );
        return in;
}
    catch (IOException e)
      {

        return null;
      }
  }

};
```

Listing 5.2 Source for FileResourceLoader.

Security

Voyager uses the normal Java sandbox security model to protect hosts from malicious objects. Without this protection, a malicious object might perform operations that compromised the security of the host machine. For example, it's not hard to implement a mobile object that reformats the hard disk of its host machine, unless the host is protected from such a malicious object. The actual code for such an object is not given here to protect the innocent.

Malicious objects represent an old security concern for Java. Even applets could maliciously attack their hosts, doing substantial damage by invoking operations to reformat the hard disk, send e-mail masqueraded as a user, or even implement a complete ftp server to distribute confidential files stored on the hard disk. The solution is to restrict the operations to the subset of operations in Java that can't do any damage to the host machine. This is the Java sandbox security model that is configured through the use of the SecurityManager.

VoyagerSecurityManager is an implementation of a SecurityManager for Voyager that protects a host from foreign objects. By invoking the operations on the VoyagerSecurityManager, the Java Virtual Machine can check to see whether a particular Voyager object should have the rights to perform a specific operation.

However, the VoyagerSecurityManager is not used by default! It can be turned on with a command line option or by registering it in source code. In order to register the SecurityManager in source code, one must install the security manager by invoking the System.setSecurityManager() operation. A Java application leaves itself open to attack if it accepts mobile objects without installing the VoyagerSecurityManager. As shown in Figure 5.1, the VoyagerSecurityManager protects the application from foreign objects.

In designing the VoyagerSecurityManager, ObjectSpace clearly made some choices about what a foreign object should and should not be allowed to do. Making these decisions is a difficult trade-off between the flexibility of the objects and the requirements of protecting a host. Some of the decisions may be somewhat controversial. You might disagree, for example, that a foreign object should be allowed to create and listen to server sockets. This particular choice means that foreign objects can implement Internet servers, like Web and ftp servers, on unsuspecting machines without the permission of their owners. Implementing such a server is a simple matter of writing a mobile object that opens a server socket and speaks the

Operation	Objects in Applet	Native Object	Foreign Object
Accept connections from any host	server only		
Connect to any host	server only		
Listen on any port			
Perform multicast operations			
Set factories			
Manipulate threads			
Manipulate thread groups			
Execute a process			
Exit the program			
Access AWT event queue			
Access the system clipboard			
Create windows			
Create class loader			
Delete files			
Read files, excluding socket file descriptors			
Write files, excluding socket file descriptors			
Access security APIs			
Link to a dynamic library			
Access private/protected data and methods			
Access packages			
Define classes in packages			
Print			
Manipulate properties	limited		

Figure 5.1 VoyagerSecurityManager restrictions.

HTTP or FTP protocol on the target host. Foreign objects are restricted from accessing the hard disk, however, so such servers could not actually distribute the files stored on the machine. Masquerading as the host machine is a potentially serious security attack in its own right. Imagine creating a Web server on a Microsoft host machine touting the benefits of Unix. Significant loss of credibility can result from such an attack.

Developers are free to implement their own SecurityManagers, however. All you have to do is derive a new SecurityManager child class from the VoyagerSecurityManager class, providing your own behavior in the new SecurityManager. One change you can make to prevent the attack mentioned previously is to turn off the access to server sockets specified. A child class of VoyagerSecurityManager should be provided to override the checkAccept method and throw a SecurityException. This exception indicates that socket accept calls are not allowed. Listing 5.3 implements such a SecurityManager.

```
public class MySecurityManager
extends VoyagerSecurityManager
{
  // Prevent foreign objects from listening to server sockets.
  public synchronized void checkListen( int port )
    throws SecurityException
  {
    throw new SecurityException();
  }

  // Prevent foreign objects from accepting connections from any host.
  public synchronized void checkAccept( String host, int port )
    throws SecurityException
  {
    throw new SecurityException();
  }
}
```

Listing 5.3 Source for MySecurityManager.

SecurityManagers address the ways a host may be protected from a malicious mobile object. The opposite concern, protecting objects from malicious hosts, is much more difficult. Voyager does not address this side of the security problem. Because Voyager makes use of Object Serialization, the state of sensitive objects may be available for anyone to read as a simple byte array. As a result, a mobile object with control of valuable resources, such as customer information, privileged access to a database, or even a valuable algorithm, is open to attacks from malicious host machines that might steal these resources from the object.

A developer can use a couple of different approaches to protect these sensitive resources. First, don't send sensitive resources as part of a mobile object. If you have valuable customer information, such as a credit card number, design your application in such a way that the credit card number is not sent along with the mobile object. A reasonably safe application design would be to store the credit card information in a local object, then use normal distributed object communication to send any results back and forth between the mobile and distributed objects. This practice gives the distributed object, on the local host, a chance to verify that any requests on the protected resource are valid before permitting access to these resources. For example, in a point-of-sale application, the credit card number is used only after the customer confirms that a particular purchase should be completed.

A more flexible solution is to implement an authentication protocol between hosts on the network. Voyager does not provide such a protocol, but as a developer, you could build your own at a moderate cost. A host is given access to protected resources only after authenticating itself as one of a small number of trusted hosts. However, this solution would require the developer to dabble in cryptographic technologies, such as SSL, X.509 certificates, and JCE, to implement the authentication protocol.

Voyager 2.0.0 doesn't come with a secure communication protocol. Other mobile object tools, Caffeine and RMI in particular, bundle at least a basic level of communication security by implementing SSL-protected TCP/IP socket communication.

Object Identity

Any serializable object may be used as an argument to a remote invocation on a Voyager object. The serializable object is serialized, copied across the network, and deserialized in the virtual machine containing the target object. The result is that the object is effectively cloned inside another address space.

After this cloning process, both instances continue to exist independently of each other. Any local Java object references in the local virtual machine that point to the serializable object before it is cloned still point back to the same local instance, even after the object is cloned to another virtual machine. It's up to the developer never to use the old instance and instead, carefully direct all future requests to the new instance in the remote virtual machine. Solving this task might involve keeping

Programming Mobile Objects with Java

track of any reference to a mobile object in the local virtual machine so that these references can later be updated with the new location of the mobile object.

In the Agent and Mobility approach in Voyager, mobile objects in the form of Agents that move between place processes on a network are used. The Agent object has some qualities that allow it to be more intelligent than simple serializable Java objects. Notably, Agent objects may be accessed only through a virtual reference in Voyager. Direct Java references to the underlying instance of the Java object are not allowed. This restriction provides a layer of indirection that is useful for implementing behavior that would be impossible otherwise.

One result is that not only can an object be cloned, but because all references to the local instance of the object are through a virtual reference, each of these may be updated with the new location of the object. The local instance of the object may be garbage collected with the reassurance that no Java references are pointed at it and that all the virtual references have updated information about the new location. This capability avoids any of the confusion that might be associated with cloning the object to a new virtual machine, as is usually the case with mobile object tools.

A second result is that any virtual references pointing back at the old instance of the object may be forwarded on to the new location, as shown in Figure 5.2. Voyager provides a Forwarder object to accomplish this task. When an agent object moves to a new place process, a Forwarder is left behind to point to the new location of the agent object. Any invocations that are sent to the old location of the agent object are forwarded to the new location.

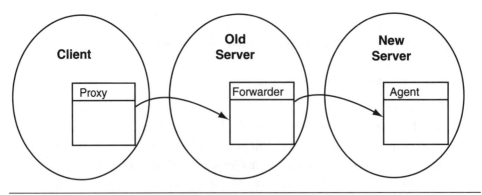

Figure 5.2 Forwarding invocations when agents move.

The response sent back from the object contains a tag indicating the new location. This tag permits the virtual reference that was used to make the invocation to update its information to point to the new location. When any of the existing virtual references are invoked, the Forwarder receives the invocation and forwards it on to the new location of the object. This action creates the illusion that the virtual reference is always pointing at the correct location of an object that may frequently move to new places in the network, reinforcing the identity of the object. Any future invocations are then sent directly to the new location of the object rather than through the Forwarder. Of course, if the object has already moved to yet another new location, the invocation is forwarded once again to the next location. Further, the response from the agent contains a tag indicating the new location of the agent so that all future invocations can be sent directly to the new location without going through the Forwarder.

Garbage collection is also provided for agent objects. Voyager keeps track of the time the last invocation occurred on each Voyager agent living in a place process. Voyager automatically removes objects that are inactive for a long period of time.

To keep objects alive that should not be garbage collected, virtual references normally invoke a heartbeat operation on each object periodically. This operation ensures that as long as virtual references exist that point to the object, the object is not garbage collected. Virtual references such as these are called *strong references* because the object stays alive as long as any strong reference exists and points to the object.

Another class of references is also available, called *weak references*. These references do not require that the object stay alive. A virtual reference that is a weak reference does not send a heartbeat to the object to keep it alive. Instead, if only weak references point to a particular object and the object is inactive for a period of time, the object is garbage collected. Weak references make it convenient to make references to objects in situations when you don't want the reference to prevent garbage collection. A good example occurs when you are implementing container classes. Depending on the situation, the reference that the container class has to the objects it contains should not force the objects to live as long as the container itself.

Object Sharing
Object sharing is a difficult problem for anyone to solve, but ObjectSpace is at least making a few cautious steps in the right direction. Voyager implements a multicast

technology called a Space. Spaces implement a basic multicast of method invocations to multiple targets.

Multicasting method invocations is a good step along the path to object sharing. For instance, consider that an exact copy of an object called Counter exists in five different processes on different computers. If a client increments the Counter on just one of these instances and the Counter is shared across all five processes, each and every process should be updated with the new value of the Counter.

One solution is to send the increment invocation to all five Counter objects in each of the five processes. Doing so would keep each of the five instances of the object up-to-date. Spaces allow you to multicast the invocation to each of the five instances of the object and simultaneously perform the invocation on all five of them.

Spaces use a protocol called IP Multicast that is already widely available on the Internet, though not 100 percent pervasive yet. IP Multicast packets can be sent from one sender to multiple recipients, rather than the typical situation of TCP/IP communication wherein one sender and one recipient communicate with each other over a live connection. This one-to-many communication mode of IP Multicast enables a Voyager object to send an invocation to multiple target objects.

As long as each invocation is made on all of the instances of the objects, they are automatically synchronized. All of the objects automatically have the same state as long as they started off with the same state and receive all of the same invocations in the same order. The different instances of the objects have the same value in this case, even though they do not take any extraordinary precautions to copy their state after each invocation.

Spaces are explored in more detail later in the section Using Spaces to Simultaneously Communicate with Groups of Objects as well as in Chapter 9: Clustering, Chapter 17: Object Groups, and Chapter 18: Replication.

Concurrency

Voyager provides a straightforward thread-pooling facility. Creating new threads is an expensive operation in Java. Often Java threads are facades over native operating system threads. Whenever a new Java thread is created, an operating system invocation is made to create a new operating system thread.

Each Voyager application has a thread pool that is used to recycle threads for later use in order to prevent the operating system overhead normally incurred when threads are repeatedly created and destroyed. The size of the thread pool controls the amount of threads that may be saved in this manner. For maximum efficiency, do not waste threads by saving them in the thread pool if they are never used. However, if the thread pool is too small, it may become exhausted, requiring new threads to be created. You may retrieve the number of idle threads that are allowed to exist in the thread pool by invoking the getMaxIdleThreads() operation and change it by invoking the setMaxIdleThreads() operation.

When a user wants to spawn a thread from the thread pool, the assignThreadTo() operation on the com.objectspace.lib.thread.ThreadPool object invocation can be made to reuse a thread from the thread pool. When the thread is no longer needed, the Thread is returned to the pool for later use if the maximum number of idle threads is not already available in the ThreadPool.

This facility can be used in any Voyager application, but by default, the voyager place process uses the thread pool to multithread invocations that are made to agent objects. All objects used with Voyager should be able to handle synchronous invocations because they may be invoked by multiple threads from the thread pool. The normal Java concurrency controls apply to objects that are invoked from threads in the thread pool, so the synchronize keyword can be used to mark operations that must be accessed by only one thread at a time.

What happens to the threads invoking some operations on an object when the object moves to another process? Two possible things happen.

In the case of agent objects accessed with pools from the Voyager thread, all the threads are completed before the object moves across the network. Then, the object may move without concern for the state of any running threads. However, this process doesn't address what happens to normal Java threads. These threads, not under the control of Voyager, may contain state of their own. Thus, developers using multithreading in their Voyager application generally should use the Voyager threading model instead of creating native Java threads.

Serializable Java objects used as part of a remote invocation make up another matter entirely. These objects are serialized immediately, without concern for either Voyager threads or native Java threads. As a result, thread state information may be lost during such an invocation. Developers should carefully ensure that objects are not accessed by threads when they are serialized during such an invocation.

Other Goodies

Voyager provides many other features that may be useful when one is implementing a distributed system. For example, Voyager supports integration with CORBA, planned integration with DCOM, a remote construction facility, and a simple persistence engine. Many of these features are useful primarily in the implementation of an agent application, but some have benefits in distributed and mobile object settings as well.

CORBA and DCOM Integration

Perhaps most important for many enterprise software developers already committed to a distributed object technology such as CORBA or DCOM is Voyager's integration with these technologies. CORBA integration is available today, with DCOM integration available by the time you read this book.

The CORBA integration system is simple and easy to use. Developers familiar with CORBA know that it normally requires the development of IDL files, stub compilation, and a specific API standardized by the OMG. Voyager makes building applications much easier by simply adding a CORBA class that can convert any object into a CORBA server with just a single method invocation. No IDL interface declaration, stub generators, compilers, or any specific API is required; ObjectSpace has reduced it all down to a single method invocation. This makes it much easier for a Voyager application developer to interact with a CORBA-based system. Instead, you can access remote CORBA objects through the familiar Voyager API.

Voyager defines a CORBA object that provides the services required to access CORBA-based services. In order to obtain a Voyager proxy to a CORBA server, the Namespace.lookup() method is invoked, passing in a CORBA interoperable object reference (IOR). This IOR is just a hexadecimally encoded string that contains the information required to locate the CORBA object on the Internet. The CORBA IOR is similar in nature to the Voyager GUID. Using IORs in this manner is common in CORBA systems.

For example, suppose that you want to access a Bank server that contains an operation for opening a bank account called openAccount. Assuming that the server stored the IOR for the CORBA server in some well-known file, the first task is to read the IOR from the file. The Namespace.lookup() operation can then be invoked on the CORBA object to obtain a virtual reference for the CORBA server, as follows:

```
// Open the file containing the IOR
RandomAccessFile file = new RandomAccessFile( "bank.ior", "r" );
// Read in the IOR from the file.
String ior = file.readUTF();

// Obtain a virtual reference for the CORBA server.
Bank bank = (Bank) Namespace.lookup( ior );
// Invoke an operation on the CORBA server.
Account account = bank.openAccount();
```

The opposite task is also achievable. Voyager can be accessed by CORBA clients as well as access CORBA servers. Each Voyager object can be converted into a CORBA server when the asIOR method on the CORBA object is invoked. Listing 5.4 demonstrates this conversion.

```
// Create a Bank in the local place process
Bank bank = new Bank( "localhost" );

// Allow access as a CORBA server
String ior = Corba.asIOR( bank );
```

Listing 5.4 asIOR method invoked on a CORBA object.

Of course, the Voyager integration with CORBA is not all roses. Voyager, though making the access of CORBA servers easy from within a Voyager application, departs radically from the CORBA standardized API. One of the goals of this API is to achieve complete source and bytecode portability, independent of the CORBA platform that is used to implement or access the objects. Voyager fails to achieve this level of portability. For example, you can't create a CORBA server with Voyager and expect the same source code to be compatible with other CORBA platforms, such as Orbix or VisiBroker.

DCOM integration is also planned to be available in the near future. The architecture of DCOM is similar to CORBA in that it makes COM components available on the network for remote invocation. The Voyager team will probably use a strategy similar to the CORBA approach for simplifying the DCOM access for Voyager developers.

Remote Construction

Another useful feature of Voyager is remote construction, a mechanism for building new objects within a remote process. A distributed system developer might have various reasons to do this, such as localizing an object with a client that is known to be the main consumer of the object, balancing the load of a distributed system across multiple hosts, or even to run new instances of a particular object on different hosts in order to implement a replicated system. Voyager makes remote construction of objects easy. Indeed, agent objects are usually remotely constructed in Voyager. When constructing an agent object, you must pass a string in the form of a URL to identify the place process in which the instantiation should occur. The object is then instantiated in this place process.

As an example of this remote construction, suppose that a SportsFan object is implemented by a Java developer. In order to construct an instance of this SportsFan object under the control of Voyager, one might use the following code:

```
SportsFan fan = Factory.create("SportsFan", "//localhost:8000");
```

The preceding code assumes that a Voyager place process, which is an instance of the voyager process, is available on the local host running on port 8000. If this is true, the SportsFan object is constructed within that place process, and the fan virtual reference points at that instance.

Remote construction can be a useful feature. For example, with an appropriately loose SecurityManager, remote construction may be used to access and consume remote resources, such as files, CPU, and memory. Remote construction can also be used to display a user interface on a remote system because the object can pop up dialog boxes and other windows from within the place process where it is living, wherever that might be.

Mobile Objects for Mobs

Virtually 100 percent of the software deployed on the Internet today communicates on a point-to-point basis—a single client to a single server. The problem with this approach is that it doesn't scale well to large numbers of participants in a distributed system. You can't distribute information to 250,000 people if you need to send a copy of the data to each and every individual.

IP Multicast solves this problem by providing a tool for broadcasting information to multiple recipients. In IP Multicast, only one copy of the data is sent from the server. The data is routed to multiple recipients by intelligent routers that support IP Multicast routing. This practice prevents the server from needing to distribute a discrete copy of the data to each and every client.

Some of the application areas envisioned for broadcast technologies such as IP Multicast include pushing content onto many clients, hosting live multimedia broadcasts on the Internet, and facilitating group-based communication such as chat sessions and collaboration among workgroups. Other applications are certain to emerge as more developers become aware of this alternative to traditional point-to-point communication. All of these are data-oriented applications of IP Multicast.

Mobile objects can also benefit from this multicast technology. When a mobile object is broadcast to a group of participants, the object may include new capabilities sent to each recipient. In the following section, we look at an example of multicasting a mobile object to a group of recipients.

Using Spaces to Simultaneously Communicate with Groups of Objects

A Voyager Space is a IP Multicast-based communication mechanism that can send data to a group of multiple recipients. Spaces provide a simple tool for using multicast technology in an ORB environment. When an invocation is made on a Space, the method invocation is delivered to each of the objects participating in the Space.

Further, when a Space issues a multicast invocation on each of the participants, the arguments passed in the invocation are serialized and delivered to each participant. Each participating application can then read and instantiate the serialized objects within the argument list. This broadcasting of serialized objects to a group of recipients enables us to build mobile object software in which an object is multicast to a group of participants rather than a single participant.

To create a Space with Voyager, you simply need a place to run the Space and a name for the Space. The place is just any old Voyager place process. Once a Voyager place process is started on a particular port, say 7000, you can create a Space in this place process by invoking the operation:

```
ISubspace space = (ISubspace)
```

```
Factory.create( "com.objectspace.voyager.space.Subspace",
               "//localhost:7000/MySpace" );
```

This invocation creates a Space in the localhost in the Voyager place process running on port 7000 and assigns it an alias called MySpace. The Space is hosted in this process, but it will actually have an effect on objects living in many processes distributed across the network.

After constructing the Space, you can connect to it by invoking the getMulticast-Proxy operation on the ISubspace interface. This invocation returns a virtual reference to the Space, so that you can manipulate it or send messages to its participants.

You can add any Voyager object to a Space by invoking the add operation on the Space. The following code is an example of creating an instance of an object called Participant using the Voyager construction mechanism and then adding this object into the Space.

```
Participant self = (Participant)
        Factory.create("Participant",
                       "//localhost:7000" );
        space.add(self);
```

Adding an object as a member of the Space means that any invocation made in the Space is delivered to the member object. Thus, each object in the Space should implement an appropriate interface with which to communicate with the others. For example, if several objects implement a Chat application, they should implement a common interface containing a common set of methods. One method might be something like print, for printing out the information entered by each participant in the chat session. Whenever any participant in the Space invokes the print operation, every participant in the Space has its print method invoked. Voyager doesn't actually restrict the members of a Space to be all of one type, though. Many different types can all be members of the same space. However, when an invocation is made on the Space, Voyager checks the type of each of the objects to ensure they support the appropriate interface, and it invokes only those members of the Space that do support this interface. Following is an example of invoking the members of a Space:

```
ISubspace space =
    (ISubspace) Namespace.lookup( "//localhost:7000/MySpace" );
```

```
// create a typesafe gateway into the subspace on local server 7000
Participant members = (Participant)
  space.getMulticastProxy("Participant");


members.print("Hi, everyone!");
```

Something subtle is happening in this example. It looks very much as if we are constructing a new instance of the Participant object and invoking its print operation. However, notice that we aren't actually constructing a new Participant. Instead, we are creating a proxy into the Space. Whenever any method for the Participant object is invoked on this virtual reference to the space, any member of the Space that is a Participant or child of Participant has that operation invoked on it. Thus, the print operation is invoked on all the members of the Space that are Participants, not just a single instance of a Participant object.

Spaces provide a convenient abstraction for communicating with a group of objects simultaneously. Let's look at how we can use them with mobile objects.

The Problem

Suppose that a group of people located in various parts of an office building are trying to decide what to do for lunch. The current method is to wander around the office cubicle environment, asking, "How about lunch?" Management realizes that hundreds of hours are wasted each year on this mundane task and forms a task force to build software to speed up the decision process.

The use case for this problem is simply that one person should be able to send the question for a vote to all the participants in the distributed system. They could respond with a simple *yes* or *no* vote. Future expectations are that the application might need to evolve to include voting on where and when to eat lunch. People would also be allowed to abstain from voting, in which case, their votes are not counted. This initial user interface is shown in Figure 5.3.

Traditional Approaches

Let's initially try to solve the lunch problem with a traditional client/server software approach, without mobile objects. We can still use Voyager and even Spaces, but we can communicate only basic data types rather than take advantage of the mobile object capabilities of Voyager.

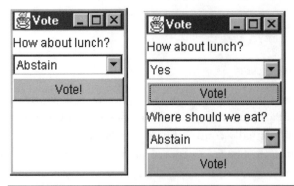

Figure 5.3 Lunch vote GUI.

Peers Versus Client/Server

A Voyager Space enables multiple participants to communicate with each other. When an invocation is made on a Voyager Space, every participant in the Space receives the invocation. Rather than send back a response after invocation, each participant may invoke other operations on the Space to simultaneously notify all the participants in the Space of the results. This method departs from the client/server model in that the communication is no longer request-response oriented. Now multiple applications are communicating with each other through an exchange of invocations on the Space.

The first task in building any distributed application is to define an interface. The interface should accomplish two tasks. First, the interface should inform all participants that a vote is taking place. Second, the interface should have a method for enabling all participants to post their votes on the issue. Since this interface is used in a peer-to-peer environment, the invocation for indicating that a vote is taking place does not return the results of each vote. Instead, participants invoke the post invocation to multicast their decision to everyone participating in the vote.

As a first take for this interface, let's propose the following:

```
public interface VoteListener
{
public void callForVotes();
public void post(String ballot);
```

```
};
```

Each peer should implement this interface and ask participants about their decision in the vote. An implementation of this interface should accept the callForVotes invocation, pop up the required user interface to ask users whether they want to go to lunch, and then invoke the post method to inform all the participants about the decision of the other users. The code in Listing 5.6 demonstrates an implementation of the VoteListener interface.

```
public class Voter
   implements VoteListener
{
  public void callForVotes()
  {
    // Ask user, "How about lunch?"
  }

  public void post(String ballot)
  {
    // Display the choice of this user.
  }
};
```

Listing 5.6 Source for VoteListener.

An immediate problem that a savvy distributed object developer notices about this interface is that it doesn't provide any way to meet the future requirements of the problem. In particular, the implementation of callForVotes() doesn't meet the future requirements of the possibility that someone might want to ask additional questions of users, not just whether they want to go to lunch. We need some additional planning to enable the voting application to ask other questions.

To enable a method for asking additional questions, let's modify the interface in order to pass in information about the vote during the invocation of callForVotes. The essential pieces of information about each vote are the issue and the choices that participants can make for the vote. For the initial lunch vote, the issue is *How about lunch?* and the choices are *Yes, No,* and *Abstain.* The issue and choices can be passed in as arguments to the callForVotes invocation. In addition, because multiple votes might be taking place at once, the issue must be returned during the post invocation to clarify to which issue participants are responding. The following is the more flexible version of the distributed object interface:

```
public interface VoteListener
{
public void callForVotes( String issue, String[] choice ); public void post(
String issue, String ballot );
};
```

This new interface enables us to ask additional questions of users and provide a path to satisfy the future requirements of the application. For example, an invocation of callForVotes might ask the question, *Where should we eat?* by passing in that as an issue with a set of choices such as *Abstain, McDonald's, Taco Bell,* and *Starbucks.* The other possible future requirement was enabling a vote on when to go to lunch as well. This can also be performed with the above interface by passing in the appropriate issue, *What time?* with the choices of, say, *Abstain, 11:00 A.M., 12:00 P.M.,* and *1:00 P.M.*

The user interface for solving this voting problem must be embedded in the client. The user interface shown earlier can be implemented using Label, Choice, and Button components from the Java AWT. An example of how to do this is shown later in this chapter under ChoiceVote; however, we do not reproduce it here because AWT code is not the focus of this book. The important point is that the user interface must be embedded in the client application.

Satisfied that we have specified an interface that can satisfy the immediate and future requirements of the problem, the development group can now implement this interface and deploy client applications to everyone participating in this lunch vote.

Unfortunately, immediately following the deployment of this application, certain observations are made. First, some people want to go to lunch at times other than those listed in the choices of the vote. Another problem is that the representation of each of the choices as a string isn't very good. Responses to the vote on when to go to lunch could better be represented as Java Dates. Finally, users would rather use an interface of a clock for establishing the time at which to go to lunch; the user interface of a set of choices would not work if the participants could respond to a vote with a time that was not in the initial list of choices. A street map would be better for the set of choices regarding where to go to lunch. That way, the participants in the vote could just click on the location of their favorite restaurant rather than choosing it from a fixed list of restaurants. Unfortunately, the migration path for adding this new capability into the distributed object application involves reimplementing and redeploying the client.

Voting with Mobile Objects

In a mobile object approach to developing this application, we can build a system that is much more flexible. Rather than passing around information about each vote that is taking place, users may multicast a vote object that implements the entire vote, including user interface. The implementation of the vote as a mobile object makes it flexible enough that the system can represent any particular vote rather than the specific votes that are foreseen at the time the distributed system is designed.

To implement this Vote, let's refine the interface to pass a Vote object along with the callForVotes invocation. The Vote object contains information about the vote, including the issue and choices if appropriate, along with the user interface for the vote. The implementation of the Vote might be as simple as the earlier user interface that used a Choice component to select from the possible list of choices. Alternatively, the user interface might paint something much more complex to the screen, such as a clock for selecting the time at which to have lunch or a city map for selecting the location of the restaurant. The interface is defined in Listing 5.7.

```
public interface VoteListener
{
  /**
    * Issue a Call for Votes.  All parties listening to this group
    * should respond to this.
    */

  public void callForVotes( Vote v );

  /**
    * Post a ballot in response to a vote.
    */

  public void post( String i, Ballot ballot );                    Continues
```

```
    /**
      * Add a supplementary issue to the current vote. This is generally
      * a related concern that should be resolved in parallel with the
      * current vote.
      */

    public void addendum( String i, Vote a );
};
```

Listing 5.7 Revised source for VoteListener.

This interface differs from the previous interface shown in Listing 5.6 in three important ways. First, a Vote object rather than the issue and choices used earlier is sent to participants in the vote. Votes are still identified by an issue in the form of a string. This convention of uniquely identifying each vote with a string remains useful as a simple way of keeping track of votes. The implementation of the Vote object is shown in Listing 5.8.

```
public interface Vote
    extends java.io.Serializable
{
    /**
      * Each vote is identified uniquely by an issue which is just a string.
      */

    public String getIssue();

    /**
      * Display the options for a vote.
      */

    public void show();

};
```

Listing 5.8 Source for Vote.

Second, a Ballot object rather than a string ballot is sent to the invocation of the post method. This enables us to represent the results of votes in a manner other than as a string. For example, the result of the "What time?" vote could be a Date object. For our convenience, the only requirement that we make with regard to the Ballot object is that it supports the toString method, so that it can be converted into a String on demand for the purposes of displaying output. Since the Ballot object is an argument in a remote invocation, the Ballot object must be serializable.

```
public interface Ballot
  extends java.io.Serializable
{
  public String toString();


};
```

Finally, an additional operation, addendum, is defined. This operation defines a supplementary vote that adds onto a vote that is already underway. For example, during the vote of whether or not to have lunch, a participant can invoke the addendum operation to add into the vote "What time?" or "Where should we eat?" The addendum operation takes a string representing the issue on which this is an addendum. For example, if a "How about lunch?" vote is underway, a participant can instantiate a new Vote object for voting on what time to have lunch, then invoke the addendum operation by passing in the issue of "How about lunch?" indicating that this addendum vote applies to that original vote.

The Vote object shown earlier is actually an interface. Any Vote can be sent to the group of participants as long as it implements this Vote interface. For starters, a ChoiceVote class could be implemented that provides the initial specified user interface. Because each of the ChoiceVote object paints its own user interface, we can make the ChoiceVote extend Panel. That way we can add the Vote object to any old Java frame to let it display its user interface.

The implementation of the ChoiceVote is summarized in Listing 5.9. Following that, we explain each part of this class.

```
import java.awt.*;
import java.awt.event.*;
import com.objectspace.voyager.*;
import com.objectspace.voyager.space.*;
```
Continues

```java
public class ChoiceVote
  extends Vote
{
  Label label1 = new Label();
  Choice choice1 = new Choice();
  Button button1 = new Button("Vote!");

  GridLayout layout1 = new GridLayout(3,1);

  public ChoiceVote() {
    try {
      jbInit();
    }
    catch (Exception e) {
      e.printStackTrace();
    }
  }

  public void jbInit() throws Exception{
    label1.setText("Let your voice be heard.");
    this.setLayout(layout1);
    this.add(label1);
    this.add(choice1);
    choice1.addItemListener(new ChoiceVote_choice1_itemAdapter(this));
    this.add(button1);
    button1.setLabel("Vote!");
    button1.addActionListener(new ChoiceVote_button1_actionAdapter(this));
  }

  void choice1_itemStateChanged(ItemEvent e) {

    System.err.println("itemStateChanged: " + e);
```

```
}


public void button1_actionPerformed(ActionEvent e)
{
   // the user hit the "Vote!" button, submit the ballot to the space.

   try
     {
       ISubspace space =
         (ISubspace) Namespace.lookup( "//localhost:7000/Vote" );

       VoteListener booth = (VoteListener)
         space.getMulticastProxy("VoteListener");
       Ballot ballot = new StringBallot( choice1.getSelectedItem() );
       booth.post( getIssue(), ballot );
     }
   catch (Exception exception)
     {
       System.err.println("ChoiceVote: " + exception);
       exception.printStackTrace();
     }
}

/**
  * Each vote is identified uniquely by an issue which is just a string.
  */

public String getIssue()
{
   return label1.getText();
}

public void setIssue(String i)
{
   label1.setText(i);                                          Continues
```

```
  }

  public void addItem(String i)
  {
    choice1.addItem(i);
  }

  /**
   * Display the options for a vote.
   */


  public void show()
  {
    // Code to display vote.
    System.err.println("ChoiceVote.show");

    // Currently creates a frame to hold the vote.
    button1.addActionListener(new ChoiceVote_button1_actionAdapter(this));
    choice1.addItemListener(new ChoiceVote_choice1_itemAdapter(this));


  }

}



class ChoiceVote_choice1_itemAdapter implements java.awt.event.ItemListener {
  ChoiceVote adaptee;

  ChoiceVote_choice1_itemAdapter(ChoiceVote adaptee) {
    this.adaptee = adaptee;
  }

  public void itemStateChanged(ItemEvent e)
  {
    System.err.println("event");
```

```
      adaptee.choice1_itemStateChanged(e);
  }

}


class ChoiceVote_button1_actionAdapter implements java.awt.event.ActionListener
{
  ChoiceVote adaptee;

  ChoiceVote_button1_actionAdapter(ChoiceVote adaptee) {
    this.adaptee = adaptee;
  }

  public void actionPerformed(ActionEvent e)
  {
    System.err.println("action");

    adaptee.button1_actionPerformed(e);
  }
}
```

Listing 5.9 Source for ChoiceVote.

Here's the important point: an instance of this ChoiceVote object is transmitted for each vote. If a participant in the vote would like to vote on whether to go to lunch, the participant simply instantiates the ChoiceVote and distributes it to the other participants.

The member variables of the ChoiceVote class are focused entirely on displaying its user interface. Each of these user interface elements is serializable, so we don't need to worry about making them members of this class for our mobile object. We don't need additional member variables to store the issue or list of choices because all of this information may be stored entirely in the user interface components. In ChoiceVote, you can see our implementation of the user interface specified by the problem requirements shown in Figure 5.3 earlier. This user interface is implemented in terms of Label, Choice, and Button AWT components. The other member variable is just a GridLayout object that helps us lay out the user interface for this object.

The two standard operations on the Vote object are show and getIssue. The getIssue operation enables us to determine what issue applies to any vote. In the ChoiceVote implementation of Vote, the issue is stored inside an instance of the Label user interface component, so the implementation of the getIssue operation is as follows:

```
public String getIssue()
   {
      return label1.getText();
   }
```

The show operation was specified to enable us to show the operations of the vote to the user. However, by making the ChoiceVote object a child of Panel, we can show the options to the user simply by adding the ChoiceVote to a Frame. This practice has several ramifications that we should consider. First, by making the ChoiceVote a child of Panel, we are assuming that all the clients can detect it by invoking the "instanceof" operation on the Vote object, then add the ChoiceVote to a Frame of their choosing. Any clients that fail to do this do not see the user interface. The show operation still must be invoked to display this panel. Otherwise, it may be hidden and won't be displayed inside the Frame. The show operation also provides a convenient spot for us to restore the transient member variables of the object, such as the Listeners of the AWT components.

The implementation of the ChoiceVote object includes several operations that are not available on the parent Vote object. The ChoiceVote has a setIssue operation that enables the user of the ChoiceVote to configure the issue of the vote before broadcasting the ChoiceVote to the other participants in the vote. The issue is stored as an instance of a Label object on the user interface. This issue appears as a title in the user interface, asking the user to respond to the particular issue. Label object is serializable, so the ChoiceVote can use this object to store the issue even as the ChoiceVote moves across the network. The setIssue operation simply has to modify this Label by invoking the setText operation. The implementation is easier than the description, as shown in the following code:

```
public void setIssue(String i)
   {
      label1.setText(i);
   }
```

In addition, the ChoiceVote has an addItem operation to enable users to insert additional choices for the vote. The implementation for this addItem operation invokes the addItem operation on the Choice member variable to add the item to the list of strings shown in the Choice.

```
public void addItem(String i)
  {
    choice1.addItem(i);
  }
```

The ChoiceVote operation also has two operations dedicated to handling the user interface events that occur with the Choice and Button AWT components. The first operation, choice1_itemStateChanged, handles any changes that are made to the selection of the Choice. If the user changes the Choice from Yes to No, for example, this event will be posted to this method.

```
void choice1_itemStateChanged(ItemEvent e) {
    System.err.println("itemStateChanged: " + e);
  }
```

Behind the scenes, an ItemListener is implemented that receives the ItemEvent and invokes this method. This ItemListener is called ChoiceVote_choice1_item-Adapter, and the implementation of it is given on the CD.

The other user interface event method is button1_actionPerformed. This operation accepts events from the Button, specifically looking for when the button is clicked to indicate that the user has finished selecting a position in the vote. This operation is responsible for providing a great deal of the implementation of the ChoiceVote because it is invoked when users are ready to broadcast their position to all the other participants. As a result, the implementation for the button1_actionPerformed operation creates a virtual reference to the Voyager space and invokes the post operation to deliver the ballot to all the participants in the vote (see Listing 5.10).

```
public void button1_actionPerformed(ActionEvent e)
  {
    // the user hit the "Vote!" button, submit the ballot to the space.
```

Continues

```
try
  {
      ISubspace space =
         (ISubspace) Namespace.lookup( "//localhost:7000/Vote" );

      VoteListener booth = (VoteListener)
         space.getMulticastProxy("VoteListener");
      Ballot ballot = new StringBallot( choice1.getSelectedItem() );
      booth.post( getIssue(), ballot );
  }
  catch (Exception exception)
  {
      System.err.println("ChoiceVote: " + exception);
      exception.printStackTrace();
  }
}
```

Listing 5.10 Returning ballot results.

The code in Listing 5.10 shows that each invocation is delivered to an instance of the VoteListener object. Three different implementations of the VoteListener object are provided with this example to demonstrate the flexibility of the Space. The first object is called Voter. The Voter object is used to display a Vote to a particular person. All participants in the vote should have their own instance of a Voter object to display each Vote to them.

The two other implementations, CoWorker and BusyWorker, are essentially automated Voter objects that serve as examples for the type of operations that a Voter can conduct on the Space. They simulate a live Voter, but you could adapt them to provide a sort of answering service for a participating user who could not be present during actual votes.

A more detailed look at the Voter object shows that the implementation of this object takes advantage of both kinds of mobile object facilities built into Voyager. In the first case, the agent-style mechanism for mobile objects is taken advantage of to create instances of Voter objects. With Voyager, Voter objects can be created in any place process without needing to distribute a form of client application to each participant in the vote. All that's necessary is that each participant is running a voyager place process.

Second, we will use the built-in mobile object facility to distribute an instance of the Vote object whenever a Vote takes place. An example of this is the ChoiceVote shown earlier.

Since VoteListeners are the members of the Space, the different forms of the Voter object are the objects that are members of this Space. The Voter object must implement the VoteListener interface. An example of this implementation is shown in Listing 5.11.

```
import java.util.*;
import java.awt.*;

public class Voter
  implements VoteListener
{
  public Hashtable votes = new Hashtable();
  public Frame voteFrame = null;

  public Voter()
  {
    voteFrame = new Frame();
    init();
  }

  public Voter(String name)
  {
    voteFrame = new Frame(name);
    init();
  }

  public void init()
  {
    voteFrame.setSize( 400, 300 );
    voteFrame.setLayout( new GridLayout(2,1) );
    voteFrame.show();
  }
```
                                                                    Continues

```
/**
 * Receive a vote request.
 */

public void callForVotes( Vote v )
{
    // keep track of all ongoing votes.
    votes.put(v.getIssue(),v);

    voteFrame.add(v);
    v.show();
    voteFrame.pack();
}

/**
 * Receive a ballot posted in response to a vote.
 * Currently this just displays a message, maybe we should
 * make a popup or scrolling window?
 */

public void post( String i, Ballot ballot )
{
    System.err.println(ballot);
}

/**
 * Add a supplementary issue to the current vote. This is generally
 * a related concern that should be resolved in parallel with the
 * current vote.
 */

public void addendum( String i, Vote a )
{
    // In theory, we could make the two votes work together.
    // Not supported right now.
```

```
    Vote v = (Vote)votes.get(i);
    System.err.println( "Addendum: " + a );
    voteFrame.add(a);
    a.show();
    voteFrame.pack();
  }
};
```

Listing 5.11 Source for Voter.

The Voter object has a Frame member variable. This Frame is used to display the user interface for the Vote, which is itself a child of Panel. As each new instance of Vote is passed to the Voter, the Vote is added to the Frame to show the user interface for the Vote to the user. This is a fairly simplistic approach to composing the different user interfaces for the Vote object, but it suffices for this example. Of course, this type of user interface composition of objects that were not compiled into the client application is impossible in the traditional approach to software development, in which the user interface for a client is statically coded into each client application.

The callForVote operation is used for receiving each new Vote. Whenever any participant in the Space would like to start a vote, an instance of the Vote object is constructed and the callForVotes operation is invoked with this instance. The implementation of the callForVotes operation does several things. First, it adds the vote to a Hashtable containing all the votes indexed by their issue. This Hashtable enables the client to look up an instance of an ongoing vote given its name. Following that, the instance of the Vote object is added to the Frame for the Voter. This provides a place to display the user interface. Next, the show operation is invoked on the Panel object. This show operation gives the Vote object the opportunity to initialize itself. Finally, the pack operation is invoked on the voteFrame to perform any frame repacking that might be required with the addition of the new Panel component.

The post operation is responsible for receiving the Ballots of the participants as they decide which way to vote. The Ballot represents the position that a particular participant decided to take in the vote. A very simple implementation of the post object is given that simply displays the Ballot each participant sends as a response to the Vote. In a more robust implementation, you might want to count the Ballot here and keep track of the status of the voting.

The addendum operation is for adding other, related issues to a vote. Whenever a Vote is underway, a participant in the Vote might decide to add a new issue by instantiating a Vote object representing the new issue and adding it to the ballot by invoking the addendum operation.

As far as the Ballot goes, the initial implementation of the Ballot wraps a String, called StringBallot. This gives us all the same capabilities of the earlier distributed object application in which the ballot was actually represented as a string, but we still have an upgrade path for creating new types of Ballot objects in the future. For example, later we implement a DateBallot for voting on dates.

The last piece of the distributed system that is missing at this point is an application for starting the vote. The Dinner application is an example of this. It's called Dinner rather than Lunch, because Dinner is one of several variations on the invitation-to-eat theme. It is responsible for instantiating a Subspace to host the vote and for starting up instances of the Voter objects in three different place processes located through the network. Each of these three place processes represents a group of three people who are participating in the Vote. The implementation for this Dinner application is shown in Listing 5.12.

```java
import com.objectspace.voyager.*;
import com.objectspace.voyager.space.*;


public class Dinner
{
  public static void main(String[] args)
  {
    try
      {
        Voyager.startup();


        ISubspace space = (ISubspace)
          Factory.create( "com.objectspace.voyager.space.Subspace",
                          "//localhost:7000/Vote" );
```

```
        VoteListener joe = (VoteListener)
          Factory.create("Voter",
                         "//localhost:7000" );
        space.add(joe);



        VoteListener tom = (VoteListener)
          Factory.create("Voter",
                         "//localhost:8000" );
        space.add(tom);


        VoteListener drew = (VoteListener)
          Factory.create("Voter",
                         "//localhost:9000" );
        space.add(drew);



        Voyager.shutdown();
      }
    catch( Exception e )
      {
        System.err.println("Voter: " + e);
        e.printStackTrace();
      }


  }


}
```

Listing 5.12 Source for Dinner application.

This Dinner application creates three Voters, expecting them all to be located on different ports of the local host for demonstration purposes. "Localhost" is a network alias available on most Unix and Windows operating systems for the current machine. In order to run this application, first start the three required "voyager" processes on the current machine to host the three voters. The easiest way to run this demo is to start up four different windows for each of the applications, as follows:

```
Window 1
Prompt> voyager 7000
voyager™ 2.0 beta 1, copyright objectspace 1997
address = localhost:7000


Window 2
Prompt> voyager 8000
voyager™ 2.0 beta 1, copyright objectspace 1997
address = localhost:8000


Window 3
Prompt> voyager 9000


Window 4
Prompt> java Dinner
voyager™ 2.0 beta 1, copyright objectspace 1997
address = localhost:1031


Window 5
Prompt> java Invite
voyager™ 2.0 beta 1, copyright objectspace 1997
address = localhost:1039
```

The output shown in these figures is only a sample. You might see slightly different output when you start up each application. Each of these applications should be started in order. After the Dinner application is invoked, you should see three blank Java windows. Each of these three windows represents the user interface for the instance of the Voter mobile object, which has moved from the Dinner application to each of the three voyager applications. The window is blank only because this is a simple example; in a more complex example, the initial window might provide a more substantial user interface.

Once the Invite application is invoked, an instance of the Vote is sent to each of the voters. Each of the three Java windows should now present the ChoiceVote user interface. Each of these three windows was individually created by one of the three voyager processes to query participants for their votes. You can optionally run this demo on three different computers with a voyager process running on each computer. In that case, you should see one Java window for the vote on each of the three computers.

At this point, all the participants can express their position on the issue at hand by selecting an option in the Choice component and then clicking the Vote! button. The button1_actionPerformed operation is invoked on the ChoiceVote object when this button is clicked. This results in the post method called on the space with an instance of the StringBallot object as an argument. The string contained in the StringBallot just represents the vote, such as Yes, No, or Abstain. When any one of the Voters invokes the post operation, all the Voters receive the invocation. Thus, the post operation enables the voters to keep track of each participant's vote on the issue.

Let's sum up what we've seen so far. The application as it stands satisfies the initial requirements for the project. Nothing has to be deployed to the participants in the vote as long as they already have a voyager process. The Voter mobile object is capable of starting up within any voyager process. The Voter object acts as a receiver for additional Vote mobile objects that are sent to it. The ChoiceVote object is just one implementation of this Vote object. We distributed an instance of the ChoiceVote mobile object at runtime to ask the participants their position in the vote. The participants respond with an instance of Ballot.

Ballot itself is a mobile object, so any participant in the vote can instantiate a new form of Ballot and pass it to other participants in the network. For example, rather than a mundane conformist ballot that just displays a string, particularly innovative participants could make their Ballots pop up a dialog box announcing in bold letters their decision on the issue. The implementation of such a Ballot is left up to the reader. Remember, you can do anything with Ballot, including displaying additional user interface elements or components of additional applications. You might even display a Web page for the recipients of the Ballot object.

The next step in the evolution of this mobile object system is to consider the future requirements of the problem. Suppose that the participants in the Vote would like to resolve the issue of when to go to lunch. In that case, a new instance of the Vote object can be created to support the determination of the preferred time of the participants. The graphical user interface should display a clock. Participants should set the clock to their preferred time and then submit a Ballot containing this time in the form of a Java Date.

The implementation of this vote is provided as an implementation of a child of Vote, called DateVote. This new class displays a clock rather than the Choice component. The implementation for this is summarized in Listing 5.13.

```java
import java.awt.*;
import java.awt.event.*;
import com.objectspace.voyager.*;
import com.objectspace.voyager.space.*;
public class DateVote
  extends Vote
{
  Label label1 = new Label();
  Clock2 clock = new Clock2();
  Button button1 = new Button("Vote!");

  GridBagLayout layout1 = new GridBagLayout();

  // ...

  public void button1_actionPerformed(ActionEvent e)
  {
    // the user hit the "Vote!" button, submit the ballot to the space.
    try
      {
        System.err.println("About to Vote.");

        ISubspace space =
          (ISubspace) Namespace.lookup( "localhost:7000/Vote" );

        // create a typesafe gateway into the subspace on local server 7000
        VoteListener booth = (VoteListener)
          space.getMulticastProxy( "VoteListener" );

        Ballot ballot = new DateBallot( clock.getDate() );
        System.err.println("Voting for " + ballot);
        booth.post( getIssue(), ballot );
```

```
        }
    catch (Exception exception)
      {
        System.err.println("DateVote: " + exception);
        exception.printStackTrace();
      }



    System.err.println("Done voting.");
  }



/**
  * Display the options for a vote.
  */



public void show()
{
  // ...

  clock = new Clock2();
  clock.resize(170,150);

  GridBagConstraints gbc2 = new GridBagConstraints();
  gbc2.anchor = GridBagConstraints.CENTER;
  layout1.setConstraints(clock, gbc2);
  this.add(clock);
  clock.init();
  clock.start();
  }


}
```

Listing 5.13 Source for DateVote.

The Clock2 shown in Listing 5.13 is an instance of the standard JDK Clock demo provided with most Java development environments, including the JDK. The applet is initialized and used as part of the implementation of the DateVote mobile object in this example. The implementation of Clock2 is slightly modified to accept user input rather than just display the time. The left mouse button sets the hour hand of the clock. The right mouse button sets the minute hand of the clock. Once the appropriate time is selected, the Vote! button is still used to submit the vote.

An implementation of VoteListener, called BusyWorker, automatically instantiates an instance of the DateVote object upon receiving a Yes vote. The BusyWorker can be thought of as either an automated robot in the same spirit as an answering machine for responding to votes while a particular person is away or simply as an automated tool for testing out the mobile object system. The implementation of the BusyWorker class is shown in Listing 5.14.

```java
import java.util.*;
import com.objectspace.voyager.*;
import com.objectspace.voyager.space.*;


public class BusyWorker
   implements VoteListener
{
   Hashtable votes = new Hashtable();

   public BusyWorker()
   {
   }

   /**
     * Receive a vote request.
     */

   public void callForVotes( Vote v )
   {
      // Very simple, we display it and assume the vote will close itself down.
```

```
   v.show();

   // keep track of all ongoing votes.
   votes.put(v.getIssue(),v);
}



/**
  * Receive a ballot posted in response to a vote.
  * Currently this just displays a message, maybe we should
  * make a popup or scrolling window?
  */

boolean asked = false;

public void post( String i, Ballot ballot )
{
   System.err.println(ballot);
   System.err.flush();

   if (!asked && ballot.toString().equals("Yes"))
     {

       try
         {

             ISubspace space =
               (ISubspace) Namespace.lookup( "//localhost:7000/Vote" );

             // create a typesafe gateway into the subspace on local server 7000
             VoteListener booth = (VoteListener)
               space.getMulticastProxy("VoteListener");

             DateVote a = new DateVote();
             a.setIssue("What time?");
```

Continues

```
            booth.addendum( i, a );

            asked = true;

         }
      catch (Exception e)
        {
          System.err.println("BusyWorker: " + e);
          e.printStackTrace();
        }
     }
  }



  /**
    * Add a supplementary issue to the current vote. This is generally
    * a related concern that should be resolved in parallel with the
    * current vote.
    */

  public void addendum( String i, Vote a )
  {
  }
};
```

Listing 5.14 Source for BusyWorker.

In addition, some participants want to vote on where to go to lunch as well as to whether to go and when to go. The implementation for voting on where to go simply reuses the ChoiceVote object. The following code snippet demonstrates how this may be done.

```
ChoiceVote a = new ChoiceVote();
a.setIssue("Where should we eat?");

a.addItem("Abstain");
a.addItem("McDonalds");
a.addItem("Taco Bell");
```

```
a.addItem("Starbucks");
```

A CoWorker object is provided with the example on the CD-ROM that instantiates a ChoiceVote with a *Where should we eat?* issue whenever it receives a Yes vote.

Of course, we could do something more substantial with this vote on where to go to lunch. For example, a street map might be displayed to present each participant with a graphical layout of all the possible restaurants that may be chosen. Remember, the implementation of the Vote object is entirely up to you, so it might perform value-added services such as showing a snapshot of the menu at individual restaurants or browsing their home pages on the Web.

Bringing it all together, an application, called Brunch, another variation on the invitation-to-eat theme, instantiates an instance of Voter, CoWorker, and BusyWorker, then broadcasts a "How about lunch?" vote to all the participants in the vote. You can run the Brunch application by starting up the following applications in four separate windows:

```
Window 1
Prompt> voyager 7000
voyager™ 2.0 beta 1, copyright objectspace 1997
address = localhost:7000


Window 2
Prompt> voyager 8000
voyager™ 2.0 beta 1, copyright objectspace 1997
address = localhost:8000


Window 3
Prompt> voyager 9000


Window 4
Prompt> java Brunch
voyager™ 2.0 beta 1, copyright objectspace 1997
address = localhost:1031
```

After the Brunch application is invoked, a window should be displayed offering you the opportunity to decide whether to go to lunch. If you vote No or Abstain, that's all there is to it. You can quit the application and happily go back to work. However, if you vote Yes, the BusyWorker detects your Yes vote and broadcasts a new mobile object implementing a DateVote, asking "What Time?" Meanwhile, the CoWorker also detects the Yes and broadcasts a new ChoiceVote asking *Where should we eat?*

What's Next

♦ In the next chapter, we continue our survey of mobile object tools with a look at RMI. We return to the world of point-to-point communication for a look at how RMI, a facility built into the Java Development Kit and many Java Virtual Machines, can be used to implement mobile object software. Everything you need is probably already part of your development environment and Web browser!

6

RMI

E verything is an object in Java. The language does not allow global
variables or functions. Applets, applications, and even JavaBeans
are all objects.

The strong focus on object technology in the Java language makes distributed objects that much more important. Distributed objects permit objects in
one application to invoke methods on objects in another application, even
if the two applications are running on separate computers or in different
countries. Without distributed objects, communicating between two object-
oriented applications is much less elegant and requires more work on the part
of the software developer.

JavaSoft recognized the benefits of distributed objects and built *Remote
Method Invocation (RMI)*, an ORB, into JDK 1.1. As part of the JDK, RMI
is available in any JDK 1.1-compliant virtual machine and development environment. This availability makes RMI often one of the most convenient
choices for the construction of distributed applications. RMI can also be used
as a tool for simple mobile object applications.

Brief Introduction to RMI

RMI is designed to provide a distributed object development tool for Java. Two
Java applications or applets can invoke each other's objects through RMI. RMI
shares many of the features of the ORBs discussed in earlier chapters. An object
written in Java can be converted into a distributed object through RMI. The
methods on the distributed object are available for remote invocation. The member variables in the object are not remotely available, except through the invocation of a method. Static methods and variables also are not remotely available.

The interface for a distributed object declares what methods are available for remote invocation. Distributed objects can have some methods that are not available for remote invocation and are available only to other objects in the same application or applet, such as any methods that are not declared in the remote interface. Because IDLs declare the methods that are available for remote invocation, most ORBs must use this separate language. RMI, however, is one of a handful of ORBs that differ from the norm by allowing Java developers to declare the methods that are available for remote invocation using a normal Java interface rather than a separate language. The use of a Java interface for declaring the interface for a distributed object simplifies the task of creating a separate distributed object and shortens the learning curve for a Java developer who is new to distributed objects.

From the point of view of the Java developer, invoking a remote object through RMI is nearly the same as invoking a local object, one that is located in the same program as the object issuing the invocation. The developer issues the invocation through a *Java object reference*. To a remote object, the RMI Java object reference is no different from any other Java object reference. The object reference itself is not magically pointing to an object that runs someplace across the network. Instead, the object reference points to an object that runs in the local address space.

This object that the object reference points to, called a *stub*, has a special task. It acts as a placeholder or surrogate for the distributed object. The stub implements exactly the same interface as the distributed object. For example, if the distributed object has an int print() method, the stub has an int print() method. Because the stub acts as a mirror to the distributed object, it can also masquerade as the distributed object. However, the surrogate object doesn't actually perform the same actions when the int print() method is invoked as the original distributed object. Instead, when another object invokes one of the print() methods on to the surrogate object, it automatically sends the invocation to the appropriate distributed object using a network protocol such as TCP/IP. The distributed object reads the method invocation from the TCP/IP socket and invokes the int print() method. Finally, the int return parameter is sent back from the distributed object to the stub so that the stub can return the value to the object that originally invoked print(). This action completes the illusion that the stub is actually a distributed object.

On the server side, the method invocation must be read from a TCP/IP socket, and the appropriate distributed object, if there is more than one, must be invoked. This task is accomplished partly by RMI and partly by another special object, called the *skeleton*. Each distributed object also has a skeleton object on the server that acts as the glue between the distributed object and the TCP/IP network. The skeleton provides many of the services we've already discussed, such as reading an invocation from a TCP/IP socket and invoking the appropriate method.

When invocations are read from or written to the network, RMI utilizes Java Object Serialization to convert all the data associated with each method invocation into a stream of bytes that is sent over the network. The process of converting the invocation into a stream of bytes is called *marshalling*. The process of converting them back is called *unmarshalling*. One marshalls each parameter in a particular method invocation onto the TCP/IP socket by serializing it and then writing the resulting bytes out onto the TCP/IP socket. The receiver is then able to read these bytes and use Object Serialization again to convert them back into a Java object.

RMI Interoperability

RMI's use of Object Serialization for marshalling makes it a Java-only solution. RMI cannot be used to communicate between Java applications and applications written in other languages such as C++. Java's Object Serialization format is simply not available in any other languages. This is a serious disadvantage for RMI in comparison with other object request brokers that are CORBA compliant. ORBs that are CORBA compliant are compatible with any other CORBA-compliant ORBs without regard to programming language. The fact that RMI does not follow the CORBA standard is of particular concern because RMI is itself simply an ORB like the many other ORBs that are now CORBA compliant. The difference between RMI and CORBA exists only at the network protocol level, an area below the concern of the developer. If the RMI protocol could simply be changed to make it conform to the CORBA standard, RMI would interoperate with other ORBs that conform to the CORBA standard.

Recently, JavaSoft announced the intention to work in cooperation with the OMG to adapt RMI and CORBA to work together. In a white paper published in June 1997, JavaSoft outlined plans to add the CORBA IIOP protocol to RMI in order to supplement RMI's proprietary Java Remote Method Protocol. According to JavaSoft representatives, IIOP would be implemented in RMI as soon as the release of JDK 1.2; however, the implementation of RMI on IIOP did not make it into the early release of JDK 1.2.

Building Distributed Applications with RMI

Developing a distributed application with RMI is much like developing a normal Java application with only a few extra steps. Those steps are explained in the following sections.

Identify the Problem

The first step in any software development project is to identify the problem that the software is intended to address. Once the problem is known, the requirements for solving the problem can be specified.

For this example, suppose that you want to build a system that delivers a simple text message from the client to the server. The end user of the application types a message in the console. That message is displayed on the server. For now, the client and server are both applications, although the client may eventually be migrated to run within a Web browser.

The client just sits and reads the input from the console. When a line of text is read, that text is sent to the RMI server as a parameter in an invocation. The server just prints out the line of text.

Choose the Objects

The next step in the development process is to consider how to represent the problem as a set of objects. The main distributed object should have one operation that accepts a string as a parameter. This string represents the text message that is passed from client to server. For historical reasons, let's call the distributed object LinePrinter and give it a method called type() with a single parameter of type String. This interface in Java looks like the following:

```java
public interface LinePrinter
   {
     public void type(String line);
   }
```

In addition to the LinePrinter, objects for both the client and the server are required to run the example. Both of these applications contain only the main() operation that includes the code to invoke when the example starts.

This interface is fine for delivering a simple text message from the client to the server. However, RMI defines certain requirements for interfaces that are used with distributed objects. These requirements are as follows:

♦ All interfaces to distributed objects must extend java.rmi.Remote.

♦ All operations on such interfaces must throw java.rmi.RemoteException.

RMI uses the first requirement to decide if a particular object is a distributed object. By requiring that all distributed objects inherit from java.rmi.Remote, RMI can determine if an object implements java.rmi.Remote. If it does, it must be a distributed object.

RMI treats distributed objects differently from the way it treats normal objects. When a method is invoked and the parameters are marshalled, each of the parameters is checked to determine if it's a distributed object. When a parameter is a distributed object, an object references back to the original distributed object. The location of the distributed object itself does not change; only an object reference to it is passed from client to server or vice versa. The object reference can then be used to remotely invoke the operations on the distributed object.

With parameters that are not distributed objects and that do not inherit from java.rmi.Remote, RMI attempts to marshall the value of the object itself rather than a reference to it. Object Serialization is employed to convert the objects into a byte array that is sent across TCP/IP sockets. When the value of the object is read in from this array, a new instance of the object is created that has the same value as the original object. This makes Java's Object Serialization a critical part of RMI.

The second requirement forces all methods that can be remotely invoked to throw a special exception, java.rmi.RemoteException. RMI throws this exception whenever something goes wrong that prevents a remote invocation from successfully completing. For example, when the network connection between the client and server fails for some reason, any remote invocations cannot be satisfied because communication between the client and server is no longer even possible. RemoteException is thrown when such a problem occurs.

The client can handle this exception by taking appropriate actions to recover from the error. You can do this using the same try/catch block that you normally use for other types of exceptions. Remember, RemoteException is not a special type of exception, and it doesn't have any distributed nature about it. A RemoteException is an instance of the RemoteException class (or a child of it) just like any other exception is an instance of the appropriate exception class. When RemoteException is caught, the client can try to do things like attempt to establish communication again with the original server, contact a backup server, or warn the user that a failure occurred. All of this code goes into the catch block. Following is a code snippet of a client that remotely invokes the type() operation on an object called printer and then catches the RemoteException. If the remote invocation fails, this sample code prints out a warning for the user and displays stack trace information for a developer.

```
Try
    {
       printer.type("Hello, World!");
    }
  catch (java.rmi.RemoteException e)
     {
       System.err.println("Couldn't even say hello!");
       e.printStackTrace();
     }
```

Because every remotely invocable operation must throw this exception, this type of code is very common in RMI applications. As an alternative, you can catch a more general exception, such as the root of all exception classes, Exception. If you do this, your catch block will attempt to handle any exception that is thrown.

Now we must go back and modify the original LinePrinter interface to make it conform to the requirements of an RMI remote object. First, the interface must extend the java.rmi.Remote interface. Second, each method on the interface must throw java.rmi.RemoteException.

```
public interface LinePrinter
     extends java.rmi.Remote
  {
    public void type(String line)
      throws java.rmi.RemoteException;
  }
```

At this point, this is a legal RMI interface that is ready to use with RMI servers and clients. You can type this into a Java file called LinePrinter.java (or you can just take a look at the source code already typed in for you on the CD). Then you can compile this Java file using your favorite Java development environment to produce LinePrinter.class.

Versioning

Versioning is an important consideration in a distributed system. Browsers and development environments contain different versions of Java classes. Individual products may share components produced by the same company that differ only in product revision.

Clients and servers may have been produced at different times, or an installed base of client applications may exist that you would like to reuse without replacing. Proper versioning tools can go a long way to addressing these concerns.

Versioning is not supported by the Java programming language in JDK 1.1. When Java classes are mixed with incorrect versions of other classes, exceptions inevitably result, such as NoSuchMethod or ClassNotFound.

Versioning of objects that are serialized or externalized is even more important. In the process of serialization, all the member variables of an object are written out to a stream of bytes. When one attempts to convert the stream of bytes back into an object, the member variables for the object are read back in. If two versions of the same object have different member variables, the task of reading the object back in from the stream may not be possible.

Object serialization has primitive support for versioning of Java objects in order to solve this problem. When an object is serialized to a stream, a descriptor identifying the class and version of the object is included in the stream. The reader of the stream can use this information to determine whether a compatible object can be created.

Some changes to objects are permissible. For example, the state of an object doesn't change when you add another method to the object. Compatible changes are modifications to the classes that don't interfere with serialization. Incompatible changes are those that prevent the serialized version of one object from another object.

Continues

Versioning *(Continued)*

All the following are compatible changes:

♦ Adding new member variables

♦ Creating new classes

♦ Removing unused classes

♦ Adding or removing writeObject or readObject methods

♦ Modifying permission for a variable or method (public, protected, private)

♦ Making a static member variable non-static

♦ Making a transient member variable non-transient

All of the following are incompatible changes:

♦ Deleting member variables

♦ Modifying the type of member variables

♦ Making a non-static member variable static

♦ Making a non-transient member variable transient

♦ Implementing or extending different class

♦ Changing writeObject or readObject methods

Through proper planning, objects may be developed that make only compatible changes. Several generations of software can then be deployed without requiring the developer to completely reinstall older versions of the software.

Implement the Objects

So far, we have only defined an interface; we haven't yet created a class that implements this interface. An interface doesn't represent anything in Java except that a certain type of object has certain operations. The actions that are taken when those operations are invoked are not addressed in the interface. We need an object that implements the LinePrinter interface that does something when the type() method is invoked. An instance for this class is used by the server as the target for remote invocations.

The implementation of the type() operation should display on standard output the message passed in with the line parameter. In Java, System.out is an object that is used to represent that standard output stream for displaying data to a console. The println method on that object displays a line of text followed by a line feed, so System.out is used to display the line of output when the type operation is invoked. More information about System.out and other Java I/O issues can be found in the JDK documentation for the java.io package.

Finally, RMI requires that the implementation classes for distributed objects extend a particular RMI base class called java.rmi.server.UnicastRemoteObject. This class provides default behavior for creating and exporting remote object and implements appropriate behavior for operations like equals, hashCode, and toString. When you write an RMI server object, it almost always inherits from this base class. In theory, an implementation object could be written that didn't extend UnicastRemoteObject, but then the developer would have to provide much of this code.

For our example, we need to choose a name for this new implementation object. Let's choose a very unoriginal name for the class that implements the LinePrinter interface: LinePrinterImpl.

Putting it all together, we can define this class by the following:

```
public class LinePrinterImpl
   extends java.rmi.server.UnicastRemoteObject
   implements LinePrinter
{
   public void type(String s)
     throws java.rmi.RemoteException
   {
     System.out.println(s);
   }
}
```

This Java source implements the LinePrinterImpl object. Java requires that it be stored in a file called LinePrinterImpl.java. This file is available on the CD in the directory "examples/printer." The name of the class must match the name of the Java file. At this point, this code is ready to compile in your favorite Java development environment to produce LinePrinterImpl.class.

The stub and skeleton also must be compiled for this object implementation. The requirements for how and when stubs are compiled varies for different ORBs. RMI requires that a stub be compiled for every object implementation. The tool that accompanies RMI for this operation is the RMIC compiler. This compiler parses the class file for the LinePrinterImpl class and creates a stub and a skeleton for this class. RMI generates the stub and the skeleton as class files rather than Java source files, eliminating the need for compilation of the stub and the skeleton.

Running the RMIC compiler is similar to running the JAVAC compiler. It accepts similar command line arguments in addition to the name of the class that is the object implementation. You can run the RMIC compiler as shown in the next code segment to compile the LinePrinterImpl stub and skeleton. For more information about this compiler, please consult the online documentation for RMI in your Java development environment.

```
% rmic LinePrinterImpl
```

After you execute this code, the compiler creates two new files: LinePrinterImpl _Stub.class and LinePrinterImpl_Skel.class. These files are the stub and the skeleton for the LinePrintImpl object.

A Peek Under The Hood

RMI generates stubs and skeletons directly as class files rather than Java source files. This convenience eliminates the need for a compilation step for the stubs and skeletons. However, many of the implementation details of RMI are hidden inside these class files. If you are curious, you can use a Java decompilation tool to examine these class files, such as Mocha or WingDis. Borland's JBuilder has a built-in Java decompilation tool.

Write a Server

At this point we have created a distributed interface and a class that implements this interface. We still need the client and server applications.

The typical server in a distributed system is a background process that runs continuously on a host computer. An example of such a server is a Web server, which runs continuously on a computer designated to host a Web site. RMI servers are designed in much the same way.

The server in a distributed object environment is responsible for instantiating the server objects and making them available for remote invocation. The server objects are instantiated by creating instances of the implementation objects, such as the LinePrinterImpl created in the last section. Construction of these new instances is like that for any other Java object; you just have to invoke a constructor.

The term *server* has become slightly overloaded at this point. In one meaning, the server is a machine that contains a set of applications that provide services on a computer network. In yet another meaning, the server is a specific application that provides a set of services to the network. Now we have another meaning—the individual objects that provide services to the network are often referred to as servers. To clarify the word's meaning, let's introduce the following terminology. The server machine is a *host* or *host computer*. The server application is often referred to simply as *server*. The host computer may have several server applications running on it at the same time. The server object is called a *servant*. Servants are the objects in the server application that provide these services on the network. A single, server application can have many servants.

The server is either an application or an applet. Applications are generally more convenient if the server is running as a background process without a user interface. Applets are more convenient if the server is intended to run within a Web browser. However, if you're considering the deployment of applets that are servers, remember that the applet security manager is very restrictive about the network communication for these server applets. An application will suffice for this example.

Implementing a server application for RMI is not significantly different from implementing any other application in Java. In particular, the details of how to write the server application are the same as those of any other Java application. The RMI server application doesn't have to inherit from any particular base classes. It must have a public static void main() method that is executed when the application starts, just like any other Java application.

Without further ado, let's create a simple RMI server application to support the LinePrinter servant. Let's call this new server PrintServer as shown in Listing 6.1.

```
public class PrintServer
{
  public static void main(String[] args)
  {
```
Continues

```
    System.setSecurityManager(new RMISecurityManager());

try
  {
     LinePrinter printer = new LinePrinter();
     Naming.rebind( "LinePrinter", printer );
     System.out.println("PrintServer is ready.");
  }
catch (Exception e)
  {
     System.out.println( "Error: " + e );
     e.printStackTrace();
  }
 }
}
```

Listing 6.1 Source for PrintServer.

The server shown in the previous code performs two additional operations that we have not seen before. The very first action of this server is to instantiate a RMISecurityManager. The security manager in any Java application or applet controls what operations and resources are accessible. RMI requires that every application instantiate and register a security manager. This additional step is not necessary with Java applets, because applets automatically are given a security manager by the Web browser. More information is provided about this in Chapter 10: Securing Mobile Objects.

The server application also invokes a method on the Naming object, which is an example of a distributed object naming service. Such naming services are common in distributed computing because of a fundamental problem faced by all distributed applications. A distributed application running on one computer on a network may want to receive access to a particular object running on another computer. The problem occurs when the client and the server do not agree on the name for the particular object. Just to review, in this circumstance the application is a client because it's trying to access the object running on another computer to invoke some of its methods. The object on the remote computer is a distributed object and is called a servant, and the application that contains this object is a server. Since the servant is running on another computer, located in a different virtual machine and address space, the task of locating this object seems insoluble.

To solve this problem, the naming service acts like a telephone book for the client and server. When a server starts up, it lists itself with the naming service, just like listing a new telephone number in the telephone book. The server chooses a particular name that's used in the naming service. In the LinePrinter example, the LinePrinterImpl servant was listed under the name PrintServer. A client can then communicate with the naming service to locate objects that it needs by requesting a particular name. The client and server must agree on this name beforehand because the client cannot easily locate a server without knowledge of the name used in the naming service.

In RMI, the Naming object provides the interface to RMI's simple naming service, called rmiregistry. The server can use the bind or rebind methods on Naming to list an object under a given name. The bind and rebind methods differ only in how they react when a particular name is already in use. The bind method throws an exception when a name is already in use. The rebind method removes the old object and lists the new object in its place. Many people find rebind easier to use because it effectively handles some of the error conditions that bind forces the developer to handle. In our example, the server uses rebind to list an instance of the LinePrinterImpl class under the name PrintServer. If an object had already been listed with the name PrintServer, it's quietly removed from the rmiregistry. The client uses the lookup method to find an object with a given name in the rmiregistry. We see more of this in the next section on writing a client.

You can now compile the server in your favorite Java development environment. Just compile the PrintServer.java source file using the normal Java compiler within your development environment. No special steps are required to compile an RMI application. The relevant RMI classes, including the stubs and skeletons you compiled in the earlier section, are loaded from your class path.

Write a Client

The client in a distributed system is an application that requests services from a server. In the context of distributed objects, any application that makes use of remote objects is a client. Frequently, applications are both clients and servers. They utilize one or more remote objects and supply objects for the consumption of other applications. The distributed object used by this example client is the LinePrinter.

As stated previously, clients are either Java applets or applications. Frequently, clients are applets so that they can be easily distributed across the Web inside browsers. Clients can also be deployed as Java applications, which can be most appropriate when clients run as background processes or when the applications are too large for a Web-based download.

One of the first tasks the client must complete is to locate the LinePrinter distributed object. The client can use the Naming object to accomplish this. The Naming object provides the interface to the naming service for use with RMI. The client also needs to use this naming service to locate the distributed object called PrintServer. The lookup operation finds the object in the rmiregistry with this name. The lookup operation has a parameter that has the form of a URL:

```
rmi://example.com:15000/FirstDir/SecondDir/PrintServer
```

A URL string is composed of four parts:

- *Prefix.* The first part is the prefix, the first word up to and including the colon. The prefix for the example URL is rmi:.

- *Host name.* After the prefix is the host name preceded by two slashes. In our example, it looks like //example.com. For RMI, this host is the Internet IP address of the rmiregistry, not the server. The Naming object looks at this string to determine which computer has the naming service running on it.

- *Port Number.* The third part of the URL string is a port number preceded by a colon. In our URL it's :15000. TCP/IP communication always happens on a particular port number. The rmiregistry defaults to port number xxx, which is usually satisfactory. However, under certain conditions, you may want to run rmiregistry on another port.

- *Name.* The fourth element of the URL is the name. In this case it looks like /FirstDir/SecondDir/PrintServer. You can use slashes to separate the name into a hierarchical directory structure. However, for all practical purposes, the name space is flat with the added / character. No operations are provided for navigating or listing the directories in the rmiregistry. Each part of the string is optional, except the last section.

The lookup operation of the Naming object returns a reference to an instance of the java.rmi.Remote interface. The Remote interface is a required base class for all distributed objects in RMI. Any distributed object that's registered with the rmiregistry implements the java.rmi.Remote interface. The instance of this base interface must then be cast into a more specific interface to invoke its operations, in this case LinePrinter. Beware of one conceptual trap: The object returned from the lookup operation is not the original LinePrinterImpl object registered by the server! Rather, the object returned by the lookup operation is a remote object reference, an instance of the LinePrinterImpl_Stub compiled by the RMIC compiler.

This stub also implements the LinePrinter interface that provides the illusion that the object returned is the original object. When the type operation is invoked on the stub, the stub forwards the invocation to the distributed object across the network. The client for this distributed object example reads lines of text from standard input and invokes the type method on the LinePrinter object passing in the text.

```
import java.io.*;
public class PrintClient
{
  public static void main(String[] args)
  {
    try
      {
        LinePrinter printer =
          (LinePrinter)Naming.lookup("//localhost/PrintServer");

        BufferedReader r = new
          BufferedReader(new InputStreamReader(System.in));

        while (true)
          printer.type( r.readLine() );
      }
    catch
      {
        System.err.println("Error: " + e);
        e.printStackTrace();
      }
  }
}
```

Listing 6.2 Source for PrintClient.

The client is ready for compilation in your favorite development environment!

Run the Example

Distributed systems are composed of several interacting applications by definition, so running this example isn't quite as simple as double-clicking an icon. Three applications interact in this example:

- rmiregistry

- PrintServer

- PrintClient

First, all RMI applications and applets make some use of rmiregistry to locate distributed objects. Servers contact rmiregistry to bind or rebind new objects. Clients look up distributed objects using rmiregistry. Because of this dependency, rmiregistry must be started before any servers or clients. Recall that while you are implementing the client, the name of the machine that contains the rmiregistry was explicitly named in the URL string passed into the lookup operation. The rmiregistry runs on the machine specified in the client source code. If not, a compile time error occurs when the client is run. The command line for executing the rmiregistry is as follows:

```
% rmiregistry
```

The server application, PrintServer, provides the LinePrinterImpl object, which is used by the client. Therefore, the server is started before the client. Unlike rmiregistry, which was a native application, the PrintServer is a Java application and must be executed with the help of a Java interpreter. If you use the JDK, the command line to execute the server is shown in the next line of code. If you're not using the JDK, execute the server with the mechanism provided by your favorite Java development environment.

```
% java PrintServer
```

The client application, PrintClient, contacts the server and uses it to print text from standard input. The client is also a Java application that you must start with a Java interpreter.

```
% java PrintClient
```

Once the client is started, type something into the input of the client application and press Return. The text entered in the client is then displayed by the server. This display demonstrates that the client has accessed the distributed object in the server.

Work through the Kinks

If the development process didn't work, read the following sections for information on some common problems and their solutions.

CLASSPATH

Experience has shown that the source of most problems with Java applications is an improperly set class path. For this example, be sure that the classes are in the class path. Often you must add the current directory into the class path explicitly by adding the "." directory to the list of directories in the class path. The class path is configured in different ways with different development environments and operating systems. In some cases, the development environment ignores the CLASSPATH environmental variable, so be sure that you perform the correct configuration in your development environment. A common indication of this type of problem is the ClassNotFound exception.

Compilation

Obviously, all the source files must be compiled before you can run this example. If some files aren't compiled, you might see a ClassNotFound exception because some class files are missing. Check to make sure that all the Java source files you've created have corresponding class files.

Class Version Conflict

The nature of Java class files encourages developers and users to exchange and mix them with other class files. However, class files compiled with different Java development environments and different versions of the same development environment are not always compatible. A common indication of this problem is the NoSuchMethod exception, but other symptoms may also occur. If you have trouble running this example, confirm that only one set of the core Java classes is present in your class path, delete all the class files for this example, and recompile them just to be sure that they are all compatible with your development environment.

TCP/IP Settings

RMI makes use of a TCP/IP library to communicate between client and server applications. It doesn't matter if they are running on different computers or all on the same computer. For some operating systems, particularly Microsoft operating systems, you must have TCP/IP networking drivers installed on your system and either a network card or dialup networking.

RMI Compilation

The RMI compiler creates class files for the stubs and skeletons of distributed objects. If an error message indicates that some problem occurred with a class ending in either _Stub or _Skel, recompile your distributed objects using the RMIC compiler. Doing so ensures that the appropriate stub and skeleton class files exist and are up-to-date.

RMI and Other Java Tools

As stated earlier in this chapter, RMI is a standard part of the Java programming language. JavaSoft made RMI a part of the core Java platform as of JDK 1.1, so RMI should be available in any JDK 1.1-compatible development environment and Web browser. However, the reality is that many vendors of Java-enhanced software are all struggling to keep up with the speed with which JavaSoft has added new capabilities to the Java programming language.

The bottom line is that even if a tool claims to be compatible with JDK 1.1, it may have left out some pieces, such as RMI. In some cases, the only way to tell is by actually trying out some RMI examples to find out whether the appropriate RMI classes are supported.

To help you avoid this time-consuming task, the following sections summarize how to use RMI with the latest Java development environments.

JavaSoft's JDK

JavaSoft's own Java Developer Kit (JDK) is perhaps the standard for Java development, though it lacks the exciting graphical IDE found in commercial development environments. RMI is available in all versions of JDK 1.1 and 1.2. Indications are that RMI will continue to be supported in future versions of the JDK.

In addition, JavaSoft has a backward-compatible port for RMI available for JDK 1.0.2, creatively named RMI on JDK 1.0.2. This package is delivered as a separate set of classes for use with JDK 1.0.2 and any compatible development environments. Examples written with this package can run on any virtual machine that supports the old JDK 1.0.2 standard. This backward compatibility is extremely helpful if you need to deploy RMI applications for older Web browsers.

When using RMI with the JDK's appletviewer, be sure to turn on unrestricted network access. This setting is controlled in the appletviewer menu called Applet in the Properties menu item. If network access is restricted, you'll probably have a difficult time with the Java SecurityManager. By default, the SecurityManager allows RMI to communicate only with the server that provided the applet. However, often the single machine can have several different Internet host names, which can confuse the SecurityManager.

Symantec's Visual Café

The Café family of products from Symantec spans almost the entire life of the Java language. Café and Visual Café versions older than 2.0 are designed for use with JDK 1.0.2 only. The backward-compatible JDK 1.0.2 version of RMI is used with these development environments without trouble. Experience has also shown that the newer JDK 1.1 classes can be loaded within Café and Visual Café. Once this is done, the new features of JDK 1.1 are available in these development environments. First, install both Visual Café and JavaSoft's JDK. Then add the JDK 1.1 classes to your class path.

Visual Café 2.0 supports JDK 1.1, including RMI. No known issues exist regarding the use of Visual Café 2.0 to develop RMI.

Borland's JBuilder

Borland's JBuilder has complete support for JDK 1.1, including RMI, even in the standard edition. Borland also makes available a client/server edition of JBuilder that includes productivity enhancements for building distributed applications with RMI (Figure 6.1).

Microsoft's Visual J++

Microsoft's Visual J++ does not support RMI, though the later versions claim to be JDK 1.1 compatible. Just as in Visual Café, you can add all the JDK 1.1 classes to the development environment by installing both Visual J++ and the JDK on the machine and then adding the JDK 1.1 classes to your classpath inside Visual J++. Note that Visual J++ ignores the normal CLASSPATH environmental variable, so you have to configure it explicitly inside Visual J++. Visual J++ uses MS Developer Studio, the same visual development environment familiar to many Visual C++ veterans. Add the JDK classes to your class path by going into the Options menu, select Tools, and then choose the Directories tab. Once this is done, you can develop RMI applications with Visual J++. When you set up a project, you can configure Custom Build Steps to run the RMIC compiler to generate the stub source files.

Alternatively, you can use the JDK 1.0.2 backward-compatible version of RMI with Visual J++ and avoid bootstrapping JDK 1.1 inside Visual J++. To do this, just

Programming Mobile Objects with Java

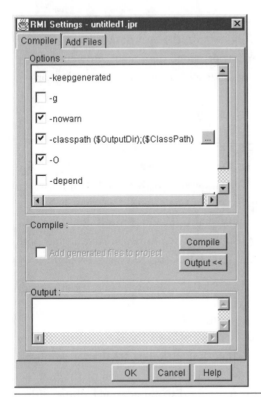

Figure 6.1 RMI with JBuilder.

install Visual J++ and the backward-compatible version of RMI. Then add the directory where you installed RMI into the class path inside Visual J++. Applets you develop in this manner will be backward-compatible with older Web browsers.

RMI in Microsoft Products

The tension over the Java programming language between Microsoft and Sun has grown considerably with the release of JDK 1.1. Two features of JDK 1.1 in particular have attracted Microsoft's attention: RMI and JNI. RMI is perceived by some to compete with DCOM. JNI, an acronym for Java Native Interface, provides an integration path for Java and native code. Microsoft maintains that they are not required parts of the core Java standard. As of late 1997, Microsoft's Web browsers and Java development tools, even those claiming to comply with JDK 1.1, did not include RMI or JNI.

RMI and Web Browsers

RMI should be available in Web browsers that support the full JDK 1.1 standard. However, the browser vendors sometimes are quick to announce that their browsers are JDK 1.1 compatible even if they support only a small portion of the JDK. When this happens, RMI is often one of the pieces left out of the browser.

Netscape's Navigator

Navigator 2 and 3 support the old JDK 1.0.2 standard. You can develop RMI applications for these browsers using the backward-compatible version of RMI. When you are ready to distribute your applet across the Internet, you will have to distribute the RMI classes along with your applet. That way, individuals who don't have RMI in their legacy Web browsers can download the classes to run your applet.

Navigator 4.0.1 and 4.0.2 contain partial support for JDK 1.1 and do not include RMI. However, a patch is available for Navigator 4.0.2 that provides virtually the entire JDK 1.1 classes. You must install this patch on every Web browser that will run your applets, though. Anyone who surfs your Web page with these browsers will also have to install the patch to run your applets. If you will be running the RMI applets on only your own computer, you can avoid installing the patch by adding the JDK 1.1 classes to your CLASSPATH environmental variable. Netscape examines your CLASSPATH and can load RMI this way as well.

According to Netscape, Navigator 4.0.3 and later versions provide basically complete support for JDK 1.1 including RMI, so you should be able to run your RMI applets with these browsers without taking special precautions. Remember, though, that browser security restrictions prevent your RMI applets from communicating with RMI servers that aren't running on the same machine that hosted the applets.

Microsoft's Internet Explorer

Microsoft's Internet Explorer 2 does not support Java. You will have to upgrade your browser in order to use applets at all.

Internet Explorer 3 and 4 include varying levels of JDK 1.0.2 and JDK 1.1 support, but none of them include support for RMI at the time of this writing. Internet Explorer runs RMI applets developed with the backward-compatible version of RMI; however, you must also make the RMI classes available along with the applets on your Web server. Doing so allows the browser to load the RMI classes along with the applets.

Internet Explorer also examines your CLASSPATH environmental variable and can load the entire JDK 1.1 library from the class path. To take advantage of this, you need to install both Internet Explorer and JDK 1.1, then configure your CLASSPATH environmental variable either in the Control Panel or through autoexec.bat in the Windows operating system. Internet Explorer is now set up to run RMI applets developed with JDK 1.1. This solution is more limiting than using the backward-compatible version of RMI. Applets cannot be distributed to Internet Explorer browsers located across the Internet using this technique because the JDK 1.1 class file cannot be placed on a Web site for two reasons. First, the JDK 1.1 class file is licensed from JavaSoft and can't be redistributed without permission. Second, the JDK 1.1 class file is larger than 8 megabytes, which is impractical to distribute across the Internet for applets. In other words, if you want to build RMI applications that run in Internet Explorer browsers on the Web, you might have to use the backward-compatible version of RMI with JDK 1.0.2-compatible development environments.

Developing Mobile Objects

Developing mobile object applications with RMI is not much more complex than creating a distributed object application. The main added complexity comes from creating the mobile object itself. First, let's consider how mobile objects are possible under RMI.

RMI requires that all parameters are either distributed objects or serializable objects. Distributed objects always implement the java.rmi.Remote interface. Serializable objects must implement either java.io.Serializable or java.io.Externalizable.

When a client invokes a method on a server passing a distributed object as a parameter, the parameter represents a remote object reference back to the original object. The instance of the object remains in the client; only a reference to the object is given to the server. The server can invoke operations on this distributed object through the remote object reference. However, the state of the object and the code that implements the object remains resident in the client at all times.

Alternatively, when a client passes a serializable object as a parameter to a remote invocation, the state of the object is serialized and passed to the server. The server creates its own copy of the object. In the process of serialization, a class descriptor is also written that identifies the class of the serialized object. The bytecode for the class may be transferred from client to server on demand.

As a result, clients and servers can effectively exchange objects, including their member variables and bytecodes. The individual objects may implement their own unique behavior for performing the operations on the object, contain additional states not present in other objects, provide a new graphical user interface, or a host of other possibilities.

All you have to do to make a mobile object using RMI is define your own serializable class as a parameter to a remote invocation. When the invocation is made, your object is copied from client to server. The capabilities and limitations of your new mobile object are entirely up to you.

Mobility Features

RMI is essentially an ORB that enables serializable Java objects to pass across the network. Therefore, RMI lacks some of the features that might be desirable in a robust mobile object tool. The support that RMI has for copying serializable Java objects enables us to build mobile object applications.

State Preservation

As with many of the other tools already examined in this book, RMI makes use of Java Object Serialization to copy objects across the network. The rules of Object Serialization apply to how and if a particular object may be serialized.

When an object is passed as an argument to an RMI remote object, any objects implementing java.rmi.Remote are passed by reference. Instances of these objects continue to exist in their original process and do not move across the network. A remote object reference is passed to the RMI remote object instead, enabling the remote object to invoke operations via the reference passed to it.

Other objects that implement java.io.Serializable or java.io.Externalizable may be copied by value across the network. Rather than pass references to these objects, RMI serializes or externalizes these objects to the object stream used to communicate between two distributed applications in RMI. The object may be read in by the receiver and reinstantiated through Object Serialization.

Class Loading

Object Serialization supports a primitive form of class loading on demand. Whenever an object is written out to a stream, a small indicator called a ClassDescriptor is also written to indicate the type of the object. This ClassDescriptor is used to indicate that an object has a specified class. The receiver of the object stream reads in the

ClassDescriptor and determines which classes are already available locally and which must be loaded by a class loader.

RMI applications can load classes from one of several sources. First, applet classes are always loaded by the AppletClassLoader. Second, any classes in the local CLASS-PATH are loaded through the default class loader. Finally, the RMIClassLoader is used to load some of the classes required in the implementation of RMI, such as the stub and skeleton classes for a RMI remote object. RMIClassLoader looks for classes in several locations, including on the local CLASSPATH for locally available classes, at a URL specified in serialized objects, or at the location specified by the property java.rmi.server.codebase.

Unfortunately, the mechanism for RMIClassLoader is not extensible. No methods are provided in RMI for defining and registering a new RMIClassLoader that can be used by the RMI run-time environment. As a result, the developer of an RMI application must depend only on the default implementation of RMIClassLoader and cannot provide custom logic for locating and loading classes.

Security

Security is always a significant concern when one is dealing with two distributed systems that communicate with each other. RMI goes well beyond communication by enabling two distributed systems to exchange objects and even code.

The risk to an RMI application is simple. Without any form of protection, RMI applications are vulnerable to malicious objects intent on doing harm. An example of an attack on an RMI application is not hard to envision. The PoisonPill object, shown in Listing 6.3, makes an operating system call to attempt to reformat the local hard disk on a Windows or DOS computer.

```
public class PoisonPill
   implements java.io.Serializable,
             java.lang.Runnable
{
  public void run()
  {
    Runtime.exec("format c:\");
```

```
    }
};
```

Listing 6.3 Source for PoisonPill.

A properly registered SecurityManager should disallow the use of the Runtime.exec invocation by throwing a SecurityException from its checkExec() method. This precaution effectively prevents the attack illustrated earlier, but developers must be sure to register a strong SecurityManager.

RMISecurityManager is designed to prevent exactly this sort of attack, as well as a number of other possible attacks on RMI applications. RMISecurityManager doesn't allow applications to open server sockets, preventing them from masquerading as a legitimate server on the host machine. It restricts file access, printing, loading libraries, exiting from applications, managing threads, and access to the system clipboard, all in an attempt to prevent malicious objects from attacking an otherwise unsuspecting RMI application.

Although RMI applications are forced to register an RMISecurityManager, RMI applets are not. Applets are governed by the AppletSecurityManager, which is enforced by the Web browser hosting the applet. The AppletSecurityManager is even more restrictive than the RMISecurityManager, so no serious security risks result from this substitution of security managers.

New features in RMI for JDK 1.2 also address some of the communication security issues. On the Internet, communication security is particularly important because it is remarkably easy for a computer hacker to eavesdrop on TCP/IP-based Internet communication. Companies moving their point of sale onto the Internet are particularly concerned about the privacy of customer information, such as credit card numbers. Encryption technology, such as Netscape's Secure Socket Layer (SSL), are available to address this problem. RMI is now including SSL functionality to help protect the privacy of communication between two RMI-based applications.

Object Identity

Just as in the case of Caffeine, mobile objects passed through RMI are copied. The original instance of an object may be duplicated with the result that several different virtual machines contain conflicting copies of the same object. It's up to the developer to resolve this issue.

Object Sharing

RMI doesn't support any form of object sharing, other than sharing of a remote object through an object reference.

Concurrency

RMI doesn't provide any special thread pooling or thread management constructs.

Building a Mobile Stream

Input and output streams are frequently employed in Java applications to save objects and other data to files. However, the streams are normally tied to a single application. For example, a client can't create an output stream, write some data to the stream, and then pass along the output stream for use by another application. If an output stream is implemented as a mobile object, this can be achieved.

Implementing the Mobile Stream

For this example, a child object of ByteArrayOutputStream that is a mobile object is created. ByteArrayOutputStream is a stream that provides a simple way to write data to a byte array. However, ByteArrayOutputStream is normally restricted to a single application. To break these bonds, the child of ByteArrayOutputStream must be serializable so that an instance of it may be passed to other applications. None of the Java streams are currently serializable. Once the child of ByteArrayOutputStream is externalized, the instance is passed back and forth between RMI client and server applications.

The state of the ByteArrayOutputStream is contained in two important member variables: *buf* and *count*. The buf is an array of bytes that saves all of the data that's written to the ByteArrayOutputStream. The count is an integer that saves the number of bytes of data that were written to buf. Externalizing the state of the ByteArrayOutputStream simply means writing these member variables out to a stream. The MobileByteArrayOutputStream class, shown in Listing 6.4, extends the ByteArrayOutputStream to add support for externalization.

```
import java.io.*;

public class MobileByteArrayOutputStream
    extends ByteArrayOutputStream
    implements Externalizable
{
```

```
public void writeExternal(ObjectOutput o)
  throws IOException
{
  o.writeInt(count);
  o.write(buf,0,count);
}

public void readExternal(ObjectInput o)
  throws IOException,ClassNotFoundException
{
  count = o.readInt();
  buf = new byte[count];
  o.read(buf,0,count);
}
}
```

Listing 6.4 Source for MobileByteArrayOutputStream.

At this point the stream object is used as an argument to a remote invocation. For example, a client instantiates an instance of MobileByteArrayOutputStream, writes some data to it, and then passes it as a parameter to a server invocation. Then the server can write some more data to the stream and pass it back to the client. When the client finally looks at the contents of the MobileByteArrayOutputStream, all the data written both by the client and by the server is available there.

What's Next

♦ The next chapter provides an extensive example of building a workgroup application with mobile objects. This example also uses RMI for a good, hands-on look at how to build large mobile object systems.

Dabbling in
Groupware

G *roupware* is a general name for software that allows many individuals to collaborate on projects. It makes up a significant part of the software deployed on a desktop. Many software applications that historically ran only as standalone applications are currently being adapted to support collaboration. Indeed, the Internet itself can be viewed as a large collaborative effort among millions of people who share common interests

Groupware is inherently a distributed application. When many users collaborate across a computer network, the applications used for this collaboration must make up a distributed system. Thus, groupware is a good first example for applying mobile objects to software development.

Looking at the Old Approach

Members of organizations share information all the time while conducting the processes of business. Software developers collaborate on project plans and specifications. Managers discuss budgets and employee records. Executives establish product plans. Often, all three groups track the hours spent on particular projects and submit expense reports for reimbursement.

In this process of information sharing, one individual creates a document and passes on that document to many others. These others may have different responsibilities with respect to the original document. Some may contribute additional material to the document or revise the existing document. Others may be responsible for approving and disapproving changes to the document.

The collaborative process is currently a long and difficult one. The software developer that designs a groupware application must perform many steps to share data among collaborating individuals.

Saving Files

Most applications operate on some data, whether this data is an e-mail message, object diagram, spreadsheet, or even class file. The first step in building any groupware application is to provide a mechanism for saving files that contain that data.

However, writing the code to save files is often considerable work for the developer. In object software, the data is represented by a collection of objects. These objects must be externalized to be saved to a file.

The user of the application might also experience additional work because of the need for objects to be externalized. In some groupware applications, the files must be saved explicitly to another file before the files are shared with a group of other individuals. Thus, the user has to take this additional step when publishing information to share with other members of a collaborative project.

Sharing Files

Many methods are available for sharing files in a groupware application. In some of the most popular applications, such as Lotus Notes, an API is specified for publishing a file to the members working on a collaborative project. Many other groupware applications support other methods for publishing data. For example, in Web servers, a file is uploaded from the user machine to the Web server, usually with FTP.

This type of file publishing is often automated. For example, in current Internet e-mail software, participants pass files to others in a collaboration by simply clicking and dragging an existing file into a mail document to add the file as an attachment. However, in the best case, even the click-and-drag operation could be avoided.

One way that many organizations still collaborate is through *sneaker net*. This is the process of sharing files between members of a collaboration by copying the files onto floppy disks and exchanging floppies. The recipient then loads the files from floppies. Sneaker net collaboration is not an example of true groupware, but it shows how difficult and inefficient collaboration can be in the absence of the proper tools.

Executing Software

Perhaps the most tenacious problem encountered by collaborators is reaching an agreement on compatible software. First, the members of the collaboration must know what software is required to read and manipulate the exchanged files. Many software applications follow the convention that the extension on the file name is used to determine what software was used to save the file; however, some applications don't follow this convention, and some extensions are ambiguously used by multiple software applications. For example, .doc is a popular extension for several word processors.

Often, resolving these issues requires some additional communication between the members to establish an agreement about what software is used and whether the file extensions contain meaning.

Once the collaboration group has agreed on a particular set of software applications, all members must confirm that they have the correct versions for all of the appropriate software. To simplify the task of opening the files exchanged in the collaboration, the participants may set up program associations between the file extensions and the software used to read the files. Such program associations provide a shortcut for the user to execute the appropriate software for examining the file. File associations often work with e-mail attachments, Web browsers, and even some software provided with the operating system. Default program associations are sometimes provided with the software supporting them, but often these default association settings are far from complete and must be customized whenever a new software application is introduced to the desktop. That some file extensions are ambiguous and cannot be mapped back to a particular software application is another source of errors.

Finally, the software itself may be executed, either manually or through a file association. The user can read the files and potentially make changes to them. Then the process starts all over again.

Collaboration with Mobile Objects

Let's look at how the tasks involved in collaboration are automated through a mobile-object approach. The steps involved for implementing this are as follows:

1. Identify what part of the system is mobile.

2. Identify those objects that move from the client to the server.

Choosing What Should Be Mobile

First, the software developer must identify what part of the collaborative system is mobile and what is more or less static. Preferably, to make the system as general and adaptive as possible, very little of the system remains static.

At this point, the requirements have not been firmly specified regarding what kind of documents are exchanged by this new groupware application. Therefore, we cannot specify that any particular document is exchanged, such as a word processing or spreadsheet document.

Choosing a Common Base Type

The documents exchanged in a mobile object system are instances of objects. So as we consider what parts of the system are mobile, we identify those objects that are moved from client to server. The approach to passing an object from a client to server utilizes the same techniques as any other object software. In particular, inheritance is employed to allow many different instances of subclasses when a particular root class is passed into a single method. That method can then employ polymorphism when the user is operating on the instances of the object in order to manipulate the instances of these different subclasses.

For this example, let's look at simply exchanging an instance of java.lang.Runnable. The Runnable interface is used by Java to represent a particular task that must be performed by a thread. Thus, as we consider the problem of the most general type of object that our new groupware application can support, Runnable is a natural choice as a common base type for the mobile objects. The Runnable has only a single method.

```
public interface java.lang.Runnable
{
  public void run();
}
```

The simplicity of this object makes it easy to adapt other objects to support the Runnable interface by implementing a run() method. In the context of the groupware application, an instance of a subclass of Runnable represents a task that must be completed by a participant in the collaboration.

Not Choosing a Common Base Type

Applications don't necessarily need to agree on a common base type for mobile objects. Yet another possibility is to avoid defining a root interface entirely. The instances of mobile objects are instances of the most generic class in Java, java.lang.Object, which is the implicit parent of all Java objects.

However, simply passing around instances of java.lang.Object can be fraught with peril. After all, the java.lang.Object doesn't define any useful methods. You can't do anything with a java.lang.Object except cast it into something else.

Java's new support for reflection changes this situation somewhat. Instances of objects even as general as java.lang.Object can be examined to determine their methods and fields. This information is then used to determine what capabilities a particular instance has by making deductions based on naming conventions for the methods and fields. For example, this technique was in the original JavaBeans specification.

However, in this example, let's stick with java.lang.Runnable as a root interface for all the mobile objects that are exchanged among our groupware applications.

Building Mobile Groupware with RMI

For the purposes of this example, let's use RMI. In practice, one of the other tools would work just as well. Please refer to Chapter 5: Building Mobile Objects with Voyager for more details about the basics of how to build a mobile object application using RMI.

Implementing the Root Interface

In the previous section we discussed the use of java.lang.Runnable as the root interface for the mobile objects in this application.

RMI determines which objects are passed by value and which objects are passed by reference through interface inheritance. Any object that implements the java.rmi.Remote interface is treated as a distributed object. Any object that implements the java.io.Serializable interface is treated as a mobile object. Therefore, our mobile objects must also implement the java.io.Serializable interface in addition to the java.lang.Runnable interface.

With this in mind, a new root interface is defined called discuss. Task, which implements both java.io.Serializable and java.lang.Runnable.

```
public interface Task
   extends java.io.Serializable,
           java.lang.Runnable
{
};
```

The Task object allows us to pass instances of objects that are declared to be both Serializable and Runnable. The Task object can also provide a useful layer of abstraction later on if we decide to add capabilities to the root interface for the mobile objects in our groupware application.

A Generic Server

When designing this groupware application, we use a straightforward client/server approach for exchanging tasks, instances of the Task mobile object. It's important to understand that this type of approach is not necessarily required or better than some of the other approaches we consider in later chapters such as peer-to-peer and group communication. Such group-based communication mechanisms are looked at in more detail in Chapter 9: Clustering.

In a client/server system, the server is generally an application that is started on a server machine and runs for an indefinite amount of time. An example of this is a Web server on the Internet that runs indefinitely, serving up Web pages to anyone who requests them. The server in this groupware example performs a similar task, running indefinitely, serving up instances of Task objects to anyone who requests them.

The server in this application is a remote object on the server machine. The clients interact with it as if it were a normal distributed object, utilizing a naming service to locate it and invoking it through a remote object reference. Users of RMI create remote object references by defining a parent interface that inherits from java.rmi.Remote. In this collaborative system, the each queue basically corresponds to an individual worker who contributes to projects. This type of client/server architecture in which many workers obtain tasks from a server is often referred to as a *master/slave system*. That terminology has negative connotation for a professional environment, but we'll call the main server interface Master nonetheless.

```
public interface Master
   extends java.rmi.Remote
```

```
{
    // ...
}
```

Conceptually, the server in this application acts as a repository for the instances of Task objects. The participants in the collaboration contact the server to determine what tasks have been sent to them.

The server maintains many different queues of tasks. Each queue is identified by a unique name. In practice, these queues could loosely correspond with the participants in the collaboration, with each participant having a unique queue of tasks to complete, as shown in Figure 7.1.

Breaking this design down into Java, the server maintains a java.util.Hashtable containing the queues for the participants. The key for the Hashtable is a String object that identifies the name of this queue. The participants can then check the queue under a given name. The server keeps track of each task as part of a java.util.Stack stored as the value in the hashtable. Using a Stack in this way is perhaps not optimal. The Java Stack is a "pushdown stack," which means that the element most recently added to the stack is the next one retrieved. In practice, this is not the way that most people tackle their tasks. Rather, tasks are usually tackled either in the order they were assigned or in order of importance. This example doesn't attempt to model this type of prioritization.

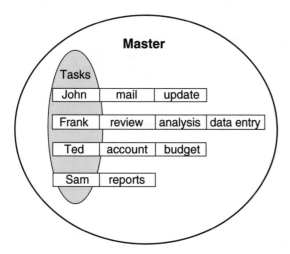

Figure 7.1 Participants with their tasks.

Constructing the server is simply a matter of implementing the distributed object for the server. In this example, the main server object is called simply Server. In RMI, remote objects usually extend java.rmi.UnicastRemoteObject. This base class provides the basic support code for an RMI server object. UnicastRemoteObject overrides methods such as hashCode, toString, and equals for use with remote objects.

```
public class Server
   extends UnicastRemoteObject
   implements Master
{
   private Hashtable slaves = new Hashtable();

   // ...
}
```

The clients contact the server to add and remove tasks, so naturally, the methods on the Master interface reflect this contact. Master has a method for adding tasks— let's call it pushTask. This method pushes a task onto a particular queue. The method signature is as follows.

```
public void pushTask(String queue, Task t)
   throws java.rmi.RemoteException;
```

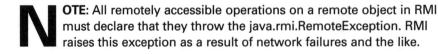

NOTE: All remotely accessible operations on a remote object in RMI must declare that they throw the java.rmi.RemoteException. RMI raises this exception as a result of network failures and the like.

The implementation of pushTask simply adds a Task to the Stack owned by the specified participant.

```
public void pushTask(String queue, Task t)
   throws java.rmi.RemoteException
{
   Stack tasks = getTasksForSlave(queue);

   Object o = tasks.push(t);
}
```

This method uses a helper method called getTasksForSlave. This operation is intended just to bundle all the code related to obtaining the stack of Tasks for a particular worker in one location. In a more robust system, this type of code would probably be part of a class dedicated to the worker, but in this simple example, the code is just placed in a single method to make it a little easier to reuse than the cut-and-paste method.

The getTasksForSlave method also implicitly adds new queues whenever a queue is not found for a particular worker. In a robust application, you might want to throw an exception or perform some other error condition to ensure that the caller is aware that the name is invalid. In this implementation, if someone accidentally misspells your name, a completely new worker is implicitly created as if another person existed under the new spelling of the name.

```
public Stack getTasksForSlave(String queue)
{
   Stack tasks = (Stack)slaves.get(queue);

   if (tasks == null)
     {
        tasks = new Stack();
        slaves.put(queue, tasks);
     }

   return tasks;
}
```

The second operation for the task server removes tasks for a participant in the collaboration. Following along with the terminology of a stack, the second method has the name popTask with the following function signature.

```
public Task popTask(String queue)
   throws java.rmi.RemoteException;
```

The implementation for popTask first obtains the Stack of tasks for a particular worker and pops the top task off the Stack. This task is then returned to the client.

```
public Task popTask(String queue)
   throws java.rmi.RemoteException
{
```

```
Stack tasks = getTasksForSlave(queue);

return (Task)tasks.pop();
}
```

These two methods provide all the basic behavior required for this demonstration.

The only other significant piece of code is implementing a static void main() method for the Server application. This main operation is called when the Server application is executed. The requirements for the main operation, shown in Listing 7.1, are very simple. First, a RMISecurityManager is registered. RMI requires that all RMI applications register a SecurityManager to prevent RMI clients and servers from acting as an open door for hackers. Second, the server instantiates an instance of the Server object and register it with the RMI Naming service, using the rebind operation. The rebind operation will not only register the object with the Naming service, it will check to see if any other object is registered with the same name and replace it with the current object. The name we assign to this object in the Naming service is just "Master," shown in Listing 7.1.

```
public static void main(String args[])
{
  System.setSecurityManager(new RMISecurityManager());

  try
    {
      Server s = new Server();

      Naming.rebind( "Master", s );
      System.out.println("Master ready...");

    }
  catch (Exception e)
    {
      System.out.println("Error: " + e);
      e.printStackTrace();
    }
};
```

Listing 7.1 Source for main() operation.

Notice how remarkably simple the design and implementation of the server is in this example. This same server proves very useful, however, because it can handle any Task objects. The server is too simple to perform operations like reviewing the current list of tasks or tracking progress on completing tasks, but operations like these could easily be added to this server.

A Generic Client

The goal of generality in the server applies equally well in the client. The server was able to store any type of Task object. The client should be able to work with virtually any type of Task object. In this example, the client is an applet, but the client can be either an application or applet. It makes little difference to the example or the code.

The clients contact the server through a remote object reference, so the first action the client must perform is to look up this remote object reference within the RMI Naming service. The lookup static operation on the Naming object is used to perform this lookup in the RMI Naming service.

```
master = (Master)Naming.lookup("//localhost/Master");
```

Right after the object reference is obtained, one of the two main operations is performed on this newly obtained operation, such as the following.

```
Task t = (Task)master.popTask("Incoming");
```

In this example, only one queue is used initially by the client. This queue is called Incoming and represents all tasks that still need to be completed. Later, more queues can be added to represent completed tasks, participants, or other conceptually convenient constructs.

Finally, the developer starts the task by calling the run() method on the Task. The run() method contains the specific implementation of each Task object. (We look at how to implement Task objects later in this chapter.)

When the client applet starts, the init() method is called automatically by Java's framework for applets. Putting it all together, the client applet has the following init() method.

```
public void init()
{
  try
```

```
    {
      master = (Master)Naming.lookup("//localhost/Master");
      Task t = (Task)master.popTask("Incoming");

      t.run();
    }
  catch (Exception e)
    {
    System.err.println("Error: " + e);
    }
}
```

To implement the example as an application, the developer simply needs to put the code inside a static-void main method for a Java application.

Where Do Tasks Come From?

If the Server stores tasks and the client retrieves them, one question that's still not resolved is where tasks originate initially. That is, the Task objects must be instantiated and added to the server. The current client is a consumer of tasks. One solution to this problem is to implement a client applet that was general enough to allow tasks to be created as well as retrieved. However, that would interfere with the basic elegance of our current three-line client.

Instead, we need a new type of client that acts as a supplier of tasks. A second client is provided that has the specific goal of creating and adding new tasks to the Server. This second client, called MakeWork, instantiates Tasks and stores instances of them in the server (Figure 7.2).

The Task objects are represented as Java classes. The MakeWork client instantiates these Java classes that represent Tasks. In order to create a solution that is as flexible as possible, MakeWork reads the class names from standard input. This allows an instance of MakeWork to run side-by-side with the server. The developer can add Tasks at any time by simply typing in the name of the class of the Task object that is instantiated.

The implementation of this example is more complex than the client and server. Primarily, this complexity is due to the command-line options and standard input operations in the MakeWork application, shown in Listing 7.2.

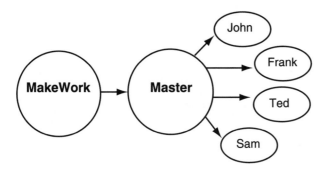

Figure 7.2. The MakeWork client, master, and slaves.

```java
public class MakeWork
{
  public static void main(String[] args)
  {
    // Default: Command line argument is the name of the queue.
    //          Input is a list of Task classes to instantiate and add
    //          to that queue.

    if (args.length == 0)
      {
        System.err.println("Usage: MakeWork <worker-name>");
        System.exit(-1);
      }

    String queue = args[0];
    System.out.println("Adding asks for " + queue + ".");

    try
      {
        Master master = (Master)Naming.lookup("//localhost/Master");

        BufferedReader r = new
```

Continues

```
            BufferedReader(new InputStreamReader(System.in));

        String tclass = r.readLine();

        while (tclass != null)
          {
            Object o = Class.forName(tclass).newInstance();

            if (o instanceof Task)
              master.pushTask(queue,(Task)o);

            System.out.println("Added " + tclass);

            tclass = r.readLine();
          }
      }
    catch (Exception e)
      {
        System.err.println("Error: MakeWork.main: " + e);
        e.printStackTrace();
      }

    System.out.println("Done.");

  }
};
```

Listing 7.2 Source for MakeWork.

The core operations of MakeWork are simply as follows.

```
Object o = Class.forName(tclass).newInstance();

  if (o instanceof Task)
    master.pushTask(queue,(Task)o);
```

This software instantiates an instance of the Task object with the class name given in standard input and pushes the Task onto the queue specified on the command line.

This process provides us with a simple way of creating new tasks by writing a new Java class and registering instances of those tasks for a particular queue.

Implementing Tasks

The applications and applet implemented so far provide a framework for sharing Tasks among many participants. However, no Task objects are available yet to share within the system.

To simply implement a task, all we have to do is create a new class that implements that Task's interface and has a run() operation. Here is an example of an implemented Task object.

```
public class MyFirstTask
   implements Task
{
   public void run()
   {
     // ...
   }
}
```

The implementation for the Task is all provided inside the run() operation. Any operations taken by the instance of the Task, such as displaying a form, asking for user feedback, or sending an e-mail message, must be implemented inside the run() operation.

The new Task subclass can define additional member methods and fields; these are also moved as part of the mobile object. In practice, RMI uses Java's built-in Object Serialization service to move objects between client and server. Thus, the normal rules for Object Serialization apply. Refer back to Chapter 5: Building Mobile Objects with Voyager for more details on this.

TrivialTask

Historically, software developers who are confronted with a new software development tool or programming language tackle a first task of printing a simple message such as "Hello, World!" In observance of this tradition, the first task is designed to do the same. When a client obtains an instance of the TrivialTask from the server, the task will simply print out the "Hello, World!" message.

The implementation of this task is very simple because the task prints only a line to standard output.

```
public class TrivialTask
   implements Task
{
  public void run()
  {
    System.out.println("Hello, World!");
  }
}
```

To try this example with the TrivialTask, just perform the following steps:

1. Start the RMI Naming service by running rmiregistry.

   % rmiregistry

   The rmiregistry must be started before anything else in this example. This represents a naming service that the RMI server and clients contact in order to locate each other.

2. Start the server.

   % java discuss.Server

   The server acts as a repository for task objects. Both MakeWork and SlaveApplet communicate with the server to save and retrieve instances of Task objects. Thus, the server must be started before either of the clients.

3. Add the task by running MakeWork.

   % java discuss.MakeWork Incoming

   discuss.TrivialTask

   After running MakeWork, enter discuss.TrivialTask in the console as the name of a Task for MakeWork to instantiate. MakeWork creates an instance of this Task and adds it to the Incoming queue in the server. Once you've typed in the name of the Task to instantiate, you can leave MakeWork running for later use or exit the application. The process for leaving the application varies depending on your development environment.

4. Run the client applet.

% appletviewer SlaveApplet.html

The SlaveApplet displays the normal applet frame and contacts the server. This applet doesn't attempt to do anything with the default applet framewindow right now, so it's just blank. But check the standard output for the message from the Task object (Figure 7.3).

AppletTask

Some companies are sitting on a huge pile of completed applets that implement useful functionality. Further, software distributors are now publishing CD-ROMs full of free applets to try out. You can reuse this functionality within this groupware framework by creating an AppletTask that simply starts up an applet.

The run method of the AppletTask, see Listing 7.3, must instantiate a copy of the applet and display it for the user. The AppletTask needs only the name of the applet that is to be instantiated. The AppletTask can then use the Class.forName() method to create an instance of the applet. The applet is then displayed when you add the Applet to a Frame thereby showing the frame.

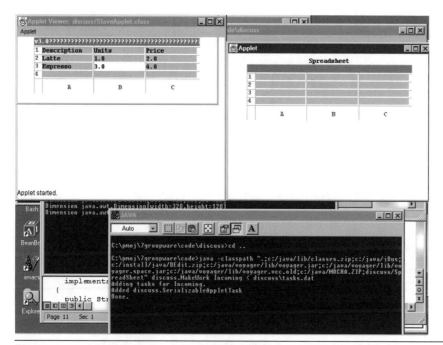

Figure 7.3 MakeWork and SlaveApplet.

```
public class AppletTask
  implements Task
{
  public String appletClassName = null;

  public AppletTask()
  {

    this("SpreadSheet");

  }

  public AppletTask( String s )
  {
    appletClassName = s;
  }

  public void run()
  {
    Frame f = new Frame("Applet");

    //    Dialog d = new Dialog(f,"Dialog");
    //  d.setLayout(new FlowLayout());

    Applet a;

    try
      {
        a = (Applet)Class.forName(appletClassName).newInstance();
      }
    catch (Exception e1)
      {
        System.err.println("Error: AppletTask.run: " + e1);
        return;
      }

    // a.setStub(new ExampleAppletStub(this));
```

```
f.setSize(400,300);
f.setLayout(new FlowLayout());

f.add("Center", a);
a.init();
f.show();


    }


}
```

Listing 7.3 Source for AppletTask.

The default Applet for the AppletTask is the SpreadSheet applet that is one of the demos provided with the JDK. The applet displays a simple spreadsheet. The Task based on this applet also displays a spreadsheet.

Running this example is a little trickier than running the TrivialTask example because of the addition of an applet. First, set CLASSPATH to include SpreadSheet. How this is done can vary widely among operating systems and among shells within the same operating system. In Windows, do the following:

1. Start the RMI Naming service by running rmiregistry.

2. Start the server.

3. Add the task by running MakeWork.

4. Run the client applet.

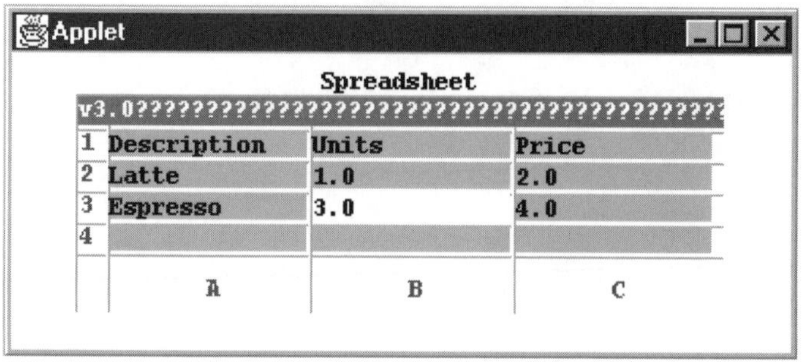

Figure 7.4 Spreadsheet screencap.

This time, although you ran exactly the same client software, a spreadsheet shows up in the appletviewer as shown in Figure 7.4. This spreadsheet is effectively a mobile object.

This example is impressive, but in truth, we cheated a little on it. The spreadsheet never really moved from the server to the client. Instead, the AppletTask object contains only the name of an applet that should be instantiated. The AppletTask uses this to instantiate the SpreadSheet applet on the Client machine, without actually moving the SpreadSheet. The AppletTask is what is moving between the client and server, but AppletTask is fairly simple. It has only a single member variable and no user interface. AppletTask is still a good example, though, because this task enables us to start up any applet as a task within the groupware system. Even prewritten applets supplied by other organizations could be added as instances of AppletTask without requiring changes to their existing code. Now we'll consider a slightly more complex, but much more useful, example.

SerializableAppletTask

SerializableAppletTask provides a Task for any applets that are serializable objects by implementing java.io.Serializable. Such a serializable applet is instantiated on one computer and then moved to other computers as a mobile object.

The SpreadSheet example provided with the JDK is not serializable, so the first task we must tackle is to make it serializable, preferably without breaking it.

First, the easy step. The SpreadSheet object must implement the java.io.Serializable class. RMI checks for this implementation relationship to determine whether a particular object is passed by value. However, simply implementing the java.io.Serializable interface doesn't mean that the applet is serialized properly. The Object Serialization specification in Java tries to do the best job possible of serializing objects, but the developer must code the application with Object Serialization in mind to make an object properly able to serialize and deserialize itself.

In the code for the SpreadSheet applet, all the member variables are not explicitly declared public.

```
public class SpreadSheet
    extends Applet
    implements java.io.Serializable
{
```

```
String          title;
Font            titleFont;
Color           cellColor;
Color           inputColor;
int                 cellWidth = 100;
int                 cellHeight = 15;
```

The Object Serialization specification requires that each member be declared variable public. Only public member variables are actually serialized as part of a stream. The rationalization behind this design decision is that private variables may contain sensitive information that should not be distributed to other parties; thus, only the public data is serializable. This limitation does not prevent the developer from utilizing Object Serialization with classes that contain private data; it just forces the developer to create additional code to communicate those private values or initialize them to some appropriate values.

However, to make the SpreadSheet serializable, we can safely say that none of the member variables looks sensitive or in need of protection from prying eyes. All the fields of SpreadSheet can simply be marked public.

The SpreadSheet class relies on several private helper classes to perform its tasks. These include CellUpdater, Cell, Node, InputField, and SpreadSheetInput. Because SpreadSheet contains members that are instances of these classes, each of these must similarly implement java.io.Serializable and have all of its elements declared public.

Finally, the applet doesn't set a preferred size. This can be somewhat problematic because when the applet is inserted into a Frame by the SerializableAppletTask, the Frame queries the applet to determine what size it is in order to determine how to lay out the Frame with the embedded applet. The frame could force the applet into a particular size, but this is a poor solution for the general case of all serializable applets. Not all applets are the same size. To solve this problem, add the following method to the SpreadSheet class.

```
public Dimension preferredSize()
{
  return new Dimension(320,120);
}
```

CellUpdater is another source of concern. The CellUpdater is a Java thread that is responsible for recalculating the value of the cell when it is modified. As a Java thread, CellUpdater is not copied when the object is moved to another machine. In this example, CellUpdater is used by only the relatively obscure URL option for the spreadsheet. This URL option allows the data from a saved spreadsheet file in the special format specified by the spreadsheet to be loaded into the spreadsheet.

Applets in Web pages depend on parameters embedded in the APPLET tag of the HTML file for configuration information. Embedded applets in Java applications sometimes have a difficult time with this configuration because the applet doesn't have an HTML file. The AppletStub object is used in JDK 1.1 as a sort of handle for the Applet to use when interacting with its environment. The software developer can create new AppletStub objects to provide parameters to even embedded applets by calling the Applet.setStub() method. The SpreadSheet applet does use some parameters, so an AppletStub must be provided to give the SpreadSheet a stub to request its parameters. Otherwise, a null object reference exception is thrown by the applet.

One final concern about Object Serialization is that base classes are not serialized with an object even if it implements java.io.Serializable. For applets, this means that the Applet objects created by the developer, along with fields defined by the developer, are copied to the remote computer, but the member variables of the Applet class itself are ignored. These include the AppletStub member variable that is set by our call to setStub. Because many applets use parameters, Applet.setStub() will probably have to be called from within the run() method of SerializableAppletTask to ensure that this value is set by the client. We provide a default implementation for an AppletStub subclass called SimpleAppletStub that does very little and doesn't return any parameter values.

The implementation of the SerializableAppletTask, shown in Listing 7.4, is similar in many ways to the AppletTask, with some important differences. First, rather than having just the name of an applet as a member variable, the SerializableAppletTask has an instance of an applet as a member variable. This applet is instantiated and initialized at the time the Task is instantiated. The applet moves with the Task whenever the Task object passes between clients and servers.

How is this example superior to just making the spreadsheet available as an applet on a Web page? After all, placing the applet on a Web page would also let people download the spreadsheet and display it dynamically. To answer this question, let's look at how we can use the SerializableAppletTask in a new way.

```java
public class SerializableAppletTask
  implements Task
{
  public Applet applet = null;


  public SerializableAppletTask()
    throws ClassNotFoundException,
    IllegalAccessException,
    InstantiationException
  {
    this( "SpreadSheet" );
  }

  public SerializableAppletTask(Applet a)
  {
    this.applet = a;
  }

  public SerializableAppletTask(String appletClassName)
    throws ClassNotFoundException,
    IllegalAccessException,
    InstantiationException
  {
    applet = (Applet)Class.forName(appletClassName).newInstance();
    applet.setStub(new SimpleAppletStub());
    applet.init();
    applet.start();
  }


  public void run()
  {
    Frame f = new Frame("Applet");

    f.setSize(400,300);
```

Continues

```
    f.setLayout(new FlowLayout());

    f.add("Center", applet);

    // If you would like to pass Parameters to the applet you can
    // add them by implementing a new AppletStub object.

    applet.setStub(new SimpleAppletStub());

    f.show();
  }
}
```

Listing 7.4 Source for SerializableAppletTask.

An instance of the SerializableAppletTask class is simply saved on the server by MakeWork. Then the instance is given to the SlaveApplet client and displayed. Clearly, this simple architecture for displaying the spreadsheet is not unlike the implementation of a spreadsheet in an applet for a Web browser. The spreadsheet is displayed to only one person on demand, so the delivery of the spreadsheet may have just as easily been done with a Web browser and applet combination as opposed to the mobile SerializableAppletTask approach.

However, much more complex situations can be constructed through use of SerializableAppletTask. For starters, the instance of the SerializableAppletTask can be forwarded to other participants in the collaboration. One person can display the spreadsheet, make changes, and then forward it on to others. The instance can then be reopened with all the changes made by the last viewer available.

The preceding example doesn't support this type of forwarding yet. The behavior of SerializableAppletTask must be extended to support the forwarding of the Task to demonstrate this capability. Alternatively, the SlaveApplet can be modified to support forwarding of any tasks. To demonstrate the flexibility of this architecture, let's implement task forwarding within SerializableAppletTask, avoiding any changes to either the client or server. To avoid modifications to the client permits the reuse of any already-deployed clients. This may not be important for a simple example in a book, but if these clients were deployed throughout several thousand computers within a Fortune 100 company that applied modifications to the clients, it could prove infeasible.

Let's add the appropriate code inside the run method for the SerializableAppletTask. Forwarding the SerializableAppletTask to another member of the collaboration requires contact with the server. This is found through the RMI Naming service with the same way it's located in the existing clients and server.

```
Master master = (Master)Naming.lookup("//localhost/Master");
```

In this sample code, localhost represents the host name of the computer that runs the rmiregistry. The localhost is a default host name that means that the service is running on the same computer as the client. If you're running different applications in a distributed environment using multiple computers, you may have to hard-code the name of the computer with the rmiregistry here.

Next, you can push the Task object onto another queue. In this case, the Task object in question will be simply this object because the forwarding code is inside the run method for the SerializableAppletTask. Assuming the task is forwarded to a queue named Outgoing, the following code needs to be executed.

```
master.pushTask("Outgoing",(Task)this);
```

Parallel Computing

The previous architecture suggests that this kind of Task server may be appropriate as a groupware application. However, the architecture is remarkably general in nature. Several other applications also can make use of this architecture. The flexibility of the groupware example to solve other significant problems demonstrates the power of the mobile object approach to building this distributed system. For example, the groupware application examined earlier can be extended to parallel computing. In examining this application area, we will see that the existing client and server require little or no modification to support the new requirements. Being able to adapt to changing requirements is a highly desirable characteristic in any software.

Parallel computing is the study of the use of many CPUs working in concert to solve discrete problems. When large problems are broken up into small parts, each part of the problem is individually attacked and solved by a single CPU among the pool of participating CPUs. A significant amount of research goes into determining the best way to optimize the parallelization of algorithms and efficiently break them up into these small parts.

The hardware used for parallel computing can vary widely. Massively parallel Connection Machines can often have thousands of CPUs grouped in discrete modules that contain a processing unit and memory. Each module is then connected with all other modules through a hierarchical bus architecture that attempts to optimize the speed and minimize the cost of intermodule communication.

Parallel computing can also be done with a LAN of low-end personal computers, called a cluster. An Ethernet LAN is capable of 10 to 100 megabits of data per second. This is plenty for many parallel computations that don't require a great deal of message traffic. The modern PC has far more CPU power than it needs and most of it is wasted while the machine sits idle and humans eat and sleep. Many organizations are sitting on a gold mine of idle processing power running on their LAN.

When solving a problem with a cluster of personal computers and workstations, one of the first problems that must be addressed is how the software is distributed across the multiple computers participating in the solution to the problem. In many of the existing cluster frameworks, each computer must individually have the appropriate software installed on it. Then when the computer participates in the parallel computation, this software can be used to perform the task.

However, the simple architecture that we have outlined here for distributing Task objects makes no such requirement. When an instance of a Task object is obtained from the server, the underlying bytecode for the Task object is automatically transferred by the Java Virtual Machine.

The implementation of a Task object to perform this kind of parallel computation is absolutely no different from that for the Task objects that we have already implemented. The only difference is that a Task object that performs this type of parallel computation would probably not depend heavily on user input. That's not to say that it couldn't include user input. Nothing in this architecture prevents ComputationTask from asking the user for additional information, so ComputationTask is suitable for querying the user for information that can be included in the computation.

The run method on the Task object does not return any values; it returns void. If the computation does have a requirement to return a value, some additional mechanism for delivering the results of the computation must be implemented within the run method. This problem is solved in several ways. The ComputationTask can include member variables that are copied from the server to the client when the instance of the ComputationTask is obtained. Such member variables can include an object reference to a distributed object that acts as a coordinator for all the results of the computations. The distributed object in this setting acts as a callback mechanism for passing results back from the call receiver to the caller, even though the operation itself returns void. The developer returns the results of the computation by invoking an operation on this distributed object. The following is an example of a ComputationTask:

```
public class ComputationTask
    implements Task
{
  public void run()
  {
    // calculate the expected return of an investment, or whatever
  }
};
```

The SlaveApplet client, implemented for the earlier Task objects, is not very appropriate for ComputationTask objects. The SlaveApplet obtains only one instance of a Task object and displays it for the user to interact with. In the case of ComputationTask, we would generally expect them to be numerous and contain little, if any, user interaction. Thus, a more appropriate client would be one that requested and ran Task objects in a loop over and over again until no more Task objects remained on the server. Let's consider the design of such a client in more detail.

First, what about the choice between applet or application? Building only a client applet to run the ComputationTasks may not be a good choice for two reasons:

♦ An applet has an associate user interface through the applet frame. Assuming the ComputationTasks generally don't perform any type of user interaction, the applet frame just gets in the way.

♦ Applets are displayed through either Web browsers or appletviewers. Neither of these is convenient for running background processes on idle machines.

On the other hand, building only a client application would also have the negative effect that we couldn't utilize the Web server as a means for distributing the clients to Web browsers. The best choice is to implement both.

It's been said that one quality that all good developers share is a lazy streak. To confirm this saying, let's avoid writing either applet or application. All that is required is another type of Task object that in turn performs additional ComputationTasks. That is to say, we don't need to actually write a new client to get the desired effect of continually executing ComputationTasks in a loop. Instead, a new Task is created that embodies this Task of looping over ComputationTasks. Let's call this task ConsumeComputations. The implementation of this task is shown in Listing 7.5.

```java
public class ConsumeComputations
  implements Task
{
  public void run()
  {
    Master master;

    // Initialize the orb and get a reference to the Master
    try
      {
        master = (Master)Naming.lookup("//localhost/Master");
        while (true)
          {
            Task t = (Task)master.popTask("Incoming");
            t.run();
          }
      }
    catch (java.util.EmptyStackException e)
      {
        System.err.println("No more tasks.");
        System.exit(-1);
      }
    catch (Exception e)
      {
        System.err.println("Error: " + e);
        e.printStackTrace();
      }
    System.err.println("Task done.");
  }
};
```

Listing 7.5 Source for ConsumeComputations.

Until now, we ran the Task objects by invoking the run method directly. This approach is single threaded in that only one thread is used to execute the Task objects—the same thread that is passed into the init method for SlaveApplet. The Task object is a child of Runnable, so a thread is instantiated to begin executing the Task immediately when we simply start a thread with the Runnable. We do this through the constructor on the java.lang.Thread class by accepting a Runnable parameter, followed by invoking the start method on the newly created thread. For example, the following line of code would construct the ConsumeComputations task and execute it within its own thread.

```
new Thread(new ConsumeComputations()).start();
```

One interesting question is whether a multiple-CPU machine can take advantage of each CPU to run different threads of a multithreaded client. This appears to depend on the Java Virtual Machine. On most Java Virtual Machines, the Java threads won't spread over multiple processors. Little benefit, other than convenience, can be had from multithreading clients on machines that don't take advantage of multiple processors.

What's Next

♦ In this chapter, we've seen how mobile objects can help build a flexible groupware framework for sharing tasks across the network. Now, we are ready to move on to see how mobile objects can impact the development of software applications such as a word processor. We'll look at how mobile objects may be added to the word processor to extend its capabilities well after the word processor has been deployed.

8

Building the
Dynamically Upgradable Text Editor

This chapter looks at how to implement a text editor using mobile object concepts. Rather than the traditional approach of distributing the application in shrink-wrap, we'll see that the major feature set of the text editor can be sent after the product has shipped. Bugs can be fixed. New user interfaces can be added. Additional menu items can be added to the application with little effort. We also look at performance considerations and ways to optimize the performance of the application yet not lose any of the flexibility of the implementation.

The Application

The implementation of a major text editor application is beyond the scope of this book. Therefore, we adopt a complete, working text editor for this application and convert it for use with this example.

As a good starting point, we adopt a text editor, called mpEDIT, designed and built entirely over the Internet pro bono by a group of software developers. The effort was organized by John Jensen, the author of the original versions of the text editor. A copy of the original mpEDIT is included on the CD-ROM. The editor is similar in functionality and user interface to the Windows Notepad. The user interface is shown in Figure 8.1.

Programming Mobile Objects with Java

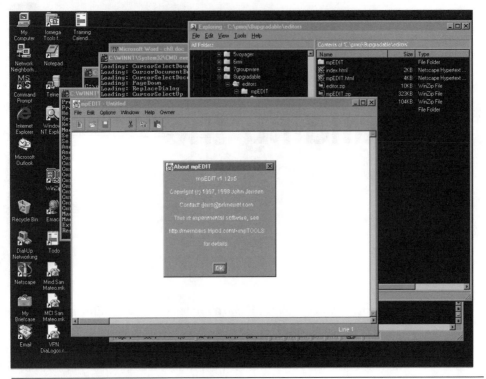

Figure 8.1 User Interface of mpEDIT.

The application functionality before a mobile object architecture is added to it is very much like the typical text editor with a few extras. The application includes the standard operations such as creating new documents, saving and opening documents from files, cutting/copying/pasting, and using an about window.

Some of the extra features supported by mpEDIT not generally found in a text editor include source code colorization. This feature, familiar to most software developers, highlights key words in source code in order to make them stand out. The support of source colorization is a sure sign that mpEDIT is the software developer's text editor.

Another feature of mpEDIT is the use of property sheets to configure the user interface of mpEDIT. Using these property sheets, a user can modify most of the user interface features of the application. Finally, mpEDIT includes an architecture for adding extensions to the application in the form of JavaBeans. For the purposes of this example, we don't pay much attention to these features of mpEDIT, except to the extent that we can leverage them to help us build a flexible, mobile object system.

Architecture

As a precursor to building this example, we examine the existing architecture of the mpEDIT application. This architecture can either help or hinder converting this application into a mobile object architecture. As it turns out, the application is configurable, modular, and object oriented, so we will attempt to leverage the application architecture to the greatest extent possible. The implementation of this example should take advantage of the architectural structure of the application. In order to determine how we can do this, let's first examine the architecture of the application as it currently exists in mpEDIT.

At the 10,000 foot level, the architecture for the mpEDIT application includes a set of objects that act as managers. Each of these objects provides a mechanism for managing the other objects in the application. Each manager follows a standard naming convention, ending in "Man." Some of the managers in the mpEDIT application include DocMan, FilterMan, LineMan, PrintMan, PropMan, and StringMan. The implementation of mpEDIT relies on these managers to control the portion of the application addressed by different areas of the application. For example, the DocMan manager is responsible for managing the document, while the StringMan manager is used to manage all the strings in the application in order to support configuration and internationalization. The functionality of these managers may impact the design of our application as we convert it into a mobile object architecture. The managers partition the implementation of the mpEDIT application, so making changes that impact only a single manager may be easier than making implementation changes that span multiple managers. Also, we may decide later to make some of the managers mobile objects.

One feature of mpEDIT that may prove useful is that it enables a great deal of user configuration. Implementing mpEDIT enables users to configure most of the user interface elements to their own preferences. For example, users can set up their own customized menus and menu items. The content of the menu items is then mapped into specific operations within mpEDIT. The entire user interface is set up through use of this configuration mechanism, so users can actually change or remove the main menus, such as the File and Edit menus, as well as introduce their own elements into the user interface. Toolbars are configured in exactly the same way. The implementation enables each button in the toolbar to be mapped into a specific operation. The image displayed by the toolbar button is also configured in the property sheet, so users are free to modify the standard set of icons to provide their own custom look and feel.

mpEDIT takes advantage of a feature of Java property sheets in order to achieve this level of user configuration. The contents of this configuration are loaded into the Java application as a ResourceBundle. The ResourceBundle object is a standard part of the java.util package. The ResourceBundle architecture is designed to make it easy to set configuration options for different objects in a Java application. MpEDIT takes advantage of this capability by loading a property sheet and creating a ResourceBundle. This ResourceBundle is then consulted whenever the application needs to determine any user preferences. The flexibility of this user configuration mechanism may prove useful when we begin implementing the mobile object version of this application.

The file that is read in for this configuration is called strings.properties. All the configuration information is stored in this file. The gif images for the toolbar are loaded by the ClassLoader, so in the standalone implementation of mpEDIT, the images for the button are loaded directly from the CLASSPATH.

These ResourceBundles within the mpEDIT application are encapsulated within the mpEDIT application. This may be done to provide a layer around the ResourceBundle objects for the convenience of the application using these resources. The layer is composed of one StringMan manager. This particular manager's name is a misnomer. The function of StringMan is not to manage strings but primarily to provide a layer around the ResourceBundles. The naming of StringMan may have been chosen because these ResourceBundles are appropriate for wrapping the internationalization of the application. When the application is translated into another language, a new property sheet can be provided in the appropriate language. Effectively, StringMan acts much like the string table used in other applications to centralize all the strings in the application in a single convenient place for internationalization. StringMan is a critical part of the application architecture because it is the sole source of this configuration information. The implementation of the example with mobile objects must take this into consideration.

Each of the operations in the mpEDIT application is available to end users as a discrete element called an Action. Each Action is given a specific name and can be referred to in the configuration file using this name. In the configuration file, users can easily map each of the elements to an action of the user interface by simply specifying the name for the Action.

Examples of these Actions are the cut/copy/paste operations. The cut operation is named "selection-cut." Several options can be specified in order to configure this operation. The display name, icon, menus, and a short description can all be provided for this action. In order to configure this information in the property sheet, use the following lines:

```
action.selection-cut.name=Cut
action.selection-cut.icon=Cut
action.selection-cut.short=Cuts current selection and puts into buffer
```

These lines specify that the "selection-cut" Action uses the display name, "Cut." The icon that is used to display this information is called "cut.gif." Finally, a short description of the operation is given as "Cuts current selection and puts into buffer." This information is used to determine how the normal cut operation is displayed to end users.

The Action can also be configured to determine how it is used in the application. The implementation of the operation can be in a toolbar or in a menu. The Action can be shown in a toolbar because an icon is specified in the operation. The following lines are used in the property sheet to configure how the Action is used in the application.

```
menu.edit=undo redo - selection-copy selection-cut buffer-paste -
   find-dialog replace-dialog goto-dialog
toolbar=document-new document-open-dialog document-save -
   selection-cut selection-copy buffer-paste
```

These options configure the use of the Cut action in the Edit menu and toolbar. The application can use this information to display the Cut option in the appropriate location in the menu and toolbar.

The object used inside mpEDIT to represent each Action is called MpAction. This interface defines the common behavior for all the actions within the mpEDIT application. Most of the methods are informational, providing mechanisms for obtaining the name, description, and icon for an action. The source for MpAction is shown in Listing 8.1.

```
interface MpAction extends ActionListener
{

   /*
```

```
     * Inherited from ActionListener
     * Main method, called from various places to execute action
     * @param evt event which caused the action
     */
    //public void actionPerformed(ActionEvent evt);



    /**
      * Text to be displayed on text button or in menu
      */
    public static final String NAME = "Name";


    /**
      * Base name of icon file family
      */
    public static final String ICON = "Icon";


    /**
      * Verbose description for help, or advanced info
      */
    public static final String LONG_DESCRIPTION = "LongDescription";


    /**
      * Short description to be displayed in tooltips etc
      */
    public static final String SHORT_DESCRIPTION = "ShortDescription";


    /**
      * Key string for returning small (16x16) icon to be displayed on button
      */
    public static final String SMALL_ICON = "SmallIcon";


    /**
      * mpEDIT addition: Small Icon in disabled state
      */


    public static final String SMALL_ICON_DISABLED = "SmallIconDisabled";
```

```
/**
  * mpEDIT addition: provide emacs-like action identifier
  */
public static final String ID_STRING = "IdString";


/**
  * Identifier passed to PropertyChangeListeners when enabled flag has changed
  */
public static final String ENABLED = "enabled";


/**
  * Returns text for action for specific key
  */
public String getText( String key );


/**
  * Sets text for action for specific key
  */
public void setText( String key, String text );


/**
  * @return emacs-like name identifier for action
  */
public String getIdString();


/**
  * Similar for getIdString, but gets one describing action fully - to be
  * used in macro save/load.
  */
public String getFullIdString();



public String getShortDescription();
public void setShortDescription(String txt);
public String getName();
public void setName(String txt);
```

Continues

```
    public String getIcon();
    public void setIcon(String txt);


    /**
      * Is action enabled for its component
      */
    public boolean isEnabled();


    /**
      * Enable/disable action for given component
      */
    public void setEnabled( boolean b );


    /**
      * Add object to be notified of change in any of the values
      * (mainly enabled state)
      */
    public void addPropertyChangeListener(PropertyChangeListener listener);


    /**
      * Add object to be notified of change in any of action's values
      */
    public void removePropertyChangeListener(PropertyChangeListener listener);
}
```

Listing 8.1 Source for MpAction.

The mechanism used to implement new instances of MpAction within the application is not to inherit a new class directly from MpAction. Instead, an intermediary abstract class called AbstractMpAction is specified to provide some base behavior for the actions. The source for the AbstractMpAction object, which provides some default behavior for all the actions, is shown in Listing 8.2.

```
abstract class AbstractMpAction implements MpAction
{
    private boolean enabled = true;
    private PropertyChangeSupport propertyChangeSupport;
```

```
protected String idString;
protected String name;
protected String icon;
protected String shortDescription;

public AbstractMpAction(StringMan strings, String aIdString)
{
  idString = aIdString;
  propertyChangeSupport = new PropertyChangeSupport(this);
  name = strings.getString("action." + idString + ".name");
  icon = strings.getOptionalString("action." + idString + ".icon");
  shortDescription = strings.getString("action." + idString + ".short");
}

public abstract void actionPerformed( ActionEvent e );

public String getText( String key )
{
  if ( key.equals(NAME) )
    return name;
  else if ( key.equals(ID_STRING) )
    return idString;
  else if ( key.equals(SHORT_DESCRIPTION) )
    return shortDescription;
  return idString;
}

public void setText( String key, String text )
{
  if ( key.equals(NAME) )
    setName(text);
  else if ( key.equals(SHORT_DESCRIPTION) )
    setShortDescription(text);
  else
    throw new RuntimeException("Value " + key + " cannot be set");
}
```

Continues

```java
public String getIdString()
{
  return idString;
}

public String getFullIdString()
{
  return getIdString();
}

public String getShortDescription()
{
  return shortDescription;
}

public void setShortDescription( String text )
{
  propertyChangeSupport.firePropertyChange( SHORT_DESCRIPTION,
shortDescription, text );
  shortDescription = text;
}

public String getName()
{
  return name;
}

public void setName(String text)
{
  propertyChangeSupport.firePropertyChange( NAME, name, text );
  name = text;
}

public String getIcon()
{
  return icon;
```

```
   }

   public void setIcon(String text)
   {
      propertyChangeSupport.firePropertyChange( ICON, icon, text );
      icon = text;
   }

   public boolean isEnabled()
   {
      return enabled;
   }

   public void setEnabled( boolean b )
   {
      propertyChangeSupport.firePropertyChange( ENABLED, new Boolean(enabled), new
Boolean(b) );
      enabled = b;
   }

   public void addPropertyChangeListener(PropertyChangeListener listener)
   {
      propertyChangeSupport.addPropertyChangeListener(listener);
   }

   public void removePropertyChangeListener(PropertyChangeListener listener)
   {
      propertyChangeSupport.removePropertyChangeListener(listener);
   }
}
```

Listing 8.2 Source for AbstractMpAction.

The implementation of this base class is declared as anonymous inner classes
rather than global classes for each of the many different Actions. The benefit of
using inner classes is primarily the compactness of the code. When they are declared
as inner classes, the code for the class can be embedded in a parent class without

even having a name assigned to the class. Listing 8.3 provides an example of deriving classes from AbstractMpAction.

```
addToDict( new

                AbstractMpAction(strings,"help-about-dialog") {
        {
        }


        public void actionPerformed( ActionEvent e ) {
          AboutDialog ab = new
AboutDialog(textFrame,strings,strings.getString("DialogAbout"));
          ab.show();
        }
    }
                );
```

Listing 8.3 Example of deriving classes from AbstractMpAction.

The application keeps track of the available MpAction implementations with a dictionary of the instances of the MpAction object. Whenever any new implementation of the MpAction object becomes available within the application, it should be registered inside the application. The application consults this dictionary in order to respond to user interface events and invoke the appropriate MpAction instance. The dictionary of actions is known as the actionDictionary. Only one action dictionary is contained within the entire mpEDIT application. The addToDict() operation in TextCanvas is used to add new actions to the actionDictionary. An example of invoking this command is shown in Listing 8.3. The implementation shown in that listing both declares a new command using anonymous inner class and invokes the addToDict() operation to add it to the dictionary.

In addition, mpEDIT supports a unique JavaBean-based component model for extending the functionality of the editor. The application architecture enables a new JavaBean to be added to the text editor with minimum overhead by placing a set of JavaBean JAR files in a special directory in the mpEDIT distribution. MpEDIT automatically loads all the JavaBeans in this directory and provides a menu item for invoking the JavaBean. In this example, we make use of this feature to add new JavaBeans to the application. We'll see that these Beans can be loaded either from the local disk or as mobile objects.

Stumbling Blocks

The architecture of the mpEDIT application does include one detail that is problematic. Most of the implementation is declared private. It is therefore difficult for us to manipulate using mobile objects because the mobile objects cannot obtain access to those parts of the applications that are not public. As a general rule, all the operations and variables in mpEDIT are declared private. We will need to revisit this design when we look at porting the application to use mobile objects. The implementation of objects using private and protected variables may enforce encapsulation in an object-oriented environment. By definition, declaring elements of your application private or protected restricts the access of portions of the application to the same class or child classes. When access is restricted in this manner, the application becomes less flexible by definition because private and protected are restrictive.

This restriction is a problem for a mobile object environment because the mobile objects may need to have access to these private or protected elements in order to implement certain features. For example, without access to the text content of a text document, a mobile object cannot move into the document and perform a spell check, lacking permission to access the private content of the document. The implementation of any object-oriented program is subject to judgment calls regarding whether to make members private or public. The addition of mobile objects merely extends these judgments to a new level of extensibility that may include the addition of new objects at runtime.

In the mpEDIT application, the text document is declared as a DocMan object, an object that manages the document. Inside DocMan is a private member whose content is a LineMan object responsible for keeping track of all the lines of text in the document. The LineMan member is declared as follows:

```
class DocMan implements DocInterface
{
  // ...
  private LineMan lines;       // the document data
  // ...
};
```

As a result of this declaration, any mobile object sent to the application cannot read the raw content of the document if it starts with the DocMan object. In the mpEDIT application, many of the private member variables and operations may need to be redeclared in order to enable access to them. In most cases, this may be as simple as selectively changing members declared as private to some other access mode or as complex as rewriting objects that are not serializable.

Supporting Mobile Objects?

The MpEDIT application is an example of an application that doesn't support any form of distribution or mobility. How do we change this application so that it supports this new functionality in a useful way? Before looking at the example, let's look at the general problem of converting nondistributed applications to support distribution and mobile objects.

The first question that should be considered is whether distribution or mobility can help an application at all. These are two separate questions. Distributed computing technology in general enables two applications to communicate with each other; mobile object technology enables two applications to exchange objects at runtime.

When you are deciding whether to add support for distributed computing technology, the question to ask yourself is always whether or not you want your application to communicate with another application. You might want your application to act as a server, distributing data or services to other applications. Alternatively, you might want your application to act as a client, consuming the data or services of other applications. In some cases, you might even want to design your application to communicate with other copies of itself running on the network. This is peer-to-peer communication.

When considering the utility of mobility, consider if implementation of other objects could be useful inside your application. Could you make use of some of the business logic from another application? Could the form displayed to a user in another application be useful inside this application? Would you like users to be able to exchange application components with each other? Would you like to be able to load part of the functionality of the application at runtime? Would you like to provide features or bug fixes at some future date after the distribution of the original application? Mobile objects can implement these features for your application.

Once you've decided to build your application with mobile objects, the next step is to clearly identify which portions of the application should offer support for mobile objects. This decision is based on how the mobile objects should affect and improve the application. Many approaches can be used for identifying how mobile objects should interact with the application, just as there are many possible benefits to the application. One approach that is often successful is to consider which objects in the application could be loaded at runtime with some benefit. For example, if an application tracks customer accounts that are historically stored in a database, the implementation of a mobile object version of the application might load different implementations of the customer object at runtime, providing more flexibility about how the customer objects are implemented. However, this is only one view of how to map an existing application to mobile objects. The primary goal in this typical approach is to extend or replace existing behavior within the application.

Another approach that may be successful is to look for ways to add new options to the application. The options that are available in an application are often just objects that follow a particular interface. The selection of possible options is often specified by a Vector or array of these option objects. If your application follows this design, you can easily build a mobile object architecture that enables you to add new instances of option objects to your application at runtime. All that is required is to implement a server that acts as a repository for instances of option objects. Then build a client into your application that contacts the repository to download new option instances. Finally, extend the set of options objects and register them in the repository. This architecture is remarkably simple to implement, as we see later in this chapter, but it proves a very powerful way for extending application behavior at runtime.

A third way to add mobile objects to an application is to look for places to add new user interface elements, such as new windows or new components to an existing window. These user interface elements can be implemented as mobile objects, as shown in Chapter 3 with the Discuss example. The mobile object in question can extend the behavior of one of the standard Java user interface elements, such as java.awt.Component. The instance then can be effectively added to the application, often to one of the existing windows, after it has been obtained from the server. Mobile objects that extend the right Java base classes can be used in the application just like local objects that extend the same base class, so it's relatively easy to download new user interface elements as mobile objects and incorporate them in the user interface.

Yet another approach is to identify objects or components of the system that can benefit from fault tolerance. For example, if the application provides a network service that is mission critical, applying techniques to ensure that the service is always available may help make your application more robust. Mobile objects may enable you to more easily implement object groups and replication to achieve this goal. In choosing the mobile objects for this approach, the important consideration is how to achieve the goal of fault tolerance. The objects that provide the critical service are typically going to be those that should be replicated, so they should be implemented as mobile objects.

We have not exhausted the possibilities for ways to choose the mobile objects of an application. The ways to determine your mobile objects are as numerous as the possible benefits to the application. Consider the goals of the benefit in question to determine how to choose the mobile objects to achieve the appropriate benefit. Keep in mind your goals for what you want the mobile objects to eventually do within the application. If you want the mobile objects to perform operations that are currently not accessible within the application, you may need to do some rearchitecting and rewriting to achieve your goals. For example, when critical data for the application is stored in private member variables, you must carefully consider how to best make this data accessible to your mobile objects. This may require reevaluating your goals for encapsulating the data and redeclaring those member variables as public. In the experience of the author, this simple problem of lack of a broad vision with respect to how member variables are encapsulated is often one of the main sources for difficulty when one is migrating an application to support mobile objects. The example from Chapter 3: Building Mobile Objects with Caffeine and the mpEDIT example demonstrate this point.

In designing ways mobile objects will be used with your application, carefully follow the normal object-oriented paradigms of programming. Mobile objects tend to be most successful when you are strictly following the object paradigm. You may need to interpret this paradigm slightly, though. As discussed, issues like the privacy of member variables take on an entirely new scope when objects may move into the application at runtime to access member variables. In the end, you benefit from following the object paradigm, but you must also carefully consider what this means in the more dynamic mobile object environment.

The next step is to consider how to implement the communication infrastructure. Possible approaches include point-to-point, multicast, group-based, and messaging approaches to communication. The design of the participants in the communication can be simple client/server or peer-to-peer. The alternatives must be chosen based on the merits of their use with a particular problem. This book has provided you with some background to make this decision.

Depending on how you decide to implement your communication infrastructure, the next step is to construct some of the additional elements of the communication infrastructure to administrate the communication. For example, if you implement a client/server architecture with your application with the client and the server acting as a repository for mobile objects, the server must be constructed to respond to the client's requests.

Next you need to modify your application to interact with the mobile objects in the communication infrastructure. The most obvious case occurs when your application is a client in the architecture and you must add this client behavior. This step may be as simple as contacting the server, if it's a client/server system, then invoking operations to obtain the appropriate mobile objects.

Mobilizing the mpEDIT Application

At this point, mpEDIT doesn't include any distributed computing or networking technology at all. The application doesn't follow any sort of client/server architecture. The implementation of the application as an example of mobile objects requires that the application contact a server to download additional functionality in the form of mobile objects. We approach this example in two steps. The first step is to break up the mpEDIT application into a client/server architecture. The second step is to implement new functionality for the mpEDIT application that can be downloaded as a mobile object.

In using a client/server architecture for this mobile object example, we follow a relatively straightforward approach of making new commands available to the client through remote invocations of operations defined by the remote interfaces made available by the server. RMI provides a sufficient toolset for us to build this distributed system, so RMI is chosen to implement this example mainly for reasons of convenience.

The first step requires that we choose a portion of the application suitable for breaking up into a set of mobile objects. This is a critical decision because those parts of the application that become mobile objects will be implemented flexibly and extensibly enough to allow a runtime upgrade of the application. Portions of the application that are not made available as mobile objects are static and cannot be changed after deployment unless we reinstall the entire application.

In the earlier discussion about mapping applications onto mobile objects, the first approach for determining which objects to add to an application was to determine how to provide new objects to replace or extend the current behavior of the application. The MpAction object is a clear example of this type of object. When a new instance of MpAction objects is added, the capabilities of the application are extended to include the capabilities of the new objects. The combination of reliance on the MpAction object within the mpEDIT application and the straightforward way we can register new instances of MpAction objects into the actionDictionary makes it an easy decision to support a MpAction object as one of the mobile objects for this application.

These instances of MpAction are added to the application when we invoke the addToDict operation on the TextCanvas. When we build our application for mobile objects, the implementation needs to find new instances of objects that derive from MpAction on the network and add these to the actionDictionary. This requires only a few lines of code to add to the existing mpEDIT application because it's just a remote method invocation that returns a mobile object, followed by an invocation of addToDict. Once the mobile object has been added to the dictionary, the mpEDIT application can take care of all the rest, including invoking the command when appropriate user input is received.

In order to implement this command, a new derived class of AbstractMpAction, called TextCanvasMpAction, is defined. The implementation of this command has support for mobile objects and enables the serialization of an instance of the action, enabling it to be passed from server to client on demand. The TextCanvasMpAction contains only minimal behavior to help define the name and configuration for the action. The implementation of TextCanvasMpAction is shown in Listing 8.4.

```
public abstract class TextCanvasMpAction
   extends AbstractMpAction
   implements java.io.Serializable
{
   public TextCanvas canvas = null;
   public StringMan strings = null;

   public TextCanvasMpAction(StringMan strings,
                             String aIdString,
                             TextCanvas canvas)
```

```
   {
      super(strings, aIdString);
      this.canvas = canvas;
      this.strings = strings;


   }

   public TextCanvasMpAction(StringMan strings,
                             String aIdString)
   {
      super(strings, aIdString);
      this.canvas = null;
      this.strings = strings;
   }

   public void setCanvas(TextCanvas canvas)
   {
      this.canvas = canvas;
   }

};
```

Listing 8.4 Source for TextCanvasMpAction.

Two stumbling blocks come up in making the TextCanvasMpAction object
serializable. In order to make the object serializable within the existing mpEDIT
application, a reference to StringMan has to be passed to the constructor for
AbstractMpAction. The implementation of the AbstractMpAction uses the StringMan
object to locate the configuration for the command. StringMan object is used by the
mpEDIT application to manage all the configuration for the application. Passing in
a reference to it as part of the constructor for the AbstractMpAction might make
sense for a monolithic application architecture in which only a single instance of the
StringMan exists in the entire mpEDIT application, but for a mobile object architecture, in which the instance of the command might be created on a different computer and then moved into the application, this architecture doesn't work well. The
solution is to define a dummy StringMan object that can be passed into the constructor for a command from within any application. This architecture enables us
to pass configuration information with each action without making a great deal of

modifications to the source code; a TextCanvas and StringMan object must be passed to the super constructor for the AbstractMpAction object. The AbstractMpAction object uses these to look up the configuration for the specific action. If our dummy StringMan contains the relevant configuration for the instance of the action in question, we kill two birds with one stone. The configuration can be properly mapped to a mobile object architecture because the configuration for a new command may be stored in an instance of the dummy StringMan object that is created on the same computer as the instance of the command.

The implementation of this dummy StringMan simply has to provide the same interface as the normal StringMan object, but it has to be easily instantiated and passed from one computer to another. A new child class of StringMan is defined called SerializableStringMan, which is a mobile object version of StringMan. The source code for this new SerializableStringMan class is shown in Listing 8.5. The simple fact that it is serializable means that it is a mobile object because the instance can be passed from one computer to the next. A remote node can construct a new instance of SerializableStringMan containing the configuration, then pass it into the constructor for TextCanvasMpAction. The constructor for AbstractMpAction can use this information to look up the configuration for the action.

```
public class SerializableStringMan
   extends mpTOOLS.mpEDIT.StringMan
   implements java.io.Serializable
{
   public SerializableStringMan()
   {
   }

   public Vector extensions = new Vector();

   public String getExtensionString(String key)
   {
      String extensionString = null;
      ResourceBundle rb;

      for (Enumeration e = extensions.elements();
           e.hasMoreElements();
```

```
            )
      {
        rb = (ResourceBundle)e.nextElement();

        try
          {
            if (extensionString == null)
              extensionString = rb.getString(key);
            else
              extensionString = extensionString + " " + rb.getString(key);
          }
        catch (MissingResourceException me)
          {
          }
      }

   return extensionString;
  }


  /**
    * Search this resource bundle IN ADDITION TO mpEDIT's own.
    * @param  new_rb ResourceBundle
    */
  public void extendResourceBundle(ResourceBundle rb)
  {
    extensions.addElement(rb);
  }
};
```

Listing 8.5 Source for SerializableStringMan.

The implementation of this SerializableStringMan object contains a Vector of ResourceBundles that contain all the relevant configuration for the action. The normal ResourceBundle is not serializable, so this represents a problem in how we add support for serialization to the StringMan object. The implementation of the SerializableStringMan object must do something to move the ResourceBundles when the instance is passed from one computer to the next. Some options for solving this problem include using an externalization procedure inside the SerializableStringMan to explicitly externalize the ResourceBundle or building a new type of ResourceBundle with support for serialization.

The latter option appears to be easier to implement because the Java class libraries include a set of default implementations of ResourceBundle that can be extended to build new types of ResourceBundles. In fact, the ListResourceBundle provides an implementation that is almost trivial to extend to build your own ResourceBundle object. The ListResourceBundle assumes that each of the resources is listed in a two-dimensional array that can be returned by a getContents() operation. A derived class called ActionResourceBundle (see Listing 8.6) is derived from this ListResourceBundle.

```
abstract public class ActionResourceBundle
  extends ListResourceBundle
  implements java.io.Serializable
{
};
```

Listing 8.6 Source for ActionResourceBundle.

The ActionResourceBundle contains the default configuration for each action. In the distributed environment, we can expect the client application to have the complete configuration for every Action because some new Actions may be added to the client dynamically at runtime. The ActionResourceBundle can move with the mobile object into the mpEDIT application to provide the required configuration while still enabling the client to override this configuration by providing a local copy of the properties file.

At this point, we can look at defining a new class for an action. The implementation of this using mobile objects parallels the way commands are constructed without mobile objects. A new derived class is created for the TextCanvasMpAction class. As an example of defining a command, let's look at how one of the existing commands in mpEDIT can be modified to support mobile objects.

In the monolithic version of mpEDIT, new actions were defined as anonymous inner classes as shown in Listing 8.3. The mobile object version of defining a new action cannot use inner classes, however. The reason for not being able to use inner classes is simply that all the existing mobile object tools lack support for inner classes. This restriction is a result of limitations within the Java's Object Serialization. No workaround exists for this problem, so inner classes simply cannot be used to define actions. A new named class is created for each new action defined by the client. The mobile object version of the help about dialog is given the name HelpAboutDialog, shown in Listing 8.7.

```
/**
  * Anonymous InnerClasses aren't supported by Object Serializaiton, so we need
  * to provide a name for each action.
  */
public class HelpAboutDialog
   extends TextCanvasMpAction
{
   public HelpAboutDialog(StringMan strings, String aIdString)
   {
     super(strings, aIdString);
   }

   public void actionPerformed( ActionEvent e )
   {
       mpTOOLS.mpEDIT.dialogs.AboutDialog ab =
         new mpTOOLS.mpEDIT.dialogs.AboutDialog(
                                              canvas.textFrame,
                                              strings,

strings.getString("DialogAbout"));
       ab.show();
   }
};
```

Listing 8.7 Source for HelpAboutDialog.

With the definition of this new action, the execute method for the action is entirely preserved from the monolithic implementation and moved into the execute method of the named classed HelpAboutDialog. The inner class implementation of the help about dialog action made use of the textFrame member variable of the TextCanvas object. One of the nuances of how inner classes are defined in Java is that they may access the private member variables of the class in which they are defined. The textFrame member variable is such a private variable.

Now that we are defining the help about dialog action in a new class, one problem we must solve is how to port code such as the use of the textFrame member variable of TextCanvas from within the new HelpAboutDialog class. Whereas before it could be accessed even though it was private, this access isn't legal for the new class. The only solution is to make some intrusive modifications to the TextCanvas object in order to declare the private member variables public and then make sure that the instance of HelpAboutDialog can find the instance of TextCanvas. This last part is solved through creation of a TextCanvas member variable within the TextCanvasMpAction object as shown in Listing 8.4; then a reference of the correct instance of TextCanvas is passed to the action. This is done on the client side because the client holds the instances of the TextCanvas class. Each instance represents an editable text document within the client mpEDIT application.

An instance of this object is created on the server and registered in a dictionary on the server of available commands. The client then invokes a remote invocation on the server in order to download the available commands by passing the server some metadata about the desired command.

The metadata for specifying a command is encapsulated in a new class called MetaData. The main reason for this encapsulation of the MetaData is to enable us to delay the decision about how to specify commands to runtime. The MetaData object is yet another type of mobile object for this application, the fourth mobile object we've defined for this text editor, following TextCanvasMpAction, SerializableStringMan, and ActionResourceBundle. The MetaData object is an example of a general class of objects called a predicate. Chapter 20: Predicate takes a closer look at how to use predicates effectively in mobile object applications.

In this case, the MetaData object encapsulates the information about the command desired by the client. The server uses this object to locate the command desired by the client. The trick is to design the MetaData object so the client can be as flexible as possible in how it determines whether a command matches its desired conditions. In the best case, we don't want to mandate how MetaData is used by the client; this decision should be delayed until runtime so that the client can modify how commands are matched without requiring any source code modifications of the server.

For example, suppose the MetaData class were simply composed of a public member variable of type String, which was used to represent the name of the action, and that the server determined whether two names matched in order to find the matching action requested by a client. This method restricts the client to specifying a matching action only by its name. In reality, any number of other criteria could be used to locate the desired action.

The equals() operation is provided to define the mechanism for matching MetaData objects. The client is free to specify a new implementation of MetaData at runtime. An instance of this new implementation of MetaData, shown in Listing 8.8, is passed from client to server, then the equals() operation is evaluated by the server to find the matching MetaData objects. The implementation of this object is left to the client. New implementations can be passed from client to server during the runtime of the server, so we have achieved a maximal level of flexibility in how the client specifies criteria to find the matching command on the server. The default implementation of MetaData does just use a string name in order to match the desired commands, but the predicate architecture enables us to be flexible by enabling the client to specify other types of criteria as well.

```
public class MetaData
   implements java.io.Serializable
{
   public MetaData()
   {
   }

   public MetaData(String name)
   {
      this.name = name;
   }

   public String name;

   public int hashCode()
   {
      return name.hashCode();                          Continues
```

```
    }

    public boolean equals(Object obj)
    {
      if (!(obj instanceof MetaData))
        return false;

      if (!(this.name.equals(((MetaData)obj).name)))
        return false;

      return true;
    }
};
```

Listing 8.8 Source for MetaData.

So far we've defined a mechanism for making instances of Actions available as mobile objects by specifying metadata. The implementation of each mobile object action is specified as a new class within the mobile object application. As a test of the architecture defined so far, let's initially try to adapt all the actions in the mpEDIT application to run as mobile objects. In practice, this enables us to make the mpEDIT application as flexible as possible because most of the implementation is loaded at runtime as mobile objects.

Adapting the commands is a straightforward task following the same process as the HelpAboutDialog action. A new class is created to represent each action derived from TextCanvasMpAction. The implementation of the action shown in the execute method defined in the inner class form of the action is moved into the new class. Any access of member variables of TextCanvas is directed to the new TextCanvas member variable of the TextCanvasMpAction class. The complete list of actions is shown in Listing 8.9. Each of these is rewritten as a mobile object for our new mobile object implementation of mpEDIT.

```
AnchorDrop
AnchorGotoLast
BraceMatchBackward
BraceMatchForward
BufferPaste
```

```
CharacterDeleteBackward

CharacterDeleteForward

CursorBackward

CursorDocumentBegin

CursorDocumentEnd

CursorDown

CursorForward

CursorLineBegin

CursorLineEnd

CursorPageBegin

CursorPageEnd

CursorSelectBackward

CursorSelectDocumentBegin

CursorSelectDocumentEnd

CursorSelectDown

CursorSelectForward

CursorSelectLineBegin

CursorSelectLineEnd

CursorSelectUp

CursorSelectWordBackward

CursorSelectWordForward

CursorUp

CursorWordBackward

CursorWordForward

DocumentNew

DocumentOpenDialog

DocumentPrintDialog

DocumentSave

DocumentSaveAsDialog

FindDialog

FindNextBackward

FindNextForward

FrameClone

FrameClose

GotoDialog

HelpAboutDialog
```

Continues

```
KeytableLoad
KeytableSave
LineBreak
LineClone
LineDelete
LineSwap
MacroRecordToggle
MacroReplay
ModeAutoindentToggle
ModeReadonlyToggle
NetworkSpellCheckEngine
PageDown
PageUp
PropertiesDialog
Redo
ReplaceDialog
SelectionCopy
SelectionCut
SelectionIndent
SelectionUnindent
Undo
```

Listing 8.9 Mobile object actions for mpEDIT.

Clearly, this list contains a lot of actions. Rewriting them as mobile objects for this example, however, took a matter of only a few hours. The task of converting them from the inner class implementation to the mobile object implementation was clear and easy to follow for all the commands using the process outlined earlier.

One final consideration is the usability for end users of the mpEDIT application. We've introduced an enormous number of mobile object actions that end users must load into their client application. End users must have a way of choosing which of the actions they would like to load into the application because some users may not want all the actions. Some of the actions may do fairly obscure operations, such as providing a bar graph within the document, while others might provide a premium service, such as reading text documents from a subscription news service on the Internet. In any event, some users may simply not want to use certain actions.

In order to provide users with a way of choosing their actions, the server defines an interface for looking at the set of available actions and then enabling the client to load the desired actions by invoking an operation to load them. The MetaData object fills the role of representing an action to the end user. The client obtains a Vector of all the available MetaData objects by invoking the getAvailable() operation on the server.

However, we've defined an enormous number of mobile object actions at this point. The client, and the end user in particular, would have to make many decisions to decide which of these actions to load from the server. Some of the actions are related to each other. For example, the cut/copy/paste menu has three closely related actions called SelectionCut, SelectionCopy, and BufferPaste. If the end user wants to support the standard cut/copy/paste menu, each of these actions would have to be individually loaded.

In order to simplify this process for the end user, actions are bundled into an Extension, composed of an array of related actions. The purpose of introducing the Extension is nothing more than to provide a way of grouping related actions into a single package so that the end user may choose to download a group of related actions as a unit rather than having to download each of them individually.

The Extension object also bundles with it all the related ActionResourceBundles for the actions in the Extension. This bundling enables the ResourceBundles used by the actions in the Extension to be added to the client side. As a result, the resources for these actions are available to the client side of the distributed system, and they are available during the construction of the action on the server side of the distributed system. When a resource is looked up by the client at runtime, the default configuration shown in the local strings.properties file is consulted first, then any of the resource bundles passed into the client as ActionResourceBundles are consulted. The end user thereby has ultimate control over the configuration, but the implementation of new actions can provide a default setting for any configuration in an instance of ActionResourceBundle. One specifies the code that performs this resolution of the configuration by modifying the original implementation of the StringMan class in mpEDIT to add some behavior for adding new ResourceBundles to it using an operation called extendResourceBundle() and by modifying the getString method inside of StringMan. The new modified code for StringMan is shown in Listing 8.10.

```
//
  // Get a optional string - it's NOT an error when string not found
  //

  public String getOptionalString(String key)
  {
    String s = getParentString(key);

    if (s != null)
      return s;

    String exts = getExtensionString(key);
    String lbs = null;

    try
      {
        lbs = localBundle.getString(key);
      }
    catch(MissingResourceException me)
      {
      }


    if (lbs == null && exts == null)
      {
        return null;
      }
    else if (lbs == null)
      {
        return exts;
      }
    else if (exts == null)
      {
        return lbs;
      }
    else
```

```
      {
        return lbs + " " + exts;
      }
}


public Vector extensions = new Vector();

public String getExtensionString(String key)
{
   String extensionString = null;
   ResourceBundle rb;

   for (Enumeration e = extensions.elements();
        e.hasMoreElements();
          )
     {
        rb = (ResourceBundle)e.nextElement();

        try
          {
             if (extensionString == null)
                extensionString = rb.getString(key);
             else
                extensionString = extensionString + " " + rb.getString(key);
          }
        catch (MissingResourceException me)
          {
          }
     }

   return extensionString;
}

/**
   * Search this resource bundle IN ADDITION TO mpEDIT's own.        Continues
```

```
   * @param  new_rb ResourceBundle
   */
public void extendResourceBundle(ResourceBundle rb)
{
   extensions.addElement(rb);
}
```

Listing 8.10 Adding new ResourceBundles to StringMan.

Now that we've defined the mobile objects that are required for the application, let's consider how to implement the server side of the distributed system. The server application in this architecture is responsible for creating new instances of the action objects and making these available to any clients that connect to it.

The server in this example supplies actions on demand. It doesn't make an effort to inform clients of new actions as they become available. In the current implementation, the client contacts the server to determine the list of available Extensions at the time that the TextCanvas object is constructed. The client then downloads any Extensions that it would like to include in its runtime and the corresponding set of Actions and ResourceBundles. After startup, no new Extensions are obtained unless a new TextCanvas object is created. In principle, the distributed system could be modified to enable the server to notify the client when new Extensions become available. The client could then download those Extensions that meet its criteria. This modification to the system would make the mpEDIT application resemble a push architecture. It's actually not too hard to extend the existing pull architecture to support such push technology, but this is left as something for the reader to experiment with implementing.

First and foremost, the client needs to be aware of what Extensions are available before downloading a set of Extensions. The getAvailable() operation on the server provides the mechanism for the client to obtain this information. Invoking getAvailable returns a vector of MetaData objects representing possible Extensions that the client can consume. The implementation of the client then uses the getExtension method to obtain an instance of an Extension matching a criterion passed in as a MetaData object. The main interface to the server is called the ExtensionDirectory, shown in Listing 8.11. This interface defines a remote object interface for RMI, the tool chosen for the implementation of this example.

```
public interface ExtensionDirectory
  extends java.rmi.Remote
{
  public Vector getAvailable()
    throws RemoteException;


  public Extension getExtension(MetaData name)
    throws RemoteException;
};
```

Listing 8.11 Source for ExtensionDirectory.

The implementation of the ExtensionDirectory, called ExtensionDirectoryImpl shown in Listing 8.12, provides the central repository for this example. The implementation acts much like a hashtable. Each Extension is listed in the hashtable using the MetaData associated with the Extension. The MetaData is the key in the hashtable while the Extension is the value. The implementation provides a listing of each of the keys to the hashtable on demand for any clients invoking the getAvailable() operation. Whenever an application invokes the getExtension directory, the Extension corresponding to the MetaData is returned to client.

```
public class ExtensionDirectoryImpl
  extends UnicastRemoteObject
  implements ExtensionDirectory
{
  Hashtable extensions = new Hashtable();
  SerializableStringMan strings = new SerializableStringMan();

  public Vector getAvailable()
    throws RemoteException
  {
    Vector vector = new Vector();
    for (Enumeration enumeration = extensions.keys();
         enumeration.hasMoreElements(); )
      vector.addElement(enumeration.nextElement());
    return vector;                                    Continues
```

```
    }

    public Extension getExtension(MetaData metaData)
        throws RemoteException
    {
        return (Extension)extensions.get(metaData);
    }

    public ExtensionDirectoryImpl()
        throws RemoteException
    {
        // Instantiate the actions
        // …
    }
}
```

Listing 8.12 Source for ExtensionDirectoryImpl.

The implementation also instantiates each of the actions. This is done inside the constructor to the ExtensionDirectoryImpl. Only one ExtensionDirectoryImpl object is stored in the Server because no additional instances are required of the application.

The server implementation shown above is responsible for instantiating each of the mobile objects and making it available to the clients. The design of this example stores the commands on the server side, allowing them to be requested by the client. The implementation instantiates each action along with all the support objects for each action. The relevant code to instantiate the HelpAboutDialog action is shown in Listing 8.13.

```
    Extension extensionHelpAboutDialog = new Extension();

    extensionHelpAboutDialog.name = new MetaData("HelpAboutDialog");
    extensionHelpAboutDialog.bundles = new ActionResourceBundle[1];
    extensionHelpAboutDialog.bundles[0] = new DefaultBundle();

    extensionHelpAboutDialog.actions = new TextCanvasMpAction[1];
    strings.extendResourceBundle(new DefaultBundle());
```

```
extensionHelpAboutDialog.actions[0] = new
    HelpAboutDialog(strings,"help-about-dialog");



extensions.put(extensionHelpAboutDialog.name,
                    extensionHelpAboutDialog);
System.err.println("HelpAboutDialog.name,
                    extensionHelpAboutDialog registered.");
```

Listing 8.13 Instantiation of Actions.

In order to make this ExtensionDirectoryImpl object available on the network, RMI requires that a server application be provided that instantiates this object and makes it available through rmiregistry. This application object is fairly standard among RMI applications and tends to contain nearly the same code every time, to perform the instantiation of the server objects and list them with the rmiregistry. The Server object for the server side of this example is shown in Listing 8.14.

```
/**
 * Anonymous InnerClasses aren't supported by Object Serialization,
 * so we need to provide a name for each action.
 *
 */

package mpTOOLS.mpEDIT.server;

import java.rmi.*;

public class Server
{
  public static void main(String args[])
  {
    System.setSecurityManager(new RMISecurityManager());

    try
      {
        ExtensionDirectory o = new ExtensionDirectoryImpl();        Continues
```

```
        System.err.println("ExtensionDirectory initialized.");
        Naming.rebind("ExtensionDirectory",o);
        System.err.println("Registered ExtensionDirectory.");
        System.err.flush();
    }
  catch (Exception e)
    {
        System.err.println("Server: " + e);
        e.printStackTrace();
    }
  }
};
```

Listing 8.14 Source for Server.

The client in this distributed system is the original mpEDIT application. The intent is that the entire behavior of the application should be loaded as a set of mobile objects. In order to make this happen, let's remove those objects from the current, monolithic implementation of the mpEDIT application, then look at how to use mobile objects to replace this behavior. In the current implementation of mpEDIT, each action is loaded through use of an invocation of addToDict with an inner class definition, as shown in Listing 8.15.

```
    addToDict( new
                AbstractMpAction(strings,"help-about-dialog") {
        {
        }

        public void actionPerformed( ActionEvent e ) {
            AboutDialog ab = new
AboutDialog(textFrame,strings,strings.getString("DialogAbout"));
            ab.show();
        }
    }
                );
```

Listing 8.15 Loading Actions in the old mpEDIT.

Removing all of this code from the TextCanvas object ensures that the implementation for the application is not provided by local objects, but by mobile objects loaded from the Server. At this point, all this code is removed from the mpEDIT application, so we can move on to the next step of implementing the mpEDIT using a mobile objects implementation.

Once this is done, we have moved nearly the entire implementation of the mpEDIT application into mobile objects, including all of those objects shown in Listing 8.9. The application at this point does almost nothing. A screen shot of the current application is shown in Figure 8.2. Notice that the File menu is entirely empty. Most of the menu items no longer exist in the mpEDIT application because in the new mobile object version, most of this code has been moved into mobile objects.

The application now depends on mobile objects for nearly its entire implementation. Even a basic operation such as creating new text files using the File|New menu option depends on mobile objects to load the implementation. The About menu is

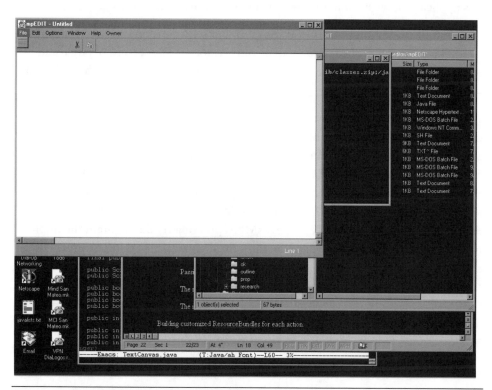

Figure 8.2 User interface with no implementation.

itself loaded in the HelpAboutDialog action object that we have discussed at several points in this chapter.

Loading the implementation inside the mpEDIT application now requires the mpEDIT application to act as a distributed object client for the ExtensionDirectory that we implemented in the Server application. The code that performs this operation first looks at the list of available Extensions by invoking the getAvailable() operation. Then it obtains any desired Extensions using the getExtension() operation.

In the default implementation of the client, all the Extensions in the ExtensionDirectory are downloaded by the client and incorporated into the runtime. In some settings, you might not want to do this. Not every client may be interested in making use of every feature, and adding unneeded features may cause substantial application bloat and could impact performance. The Smorgasbord, discussed in Chapter 23: Smorgasbord, discusses how to solve this type of problem by leaving the choice of features up to the client based on the MetaData. However, in this application, we assume the client is interested in all features.

The implementation of the client looks up the server within the rmiregistry using the lookup() call with the name "ExtensionDirectory." The server already listed a reference to an instance of the ExtensionDirectoryImpl object within the rmiregistry using this name.

Upon obtaining the reference to the ExtensionDirectoryImpl, the client can obtain the list of MetaData objects for each of the available Extensions. The client converts this into an Enumerator and then loops through each of the MetaData objects to call getExtension(). The Extension is returned to the client as a mobile object by this operation. The implementation of the client can then add the Extension to the local runtime. The Extension contains a set of ActionResourceBundles and TextCanvasMpAction objects that contain the implementation of the feature. The client iterates through all the ActionResourceBundles and TextCanvasMpAction objects stored inside the Extension in order to add them to the StringMan and the actionDictionary, respectively. The relevant code added to the TextCanvas object to accomplish this task is shown in Listing 8.16. The TextCanvasMpAction objects are added to the actionDictionary through use of the addToDict operation. The ActionResourceBundles are added to the StringMan with the new operation we implemented on StringMan, extendResourceBundle().

```
// Implement a quick RMI client to download the SpellCheck
// as a mobile object.

try
   {
     ExtensionDirectory dir =
     (ExtensionDirectory)Naming.lookup(
         "//localhost/ExtensionDirectory");
     Vector v = dir.getAvailable();
     mpTOOLS.mpEDIT.server.Extension anExtension = null;

     // current implementation: load all extensions, don't
     // bother asking user what he wants and doesn't want

     for (Enumeration e = v.elements();
         e.hasMoreElements();
           )
            {
              anExtension =
                dir.getExtension((MetaData)e.nextElement());

              System.err.println("Loading: " + anExtension.name.name);

              for (int i = 0; i < anExtension.bundles.length; i++)
                {
                  strings.extendResourceBundle(anExtension.bundles[i]);
                }

              for (int i = 0; i < anExtension.bundles.length; i++)
                {
                  action = anExtension.actions[i];
                  action.setCanvas(this);
                  addToDict(action);
                }
            }
```

Continues

```
    }
  catch (Exception e)
    {
        System.out.println("TextCanvas: " + e);
        e.printStackTrace();
    }
```

Listing 8.16 Making mpEDIT a client.

At this point, all the necessary pieces are in place. We are ready to run the application! When we run the application, what can we expect to see? We took the implementation of all the Actions, removed them from the monolithic form of the mpEDIT application, and placed them inside mobile objects. However, we didn't add or delete any of the Actions. The set of Actions is still exactly the same.

As a result, when we run the mobile object version of the mpEDIT application, we expect it to appear exactly the same as the previous monolithic version, because we haven't changed the features at all. The first step in running the example is to start the rmiregistry in order to make it available to both the server and client:

```
Window 1
Prompt> set CLASSPATH=%CLASSPATH%;src
Prompt> rmiregistry
```

Next, start the Server application by invoking the java interpreter on the server as shown here. The server then prints a great deal of diagnostic information about the Action objects that it is instantiating and making available to the client:

```
Window 2
Prompt> java -classpath src;%CLASSPATH% mpTOOLS.mpEDIT.mpEDIT.server.Server
SpellCheck.name,extensionSpellCheck registered.
SendTo.name,extensionSendTo registered.
Undo.name,extensionUndo registered.
Redo.name,extensionRedo registered.
LineSwap.name,extensionLineSwap registered.
CursorUp.name,extensionCursorUp registered.
CursorDown.name,extensionCursorDown registered.
CursorForward.name,extensionCursorForward registered.
CursorBackward.name,extensionCursorBackward registered.
```

```
CursorWordForward.name,extensionCursorWordForward registered.
CursorWordBackward.name,extensionCursorWordBackward registered.
CursorLineBegin.name,extensionCursorLineBegin registered.
CursorLineEnd.name,extensionCursorLineEnd registered.
CursorPageBegin.name,extensionCursorPageBegin registered.
CursorPageEnd.name,extensionCursorPageEnd registered.
CursorDocumentBegin.name,extensionCursorDocumentBegin registered.
CursorDocumentEnd.name,extensionCursorDocumentEnd registered.
PageUp.name,extensionPageUp registered.
PageDown.name,extensionPageDown registered.
FindNextForward.name,extensionFindNextForward registered.
FindNextBackward.name,extensionFindNextBackward registered.
BraceMatchForward.name,extensionBraceMatchForward registered.
BraceMatchBackward.name,extensionBraceMatchBackward registered.
CharacterDeleteForward.name,extensionCharacterDeleteForward registered.
CharacterDeleteBackward.name,extensionCharacterDeleteBackward registered.
LineBreak.name,extensionLineBreak registered.
LineClone.name,extensionLineClone registered.
LineDelete.name,extensionLineDelete registered.
DocumentSave.name,extensionDocumentSave registered.
FrameClose.name,extensionFrameClose registered.
ModeAutoindentToggle.name,extensionModeAutoindentToggle registered.
DocumentNew.name,extensionDocumentNew registered.
DocumentOpenDialog.name,extensionDocumentOpenDialog registered.
DocumentSaveAsDialog.name,extensionDocumentSaveAsDialog registered.
DocumentPrintDialog.name,extensionDocumentPrintDialog registered.
FindDialog.name,extensionFindDialog registered.
GotoDialog.name,extensionGotoDialog registered.
ReplaceDialog.name,extensionReplaceDialog registered.
SelectionCopy.name,extensionSelectionCopy registered.
SelectionCut.name,extensionSelectionCut registered.
BufferPaste.name,extensionBufferPaste registered.
PropertiesDialog.name,extensionPropertiesDialog registered.
FrameClone.name,extensionFrameClone registered.
HelpAboutDialog.name,extensionHelpAboutDialog registered.
```

Continues

```
KeytableSave.name,extensionKeytableSave registered.
KeytableLoad.name,extensionKeytableLoad registered.
ModeReadonlyToggle.name,extensionModeReadonlyToggle registered.
SelectionIndent.name,extensionSelectionIndent registered.
SelectionUnindent.name,extensionSelectionUnindent registered.
AnchorDrop.name,extensionAnchorDrop registered.
AnchorGotoLast.name,extensionAnchorGotoLast registered.
CursorSelectForward.name,extensionCursorSelectForward registered.
CursorSelectBackward.name,extensionCursorSelectBackward registered.
CursorSelectUp.name,extensionCursorSelectUp registered.
CursorSelectDown.name,extensionCursorSelectDown registered.
CursorSelectWordBackward.name,extensionCursorSelectWordBackward registered.
CursorSelectWordForward.name,extensionCursorSelectWordForward registered.
CursorSelectDocumentBegin.name,extensionCursorSelectDocumentBegin registered.
CursorSelectDocumentEnd.name,extensionCursorSelectDocumentEnd registered.
CursorSelectLineBegin.name,extensionCursorSelectLineBegin registered.
CursorSelectLineEnd.name,extensionCursorSelectLineEnd registered.
MacroRecordToggle.name,extensionMacroRecordToggle registered.
MacroReplay.name,extensionMacroReplay registered.
ExtensionDirectory initialized.
```

The final step is to start the client, so that it can contact the server and download the Extensions from the Server. You can start the client with the Java interpreter. You should then see a list of diagnostic messages from the client as it loads the Extensions and their corresponding Actions and ResourceBundles. The command to run the Java interpreter for the client should look something like the following:

```
Prompt> java -classpath src;%CLASSPATH% mpTOOLS.mpEDIT.mpEDIT
Using default properties.
scaning file: jars\DateBean.jar
loading bean: mpTOOLS/DateBean/DateBean.class
Added EditBean: mpTOOLS.DateBean.DateBean
scaning file: jars\ToLowerBean.jar
loading bean: mpTOOLS/ToLowerBean/ToLowerBean.class
Added EditBean: mpTOOLS.ToLowerBean.ToLowerBean
scaning file: jars\ToUpperBean.jar
```

```
loading bean: mpTOOLS/ToUpperBean/ToUpperBean.class
Added EditBean: mpTOOLS.ToUpperBean.ToUpperBean
Loading: Redo
Loading: GotoDialog
Loading: PageUp
Loading: LineBreak
Loading: SelectionIndent
Loading: DocumentOpenDialog
Loading: AnchorDrop
Loading: CursorWordBackward
Loading: CursorSelectWordBackward
Loading: KeytableLoad
Loading: CursorPageBegin
Loading: CursorSelectBackward
Loading: DocumentSave
Loading: SelectionCopy
Loading: BraceMatchForward
Loading: ModeReadonlyToggle
Loading: MacroRecordToggle
Loading: CharacterDeleteForward
Loading: AnchorGotoLast
Loading: CursorUp
Loading: CursorSelectLineBegin
Loading: CursorForward
Loading: DocumentPrintDialog
Loading: DocumentNew
Loading: SpellCheck
Loading: SelectionUnindent
Loading: CursorDocumentEnd
Loading: CursorLineBegin
Loading: FindNextForward
Loading: CursorLineEnd
Loading: MacroReplay
Loading: Undo
Loading: DocumentSaveAsDialog
```

Continues

```
Loading: CursorDown
Loading: CursorWordForward
Loading: CursorBackward
Loading: LineSwap
Loading: KeytableSave
Loading: CharacterDeleteBackward
Loading: CursorSelectDown
Loading: CursorDocumentBegin
Loading: CursorSelectDocumentEnd
Loading: PageDown
Loading: ReplaceDialog
Loading: CursorSelectUp
Loading: CursorSelectForward
Loading: PropertiesDialog
Loading: SendTo
Loading: BraceMatchBackward
Loading: CursorPageEnd
Loading: SelectionCut
Loading: FrameClone
Loading: FindNextBackward
Loading: BufferPaste
Loading: HelpAboutDialog
Loading: CursorSelectLineEnd
Loading: CursorSelectWordForward
Loading: LineClone
Loading: LineDelete
Loading: ModeAutoindentToggle
Loading: FindDialog
Loading: FrameClose
Loading: CursorSelectDocumentBegin
```

At this point, the new mobile object version of the mpEDIT application should be properly running. Each of the "Loading" messages indicates the name of an Extension that was downloaded from the Server. All the Extensions available on the Server are obtained and added to the mpEDIT application. The application should be fully functional at this point. Try it out! The user interface should look exactly like that shown in Figure 8.1.

So What Is the Big Deal?

The implementation of this example so far has demonstrated only how to take a monolithic application and reimplement it with mobile objects. This clearly was not a trivial task, though it was straightforward and easily accomplished within a few days of work for this text editor example.

You might be asking, "So what's the big deal?" It doesn't *do* anything differently at all. It's the same application, even if the back end is now a mobile object system rather than an inseparable part of a monolithic application.

At this point, let's demonstrate how this application can now migrate to include new features dynamically at runtime by constructing some new Actions and adding them into the Server. The implementation of the Client, unchanged, can then load these new features from the Server in the mobile object system. For this system, we are taking advantage of the flexibility of the mobile object system to add new features dynamically at runtime.

A new feature is implemented for the mobile object system. The SendTo Action is used to define how a document may be forwarded to someone over e-mail. The existing implementation of mpEDIT doesn't include any functionality to perform either of these tasks. The SendTo action requires the mpEDIT application to convert the document into an e-mail message and then send it to an e-mail server. However, the mpEDIT application currently doesn't actually do anything even close to this. Again, no code changes are required on the part of the client; all we have to do is add the new Action to the server.

Adding the SendTo Action

SendTo is present in other applications, such as Web browsers, for forwarding interesting Web pages on to someone who might be interested in the application. The implementation of SendTo Action has to do with things like bundling the document into an e-mail message and delivering it to a mail server. The original mpEDIT application didn't have any type of feature like this, but we can implement it as an Extension, add it to the Server, and enable it to be dynamically downloaded to the Client at runtime without making any modification or installation on the Client itself.

The SendTo action reads the document and forwards it over e-mail to a recipient. The implementation must be able to obtain the recipient's e-mail address, read the document, and send it as an e-mail message. The implementation for the SendTo is shown in Listing 8.17.

```
/**
  * Anonymous InnerClasses aren't supported by Object Serialization,
  * so we need to provide a name for each action.
  */
public class SendTo
  extends TextCanvasMpAction
{

  StringMan strings;

  public SendTo(StringMan strings, String aIdString)
  {
    super(strings, aIdString);

    this.strings = strings;
  }



  public void actionPerformed( ActionEvent event )
  {
    System.err.println("Send To");

    SendToDialog sendToDialog =
      new SendToDialog(
                          canvas.textFrame,
                          canvas.textCanvas,
                          strings,
                          strings.getString("DialogSendTo")
                          );
    sendToDialog.show();


    // Test writer - later replaced with actual email.
```

```
    }
};
```

Listing 8.17 Source for SendTo.

This implementation inherits from the TextCanvasMpAction class. Recall that this is the base class for all mobile object actions. The implementation of this class includes essential code for transporting the state of the Action as a mobile object, in particular the configuration stored in SerializableStringMan. Calling the super constructor for TextCanvasMpAction initializes these operations inside the constructor for the SendTo Action.

In order to obtain the e-mail address to send the document, we can use a simple dialog box to query this information from the application end user. A class called SendToDialog is provided to query the recipient's e-mail address. This class also bundles the application logic to e-mail the document. We are violating some of the basic tenants of separating user interface and application logic, but this is only an example, after all.

Continues

```
 * (INCLUDING, BUT NOT LIMITED TO, PROCUREMENT OF SUBSTITUTE GOODS OR
 * SERVICES; LOSS OF USE, DATA, OR PROFITS; OR BUSINESS INTERRUPTION)
 * HOWEVER CAUSED AND ON ANY THEORY OF LIABILITY, WHETHER IN CONTRACT,
 * STRICT LIABILITY, OR TORT (INCLUDING NEGLIGENCE OR OTHERWISE) ARISING
 * IN ANY WAY OUT OF THE USE OF THIS SOFTWARE, EVEN IF ADVISED OF THE
 * POSSIBILITY OF SUCH DAMAGE.
 *
 * CopyrightVersion 1.0
 */


package mpTOOLS.mpEDIT.actions;


import java.util.*;
import java.awt.*;
import java.awt.event.*;
import mpTOOLS.mpEDIT.*;
import java.net.*;
import java.io.*;




class SendToDialog extends Dialog implements WindowListener, ActionListener,
KeyListener, ItemListener
{
    private Button fbutton,cbutton;
    private TextFrame textFrame;
    private TextField pattern;
    private StringMan strings;
    private String prevPatterns[];
    private int prevPatternIndex;
    private Checkbox forward;
    private Checkbox regex;
    private Checkbox matchCase;
    private TextCanvas textCanvas;

    public static boolean classInitialized = false;
```

```java
public SendToDialog(TextFrame tf, TextCanvas tc, StringMan str, String title)
{
  super(tf,title,true);

  if (!classInitialized)
    {
      classInitialized = true;

      // Actually it would make sense to do this for all the properties.
      Properties p = System.getProperties();
      p.put("mail.host",strings.getString("mail.host"));
      System.setProperties(p);
    }

  setBackground(Color.lightGray);

  textFrame = tf;
  textCanvas = tc;
  strings = str;

  Panel p1 = new Panel();
  p1.setLayout(new FlowLayout());
  p1.add(new Label(strings.getString("PromptSendTo")));
  prevPatterns = textCanvas.getSearchPatterns();
  prevPatternIndex = prevPatterns.length-1;
  pattern = new TextField(prevPatterns[prevPatternIndex],50);
  p1.add(pattern);
  p1.doLayout();
  add("North", p1);

  Panel p2 = new Panel();
  fbutton = new Button(strings.getString("ButtonSendToSend"));
  fbutton.addActionListener(this);
  p2.add(fbutton);
```

Continues

```java
      cbutton = new Button(strings.getString("ButtonClose"));
      cbutton.addActionListener(this);
      p2.add(cbutton);
      add("South",p2);

      Dimension size = new Dimension(500,140);
      setSize(size);
      setLocation(textFrame.getPlace(size));

      pattern.requestFocus();
      pattern.selectAll();
      pattern.addKeyListener(this);

      addWindowListener(this);
   }

   public void executeSendTo()
   {
     try
       {
         URL u = new URL("mailto:" + pattern.getText());
         URLConnection c = u.openConnection();

         c.setDoInput(true);
         c.setAllowUserInteraction(false);
         c.setUseCaches(false);

         c.connect();

         OutputStream out = c.getOutputStream();
         PrintStream po = new PrintStream(out);
         long max;
         String line;

         max = textCanvas.docMan.lines.size();
```

```
        for (int i=0;i<max;i++)
          {
            line = textCanvas.docMan.lines.getString(i);

            po.print(line);
          }

      po.close();
      out.close();


      // Closing a writer appears to close the underlying
      // stream, this makes System.err useless.
      // writer.close();
    }
  catch (Exception e)
    {
      System.err.println("SendTo: " + e);
      e.printStackTrace();
    }
}

public void itemStateChanged(ItemEvent e)
{
  if (e.getSource() == regex)
    {
      if(e.getStateChange() == ItemEvent.SELECTED)
        {
          matchCase.setEnabled(false);
          matchCase.setState(false);
        }
      else
        {
          matchCase.setEnabled(true);
          matchCase.setState(textCanvas.getLastMatchCase());
        }
```

Continues

```
        }
    }

    public void windowDeiconified(WindowEvent event) {}
    public void windowIconified(WindowEvent event) {}
    public void windowActivated(WindowEvent event) {}
    public void windowDeactivated(WindowEvent event) {}
    public void windowOpened(WindowEvent event) {}
    public void windowClosed(WindowEvent event) {}
    public void windowClosing(WindowEvent event)
    {
      dispose();
    }

    public void actionPerformed(ActionEvent evt)
    {
      if (evt.getSource() == cbutton)
        {
          dispose();
          return;
        }

      if (evt.getSource() == fbutton)
        executeSendTo();
    }

    public void keyTyped( KeyEvent e ) {}
    public void keyReleased( KeyEvent e ) {}
    public void keyPressed( KeyEvent e )
    {
      if ( e.getKeyCode() == KeyEvent.VK_ENTER )
        {
          executeSendTo();
        }
      else if ( e.getKeyCode() == KeyEvent.VK_ESCAPE )
        {
```

```
        dispose();
        return;
    }
  else if ( (e.getKeyCode() == KeyEvent.VK_UP) ||
            (e.getKeyCode() == KeyEvent.VK_DOWN) )
    {
       // this is part of editable-combobox functionality
       // if we ever move to swing we can replace it
       if ( e.getKeyCode() == KeyEvent.VK_UP )
         {
           if ( prevPatternIndex > 0 )
             prevPatternIndex--;
         }
       else
         {
           if ( prevPatternIndex < (prevPatterns.length-1) )
             prevPatternIndex++;
         }
       pattern.setText(prevPatterns[prevPatternIndex]);

       e.consume();
       return;
    }
  }


}
```

Listing 8.18 Source for SendToDialog.

The executeSendTo() operation actually performs the sending of the document as
an e-mail message. When this operation is invoked, a URL is opened to the mail
server using the "mailto:" URL protocol specifier. Java application can open URLs
using this protocol to easily send e-mail. This protocol enables your Java application
to write data to a stream that is sent to the recipient specified as part of the URL.

The raw text stored in the document is contained deep inside the TextCanvas
class, stored several layers deep inside its members. The DocMan object is used
inside TextCanvas to manage the document. Inside DocMan is an object called

LineMan, and the instance of LineMan contains a Vector containing the actual lines of text. The call to textCanvas.docMan.lines.getString() returns an individual line of text for the document. In order to write out the document to an e-mail message, mpEDIT iterates over all the lines of text in the document and writes these out to the "mailto:" URL.

The user interface presented by this SendToDialog is fairly simple, just printing a TextField to allow the user to enter in the desired e-mail address. An example of this user interface is shown in Figure 8.3.

The implementation of SendTo is complete, but we don't have any way of associating it with the application. Right now, it's a mobile object that extends from TextCanvasMpAction, but we haven't associated it with any user interface elements yet. Here is where the property sheet configuration support in mpEDIT is going to come as a big help. This architecture is exceptionally flexible, enabling us to make

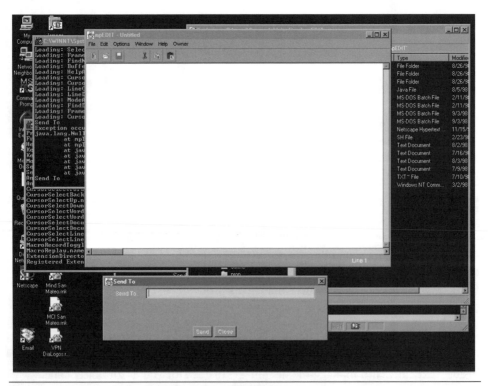

Figure 8.3 User interface for SendToDialog.

changes in the user interface to mpEDIT by making relatively simple changes to the configuration options.

We can't expect the end user to make such configuration changes manually. This would simply require too much administrative overhead on the part of the end user, who may not even be aware of what type of configuration is required for the SendTo Action or that the SendTo option exists at all. The Action therefore provides its own default configuration through the SendToBundle, an ActionResourceBundle implemented for this particular action. The implementation of the SendToBundle, shown in Listing 8.19, contains a two-dimensional array of strings representing the properties for the SendTo Action. The SendToBundle is added to the mpEDIT client's StringMan by invoking the extendResourceBundle( ) operation on StringMan when the Extension containing the SendTo action and the SendToBundle are obtained by the mpEDIT client application.

```java
public class SendToBundle
   extends ActionResourceBundle
{
   static final Object[][] contents =
     {
        {"menu.file", "- send-to"},
        {"action.send-to.name", "Send To"},
        {"action.send-to.short", "Send document to an email recipient"},
        {"action.send-to-dialog.name", "SendTo.."},
        {"action.send-to-dialog.short", "Seeks for given string"},
        {"ButtonSendToSend", "Send"},
        {"DialogSendTo", "Send To"},
        {"PromptSendTo", "Send To:"},
        {"mail.host", "mail"},
     };

   public Object[][] getContents()
   {
     return contents;
   }
```
                                                                    Continues

```
public SendToBundle()
{
}
};
```

Listing 8.19 Source for SendToBundle.

This SendToBundle class is an instance of a Java ResourceBundle. The properties configured inside it assign string values such as the name and a short description along with strings to be displayed in prompts and on buttons. The user interface shown earlier for the SendTo dialog box assumes the default configuration. The "Send To:" prompt inside this dialog box is configurable through the "PromptSendTo" property. The name of the dialog is also configurable through the "DialogSendTo" property. The configuration of the "mail.host" property assigns the name of the POP3 mail host that should be used to receive the mail. The configuration of the "menu.file" property makes the SendTo action available through the File menu of mpEDIT (see Figure 8.4).

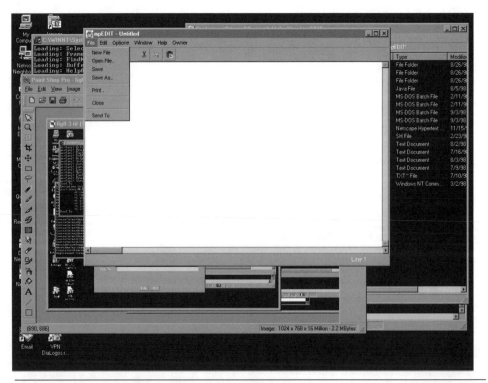

Figure 8.4 Invoking SendTo from mpEDIT.

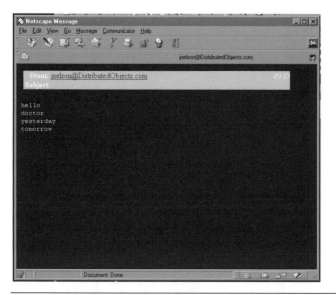

Figure 8.5 Mail viewed with Netscape Communicator.

In order to use the SendTo feature, open or type in a sample document that you might want to send to a friend. Next, go to the File menu and select SendTo. You should see the dialog box from Figure 8.3 pop up to ask the desired destination's e-mail address. Once you've entered in the e-mail address, select the Send button. That's it! You've just e-mailed the document. Give your e-mail server a few moments to process the e-mail, then check your e-mail using your preferred e-mail software. When you check e-mail using Netscape Communicator, the document looks something like Figure 8.5.

In summary, we have just created a totally new feature for the mpEDIT application: the capability to e-mail documents to a recipient. Rather than installing this feature on the client side, the SendTo action was registered on the server side then downloaded as a mobile object to the clients. In the end, this approach makes extending the feature set of software easier and more manageable.

What's Next

♦ Now that we've seen some of the products and issues available for mobile objects, we are ready to look at some of the more subtle issues of building applications, even robust enterprise applications, using mobile objects. In the next chapter, we examine the security issues surrounding mobile objects, the vulnerabilities, and methods of protection.

9

Clustering

Monolithic, centralized software applications are subject to failure and bottlenecking and are limited by the performance of a single host system. The approach used to improve the performance of these monolithic software applications is to try to build bigger, faster, more reliable host systems. Such systems have faster processors and use redundant hardware to ensure that the system won't crash, causing unavailability of a critical system.

However, such systems are more expensive to both build and maintain. Further, the bigger, better system that is supposed to be less likely to fail may also be more complex and actually increase the likelihood of failure.

An alternative approach is to build software applications that rely on having only one of several applications running at any given time. For example, the unavailability of a mission-critical billing system might bring any business to a screeching halt. Suppose that several copies of the billing system could be made available at any given time, with each participant capable of handling billing requests. If any single copy of the billing system were to fail, the system as a whole would be capable of proceeding with orders submitted to a different copy of the billing system. The business becomes less likely to suffer downtime.

Clustering is an approach to building systems that taken advantage of multiple computers on a network to solve problems such as running different copies of the same service as just described. Clustering may be one of the next big steps in distributed software for improving performance and reliability.

In this chapter, we look at how clustering and mobile objects can work together. We see how mobile objects make the implementation of cluster software much easier.

Fundamentals

Several approaches have surfaced for ensuring software reliability through the use of clusters of inexpensive PCs rather than bigger, more expensive systems. System failover, restarting, and replication are a few approaches that work well for distributed systems.

Failover

Failover is an approach to achieving reliability on a cluster by replacing a single server with a set of multiple servers. One of the servers is designated as a primary while the others are designated as backups. When the primary server becomes faulty, one of the backups is promoted to become the new primary and takes over processing requests. The failover of the system to the backups enables the system as a whole to continue processing requests even after the primary server has failed. In a failover system, the states of the primary and its backups are not necessarily synchronized, so the backups have to be capable of processing requests even though they may not know the final state of the server when it failed.

Only a limited number of problems are suitable for a failover architecture. Because the primary and backups are not kept in a synchronized state, many types of stateful services cannot be properly adapted for a failover environment. Those that can be adapted often depend on a data repository of some kind to store the state of the system persistently. However, accessing a data repository, such as a relational database, every time the state of the system changes can require substantial system resources.

Restarting

Restarting a failed server is another important approach to preserving system reliability. When a server fails, a new copy of the server may be restarted to process any incoming requests.

Failed servers often have some internal state that must be preserved through a system failure. In some architectures that support service restarting, this essential characteristic is ignored, or the application is responsible for recovering its own internal state after a restart. This recovery can mean a great deal of additional code required on the part of the application developer. The persistent store is often maintained in a data repository of some kind, just as in failover. In order to maintain the system consistency, this persistent state has to be updated whenever the state of the system changes. As a result, maintaining the persistent state properly for server restart can have the same negative impact on system performance as in failover.

Further, a server that can be restarted after it fails may suffer from some downtime just after the failure and before the system is restarted. In some architectures, the system is restarted automatically within only a few minutes of failure. In order to prevent the downtime of the system during the restarting period, system restarting is often combined with one of the other approaches to reliability, such as failover. The combination of restarting and failover enables requests to be handled by the backup until the primary is ready to continue receiving requests.

Another approach to eliminating system downtime is to queue incoming requests until the server can properly be restarted. In these systems, a request may not be processed immediately, but the request is eventually delivered to the restarted server and processed when the server is available. This approach eliminates system downtime at the expense of delaying some requests for an indefinite period of time until the server is restarted.

Replication

Replication is a more robust form of ensuring reliability. In a replicated system, several copies of the participants are running at all times. If one participant fails, the other participants are capable of taking over where the failed participant left off. The goal of replication is to maintain all the servers in synchrony; that is, to have all the servers in the same state so that they can take over for one another. One part of this method is synchronizing at least a subset of the state of the system. The synchronized data, or synchronized objects in Java, agree across all the servers in the system. In this architecture, if any single participant fails, the system can continue processing requests even if they happen to be dependent on the state of the failed participant.

A useful abstraction to describe the participants that are kept in synchronization with each other is to treat them as a group. With this abstraction, we can conceptually view clients as issuing requests not on a single server but on the entire group of replicated servers. Depending on how the group is actually implemented, this may be literally true; the client may be issuing requests on all the replicated servers at once using a multicast-based protocol.

Three basic operations are required to implement a group. First, participants need some means of joining and leaving the group. Upon joining the group, the new member must synchronize its state with the current state of the rest of the participants. Second, some mechanism must be provided to send messages to the group. When a message is sent to the group, it should be delivered to all the current participants. Messages may be sent by participants in the group to everyone in the group or by clients of the group who are not themselves participants in the group.

Finally, groups need some kind of membership system, listing the current participants in the group. Knowing the list of all the members of a group is a necessary condition for being able to guarantee that the state of all of the participants is kept in strict synchronization. Each participant can verify that it knows the current state of the system. Without a membership layer to indicate the current list of participants, some of the participants in the system may not be aware of the existence of other participants, allowing them to eventually become out of synchronization with each other.

Anonymous groups are those that don't maintain any membership information. *Explicit groups* use a membership layer, often incorporating membership information into the functioning of the group to determine how each participant performs its tasks. For example, an explicit group may explicitly divide a large problem among its participants so that any single participant has to do only a fraction of the work.

When all the servers are discrete application processes running on different machines, the resulting group is a *process group*. In a process group, the state of each of the member processes is kept on synchronization even though the processes may be running on different machines.

A process group applies to the general case of multiple server processes that are working together as a group. This concept can be extended to encompass distributed object computing. Requests in a distributed object environment are method invocations, and servers are individual distributed objects. Instead of processes as members of the group, objects are members of the group in a distributed object environment, so we call this an *object group*. In an object group, all the member distributed objects are kept in synchronization.

Implementing an Object Group

Implementing a replicated system can be expensive. As a software developer, consider taking any of the client/server projects you have worked on in the past and implementing a mechanism to robustly replicate the state of the server among multiple processes. Just consider some of the issues involved. How do you guarantee that the state of each participant agrees with that of all the other participants? What would you do if a new participant joined the group? What happens when one participant fails? How does all of this impact the performance and scalability of the system?

One solution might be to build a system that updates the state of all participants after any request is sent to the system. This solution would guarantee the consistency of the participants, as long as the state of every participant were updated to the new state before any further requests were processed. Unfortunately, updating the entire state of all participants is prohibitively expensive, and guaranteeing that every participant agrees on the current state after each request requires a great deal of additional communication overhead.

A better solution is to have every participant process every request synchronously. Consider the situation in which every participant already has the same state and a request is received. If every participant processes the request in exactly the same way, the states of all participants should agree once the participants are done processing the message. The entire state of each participant doesn't need to be communicated after every request. In fact, just the request itself has to be sent to each participant. The participants are kept synchronized without exchanging messages with each other directly or explicitly synchronizing their state, so this architecture is called virtual synchrony.

The key assumption of virtual synchrony is that the state of each participant in the group can be kept synchronized as long as each server processes the same requests. At the minimum, this synchronization requires that each participant receive every message, but additional constraints may be required on the order in which requests are processed. For example, service-providing applications that don't depend on any external state may be kept in synchronization if they process each request in the same order. However, if two servers receive two different requests in a different order, they may become accidentally out of synchronization.

An example of becoming out of synchronization is shown by simple numerical operations on two integers. Suppose that the two integers can be treated as service providers whose state is just the value of the integer and whose services are numerical operations such as add, subtract, multiply, and divide. Additionally, suppose the initial state of both servers is synchronized to the value 137. When a new request arrives, the two servers process this request by manipulating the value of their internal state. If the initial request were "Subtract 12," both servers would subtract 12 from their initial state to arrive at 125. Because both servers process the same request, they remain synchronized and arrive at the value 125 together.

In this case, we must make some additional assumptions about the order of the requests. For example, suppose that two requests, "Subtract 12" and "Multiply 2," are sent to both servers simultaneously. If the first server processes the "Subtract 12" request first, and the second server processes the "Multiply 2" request first, the servers arrive at an inconsistent state. The first server arrives at the state of 250 after processing the requests, and the second server arrives at the state of 262 after processing both requests. The order in which the requests are processed is important.

The group must guarantee that requests are delivered to all participants in some consistent order to ensure that they don't arrive at inconsistent states. As a result, a great deal of research in the field of virtual synchrony focuses on guaranteeing message ordering when messages are delivered to a set of participants.

The least strict form of message ordering is, of course, unordered delivery of messages. In this process, the messages are sent to each server with guaranteed delivery, but the messages may be delivered in any order. Most stateful systems become inconsistent when requests are delivered unordered, but unordered delivery may be suitable for servers that are stateless.

A slightly stronger guarantee is that messages are delivered in the correct order they were sent relative to other messages sent from the same originator. To illustrate, suppose two senders, Talker1 and Talker2, both send out a stream of messages to two participants, labeled Participant1 and Participant2. If Talker1 sends the messages "Add 1" followed by "Divide 5," Participant1 and Participant2 are guaranteed to receive "Add 1" before "Divide 5." However, suppose Talker2 sends out a message containing "Subtract 2" immediately after Talker1 sends its messages. The ordering of the messages delivered to the Participants is guaranteed only to be ordered relative to other messages sent by the same sender, so Participant1 may receive the requests in the order "Add 1," "Subtract 2," and "Divide 5." Meanwhile, Participant2 might receive the messages as "Subtract 2," "Add 1," and "Divide 5." Notice that neither of these cases intersects with the global order in which the messages were sent; the delivery of messages is simply guaranteed relative to the sender.

This type of message ordering is called *FIFO* (first in, first out) or *fbcast*. In this case, this message delivery ordering is unsuitable because the state of the participants becomes inconsistent after the participants process these messages. FIFO delivery may be applicable to servers that maintain a session state when processing individual requests. Session state is stored as part of the request so that it may be passed into the server at the time the request is made. This technique is common to the Web, where cookies are used to represent the session state of individual requests. However, session state is cumbersome. Adapting a stateful server to use session state is often difficult. In addition, session state may be bulky, requiring a great deal of network overhead to transmit with each request.

At this point, it may seem that total ordering is the only way to guarantee the consistency of the system. *Totally ordered* message delivery means that the messages are delivered in the order in which they were sent, even by different senders. In particular, every participant delivers every message in exactly the same order, and that order is the same as the order in which the messages were sent relative to the global time of the system. When totally ordered message delivery is required, the state of the individual servers can be guaranteed to be consistent. However, building a system in which message delivery is guaranteed to be totally ordered is exceedingly difficult. In a distributed system, even getting the individual participants to agree on some notion of global time can be a very difficult problem to solve. The delivery of messages is expensive, also, because all participants must agree on the correct order in which to deliver each message. As a result, totally ordered message delivery has a considerable overhead that is prohibitive for most applications.

In order to weaken the assumptions enough to make performance reasonable, we can remove the constraint that messages must be delivered in the correct order relative to some global clock. Instead, we can simply mandate that messages are delivered in the same order by all participants but that this order may not necessarily correspond to the time or order in which they were sent. This form of message ordering is called *atomic* or *abcast*. It guarantees only that messages are delivered in the same order by all participants.

However, atomic delivery may not make sense if messages are delivered out of order relative to the sender. For example, in the situation discussed earlier with two participants and two senders, Participant1 and Participant2 might receive the messages as "Subtract 2," "Divide 5," and "Add 1." The resulting state of both participants would agree because they both processed the same messages in the same order, but the resulting state might be inconsistent with the expectations of the talkers.

We might require FIFO ordering in addition to atomic delivery of the messages. In this *FIFO atomic* case, the order in which messages are sent is guaranteed to be the same for all participants and guaranteed to be consistent with the order in which messages were sent by individual senders. Messages sent from different originators might disagree with the order according to global time, but this strong ordering guarantee is often enough for many systems. Unfortunately, FIFO atomic ordering requires a great deal of overhead to implement, as does atomic ordering.

In struggling with these problems, we can make a few observations about how messages are treated in a synchronized system. The first is that messages usually are not sent at about the same time by different originators except in particular cases. Most distributed systems receive requests from end users at a very slow rate. Because humans can be slow and bulky, they issue requests at a rate of about one every few seconds. A group is capable of processing discrete requests before receiving the next request. One exception to this rule that often occurs is when one message triggers a cascade of other messages. For example, in order for a billing system to satisfy a request to purchase a product, the billing system might need to issue requests to determine if the inventory is available to ship the product, verify the funds are available in the customers account, and consult shipping to determine how soon the product can be delivered. In this situation, a single message causes a cascade of other messages to the participants in the group. All of these messages are delivered at roughly the same time. The state of the system is threatened if two participants receive the messages in the cascade in the incorrect order.

Instead of trying to guarantee total or atomic ordering, we can conclude from this observation that for many systems, guaranteeing that messages are delivered in the order in which they were triggered relative to the messages that caused them may be sufficient. That is to say, the messages in a particular cascade of messages are delivered in the correct order relative to the other messages in the cascade. This is called *causal ordering*, because discrete messages are delivered in the order in which they caused other messages.

This solution turns out to be remarkable performant. Rather than requiring additional state synchronization protocols, the system is limited only by the speed at which requests can be delivered to all participants.

The Role of Mobility

Mobile objects can play a number of roles in implementing clusters. In the case of a cluster implementing a replicated system, the participants of a replicated system can be mobile objects. The implementation of a participant in a group is analogous to the implementation of a server in a client/server architecture. In the distributed objects approach to client/server software development, the individual servers are objects, called distributed objects. The messages sent to these servers are invocations of operations on these distributed objects. In a group environment, the participants may also be objects. The messages sent to the group are invocations of the operations on these objects. In this case, the objects implementing the participants of the group can be mobile. We'll see later in this section how this format can impact group-based systems.

Mobile objects can also be used in the messages to a group. When a mobile object is sent to a group, each of the participants in the group may instantiate the object to maintain its own copy of the object. When a mobile object is sent to all the members of a set of listeners, as is the case in either a group or multicast setting, the behavior of the mobile object may be incorporated into each of the receiving host applications. An example is shown in Chapter 5: Building Mobile Objects with Voyager. In this example, a Vote object implementing a graphical user interface is multicast to several listeners. The Vote object can be presented simultaneously to all of these listeners and shown on the screen with its user interface.

Mobile objects can also be used in the implementation of the group-based system. One example is in using mobile objects to implement the group protocols. Whenever a mobile object implements a network protocol, a high degree of flexibility can be achieved in the distributed system because new mobile objects may move into existing applications to provide them with the capabilities of the new protocol. For example, many mobile object applications interact with each other by exchanging mobile objects that implement Java interfaces, as in the case of the Vote interface from Chapter 5: Building Mobile Objects with Voyager. The class implementing the Java interface is free to do anything within the capabilities of the Java programming language as long as the class fully implements the complete interface (otherwise, it must be declared abstract and a further implementation must be provided). The implementation can include proxies for groups or other distributed computing models. Doing so facilitates the construction of group-based software using existing applications without modification with mobile objects.

Another role that mobile objects can play in the implementation of replicated systems is as part of the implementation of the participants in the system. Mobile objects can move from application to application with their state and implementation. This ability greatly assists in the implementation of groups by allowing participants to easily transfer state and even implementation.

Implementing a Replicated System

Implementing a virtual synchronous group, in other words a replicated system that is maintained in synchrony by having each participant process the same requests, is not an easy task, just as implementing an object request broker is not something you want to do with your weekend off. In general, you would like to purchase a product or tool that implements all of this for you. To date, none of the mobile object tool vendors have any substantial products that provide synchronization across multiple servers. Some vendors, Object Space in particular, have products that support group message delivery without any delivery or ordering guarantees, but this is not enough to build a virtually synchronous system. Other tools, such as iBus from SoftWired, support more robust group messaging, but they lack a mobile object computing model.

Rather than worrying too much over the lack of robust products in the market that provide guaranteed, causal message delivery, let's consider how we can build a replicated system on top of the unreliable, unordered messaging systems with the benefit of mobile objects. We can expect that the market eventually will catch up with the release of more robust products.

Let's consider the basic tasks of a synchronized system and ways we could implement them using mobile objects and existing products.

Building Groups with Mobile Objects

Assuming that the replicated system is implemented on top of a group, a portion of the task is to implement a group using mobile objects. Recall that the essential services of any group were to enable a participant to join and leave the group, provide a way for clients or participants to send messages to the group, and facilitate the access of the membership of the group.

Joining a group is more difficult than it initially sounds. Once a participant joins a group, the participant must synchronize its current state with that of other participants in the group. A couple of alternatives exist for synchronizing the current state of a new participant that is joining the system. First, the new participant can obtain a copy of the current state from one of the existing participants in the group. In order to do this, the new participant announces that it is joining the group and solicits an existing group member to transfer its state to the new participant. State transfer is not a trivial matter for many systems. In traditional software applications, the state of the system is tied up in the application objects, many of which aren't serializable. This state becomes difficult to separate from the state of the rest of the system.

N O T E : Some replicated service products may ignore the essential requirement to synchronize the initial state of a new participant. However, these products have limitations to accommodate this lack of functionality. Some of these products are limited to stateless or session state approaches to managing the state of a server. Others simply do not allow a new participant to dynamically join a group unless the entire system is reset.

However, when the participants are mobile objects, the state transfer is a much easier problem to solve. In this situation, the state of the system is tied up in mobile objects, which by definition can be copied from system to system. When a new participant joins the group, the new participant can announce itself and solicit state transfer from one of the existing participants. In order to perform the state transfer, the existing participant simply provides the new participant with copies of the appropriate mobile objects implementing the state of the system, as shown in Figure 9.1.

Another approach to state transfer is to replay the history of previous invocations. Assuming that all participants start with some common initial state and then diverge from this state as they are processing requests, one can re-create the current state of any given participant by starting with the initial state and replaying the entire history of requests. A new participant can synchronize its state with an existing participant by processing the entire request history. Obviously, processing the entire request history may have a significant impact on system performance. For a system in which processing individual requests requires a great deal of resources, replaying the entire request history at one time could be very computationally intensive for the new participant.

In a mobile object environment, messages sent to the group correspond to object invocations. Replaying messages means that a history of all the invocations on the group should be maintained because the group was created. Mobile object invocations, which are serializable, can be stored in a persistent database. When a new participant joins the group, the set of requests can be read and replayed for the new participant.

The decision regarding which approach of state transfer to use is largely one of performance. Either approach can perform the task, but in some situations, one might be faster than the other. When participants have a very large state, say 10 megabytes or

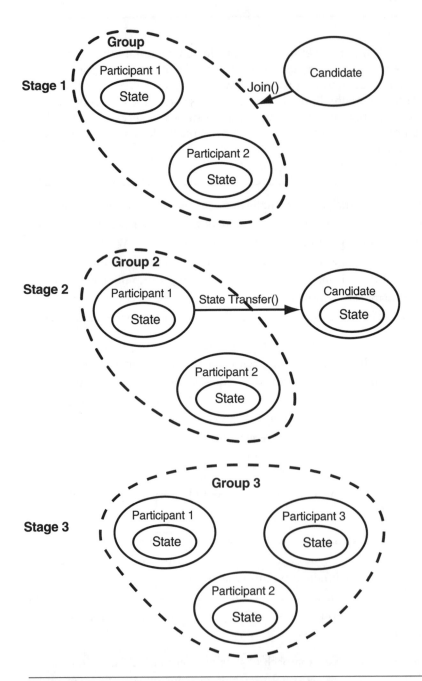

Figure 9.1 Transferring state as mobile objects.

more of data, transferring the state of the objects may be inefficient for bandwidth reasons. Replaying the history of requests in this case may require much less bandwidth. In other situations, long-lived groups may continue processing requests for days, even months. The request history may grow to become prohibitively large over this extended period of time, making state copying more efficient.

Mobile objects can also apply to the problem of starting up new participants. Starting a new participant using a traditional virtual synchrony environment, such as HORUS, requires some effort. The software for the participant has to be installed and configured on the new host. The participant application has to be started through the use of some activation mechanism. Finally, a state transfer protocol must be used to synchronize the new participant with the rest of the group in the virtual synchronous system.

Mobile objects, which can be cloned from host to host with ease, can easily start up on a new host. Suppose that we are using Voyager and a voyager process is already running on each host in your environment. A mobile object is cloned onto a new host whenever a remote invocation is made, and the mobile object is passed as an argument to the invocation. Once the invocation is made, the mobile object's state and implementation are uploaded to the remote host, running within the voyager process. The implementation of the mobile object moves as part of the invocation, so no custom software installation is required for the implementation of the participant. The state of the mobile object moves as part of the invocation, so no explicit state transfer protocol is required. State transfer is handled as part of the invocation. Finally, the application on the remote participant doesn't need to be activated because the invocation is performed on a distributed object running within the voyager process. The bottom line is that most of the steps of starting a new participant in the group for a virtual synchronous system are eliminated when the participants are mobile objects, as shown in Figure 9.2. For this Voyager example, Voyager has to be installed on each of the systems on the network, but once that is done, participants for arbitrary groups can be started on any of the systems.

As a direct result of the ease with which new participants can be cloned with mobile objects, implementing failover and other types of primary/backup architectures is made easier. Failover systems require that backups or secondary servers are running on other hosts. As in the case for creating new participants in the virtually synchronous system, starting new clones of the server on the remote hosts enables

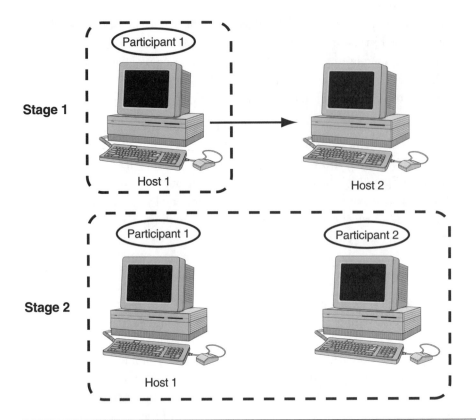

Stage 1

Participant 1

Host 1

Host 2

Stage 2

Participant 1

Participant 2

Host 1

Figure 9.2 Using mobile objects in a synchronous system.

new backups to be started on demand. This cloning of essential services to new hosts could even happen just in time while the primary host is in the process of failure. The process of shutting down a failed host could make the relevant remote invocations clone the host onto additional remote systems.

Restarting services is a final area that benefits from mobile objects. When a service is restarted, one of the essential tasks is restoring the state of the failed system. If the state of a stateful server is not preserved, the restarted service may be running out of context with any of the existing clients in the system. In order to ensure that the state can be preserved when the service is restarted, the state of the server should be saved in some stable medium, such as a database or other persistent store. The restarted server can then read in this persistent state in order to restore the state of the server after restarting.

In the traditional software environment, storing the state of the system in a persistent database is a considerable task of serializing objects to a database. Tools such as object databases can be used to fill this role, but the application must incorporate the functionality of the mobile object and the application developer must build the relevant code into the application to access the object database. With an appropriate frequency, the state of the system must be written into the database so that the restarted server may be able to read in the state of the system from the database. Some applications don't require that the exact final state of the system be restored. Some work may be lost if the state isn't restored, but the system may still be able to continue even without the latest state. Not having to get back to the exact final state of the system enables the server to checkpoint only occasionally, for example, with some frequency such as every 30 minutes. That's 30 minutes of lost work if the server fails and has to be redone, but the system minimizes the impact of storing its state in a database by checkpointing only infrequently. In other systems, the server must be restored back to the final state without any lost work. The implementation of such servers must save any state changes immediately after they are made to prevent any changes from being lost. As a result, the state of the primary server must be checkpointed whenever the system finishes processing a request. Systems that process many requests must lean heavily on the persistent store in these cases to save the state of the primary server after every request.

If the primary server is a mobile object, or if mobile objects are used to implement the primary server, the application developer may not have to do nearly as much work to save the state of the primary server. Mobile objects are always serializable. Tools, such as Voyager, provide database adapters that make it much easier to save mobile objects in a stable state. The implementation of saving the state of the primary server becomes much easier as a result of depending on mobile objects to do most of the work. Unfortunately, system performance is not impacted greatly. If the state of the primary server must be preserved after every request, this state must still be checkpointed to the database after every single request. A system that has a high frequency of invocations must be checkpointed so frequently in this case that the impact of the database becomes very significant.

What's Next

- Later in this book, we revisit the topic of clustering in the form of design patterns for mobile objects in Chapter 17: Object Group and Chapter 18: Replication, but preventing system failure is only one consideration of a robust system.

Security is yet another. Not only should a robust system be resilient from failure, it should also be difficult, if not impossible, for malicious attackers to compromise. In the next chapter we look at the challenge of implementing mobile objects securely.

Securing
Mobile Objects

A s we've examined throughout this book, mobile objects take us to a new level of flexibility in the software development process. At the same time, the power and flexibility that mobile objects afford you in application development lead to new ways to compromise a system, threatening system security.

Risks

The risks are real. Members of any system can attack each other. That's the basis of an ecology, the process that we call life. In a mobile object system, the two main components are mobile objects and the applications that host them. How can they threaten each other?

Who Is at Risk

Mobile objects can threaten the applications that receive them. A mobile object may attack an application in several ways. First, the mobile object may overconsume the resources of the application by using more threads, CPU, memory, disk space, or network bandwidth than it should be allotted. When the mobile object overconsumes resources, the host application as well as other applications on the same host may be impacted. They may not be able to obtain the resources essential to normal functioning. In the worst case, other applications may actually crash as a result of resource unavailability.

Second, the mobile object may steal data from the host application. The host may contain sensitive data that should be confidential, but once the mobile object is a part of the application, it may be able to circumvent and distribute the confidential information. The mobile object may also compromise the reputation of a host application by acting on behalf of the host application and performing actions that were not authorized by the host application. For example, a mobile object may implement an e-mail client that sends spam e-mail. The e-mail appears to originate from the host application. If the host application is running within an account owned by a particular end user, the e-mail has a FROM line of the account owner. That means the mobile object can forge e-mail that appears to be from the owner of the account. In such a situation, the owner of the account may have a difficult time proving he or she did not originate the e-mail message because it was sent by an application under the control of the owner of the account. The fact that a particular mobile object within that application actually originated the message would be difficult to explain to an upset system administrator investigating the forged e-mail.

Hosts can also compromise mobile objects. A host application may steal confidential data from the mobile object. For example, a mobile object that maintains a customer account in an electronic commerce setting might contain the current credit card information for a customer. In a mobile object setting, this information must be kept confidential in some way before the mobile object can be distributed to an application host that might attempt to steal this information. A host application may also abuse the resources of the mobile object. An example of this is unauthorized use of a mobile object that may have a licensing term. If only certain licensed users are allowed to access the mobile object, unauthorized access is a theft of a service from the mobile object. The host application can also compromise the reputation of a mobile object by modifying the mobile object to force it to perform actions that it would not otherwise perform. In an electronic commerce setting, this may include making unauthorized purchases or otherwise conducting business that the mobile object would not perform.

Mobile objects can also attack other mobile objects. Once two mobile objects are present in the same process, they may be able to identify and attack each other. Under these conditions, a mobile object may circumvent another mobile object to steal confidential data, abuse its resources, or damage its reputation, just as in the case of a host abusing a mobile object.

Rounding out the set of possible parties at risk, hosts may attack other hosts. One host attacks another by first circumventing the security of a mobile object, then inserting instructions into the mobile object to attack the host before submitting the object to the target host. Once in the target host, the mobile object may threaten the destination host.

What's at Stake

Attacks involving any combination of mobile objects and application hosts may perform any number of "nasty" activities. The resources of the host application and mobile object may be damaged or overused. This CPU may be overconsumed by running numerous unauthorized tasks. The disk space may be abused if large amounts of unauthorized data are stored on the hard disk. Existing files may also be damaged, modified, or read on the hard disk. Network bandwidth may be consumed if unauthorized network services are set up or if large amounts of junk data are purposely transmitted to clog the network.

Further, our computer systems are not just meaningless bundles of resources. Today computers are invariably used to conduct mission-critical activities for a business. Inventory systems can be circumvented to misappropriate inventory. Shipping systems can be attacked to redirect packages. Client and contact management systems can be attacked to allow unauthorized individuals to learn information about clients. Electronic commerce and banking systems can be attacked to conduct business transactions that were not authorized, potentially including theft of funds.

Are we without hope? No, we have the technology to protect ourselves from these attacks. Security is always difficult to implement because it requires so much work to foresee all possible attacks, but even a system as powerful and flexible as a mobile object system can be secure with adequate preparation.

Technology

The technology used to secure a mobile object system enables us to protect against some (or all, we hope) of these risks to our security. Let's quickly look at some of the tools available for building a secure mobile object system.

Cryptography

A second tried-and-true tool of software security is the field of cryptography. Cryptography is the science of protecting data through use of irreversible algorithms called ciphers. Cryptography can be used in many roles in a mobile object system, and it can be used to authenticate the originator of a particular set of data.

Ciphers

One of the staples of cryptography is the cipher. A cipher is an algorithm that can protect some data by encrypting it into an apparently random set of bits. Ciphers have been in use for thousands of years. Some of the most famous uses of ciphers come from warfare, in which ciphers were used to secure battlefield communication. Commanders sending messages to each other across a field of battle must be able to guarantee that messages are not read by the enemy.

Historically, ciphers were often algorithms that the enemy did not know how to use to read the message. For example, the Caesar cipher involved wrapping a thin strip of paper around a round pole in an overlapping helix. A message was then written down the wrapped pole. The strip of paper was then unwrapped and sent to the intended destinations. If the paper should fall into the wrong hands, the strip of paper, with seemingly random letter fragment markings along its length, would appear meaningless. The enemy could not read the message without knowing the secret of wrapping the paper around a round pole.

Today, the security of ciphers is no longer dependent on the secrecy of the algorithm. All parties, including the attacker, may be aware of the cipher used to encrypt a message. Instead, the security of the data protected by the cipher is dependent on two things. First, the cipher must be an algorithm that is difficult to reverse engineer. That is, an observer should not be able to take the output of the cipher and compute the input. Second, the security of the algorithm should be based on whether or not a person knows some secret information, called a private key. The participants who would like to communicate privately agree on a secret key, a very large number often with several hundred binary digits, that no other parties know. The security of the system is based on the secrecy of the key, not on the secrecy of the algorithm. Given the current laws of probability, the key is nearly impossible to guess. For a 128-bit key, if an attacker tried to make one guess per second, it would take longer than the age of the universe to guess the key.

Such ciphers can encrypt a digital message sent from one computer to another across the Internet by processing it to create a seemingly random sequence of bits. The original message is called the cleartext. The encrypted form of the message is called the ciphertext. If the ciphertext falls into the wrong hands in the process of being sent to the intended recipient, the irreversibility of the cipher prevents the observer from deriving the cleartext from the ciphertext. In human terms, the observer can't figure out what the message is from only the encrypted message.

Public Key

Another powerful advance in cryptography is public key cryptography. Public key cryptography is based on the distribution of a public key to everyone, including potential attackers, instead of trying to keep all keys secret to the participants of a secure system. Public key cryptography is based on a pair of keys, called the public key and private key. The public key is used to encrypt while the private key is used to decrypt message. If a particular entity would like to participate in a secure system, the entity generates a public/private key pair, then announces the public key to the world. Someone wishing to send a message privately to this entity can then encrypt the message with the public key and send the message. If the message falls into the wrong hands, it cannot be read without the private key, which is a secret known only by the entity. Once the entity receives the message, the private key can be used to decrypt it.

In order to understand how public key cryptography works, consider the following analogy. To encourage people to communicate with me securely, suppose I announce that I will gladly give away a safe with a preset combination to anyone who would like one. Someone who wants to send me a private message can just put it in the safe, lock the safe, and ship the safe back to me. I already know the combination to the safe, so I don't have to worry about how to get this information from the recipient out of the safe. Once the safe is closed, no one can break into it without knowing the combination, a secret known only to me. Even the sender of the message cannot open the safe once it is closed because I don't share the combination with anyone, including the people who would like to send me messages. The safe is like the public key. Anyone can use it to protect a message, but once it is closed, no one can open it without some secret information.

Public key cryptography is also useful for authenticating the source of a particular message through a special property of the public and private keys. Messages encrypted by the public key can be decrypted only by the private key, but messages may be encrypted by the private key and decrypted only by the public key! This property provides a useful capability: Given a known public key, holders of the corresponding private key can prove they know the private key without revealing it to other people by encrypting a known message with the private key. The encrypted message can be decrypted by the known public key to prove that the holder had access to the private key to encrypt the message correctly. This technique is called authentication. It can be used to prove the identity of an entity on a computer network, assuming that only one entity knows the private key.

Other Tools

Cryptography can do more than just encrypt messages to hide their content. The study of cryptography has led to many useful tools in implementing a secure computing platform such as authentication and access control.

Authentication is an area of cryptography in which an observer can verify the identity of a particular party by exchanging encrypted messages. The contents of the encrypted messages are such that they prove the identity of the sender. The party that created the message knows some secrets shared only by the party whose identity is known. This is enough to prove that the secrets are known only to the authenticated party, proving the identity of the authenticated party in a secure communication.

Access control is the restricting of the access of certain resources to only a limited number of entities. For example, a list of allowed accessors can be kept, and other parties not on the list can be prevented from manipulating the protected resource. It can be treated as an extension to authentication because authentication makes up the bulk of access control. A mobile object system may have only a limited set of parties with which it may interact. Upon authenticating the identity of a particular mobile object, the originating host may determine that a particular mobile object is not permitted to communicate with the host application. Parties that do not have permission are simply prevented from accessing the protected resource. Failed attempts may also be logged so that attempts to breach system security can be tracked.

Confidentiality is a term applied to the guarantee of privacy from parties stealing data not intended for prying eyes. The mobile object system may use cryptography to provide confidentiality of communication between two objects in a mobile object system. One individual may send encrypted information to another. The data is then protected against copying by third parties.

Nonrepudiation is another technique available through cryptography that enables a third party to validate the originator of a particular request. When a mobile object requests resources from a host application, the mobile object may be required to invoke an operation in a nonreputable way. In this event, the mobile object cannot deny that it issued a request at a later time, and the server making the resources available cannot forge a request from a mobile object that never issued such a request. This may be appropriate when the invocation of a request has a certain cost associated with it. The server application does not want the client to be able to later deny issuing the request.

However, we may find that cryptography is not as useful for providing security to individual components of an application against other components of the application. For example, how does a host application send a message to a mobile object without risking that another mobile object may intercept this message? An even harder problem may be how two mobile objects in a host application can send a message to each other without risking that the host application may learn the content of the message. We will examine some techniques for providing this type of security in a mobile object application.

Trust Models

Another technique that can be used to protect a mobile object system is the use of trust models. If a mobile object can trust the host application, and the host application trusts the mobile object, security may not be required. In larger systems, some combination of trust might be able to provide enough properties to eliminate the need for security. At the lowest level, trust isn't implemented; it's a property of a particular system. Two parties either trust each other or they don't. When two parties trust each other, security may not be necessary.

In order to consider how trust works in a real-world setting, consider that you would probably trust your friends enough to leave them in your house while you were away. You expect that your friends will act responsibly and not break, steal, reprogram, or stain anything while you are away. Your friends probably trust their friends enough to leave them in their own houses while they are away also. However, you might not necessarily know the friends of your friends enough to leave them in your home when you are away. In this case, trust is not transitive from your friends to their friends. However, a distributed system may be composed of multiple participants that must trust every other participant if security is to be foregone in the system. For example, in a mobile object system that has only a single host application and two mobile objects, the first mobile object must trust the host application. This mutual trust is called a trust relationship between the object and the host. The host application must trust the first mobile object. The second mobile object must trust the host application. The host application must trust the second mobile object. Furthermore, the first mobile object must trust the second mobile object. Often overlooked, the first mobile object must also trust the combination of the second mobile object and the host application. The second mobile object must trust the combination of the first mobile object and the host application. The host application must trust the combination of the first mobile object and second mobile object. That's an awful lot of different ways that the entities in the system must trust each other!

The more entities that are involved, the more possible combinations that must be trusted. It becomes quickly apparent from examining examples such as the one above that trust can require quite a few trust relationships before any guarantees can be established in even moderately sized systems.

Java

Java is a safe language. A Java interpreter has some controls available to restrict the capabilities of the bytecode. The SecurityManager makes up the controls that enable a software developer to turn certain features on and off in the Java run-time environment. In what is called the sandbox security model. An application is restricted to only a certain set of options that are "in its sandbox". Other operations, such as file or network access, may be restricted to prevent the bytecode from abusing the interpreter. This means that the SecurityManager can be used to control the capabilities of a particular mobile object. A mobile object system may be restricted to certain types of actions by the SecurityManager that is currently set in the system.

The SecurityManager is the object used to configure the Java sandbox security model. The capabilities of the classes in a particular Java application are defined by the settings in the SecurityManager. Whenever a sensitive action is about to be conducted, the SecurityManager is consulted to see if the action is permitted. The SecurityManager indicates that an action is not permitted by throwing an exception, which often turns out to be a fatal exception to the Java application.

Let's look at each feature that can be configured in the SecurityManager and the issues surrounding its use.

checkAccept(String, int)

checkAccept(String, int) validates whether the calling thread should be allowed to accept socket connections from a particular host. The host is specified by the host name passed in as a string on a port number passed in as an integer. When a mobile object is allowed to accept socket connections, the mobile object can implement network services provided on behalf of the host application. For example, a mobile object could easily implement an SMTP e-mail server to manage e-mail sent between other parties, some of them people, some of them other mobile objects.

However, at the same time, allowing a mobile object to accept network connections poses a significant risk. The mobile object can masquerade as a legitimate service of the host machine. For example, the mobile object can masquerade as a Web server by accepting HTTP requests and distributing forged HTML documents in response. During this masquerade, the mobile object can compromise the reputation of the host machine by distributing documents that the administrator of the machine would not normally distribute, such as confidential or pornographic material. Enabling a mobile object to accept connections can be particularly risky on a machine that provides legitimate network services if the ports used by the legitimate services are not protected from tampering. Under these cases, the mobile object may not only perform the subterfuge, it may also block out access to the legitimate service. Multihomed hosts pose a difficult twist to this security check because multihomed systems may be known by several different host names on the Internet. In such conditions, the SecurityManager may know to disallow certain names, but it may not be aware of all of the names of the multihomed system.

The least dangerous path to take for allowing a mobile object to accept connections is to allow only connections on certain port numbers that you know are not used by other services and that you can make freely available for the mobile object. However, even this path has its risks because a mobile object may run a masqueraded service on a nonstandard port, then fool users into believing the service originates from the host machine.

checkAccess(Thread)

The purpose of checkAccess(Thread) is to validate whether the calling thread can invoke operations to modify the specified thread. A mobile object can use this privilege to manage the priority of threads, remove threads that are no longer needed, and cause threads to go to sleep or wake up triggered by other events in the system.

A mobile object that can modify a thread can classify it as a high or low priority. This may be a form of attack on a system because a high-priority thread can overconsume the resources of the system. At the same time, important threads may be reprioritized to a very low level in order for the current thread to gain more system resources. A mobile object with unlimited access to threads can cannibalistically kill off all the other threads of a system or all the threads owned by rival mobile objects.

In order to ensure safety for a mobile object, the mobile object should not be able to access any threads. In most settings, the limited access should not have a detrimental effect on application development because thread priority should not have a significant impact on the behavior of a system except under extreme performance conditions.

checkAccess(ThreadGroup)

checkAccess(ThreadGroup) validates whether the calling thread can invoke operations to modify a particular ThreadGroup. The ThreadGroup is just an administratively convenient package of Threads, so the same issues associated with checkAccess-(Thread) pertain here.

checkAwtEventQueueAccess()

checkAwtEventQueueAccess() validates whether the calling thread can obtain direct access to the AWT event queue. The mobile object may be able to perform special operations when events come in by watching the AWT event queue for specific events such as control keys or certain key sequences. The mobile object can take its own actions based on the content of the EventQueue, choosing to either leave the original queue intact or remove specified elements from the queue before they are processed by the normal event handling systems. The mobile object may also add new events to the Event Queue, driving the rest of the application with AWTEvents.

The key risk here is that a mobile object may effectively take over the keyboard and other user interface systems such as the mouse, keypad, and joystick. The mobile object can use these resources to benignly monitor the activities of the user or malevolently steal confidential information such as passwords. In addition, the mobile object can drive the user interface of an application by inserting new AWTEvents into the event queue, potentially enabling the mobile object to perform operations by going through the user interface that would not normally be accessible through the application layer. For example, a method involved in the handling of keyboard input might be declared private. The mobile object is not allowed to access any private member directly except its own, so the mobile object cannot invoke an arbitrary private member on a different object. However, because the private method is involved in the handling of keyboard input, the mobile object might be designed to indirectly cause the method to be invoked by the manipulation of the EventQueue to cause the appropriate keyboard event to invoke the operation.

In a mobile object setting, you may want to disallow access to the EventQueue in order to prevent the mobile object from performing unnecessary manipulation of the EventQueue. In most cases, the normal Java event architecture should be sufficient for an application. A foreign mobile object should not need to access the EventQueue under normal circumstances. However, certain classes of objects that perform tasks involved in the monitoring of keyboard input, such as macro and shortcut key packages, might benefit from having access to the EventQueue. Under these conditions, you might want to grant this privilege to selected objects.

checkConnect(String, int)

The purpose of checkConnect(String, int) is to validate whether a calling thread can open a TCP/IP socket to a particular host name and port number. The SecurityManager may choose to allow some hosts and ports but disallow others. Opening sockets is an important capability in a distributed system. In order for one application to communicate with another over a TCP/IP network, the applications must be able to open a socket. The two applications connected to the socket can use this socket to exchange messages.

The mobile object can send messages to any computer permitted by this operation while masquerading as the host. As a result, abuse by the mobile object can damage the reputation of the mobile object. This may include actions like sending e-mail on behalf of the host, submitting Web requests, or interacting with any other type of network server. In an e-commerce environment, financial transactions may be forged on behalf of the host application.

Mobile objects should be allowed only restricted access to the network under most circumstances. In the experience of the applet development community, a restriction is enforced that an applet can open network sockets only back to its originating server. Many applet developers find this capability more than sufficient to build applets that participate in distributed systems. Even this strict restriction can sometimes be used to attack a system.

checkConnect(String, int, Object)

checkConnect(String, int, Object) is identical to the previous checkConnect operation, but it checks whether a socket connection is allowed within a particular security context specified by an object, not just in the calling thread.

checkCreateClassLoader()

checkCreateClassLoader() validates whether the calling thread is permitted to instantiate new class loaders. A mobile object might want to do this for several reasons. ClassLoaders have a very special status within the Java run-time environment as the tools for locating and loading classes on demand. The default ClassLoaders are limited in functionality in terms of how and where they search for classes. Many mobile objects may want to extend the behavior of the default ClassLoaders to provide additional capabilities. One of the other big benefits of ClassLoaders is that they define a unique scope for class names and can be used as tools for preventing different versions of the same class from conflicting with each other within a single virtual machine.

ClassLoaders are used to load every object in the Java system, including system classes such as java.lang.System, java.lang.SecurityManager, and other critical classes. A mobile object that can define its own ClassLoader may be able to provide its own implementation for these core classes, using them to obtain resources that would not normally be available to the application. The author is not aware of any specific attack that manages to take advantage of ClassLoaders in this way.

Mobile objects probably should not be allowed to instantiate new ClassLoaders of their own; the risks are too great that the ClassLoader may be used to abuse the Java run-time environment. The host application may provide a useful set of ClassLoaders to the mobile object but set the SecurityManager such that additional ClassLoaders may not be instantiated.

checkDelete(String)

The purpose of checkDelete(String) is to validate whether the calling thread is allowed to delete a particular file given by a string name. A mobile object that was responsible for maintaining a set of files might have to clean up after itself by deleting the files that it originally created.

Mobile objects obviously should not be given carte blanche to delete any file. You don't want to give a mobile object that you don't trust the right to delete everything on your hard disk. You should also be cautious when giving a mobile object permission to delete any of the files in a particular subdirectory that contains symbolic links to other directories. In this situation, a given file name might appear to be in the subdirectory, but the specified files may actually be located in other directories.

A good solution when a mobile object performs some file access is to permit it to access all the files in a given directory as well as delete those files. Don't permit any symbolic links in the directory.

checkExec(String)

checkExec(String) validates whether the calling thread can use System.exec() to invoke a particular operating system command. This is a powerful capability because it opens up the resources of the operating system to your Java application. A mobile object can take advantage of this option to do almost anything with your computer.

Nothing, including mobile objects, should be given unrestricted access to all the commands on a system. Such access is too dangerous because it leaves control of your entire system in the hands of foreign code. The application can easily delete or reformat the hard disk or take virtually any other malevolent action.

The safest situation for mobile objects is to permit only certain commands, denying most others. Although doing so denies the mobile object system the ability to build software that directly accesses the local operating system, such an architecture is much safer.

checkExit(int)

checkExit(int) determines whether the calling thread is allowed to exit the application with the given status code. In certain conditions, mobile objects may determine that an application should not continue. In this event, the application can be halted with the appropriate status code.

Mobile objects may abuse this privilege to implement a denial of service attack, killing applications to prevent legitimate users from using their services. A mobile object may monitor processes, such as business transactions, to determine if they are favorable or unfavorable, then terminate those that are unfavorable.

Mobile objects probably should not be given the privilege to terminate an application because you usually don't want foreign code to be able to terminate the host application. The design of most applications should not have this requirement.

checkLink(String)

checkLink(String) validates whether the calling thread is permitted to link to a particular dynamic linked library specified by a string file name. The mobile object may wish to obtain additional functionality provided by the dynamic linked library through the Java Native Interface. The implementation of the dynamic linked library may perform any task that any dynamic linked library might perform.

Mobile objects should not be permitted to link to any library except those that are believed to be secure. Determining whether a dynamic linked library is secure or not involves assessing the type of operations used by the library to ensure that it isn't accessing resources that should not be available to the mobile object. For example, a dynamic linked library used to control your e-mail system may have operations available in it to send e-mail, receive e-mail, save e-mail messages in files, or even delete files. Giving a mobile object access to just this one hypothetical dynamic linked library may be enough to allow it to perform all sorts of mischief. In addition, many dynamic linked libraries have bugs that permit them to be compromised and used as tools for breaking system security.

Mobile objects should not be allowed to link to dynamic linked libraries other than a small, trusted list of dynamic linked libraries. Be careful giving any Java application the right to link to arbitrary dynamic linked libraries.

checkListen(int)

checkListen(int) determines whether the calling thread should be allowed to listen for incoming connection requests to a given port. The security issues for checkAccept(String, int) apply here.

checkMemberAccess(Class, int)

The purpose of checkMemberAccess(Class, int) is to validate whether a calling thread can access a particular member variable of a class. This flexible operation enables you to control member-level access to the individual classes in your Java application. You might easily decide that a particular mobile object should not be permitted to access some of the contents of some objects.

Mobile objects that arrive in an application can access any objects that they manage to which they obtain an object reference. In some cases, they might have access to confidential data such as credit card numbers unless they can be prevented from obtaining access to this sensitive information.

Mobile objects should, in general, have unrestricted access to the members of all classes unless an exceptional case occurs. When data should be protected from other objects in the same application, the best way to protect it is to partition the sensitive data into a completely separate application.

checkMulticast(InetAddress)

checkMulticast(InetAddress) validates whether the calling thread can use IP multicast communication. IP multicast is an efficient way to distribute information to a group of listeners all at the same time.

Mobile objects may be able to abuse existing multicast resources. Just as in the point-to-point communication example discussed in the checkAccept() section, IP multicast may be abused to impersonate the originating host, damaging its reputation.

Few firm standards currently exist in the multicast world, so it's difficult to administrate which IP multicast addresses should be allowed and which should be disallowed. To be safe, a small subset of the multicast domain might be allocated for a particular mobile object system. Within that small set of address, mobile objects may have free rein to access IP multicast.

checkMulticast(InetAddress, byte)

checkMulticast(InetAddress, byte) validates whether the current execution context is allowed to specifically join, leave, send messages to, or receive messages from an IP multicast group specified by a particular InetAddress.

checkPackageAccess(String)

checkPackageAccess(String) validates whether the calling thread is permitted to access a specific package given by a string argument. If the current thread has access to this package, it may be able to access member classes of the package, view the static state of the classes in the package, and instantiate classes from the package.

Mobile objects may be able to abuse certain packages. For example, you may not want mobile objects to have access to the java.rmi.* package because they might implement or consume additional network services implemented with RMI beyond those intended by the author of the host application. Database and security packages may be other examples of candidates that could be abused by mobile objects.

Mobile objects should generally be allowed access to all packages unless certain packages are identified that can be used by a mobile object to circumvent system security. In that case, obviously, the mobile object must be denied access to the package.

checkPackageDefinition(String)

checkPackageDefinition(String) validates whether the calling thread should be permitted to create new classes within the package specified by a string argument. The implementation of the package may include protected members that can be accessed only by other members of the same package. By allowing a mobile object to add classes to a particular package, the mobile object can access the protected members of the package.

In some cases, protected members may contain sensitive data that could compromise a system. This data must be protected from untrusted mobile objects. However, if the mobile object can create new classes within the package, the data is easily accessible by the objects added into the package.

Depending on your philosophy regarding safe coding practices, mobile objects should or should not have access to the protected members of a particular package. The author would tend to allow mobile objects to have access to any protected members of a package under the assumption that more flexible software would be possible as a result.

checkPrintJobAccess()

The purpose of checkPrintJobAccess() is to validate whether the calling thread can initiate print jobs. The mobile object may implement a feature set that naturally incorporates a feature like printing. In these conditions, the mobile object could benefit from having the ability to issue its own print jobs.

Mobile objects may abuse any resources that are made available to them, including document printing. A mobile object can spam a printer, issuing thousands of document print requests, jamming up the printer and preventing other users from accessing it. Not only are the resources spent by the printer expensive, the inability of legitimate users to access these resources is just as expensive.

Mobile objects should have print access under circumstances that permit the system to properly monitor and manage resource consumption of the mobile object using the printer resources. The SecurityManager doesn't provide sufficient granularity to do this adequately, so the best solution may be to implement an indirect mechanism for the submitting of print requests by mobile objects, allowing the host application to verify and approve the resources consumed by the mobile object in issuing its print requests.

checkPropertiesAccess()

checkPropertiesAccess() determines whether the calling thread should be permitted to access and even modify the System Properties. The Properties contain general configuration about the Java run-time environment. The mobile object may need to access the Properties to configure properties that may be missing. In the Upgradable Text Editor application examined in Chapter 8: Building the Dynamically Upgradable Text Editor, the Properties list had to be accessed to add a "mail.host" property required by the Java mail libraries but not set by default. If the Properties had been unavailable, the mobile object in that application would not have been able to send e-mail using the Java mail libraries.

The ability to arbitrarily access and manipulate the System Properties may be too much of a responsibility for a mobile object. Some of the System Properties include properties that identify users and their e-mail addresses. This may not be information that you want to make readily available to any mobile object.

Mobile objects should generally be permitted access to System Properties. CheckPropertyAccess(String) can be used to achieve finer-grain control over which System Properties are accessible and which are restricted.

checkPropertyAccess(String)

checkPropertyAccess(String) validates whether the calling thread has access to a particular System Property. See the description of checkPropertiesAccess().

checkRead(FileDescriptor)

checkRead(FileDescriptor) determines whether the calling thread has read access for the file specified by the FileDescriptor. Mobile objects may incorporate code to read and write data to disk. The local hard disk is the best place to store data for later use.

Mobile objects with unrestricted access to read files may obviously abuse this privilege to access confidential data. An example is a mobile object that attempts to read the saved e-mail file on its host system, compromising the privacy of users' e-mail.

Protecting the confidentiality of data that the mobile object should not read is just a matter of restricting the files that the mobile object has access to read. It requires simply maintaining a list of the specific files that the mobile object can read. Whole subdirectories may also be readable. Be careful that soft links to different files in the operating system don't allow the mobile object to access files or directories to which the mobile object should not have access. Also, you must be very careful that the mechanism used to store the names of the files that the mobile object may access cannot be manipulated by the mobile object.

checkRead(String)

checkRead(String) determines if the mobile object should have permission to read a specific named file, the same as checkRead(FileDescriptor), but the file is specified with a string name.

checkRead(String, Object)

The same issues that apply to checkRead(String) apply to checkRead(String, Object), but the privilege is checked within the specified execution context rather than in the calling thread.

checkSecurityAccess(String)

checkSecurityAccess(String) determines whether the mobile object can access specific operations in the Security API. A mobile object can use this API to communicate securely with other mobile objects or service providers.

Giving a mobile object unrestricted access to your security subsystem means that the mobile object can impersonate the host application by using any mechanism that other applications use to authenticate the host application. The mobile object has a significant ability to damage the reputation of the host application under these conditions because other applications may put great confidence in the identity of the host application after authenticating it.

The mobile object is also at risk. The host application controls the run-time environment in which the mobile object lives. When the mobile object attempts to access the Security API, the host application may circumvent the normal security mechanisms to provide its own Trojan horse Security API. In this case, the mobile object may think it's configuring the Security API and communicating securely with other mobile objects, but in reality, the mobile object is subject to the whim of the host application.

Mobile objects should have access to the Security API only when the mobile object and host application place complete trust in each other and the mobile object needs to configure a portion of the Security run-time environment. This situation should be fairly rare in most distributed systems.

checkSetFactory()

checkSetFactory() determines whether the application is allowed to register its own SocketFactories. A SocketFactory controls the construction process for sockets used by the Java run-time environment. Mobile objects may be able to build their own type of sockets and register custom SocketFactories to create these sockets. Custom sockets might perform operations like encryption or filtering data that is sent across it. They may also be used to broadcast information to multiple destinations.

Sockets make up the basis for communication in a distributed system, so giving a mobile object the ability to change the implementation for sockets may grant the mobile object a great deal of control over the rest of the host application. The mobile object may register a custom socket factory in order to be able to monitor, filter, or manipulate the communication of other components of the host application.

The host application should be careful that the mobile object doesn't replace the expected implementation of a socket with its own custom implementation. In order to enforce this restriction on replacement, either mobile objects should be prevented from registering their own socket factories or the settings of the socket factory should be partitioned so that the socket factory set by the mobile object affects only the mobile object itself.

checkSystemClipboardAccess()

The purpose of checkSystemClipboardAccess() is to determine whether the calling thread has access to the system clipboard. A mobile object can use this to cut and paste information to other mobile objects or applications running on the same host.

The system clipboard might accidentally contain confidential data such as spreadsheet or word processor documents. A mobile object might be able to copy this information without the knowledge of the end user if the mobile object has access to the system clipboard. Giving any application access to the system clipboard is dangerous for exactly the same reason: applications can steal each other's data if the data happens to end up in the system clipboard.

The only solution to maintaining system security with a system clipboard is to educate users not to store sensitive information in their clipboards. End users must be aware that any information stored in the system clipboard is public information that any application on the host can read, copy, and modify. If you are not confident that end users can have this level of security awareness, the only recourse is to disable the system clipboard and deny access to it for mobile objects.

checkTopLevelWindow(Object)

checkTopLevelWindow(Object) determines whether the calling thread can create top-level windows. A top-level window is a window that appears above all the other windows in a window manager. A mobile object can use this feature to display important windows above all the other windows, preventing important messages from being hidden or covered by other windows.

Mobile objects can create windows as large as the entire desktop window that cover up all the other windows. When this happens, the end user can be blocked out of interacting with any other windows. Other windows are covered by the large top-level window, but the top-level window may be sized and positioned in such a way to make it difficult to remove. In addition, the mobile object can configure the window to ignore frame close events, so the window cannot be removed without killing the host application. Mobile objects may also provide a look and feel that simulates the desktop to attempt to fool end users into believing that they are interacting with the desktop when they are actually inside a window controlled by the mobile object. Under these conditions, users might be tricked into divulging passwords and other sensitive information.

Top-level windows don't contribute a great deal to application development, so they can easily be disabled for mobile objects.

checkWrite(FileDescriptor)

checkWrite(FileDescriptor) validates whether the mobile object should be able to write a file specified by a FileDescriptor. The mobile object can then save data between sessions. Writing files may be very useful for caching mobile objects between sessions, so the individual mobile objects, their classes, and their state don't need to be loaded every time.

Mobile objects that can write files can accidentally or maliciously attack the host system by writing data to the hard disk until it reaches maximum capacity. The SecurityManager API for controlling file writing is not sufficiently fine-grained to grant the mobile object permission to write only a certain amount of data; it can only write specific files. Important files may be overwritten by a mobile object if the object has unrestricted access to write files in a particular subdirectory. A file containing valuable data may be overwritten with random garbage, irrecoverably deleting the original data.

Mobile objects should be given write access to files only under limited circumstances, and then the administrator of the host system should guarantee that the disk is partitioned sufficiently to guarantee that the mobile object cannot hurt any other applications on the host system. If the mobile object has access to write files only in a single disk partition that is not used by other objects, the mobile object cannot cause much damage to other applications.

checkWrite(String)

checkWrite(String) validates whether a mobile object can write to a named file. See the description of checkWrite(FileDescriptor) for further explanation of the issues surrounding allowing a mobile object to write to a file.

What's Next

♦ Now that we have seen what makes up mobile objects, how to build them, and how to secure them, the next section examines what's in store for the future of mobile objects and how they will impact the software development industry. We'll examine some of the latest trends and try to determine what technologies are likely to be the winners and losers as we proceed into this new area.

Trends in
Mobile Objects

For decades, application development has followed a rigid iterative process of code, compile, deploy. Recent advances in distributed object technology now enable us to climb out of this historical mold. The future of application development and deployment may soon seem foreign to legacy application developers.

In the face of the tremendous advances in distributed computing with the advent of LANs, TCP/IP, RPCs, and distributed object technologies, the natural question is whether the flow of technology advances is slowing. Are we faced with a technological future in which advances slow to a mere trickle where once there was a river? Quite the reverse is happening; advances are fostering further advances.

In fact, distributed computing is the core technology for what we know of today as the Internet. Since its inception, the Internet could only be described as an avalanche sweeping across the entire globe. Businesses are depending on the Internet for delivering of products and services both internally and externally. This dependence virtually ensures the continued interest in extending the frontier of distributed computing.

What should we expect? What new technologies are destined to be tomorrow's hottest new developments?

Some trends are clear, almost obvious. Some advances are on the cusp of breaking into the mainstream and achieving wide acceptance. These are the trends that will probably happen because they are already well into the early adopter phase of the software sales cycle. This chapter covers upcoming trends and their effect on distributed computing.

Protocol Interoperability

One trend is toward further interoperability. CORBA has led the way in encouraging interoperability among many operating systems, programming languages, and development environments. The OMG philosophy of interoperating with other technologies rather than trying to compete with them head-to-head has won the day.

The list of languages that support CORBA is ever increasing as new organizations recognize the value of interoperating with CORBA. Not too long ago, C, C++, and Smalltalk were the only languages available for CORBA. Over the last few years, COBOL, ADA, and Java have been officially standardized within the OMG. Perl, TCL, Python, LISP, and Scheme are among the other languages that support CORBA.

Even Microsoft is onboard, interoperating DCOM and CORBA with a special conversion tool for creating the support code required to make a CORBA server look and act like a DCOM server or vice versa. DCOM and CORBA have effectively become interchangeable parts in a heterogeneous software environment. The interoperability of DCOM and CORBA also means that DCOM-compatible tools like Visual Basic, Delphi, and PowerBuilder become platforms for CORBA software development.

That's not the end of it. RMI and CORBA interoperability is available from JavaSoft. Software developed for RMI can now interoperate with CORBA clients and servers. By interoperating with both technologies, CORBA provides a middle ground between RMI and DCOM, enabling RMI and DCOM to interoperate with each other through CORBA. Enterprise JavaBeans (EJB) also requires CORBA interoperability for any compliant EJB implementation.

Proprietary application technologies, such as Weblogic's Tengah and ObjectSpace's Voyager, are adding interoperability as well. Both products interoperate with CORBA. Each also supports some form of RMI and/or DCOM interoperability, as well as indirect interoperability with these technologies through CORBA.

Again, by interoperating with CORBA, these technologies offer a way of enabling their own clients and servers to access numerous other technologies that also interoperate with CORBA. A Tengah client can invoke a DCOM server because the two share a common interoperability with CORBA.

Indications are very good that this trend toward interoperability will continue. System integrators have often relied on proprietary protocols and toolkits to accomplish their task of linking heterogeneous software and hardware. Today, systems integrators in fields as diverse as finance, health care, and defense are considering interoperability a priority, often by replacing proprietary protocols and APIs with support for open standards like CORBA.

Protocol interoperability goes only so far. Protocol interoperability isn't the magic bullet that can make every application interoperate usefully with every other application. After all, as pointed out early in Chapter 1 of this book, network protocols are limited to communication between more or less static software applications. Protocol interoperability standardizes the format for communication between different applications. Using a standardized format is only part of the game. Two applications that communicate using a common protocol may not be able to interact in a meaningful way if both applications don't include the appropriate code to interact with each other. Protocol interoperability must include a standard for the content of the protocol, or disparate applications may share a common format but not be able to communicate.

An example would be two random applications written for CORBA with support for two different interfaces, such as a client that incorporates a financial transaction and a server that implements a database of public records on real estate. The implementation of CORBA applications that communicate requires that the applications share the same interface and the appropriate implementation code to either invoke the interface in the case of the client or implement the interface in the case of the server. These two applications, though they communicate with the same protocol, probably would not share the same interface or have the appropriate implementation code to enable interaction. Both applications are loosely related to the field of real estate; thus, making them interact might be useful to a real estate analyst.

An example of such interaction might be how a menu item can be shared between the two applications. An implementation might display the menu item from one application in the second application. When the menu item is invoked, the second application should be notified about the invocation. At that time, the second application can take whatever actions are appropriate for responding to the invocation. A number of steps have to be taken by the two applications before they can interact in this manner. The second application has to be able to notify the first application of the availability of the menu item. The first application has to be capable of displaying menu items and adding them to its own user interface. The second application has to have a distributed object interface that enables the first application to notify it in the event that someone invokes the menu item, and the first application needs to share a copy of that interface in order to be able to invoke the interface when someone selects the appropriate menu item.

A rewrite of one or the other applications is generally required in order to make all of this happen. Without a rewrite, the applications cannot communicate in any useful way. In a traditional software development approach, this also implies that one or the other of the applications must be redeployed to make the changes widely available to the base of users.

This problem is not without a solution, though. The next section discusses a new direction in interoperability that will emerge (and already has emerged to some extent) in order to address the problem of making two totally unrelated application interact with each other.

Implementation Interoperability

Mobile objects allow interoperability to go even further. Suppose that the two applications discussed in the previous section are developed independently by two parties using mobile objects. The applications may share menu items by exchanging mobile objects that implement the appropriate menu items. However, this is not the end of the story. Unless the applications agree on how to use the menu, the mobile objects sent by one application may be meaningless to another application. For example, a mobile object implementing a menu item from a foreign application must have some way of registering itself with the application menu. An application might easily have several different windows, each with a menu. The mobile object has no way of determining which to use and indeed may not even be able to obtain a reference to any of the menus. Yet in Chapter 8: Building the Upgradable Text Editor, we managed to solve this problem. Two applications managed to share mobile objects implementing menu items.

The solution is implementation interoperability. Applications require some way of agreeing with each other on how to implement a certain behavior. In the menu item example, a mobile object needs a standard way of registering its menu items with an application's main menu. The inverse problem is just as difficult; an application needs some way of querying a mobile object for any menu items that might be available on it. Several mechanisms have been put forth for achieving this sort of agreement. The mobile agent research community has put a substantial effort into designing LISP-like languages, such as KQML and KIF, for representing the semantic content of an agent so that other agents may determine how to interact with it.

However, from a pragmatic application development standpoint, defining the semantic content of every reusable element of a program in a LISP-like language is probably not a practical suggestion. The effort invested in defining the semantic content of the object could drastically increase the total resource requirements for developing the object in the first place. Also, many industry observers have challenged the utility of this type of application discovery. The implementation and description of an operation using a metalanguage doesn't necessarily make it easier to integrate that operation into another application at runtime. Integrating two entirely different entities almost always requires some custom code. That means two applications are never able to magically integrate with each other in a seamless way. System integrators, professionals who work hard to integrate different systems, will probably be entirely nonplused to hear this.

Integrating totally unrelated systems requires some planning. The applications that integrate must follow a standard and must conform to some agreed-upon conventions in order to communicate. For example, an accounting application dedicated to tax processing must have a standard way of making the information content of the form available to other software packages in order to enable them to access it. The actual implementation of the accounting software may vary considerably, but the mechanism for accessing the data must be standardized so that discrete applications have access to it.

The answer then is in the construction of standards for integrating unrelated applications. This process has already started in the distributed object world, but mobile object technology is still in its infancy. No such effort has begun to ensure that mobile objects can integrate seamlessly.

Some people contest whether advances in new technology should be standardized using formal mechanisms. The OMG has been moderately successful in standardizing CORBA, but de facto standards like Java have swept through the industry even faster. In the end, mobile object technology is probably moving fast enough that eventually the de facto standards will start to appear. It is expected that when mobile object technology enters the mainstream, de facto standards written by the companies implementing the technology will sweep past the standards efforts of committee-based organizations.

How do we apply this standards issue to the menu example? The mobile object implements a menu item and defines an API for accessing the menu item. The implementation of the mobile object displays the menu item to a menu when the appropriate invocation is made on the API. On the other hand, the application supports menus and could potentially make use of the menu item. However, the application, developed by a second party, was not written specifically to use the mobile object and its menu item API. Specific implementation code would be required to handle the menu event and direct it to a mobile object before such a feature set could be supported. The application that displays menus could potentially make use of this feature of the mobile object. However, how does the application notify the other applications that it is capable of supporting a menu item? What API is used to update the menu item or invalidate it? In a custom-built system, the designer of the system could define and use the API throughout the application, but two applications that are intended to interoperate seamlessly may not have this luxury.

In effect, to solve this problem, we need standards for mobile objects. A world populated by mobile objects can achieve great benefits without standards, but when millions of developers and organizations are all spewing out mobile objects with the expectation that a useful level of interoperability is achieved, standards become important, whether de facto or otherwise. Whenever any two implementations of technologies tackle the same problems, standards become beneficial for ensuring that other software implemented to work in the context of those problems is interoperable across both implementations. Mobile object technologies require standards that specify in what way different implementations must be the same and in which ways they may differ. The implementation of such standards enables objects developed for entirely different organizations to coordinate sufficiently to exchange information with each other.

How will mobile object standards be defined? Anyone's guess is likely to be at least partially right. Standards bodies like the OMG have already begun accepting requests for proposals (RFPs) and standards submissions that begin to point the way toward this future. Other organizations, such as Object Space, are quickly releasing products that include mobile object functionality. These may be charting the way to eventually becoming de facto standards.

Object Web

Interoperability is not the only new front of development. Distributed objects are changing the face of the traditional three-tier client/server system as well. The traditional three-tier system is a relatively static system composed of three layers. The first layer is a legacy system, often a mainframe system, used for little more than data warehousing. The middle layer is composed of the business logic. Many middle tiers are written as C++ servers running on a Unix or NT system. The third tier, the presentation layer, is the application employed by the end user. In a traditional three-tier system, the presentation layer is a client application installed on the desktop of the end user. The layers must agree on a protocol in order to communicate with each other. Historically, the developers implementing the three-tier system would often design and implement their own proprietary protocol for each and every tiered system. Rarely did any two systems share a common protocol, so very few tiered systems interoperated with each other.

CORBA and Java open up the three-tier system. Robert Orfali coined the term Object Web to describe the synergy among distributed objects, the Web, and Java. CORBA facilitates the interoperability of tiered systems with other systems. When CORBA is used in the construction of a three-tier system, the IIOP protocol becomes the standard protocol for communication between tiers of the system. Recall the list of technologies that interoperate with CORBA discussed earlier, including COM, DCOM, RMI, IDEs like Visual Basic and Delphi, and a great many programming languages; each of these is programmatically compatible with any three-tier system that is implemented with CORBA. Build a three-tier system with CORBA today, and tomorrow you may be using RMI, Visual Basic, or Perl to extend the system. Each network resource appears as a CORBA-compatible distributed object.

Java, a programming language designed with the network in mind, provides a unique set of benefits of its own. Applets can be downloaded as part of Web pages. No installation procedures are required. When the presentation layer is implemented in Java and designed to run as an applet in a browser, no client installation is required for the end user. Java enables the presentation layer of the tiered system to be embedded directly into arbitrary Web pages for download across the Internet. Absolutely no additional work must be placed in administrating the presentation layer of the system; no prior installation and no customization requirements are necessary.

These Java applets, implemented as a set of Java objects, can even contain distributed objects. The implementation of the presentation layer of a three-tier system is just a set of objects that fly across the network to run inside someone's browser, accessing a bunch of Web resources, which are also objects. The derivation for the term "Object Web" thus becomes apparent.

That's not the end of the Object Web vision, though. We've extended the traditional three-tier model in powerful ways, but a great deal more is possible, as we will see in the rest of this chapter.

Pass-By-Value

Perhaps the most significant advance in the software industry today is going virtually unnoticed and totally unappreciated—Pass-By-Value. Pass-By-Value simply means that one can invoke a distributed object by passing a serialized object to it. Distributed object invocations are normally restricted to a standard set of data types, including the well-known scalar data types and a few complex data types like structures, enumerations, exceptions, and unions. With Pass-By-Value, actual objects can be used as arguments in distributed object invocations.

Several types of Pass-By-Value are possible. First, state transfer Pass-by-Value transfers the state of objects between programs. The state of the object includes all the values of the object's member variables. When the state of an object is transferred from one program to another, the receiver is able to instantiate a clone of the original object by creating a new instance of the appropriate class and copying the state to the instance. The receiver must have the implementation code for the correct class or a compatible version of the class, or the object cannot be instantiated. This is a limitation of state transfer Pass-by-Value because it means that the receiver is restricted to instantiating only those objects that are already available on the platform. Another limitation of state transfer Pass-By-Value is that the serialized objects written in one language are generally not compatible with serialized objects of another language. However, this last limitation is easy to overcome.

Interoperable Pass-By-Value may be achieved when one creates a standard data format for serializing objects in a language-independent way. Standard data formats are important for interoperable technologies because different programming languages, operating systems, and hardware architectures often use completely different formats to represent data types such as integers. By creating a standard for how objects can be serialized into raw data, Pass-By-Value enables many different types of platforms to interoperate with each other. For example, multiple programming languages can share each other's objects. An example scenario is one in which an object written in one language, for example, C++, serializes the objects into the standard data format and sends them to a program written in another language, for example, Java. The standard data format enables the different languages to share objects even though the native representation for the objects is quite different in each language. The OMG has drafted an Object-By-Value specification for CORBA that supports interoperable Pass-By-Value.

The other limitation of state transfer Pass-by-Value was the requirement of the availability of an appropriate class to instantiate the object on the receiver. This limitation can be overcome through use of a mobile code. When a new object is passed into a program, the appropriate class can actually be downloaded from a network server and dynamically installed in the running program. The language must be capable of providing support for mobile code to make this feasible. The combination of state transfer and mobile code is a mobile object.

Versioning

The problem with passing objects around on the network as well as reusing other types of code is that many objects depend on having the correct version of other components of the system. Many Java developers run into this problem when they discover that their Java applets require porting to run on new versions of the Java Runtime Environment. Dependency checking is one solution to the versioning problem. Dependency checking provides a means of ensuring that dependent implementations are coupled with their required components. When a problem is detected, a specific algorithm can be used for resolving the ambiguity of the dependent system. The implementation of the versioning system based on a typing mechanism performs version checking based on verifying that the appropriate interfaces are coupled with each other. With type versioning, a component must ensure that some implementation of a component of the correct version of the specified type is provided. Any implementation matching the appropriate type and version is used. However, type versioning may not ensure correct implementation versioning.

Implementation of any software is subject to versioning concerns. Whenever you produce something, you implicitly create a new item in the system. Anything else in the system may become dependent on that object. The implementation of other parts of the system expect not just the interface but often the behavior present in your implementation of the software. Changes to your software always risk problems of other software failing to handle the implementation changes. Why? Object purists might have you believe that as long as you build software that uses the expected interface and no hidden behavior, no problems should arise regarding the implementation of the software. The implementation, however, might include side effects that are expected by other software, and this is where the problem occurs. Side effects include any changes to the global state of the system. The "global state" here should be interpreted in the most general possible sense. Global state of a system includes any static variables, any reading or writing to the default input or output streams, any file I/O, any database accessing, and any GUI events.

The system may also become fragile if the caller becomes dependent on a specific implementation for the computation of return values. For example, the implementation of a financial application might expect Cash Flow to be calculated using a specific formula in order to be able to translate the calculated Cash Flow into other useful data. If the implementation of the Cash Flow calculation changes, a different formula needs to be used in order to use this value in further calculations. Changing the formula for Cash Flow may change the way that the result should be handled, causing the implementation changes to Cash Flow to invalidate clients that become dependent on the specific implementation.

Implementation versioning is more resource intensive than type versioning. First, many implementation versions may exist for a single interface version. Second, the number of versions that must be retained increases dramatically as a result of the interdependency of implementation versions. Finally, the implementations are much bulkier than interfaces.

Implementation versioning may lead to apparent paradoxical relationships between multiple components of a system. Suppose a popular component called the Web Browser 1.0 widget depends on a FTP Client 1.2.1 widget. The developer of the FTP Client widget might decide to include some of the functionality of Web Browser 1.0 in the FTP Client 1.2.1. However, on further review, the author of FTP Client decides to incorporate Web Browser functionality into FTP Client. The implementation of the next version of FTP Client 1.3 becomes dependent on Web Browser 1.0. However, the implementation of Web Browser 1.0 itself included functionality from and was dependent on FTP Client 1.2.1. FTP Client 1.2.1 should not be coerced into FTP Client 1.3 because of implementation versioning. The solution is to include the implementation of both the old and new implementations of FTP Client. The two implementation can coexist in the same application with the appropriate implementation used in the appropriate context. This inclusion of multiple versions of the same application may result in some waste, but problems resulting from coercion of incompatible implementation versions are avoided.

The deployment of the Java class libraries already runs straight into the same versioning problems. For example, when you write code for JDK 1.0.2, you may have difficulty porting your code to JDK 1.1 or 1.2 as a direct result of the versioning of the Java class libraries. For example, a Java 1.0.2 software developer might write an application that makes use of the InputStream class to read characters from a data file, only to find out that this portion of Java has been significantly restructured in JDK 1.1 and later versions. Older code that uses depreciated, unsupported APIs may no longer work.

As Sun continues to develop and add to the Java language, new classes are added and old classes are modified. Software written with the older standard has trouble running against the new class libraries until the source code is updated to support the new libraries. As a result, Java developers have to port their applications from one version of the JDK to another.

This porting from version to version is an example of a dependency on having the appropriate version of a software package. Some large enterprise Java software distributes multiple versions of the JDK in order to guarantee the availability of the appropriate version of the JDK in all environments. By making multiple Java runtimes available, the software can run on the appropriate version.

This problem needs to be solved by the virtual machine itself. Because many Java classes are available from many sources, the versions of all of these packages becomes dependent on the application. The implementation of any software becomes dependent on the combination of all the versions of all the packages that are used to implement it.

The answer to this problem is a version management system analogous to that found in other application development environments, such as Smalltalk. The implementation of such languages can perform automatic version checking when new components are added to the system, then compatible versions of each component can be located and loaded in order to run the application. At the very least, the application can perform the check and deliver a diagnostic message when an inappropriate version of the software is detected.

One example of such a deployment of a versioning system is in the distribution of the Java class library itself. In order to solve the problems inherent in the way the Java class libraries are currently implemented, a version-checking mechanism could be provided to detect conflicts and automatically provide classes that are compatible for applications that require them. In the Java class libraries, that might mean locating an appropriate version of an InputStream in order to satisfy the versioning dependencies of a particular Java application. In Java, a different version would be loaded through use of the standard mechanism of the Java CLASSPATH or they could be loaded from a Web server in the case of an applet. Such techniques of resolving the dependencies of applications are very well tried in other application development environments and have the potential to eliminate at least some of the porting efforts required by Java application developers today.

Object Groups

The group pattern demonstrates the pragmatic benefits of object groups in a single application. Object groups may take a much bolder position on the future of computing. Object groups and group-based communication protocols address ways to disseminate information to thousands or millions of listeners in an audience.

One of the most exciting areas of research is that regarding the super-scalable implementation of group communication between large groups of participants. These protocols demonstrate interesting characteristics. Some protocols even become more reliable when additional participants join the group. The measure of this reliability is in terms of the probability that a message is not received by one of the participants in the group. Some protocols demonstrate that the probability is actually lower when more participants join the group. Such protocols offer a great deal of hope for large-scale deployment on the Internet.

The type of messages passed around in group-based communication may include a number of resources. One example of a resource is the publishing of mobile objects to a large number of recipients. Mobile objects may be treated as discrete messages. The Object Group pattern discussed in this book takes a look at one example application of this, but a much larger vision of mobile object publication is likely. Mobile objects extending an application may be published to millions of listeners in real time with excellent guarantees regarding the delivery of every mobile object to every intended recipient. Such an approach to distribution of software could effectively extend or replace the existing version of a software application across millions of desktops in real time. Existing push technology comes close to this goal but falls short in several ways, including the lack of real time and quality of service guarantees. In a push environment such as those offered in multiple products falling under the category of push technology, only files are pushed from host to host. In such an environment, the machine may need to be rebooted before new files are detected. In a mobile object environment, mobile objects are incorporated into the application at runtime. With proper support for group communication, excellent guarantees can be made regarding the delivery of messages to all recipients and even regarding a certain speed of delivery.

Another application area of mobile objects in multicast groups is broadcasting streaming content. The implementation of streaming content with mobile objects is remarkably similar to the implementation of file based access because both involve serializing a stream of objects. Many applications may be more or less ready to receive streams because of their implementation of file access. In effect, by defining a format for streaming data to files, the same format and code may often be reused in the implementation of a streaming network protocol for objects. The implementation of such a streaming protocol is conducive to a multicast environment because the data may be streamed to multiple recipients rather than just one recipient. Some application areas in which this functionality will probably prove important include groupware and collaborative applications. These environments typically involve the sharing of information among multiple recipients. The implementation of such collaboration may not be difficult because in a mobile object environment, the content of the broadcast data may contain the very implementation for handling the data. An example is shown in Chapter 7: Dabbling in Groupware.

In this application, the mobile objects sent to the collaborators contained the implementation for a task to be executed on each participant's machine. The data contained in the task included the state of the mobile object as well as the implementation for handling this data. One less abstract example is the spreadsheet, in which the data in the spreadsheet is forwarded to another destination along with the implementation of the spreadsheet. Every recipient in the group receives this information and is able to interpret the data with the benefit of the implementation of the spreadsheet. In a larger-scale environment, many hundreds of data formats might interact with implementations or interpreters that are dynamically loaded as part of the stream. The simple example of the spreadsheet made use of only a single format specified by the Object Serialization standard for the SpreadSheet applet object implemented as part of this example.

Replication

The implementation of object groups and streaming invocations to object groups quickly introduces the power of replication. We examined replication in Chapter 9: Clustering but expect a great deal more from this area of development.

One possibility in the future of replications is that a framework may be implemented that enables any mobile object to be replicated without additional effort on the part of the object implementers. Many experienced developers of replicated systems would likely scoff at this suggestion. The implementation of replication in terms of mobile objects is relatively easy because mobile objects are more easily serialized and cloned than are other types of objects. In fact, all mobile objects are clonable and serializable. All remote invocations on mobile objects are also inherently serializable because they must be accessible in a distributed object environment.

The implementation of a replicated system can be based on no additional assumptions about the underlying objects and invocations. Some benefits may be derived when one makes additional assumptions, such as how strictly the invocations of the mobile object must be ordered with respect to other invocations. However, these assumptions may benefit system performance but are not absolutely necessary to implement a replicated system. The most restrictive and safest assumptions can be made on the ordering of the invocations of the mobile objects without having to know anything at all about the objects. That is to say, assuming that a group-based communication mechanism is used that enforces the absolute order of every invocation on every object, any mobile object that does not depend on the external state of the system can be replicated.

Replication introduces another type of collaboration among members of an object group. An approach to collaboration other than streaming ordered invocations is to replicate objects among members of the collaboration. Both approaches are effectively the same because streaming group communication protocols are often used to replicate objects, but collaborating with replication is a little more abstract because the underlying messages don't have to be interpreted as invocations on the member of the collaboration. Effectively, applications that collaborate through stream invocation broadcast implement or nearly implement object replication on their own. Starting with object replication provides a more convenient level of abstraction and requires less effort on the part of the developer of the collaborative software.

The introduction of implicit replication of services has positive effects on other areas of computing. First and foremost, a replicated system is much more fault tolerant. A service that is replicated on multiple systems may be able to survive the failure of a subset of those systems. The responses of replicated systems may also be verified against each other to ensure the correct response of the servers. In this manner, even if a minority of the servers become faulty and start producing incorrect responses, the client can continue as long as the majority of the servers consistently agree on the correct answer.

Replication also offers the benefits of balancing the load for processing a request across multiple servers. The implementation of load balancing requires that replicated servers be available to process the requests in parallel with each other. Different load balancing policies may be applied to resolve the way the requests are processed and concurrent access to resources is handled.

The future of computing will certainly include a greater focus on replication, fault tolerance, and load balancing. In the past, these techniques were implemented in hardware with expensive custom systems with redundant hardware components and hot swapping of devices. These systems were often astronomically expensive. The future points to cheap software solutions of replication, fault tolerance, and load balancing, with mobile objects.

Messaging

The implementation of most software on the Internet today is synchronous, dependent on active communication between two parties on the network. The upshot is that both parties must be actively participating in the process or the process fails to complete correctly. In addition, the communication link between the two parties must be active at all times. This situation is analogous to a telephone conversation. In such a conversation, both parties must actively participate in the communication. One party picks up the phone and dials the appropriate number. The phone rings for the other party while the first party waits for an answer. If the second party does not answer, the phone conversation cannot be completed. If the second party answers the phone, the conversation begins, but the conversation may be cut short if the phone line fails for some reason.

A better solution is to model communication after the mail system. When you mail a postcard, you drop it in the mailbox and then go do something else. You trust the postal employees to make all due effort to deliver your message to the intended destination. You also have a certain belief in the quality of service that the postal system can provide to you, delivering the message within about four days. The response then comes back on another postcard.

Messaging systems like this are also appropriate for the construction of software systems. The implementation of a system with messaging enables the system to continue functioning even when the other party is not active or when the communication link has failed. The implementation of messaging software can make the overall system more reliable because it reduces the requirement that both parties and their communication link be operating at the same time. Each communication of a message takes less than four days to reach its intended destination.

In a mobile object system, messaging can enable the invocation of a mobile object system to be treated as a message sent between the client and the server. Inside the implementation of the mobile object tool, each invocation is treated as a packet sent across a TCP/IP socket. These messages can be treated as a message. The client can invoke the server by sending a message to it. If the server or communication link is not available, the message may take some time to deliver. In fact, the client application may be closed before the message is sent to the server. That's not a problem. The messaging system continues to attempt to deliver the message even if the client application has closed. When the communication link is available, the message is delivered to the destination and received by the server when the server starts processing messages. Any response sent from the server is then sent back to the client. The client processes these responses when it starts processing messages again.

Messaging systems also enable the queuing of messages before delivery to the other party. The queue acts like a waiting line with each message processed in turn when the resources become available to process the message. Queuing can help to ensure that a system continues to function even when concurrent access to resources is limited. Frameworks that support queuing should be implemented for mobile object systems in the near future. Voyager is already making inroads into this area.

Messages may also be archived during the process of transmission. The implementation of messaging enables a message to be saved for an extended period of time before the message is processed. The quality of service guarantees that the message should eventually be processed or should expire after a certain period of time. The implementation of queuing in a messaging system enables a message to be saved for an extended period of time before it is delivered to the intended destination. When the recipient is not available or when the communication link has failed, the message is stored on the sender until it is ready for delivery.

Shippable Places

What is the function of these objects flying across the network? One view of them is as "shippable places." The concept of a place is similar to that of an application. A place is a graphical user interface that enables the user to interact with a system. Both applets and applications are examples of places. An accounting place might be used to accomplish a particular accounting task. However, places are more general and powerful than applications. While applications are static and provide little flexibility for changing requirements, places are often viewed as dynamic compositions of many elements that are also places.

"Shippable places" address a unique capability of mobile code to ship the implementation for a particular place around different computers. The implementation of a "shippable place" could be given as a set of objects implemented with mobile code Pass-By-Value. When a particular place needs to be shown on a new computer, the appropriate set of objects is sent to the recipient computer, which uses them to display the desired place.

Shippable places are very effective in a workflow environment in which many users collaborate to complete a set of tasks. As each user is involved in completing the steps of the process in the workflow, the appropriate place may be shipped to each user involved in the completion of a specific step of the process.

Shippable places effectively eliminate or radically realign the traditional concepts associated with software installation, administration, and management. Because places may be dynamically downloaded, often on demand, the manual software installation process is eliminated. Client-side administration and management concepts are virtually eliminated because the shippable places should require no client-side configuration.

End users may have their own personal place, a customized desktop for interacting with the computer. The benefits of such a customizable personal place parallel those of having a customizable desktop. However, a shippable version of the personal place might follow users as they move from computer to computer.

One benefit of places is in their composability, the construction of new places out of the composition of old places. Examples of applications of such technology include assembling messages to remote users out of places. An accountant who needs an associate to comment on a particular item in a ledger could forward the associate the appropriate place with annotations regarding the requested actions. Shippable places facilitate this type of collaboration.

Mobile code results in many other types of subtle benefits that are already starting to become available in select mainstream software packages. For example, dynamic software upgrade, already available in Netscape Navigator, enables new plug-ins to be added to a software application by allowing them to be downloaded from the Internet. In the case of Netscape Navigator, the upgrade process is triggered when the user clicks on a particular software package to install while surfing the Web. However, push-based technologies have the potential to perform automatic software upgrades without user interaction. Existing push technologies, such as Marimba Castanet, Netscape Netcaster, and Microsoft Active Channels, are not based on a distributed object paradigm. They are limited to performing straightforward file transfer. Clearly, this is an area ripe for further technical innovation.

Sea of Objects

The entire notion of "application" may already be obsolete. Applications are installed on a computer. They are static, sold as shrink-wrapped products. The phrase "Write once" implies concrete and unchanging, but the future of software is much more dynamic. Applications are subject to radical change. The software life cycle of writing, releasing, and revising was once several years long. Today, information technology organizations are struggling to reduce this life cycle to months, weeks, or even days. In order to accomplish this task, the notion of an application as an unchanging monolithic structure must be revised.

Instead, imagine a sea of objects floating on the Internet—objects providing services, such as search engines, electronic commerce, naming and directory services, news and weather, legal and financial information repositories. Objects implementing specific business processes, such as customizable Internet meta searches, point of sale, insurance claims, and updated versions of existing network services such as e-mail, news, and Web browsing. Objects providing workgroup environments, such as multiple-person collaboration on tasks such as report writing, accounting, and other business processes. All of these objects are flowing around, implementing shippable places, interacting with a user for a brief time to enable the user to perform a contribution to the process.

No longer are we focused on installing a specific application on a specific desktop. Instead, the software environment becomes much more dynamic as each user interacts with many available places for a session. This concept of the "session" of interacting with a sea of objects may eventually replace the concept of an "application" installed on a desktop. Already, more and more business processes are focusing on sessions of interaction with the Web. Such a Web session involves surfing from place to place on the HTML-based Internet. HTML pages are flying back and forth across the Web to implement this session—not a very rich and full-featured interaction, but it's a beginning.

Professional software developers should be asking themselves, "If we don't sell shrink-wrapped applications, how will I continue making payments on my Lotus Esprit?" The answer is simple. You'll be selling places or maybe even renting them. A shippable place provides a robust amount of interaction with the computing environment. The demand for good places will certainly be just as wild as the demand for good applications today. If you build the better accounting place, the world will be knocking at your door to use it. Licensing services and electronic commerce frameworks will still ensure that you receive due payment for your work.

Today we talk about the component marketplace, a market for purchasing components that can then be composed into entire applications. The component marketplace business model may be extended to include shippable places. Further, many more types of exchanges are possible in the marketplace, licensing per seat or per user, subscribing to automatic software updates, renting services for a specific period of time or a specific number of incidents, and composing services of multiple places into larger, composite places. Some of these financial transactions may not follow the current model of software commerce in which a single large payment is made by the end user. Instead, we may see microtransactions of very small amounts of money—pennies or fractions of pennies per use. You may not be selling a shrink-wrapped product in the future, but you will still be behind the wheel of a Lotus.

Ad hoc Collaboration

Collaborations of heterogeneous systems represent another area ripe for advances in distributed computing. The implementation of heterogeneous distributed systems is always a challenge. When two applications differ in their expectations, such as in the format of data files, the protocols used to communicate, or the programmatic API used to interact with the system, the implementation of collaboration between the heterogeneous systems becomes more and more complex. When many systems are involved, the task of making each interact with the others becomes an $O(n^2)$ problem.

Many solutions have been tried for the interaction of heterogeneous systems. Each provides some advantages and disadvantages. However, the implementation of collaboration is often intrusive to a particular application. That is, to make two applications in a distributed system collaborate with each other, modifications must be made to one or the other application so that they are compatible in terms of protocol, API, or file format. Mobile code may provide a solution to this problem as well.

Mobile code can enable the modifications required to make two applications compatible by moving code from application to application. For example, in the typical scenario of mobile objects, new objects may be added to an application at runtime as long as the mobile objects conform to a particular interface. The implementation of any object conforming to this interface may be added into the application. As a result, making two applications compatible may be a matter of including an appropriate mobile object in the application. For example, if the mobile object implements a destination to send the contents of the document in the application, incorporating an appropriate mobile object may enable the contents of the document to be saved in a different format to a different resource.

What's Next

♦ Now that we've caught a glimpse into the future of software, the rest of the book looks at how to implement it successfully using mobile objects and a software design technique called design patterns. Design patterns are proven methods for building quality software that takes into consideration many of the issues discussed in this book, such as flexibility, extensibility, and code reuse. The rest of the book examines each design pattern and ways it can be applied in the mobile object arena along with a practical example of the pattern implemented using Java and mobile objects.

12

Overview of
Design Patterns

I magine that instead of a software developer, you were a blacksmith fashioning a wagon. The blacksmith knows virtually nothing about the basic laws of physics, such as the laws of motion, the properties of the materials used in construction, or the fundamentals of mechanical engineering, yet for hundreds of years, blacksmiths successfully managed to build high-quality wagons.

The blacksmith doesn't start with a set of physical laws and finish with a wagon. Rather, the process of construction is one of reusing and recombining successful wagon design techniques or design patterns. For example, the wheel might be an example of a successful technique for making the vehicle move with minimal friction against the ground. The challenge of becoming a successful blacksmith is to expand the capabilities of the novice by learning many successful techniques. The trial-and-error method is one way to do this, but it is not easy and may take years or decades of potentially expensive failures before all the largest lessons in the field are learned.

A period of apprenticeship may be another way that the novice can learn many successful techniques by observing the master blacksmith at work and by attempting to use the techniques. However, these two methods aren't feasible for the world of software development. Software patterns were learned through experience. The software author would consider the design issues for years and only through the process of building, come to certain conclusions, learning what works and doesn't work. Learning how to design software by trial and error is costly and time consuming. The success of a multimillion-dollar, mission-critical software project cannot be risked for the education of a few young software developers. Finding a master in your field to do an apprenticeship with is not always an easy proposition in the new world of global computing. The master software architect may be located half a world away from you, and of course, a shortage of good software designers exists in the industry today. We can ill afford to have them occupy their time training apprentices. In addition, an apprenticeship could last for several years; not all professionals can afford to take that much time to learn a new technology.

What Are Design Patterns?

Design patterns provide the solution to the problem of learning to be a successful software developer. A design pattern is a concise definition of a technique that demonstrates some well-tried solution to a particular problem. Christopher Alexander, a professor of architecture at the University of California at Berkeley, first suggested that creating building architecture was a process of reusing successful design elements that he called design patterns. By reusing and recombining design patterns thousands of times, he could create new structural designs. His goal was to identify the patterns that worked and didn't work so that a novice architect could quickly learn the profession and a master architect could quickly develop new designs by reusing successful techniques over and over. Andrews proposed that these successful design patterns should be written clearly and concisely for the benefit of both novices and experts.

The effort to document successful software design patterns stems from this concept. The goal is to be able to give a primer to novice software designers and allow them to learn many of the most successful techniques of software design by reading about the patterns. Each design technique or pattern is the distilled result of the experiences of experts in the field. A novice could start building successful designs by reusing and combining the design patterns to create new designs and should achieve a high level of competence much more efficiently than a software designer who has not learned the lessons of the software design patterns.

Documenting all the successful patterns in the software industry is a large undertaking. Further, the success of patterns in software design has led practitioners in related fields to apply patterns in their own areas of specialty. The variety of fields that have adopted patterns is reflected in the variety of mailing lists that have been created, including the following:

♦ **Business Patterns.** This discussion list is dedicated to presenting and describing patterns of business processes. These patterns cover topics like product life cycles and development process management.

♦ **Organizational Patterns.** This list focuses on patterns of effectively organizing groups of people and structuring organizations. Organizational patterns describe how to build a team that maximizes the talents of each individual and the productivity of the entire group.

♦ **CORBA.** Patterns centering on the construction of distributed systems are described here. Many of these patterns describe techniques for scaling distributed systems and for avoiding performance bottlenecks. Much of this list is dedicated to discussion of the content of the *CORBA Design Patterns* book by Thomas Mowbray.

♦ **DACM.** DACM is an acronym for decoupling and complexity management. The list discusses techniques for effectively designing systems to maximize decoupling of the system components. Such systems tend to be much easier to manage as the complexity of the system increases. The application of the Gang-of-Four patterns to complexity management is a frequent topic of this mailing list.

♦ **IPC.** Inter Process Communication describes the broad class of technologies that enable diverse applications to communicate with each other. These technologies include other technologies like CORBA, so distributed objects are also frequently discussed on this mailing list.

♦ **PowerBuilder.** PowerBuilder is a popular development platform that uses object-oriented concepts to construct applications and user interfaces. This mailing list focuses on the discussion of patterns specific to the PowerBuilder development platform.

♦ **Antipatterns.** In addition to learning successful techniques, a software engineer learns techniques that don't work well. These are antipatterns, patterns that don't work and should be avoided. Many antipatterns are obvious. For example, the blacksmith building a wagon should see quickly that no fixed part of the wagon can be nailed to any of the wheels because they wouldn't be able to rotate. Others are subtle and are learned from long years of work. For example, don't build an extremely high-quality seat with a second-rate set of wheels. This pattern is subtle because it's the result of complex buying patterns of customers shopping for wagons. Such subtle antipatterns may be harder to justify concisely because they may be based not on an obvious logical argument, but on only years of experience with the entire process of car design. It's the challenge of the antipattern author to phrase them concisely.

Using Patterns

The process for using patterns is intended to be just as concise and straightforward as the patterns themselves. This set of easy-to-follow steps describes how to apply design patterns to a problem:

1. Identify a problem that must be addressed in the construction of an application.

2. Match the problem with the applicability section of each pattern to determine a set of candidate patterns that may apply to the problem.

3. Consider the consequences of using the pattern and decide whether it makes sense in this application.

4. Start the implementation of the pattern in your application.

5. Reuse the sample code if appropriate to simplify the task of building your own applications.

Combining these steps with design patterns enables even the novice developer to apply design patterns. These steps can be used with the design patterns discussed in this book as well with other software patterns.

Pattern Format

Patterns are described in a concise format, simplifying the task of learning each pattern. What follows is a list of the formats used for this book. This format has been roughly accepted as the standard format for design patterns throughout the software industry:

♦ **Name.** The patterns in this book demonstrate how mobile objects can be used effectively to create new patterns based on existing patterns. The name of the existing pattern is used, and a reference to the origin of the pattern is provided.

♦ **Intent.** The purpose of the Intent section is to concisely describe the problem addressed by this pattern and ways the problem should be solved. It gives a quick, clear view of the pattern's goal and the areas it addresses. The Intent section provides a useful abstract summary of each pattern.

♦ **Motivation.** Motivation describes a typical situation in which the pattern could be applied to solve the problem mentioned under Intent successfully. The Motivation section tells you why this pattern is important. It also discusses what role mobility plays in this pattern and why it is important. Each of the patterns in this book is oriented specifically to mobility. The benefits of mobility and the ways it impacts the pattern are discussed in this section, as are ways that mobile object software can benefit from this pattern.

♦ **Applicability.** The Applicability section enumerates the situations in which the pattern could be used. Unlike the Motivation section, Applicability goes into detail about example situations that would benefit from the pattern. It is the task of the designer to evaluate whether a specific situation calls for the use of the pattern.

N O T E : Patterns are not inherently good. Your application is not better if you include in it as many patterns as possible. In my experience, this is an antipattern that some pattern enthusiasts fail to learn. Use a pattern only when it helps. Whether the pattern is beneficial in a specific situation is often a judgment call, but the Applicability section should give you a good idea of the situations in which it might be useful.

♦ **Structure.** The Structure section contains a UML diagram that documents what objects are present in the pattern and how they relate to each other. Only a small, easy-to-comprehend subset of UML is used in this section. The elements of UML that we use are as follows:

◊ **Classes.** Classes are represented in a UML by a rectangle partitioned into three vertical parts, as shown in Figure 12.1. The name of the class is located in the top partition of the rectangle. The member variables of the class are located in the middle portion of the rectangle, and the operations are located

Programming Mobile Objects with Java

Class 1
data 1
op 1()   op 2()

Class 2
data 1   data 2
op 1()

Class 3

Figure 12.1 Rectangles are classes.

in the bottom portion of the rectangle. In some diagrams, the operations and variables are left out of the diagram when the complete implementation of the class is not specified.

◊ **Relationships.** Classes frequently participate in some kind of relationship with other classes. Three types of relationships are used in the diagrams: inheritance, association, and aggregation.

◊ **Inheritance.** The implementation of classes is naturally subject to the typical object-oriented relationships. When inheritance is a part of the object hierarchy, an arrow with a hollow head is used to represent that one class specializes another class, as shown in Figure 12.2. When two or more classes are derived from a common base class, the implementation may be shown as a class diagram. The class diagram is logically equivalent to two classes specializing individually from a single class. Specialization and derivation are just two different types of inheritance relationships identified by object-

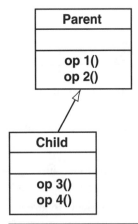

Figure 12.2 Arrow represents inheritance.

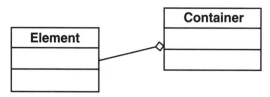

Figure 12.3 Line with diamond represents aggregation.

oriented designers. Both types of inheritance have the same implementation
in terms of the actual source code.

◊ **Aggregation.** An aggregation is a type of association in which one instance is
a member of another instance. Aggregation is a unidirectional relationship
between an object and a container for the object. Aggregation is depicted as
a line with a hollow diamond, as in Figure 12.3.

◊ **Association.** An association is a bidirectional relationship between two
objects that establishes some kind of relationship between them that is not
containment. For example, an application to perform matchmaking may
include an association between two Person objects. Association of two objects
is portrayed by a simple line connecting the two classes (see Figure 12.4).

◊ Multiplicity of the association may be useful in understanding the association between two different classes. In some cases, several instances of one
class may share access to a single instance of another class; for example,
a many-to-one relationship. In the case of the matchmaking association
between two applications, the association is presumably one-to-one, except
in a polygamous society. The manner in which elements combine with
each other is called the multiplicity of the relationship. The multiplicity is
documented simply by an indication of how many instances participate in
the relationship next to the class. In order to document the multiplicity of
the association, a number is placed next to the line for the association to

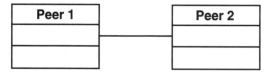

Figure 12.4 Line represents assocation.

indicate the multiplicity. Table 12.1 shows the symbols used to indicate multiplicity of an association.

◆ **Participants.** The Participants section lists each of the objects in the pattern with a short description. The description provides further information to elaborate on the object-oriented design shown in the Structure section.

◆ **Collaborations.** Each object in the pattern functions by interacting with a number of other objects. The Collaborations section documents the different relationships between the objects in the pattern. It also details any associations shown in the Structure.

◆ **Consequences.** A pattern may solve certain problems, but it also may have side effects, like slowing down the application. The Consequences section lists the pros and cons of using the pattern.

◆ **Implementation.** The Implementation section provides pointers on how to effectively build the pattern. Patterns in this book are software constructs for use in application development. Once the use of a pattern is specified, it must be coded as part of an application. This section gives pointers for effectively building the pattern. It also includes specifics on how to build the pattern correctly. Follow these specifics carefully to avoid compromising the pattern with detrimental flaws. Tips and suggestions are also provided to help guide you in less concrete ways toward building and using the pattern effectively.

◆ **Sample Code.** Each pattern has a sample running application that demonstrates how the pattern works when coded into software. The sample code in this section

Table 12.1 Multiplicity

Symbol	Association
1	One
0.1	Zero or one
0..∞	Zero or more
1..∞	One or more
4..16	Four to sixteen
2, 3, 5, 7	Two, three, five, or seven

also shows how the objects interact with each other and often move from application to application as part of the pattern.

♦ **Related Patterns.** Building one pattern may involve the use of another pattern. Sometimes different patterns may be alternatives to each other in the construction of a system. Some patterns are enhanced by the use of another pattern. The Related Patterns section lists those patterns that are used with, enhanced by, or replaced by the pattern.

Why Mobility?

The recent development of mobile object technology has created a rich foundation for the construction of new patterns. Object mobility offers a number of techniques in the construction of software that are not available through traditional technologies. Specifying these new approaches has been the goal of this book.

The design patterns examined in this book are established primarily to make it easier to develop software that successfully utilizes mobile objects. When writing software that incorporates mobile objects, follow these patterns because they may make implementing a successful design a bit easier.

Many of the patterns are derived from traditional design patterns, with new enhancements provided by the inclusion of mobile object technology. For example, the first design pattern examined is the traditional Model View Controller (MVC) architecture, perhaps the oldest design pattern in the software industry. However, with mobile objects, MVC achieves a whole new level of capability by dynamically sharing models, views, and controllers between multiple applications at runtime. Mobility is certainly not required to implement design patterns like MVC, but mobility does provide some powerful capabilities that would not be available otherwise.

The newness of mobile object technology prohibits us from basing the patterns in this book on the expertise of many practitioners over many years, but the author has observed the successful use of these patterns with mobile objects over the last two years. Each pattern is believed to represent a significant mobile object software development technique that greatly improves the construction of a mobile object system.

> **N OTE:** There are many points available for the Application, Implementation, and Consequences of each pattern. Don't be afraid to deviate from the mold once you are comfortable with the use of these patterns. If you do identify some particularly innovative new points, please pass them on to the author so that they may be included in future versions of this book!

What's Next

♦ The rest of this book is dedicated to laying out some design patterns for mobile objects. Many of these patterns have analogs in the traditional software development approach, but generalize these patterns to make some of the participants in the pattern distributed between multiple applications and to even implement some of the participants as mobile objects. We'll see the power of mobile objects demonstrated in each of these design patterns.

MVC [Krasner88]

Intent

Implement models, views, and controllers as mobile objects that can be replaced and extended at runtime.

Benefits of Mobility

By deploying your components as mobile objects, new components can be dynamically added or substituted at runtime. This means the application behavior (models), user interfaces (views), or even user interface handlers (controllers) can be modified in a running application without stopping or redeploying the application.

MVC is generally seen as a design time pattern for building effective designs that plan for migration of an application. However, with components implemented as mobile objects, components may be added to an application to add new components or replace existing components at runtime without redeploying the entire application.

The natural decoupling of the components under the MVC pattern lends naturally to making components modular, making such runtime manipulation of existing applications possible. In such a loosely coupled architecture, individual components don't depend closely on one another, so components can be exchanged without having to redevelop the entire application (see Figure 13.1). In any software development setting, this means it's easier to evolve the system by making changes to individual components without having to substantially redevelop the entire system.

Structure

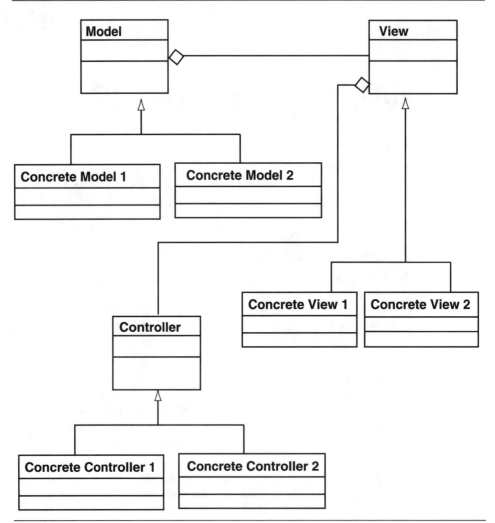

Figure 13.1 The structure of the Collaborative MVC Pattern.

Motivation

The original MVC pattern decouples application logic, application user interface, and user interface elements during the software development process. Decoupling enhances the extensibility of the application during future development cycles.

As a result, the original MVC pattern addresses only development time concerns. The models, views, and controllers are compiled into the application at compile time. No additional models, views, or controllers can be added without redeveloping the application.

The Collaborative MVC pattern enables applications to exchange models, views, and controllers at runtime as mobile objects, facilitating the runtime extensibility of the application without requiring redevelopment.

Applicability

The Collaborative MVC pattern is useful under the following conditions:

♦ Requirements for models, views, or controllers change frequently.

♦ Models will be extended or replaced in the future.

♦ User interface primitives will be enhanced in the future.

♦ Other developers must be enabled to extend models, views, or controllers in the application.

Participants

Model
Defines the interface for interchangeable application logic.

ConcreteModel1
An original implementation of the application logic.

ConcreteModel2
Defines an alternative implementation of the application logic.

View
Defines the interface for the user interfaces of common objects.

ConcreteView1
Defines an implementation for the user interface.

ConcreteView2
Defines an alternative user interface.

Controller
Defines the interface for elements that may be incorporated into the user interface.

ConcreteController1
Defines an implementation of a user interface element.

ConcreteController2
Defines an alternative user interface element that may extend or replace the original user interface element.

Application
Application based on MVC principles.

Supplier
Application that can supply MVCs as mobile objects.

Collaborations

Application interacts with Supplier through remote invocation to obtain new implementations of models, views, and controllers in the form of mobile objects. Views are observers of a Model. One Model can have many different types of Views, and different Views of the same Model are often interchangeable. Views are often implemented in terms of Controllers.

Consequences

Applications may be extended with flexible runtime additions or deletions of the set of models, views, or controllers. The implementation of MVCs as mobile objects has a powerful benefit. When a new MVC arrives at a destination application, the MVC may become part of the destination application. This implementation enables the extension of the application with the newly acquired mobile object. For example, a View mobile object may be presented with the user interface of the destination application. A Model object may become part of the application logic of the destination application. A new Controller could be used by the destination application to provide new types of behavior in the user interface.

Models, views, and controllers may be distributed with their data. New types of data are often sent back and forth between applications. Once a new data format has been received by an application, an appropriate Model capable of interpreting the data may be obtained. This Model may not be present in the application initially and might be provided with the data as a mobile object. Additional customized Views may also be distributed with the data, providing a customized user interface. Finally, an application that makes use of new Controllers can bundle them in with the data as a mobile object.

Implementation

Whether benefits are realized through the use of the MVC pattern is strongly dependent on how well it is implemented. A good design improves your ability to migrate your application. A poor design not only wastes your time but may make it more difficult to change the application later. The following points should be taken into consideration when implementing MVC with mobile objects:

◆ **Plan for extensibility.** Implementation of the Collaborative MVC pattern is highly dependent on the ability of application designers to plan for the extensibility of their models, views, and controls. For brevity, the term "component" refers to any programming entity that implements either a model, view, or controller. A successful design enables each to be extended without impacting the rest of the application. If the application itself must be significantly reworked in order to extend the behavior of a specific component, the goals of dynamic extensibility fail, and new components cannot be added at runtime. This same concern applies to the original MVC pattern, in which each component should be sufficiently decoupled from the others to allow for extensibility of components without reworking the entire application.

◆ **Hide behind interfaces.** Hiding the implementation of collaborative MVC behind an interface provides a convenient separation between the implementation and interface of MVC components. Each component implements the appropriate interface for the model, view, or controller for which it is providing an alternative implementation.

◆ **Build all models, views, and controllers as mobile objects.** The actual implementation of mobile models, views, or controls should not be significantly different from implementation under the MVC programming model. However, because they are mobile objects, they must be implemented according to the appropriate guidelines for developing mobile objects, depending on the mobile object tool that is used for the application. For example, if you are developing mobile objects with RMI, they must be serializable Java objects passed as parameters to method invocations.

Sample Code

The implementation of Model is shown as a public class:

```
public class Model
   extends java.util.Observable
   implements java.io.Serializable
{
};
```

The Model extends java.util.Observable and implements java.io.Serializable. Here the Observable event model in Java is used, although other event models might also be used to implement this same code. The Model is an Observable because Model represents a document that may be an event source. Model is Serializable in order to implement Model as a mobile object. As was already stated, as long as a Java object is Serializable, it can usually be treated as a mobile object with most mobile object tools. For this example, we are not using a specific tool, though. The code shown is compatible with RMI, Voyager, and Caffeine. Any implementations of Models extend this class.

The implementation of View is an interface. Any object that implements this interface is compatible with the MVC.

```
public interface View
   extends java.io.Serializable,
           java.util.Observer
{
};
```

The View implementation is designed to work with the Model. This View is a child of java.util.Observer, indicating that it is capable of receiving events from an Observable, such as Model. View is also Serializable in order to make it implement a mobile object. Concrete implementations of Views implement this interface to indicate that they are compatible Views.

The implementation of Controller is shown as an interface:

```
public interface Controller
   implements java.io.Serializable
{
};
```

The Controller is also a child of Serializable to implement a mobile object. Controller does not participate in the Observer/Observable relationship between Model and View, so it doesn't need to implement either of these. Concrete implementations of Controllers extend this class.

The following is an example of a concrete implementation of a Model. A simple bank account is used as the subject for this example. The generic Account class for this example is shown in Listing 13.1 The Model represents the application logic for a savings account, represented by the SavingsAccount class shown in Listing 13.2.

```
public abstract class Account
   extends Model
{
   public abstract double getBalance();
   public abstract void setBalance(double d);
   public abstract void compound();
};
```

Listing 13.1 Account class.

```
public class SavingsAccount
   extends Account
{
   public double balance = 0.;
```

Continues

```
public double getBalance()
{
    return balance;
}

public void setBalance(double d)
{
    balance = d;
}

public void compound()
{
    balance *= 1.02;
}
};
```

Listing 13.2 Source for SavingsAccount.

The model is implemented with an intermediate abstract class. This abstract class provides a convenient abstraction that other accounts can specialize. Implementing a common base class also enables the implementation of Views to provide a view into any implementation of the abstract class without the developer having to know specific details about each implementation—another benefit that provides greater extensibility at very little cost.

The AccountView class implements a View for the Account object, which can be reused to provide a user interface for the Account in any appropriate context. The implementation is shown in Listing 13.3.

```
import java.awt.*;
import java.awt.event.*;

public class AccountView
    implements View
{
    Account account1;
```

```
Panel p = new Panel();
Label label1 = new Label(Account");
TextField textField1 = new TextField("0.00");
Button button1 = new Button("Calc Interest & Fees");

GridLayout layout1 = new GridLayout(3,1);

public AccountView(Account a)
{
  account1 = a;

  try {
    jbInit();
  }
  catch (Exception e) {
    e.printStackTrace();
  }
}

public void jbInit() throws Exception{
  label1.setText("Account");
  p.setLayout(layout1);
  p.add(label1);
  p.add(textField1);
  textField1.addTextListener(new AccountView_textField1_textAdapter(this));
  p.add(button1);
  button1.setLabel("Calc Interest & Fees");
  button1.addActionListener(new AccountView_button1_actionAdapter(this));

}

public void update( java.util.Observable o,
                    Object arg )
{
  p.repaint();
}
```

Continues

```java
public void textField1_textValueChanged( TextEvent e )
{
    // Request that the document change the balance.

    // Looks like the behavior of the AWT changed slightly.
    // This no longer works.
    //     double d = Double.valueOf( e.toString() ).doubleValue();

    if (e.getSource() instanceof TextField)
      {
        TextField tf = (TextField)e.getSource();

        double d = Double.valueOf( tf.getText() ).doubleValue();

        account1.setBalance(d);

      }
}

public void button1_actionPerformed( ActionEvent e )
{
    // Request that the document perform the calculation.

    account1.compound();
    textField1.setText( new Double( account1.getBalance() ).toString() );

    p.repaint();

}

};

class AccountView_textField1_textAdapter implements java.awt.event.TextListener
{
```

```
  AccountView adaptee;

  AccountView_textField1_textAdapter(AccountView adaptee) {
    this.adaptee = adaptee;
  }

  public void textValueChanged(TextEvent e)
  {
    System.err.println("event");
    adaptee.textField1_textValueChanged(e);
  }

}


class AccountView_button1_actionAdapter implements java.awt.event.ActionListener
{
  AccountView adaptee;

  AccountView_button1_actionAdapter(AccountView adaptee) {
    this.adaptee = adaptee;
  }

  public void actionPerformed(ActionEvent e)
  {
    System.err.println("action");

    adaptee.button1_actionPerformed(e);
  }
}
```

Listing 13.3 Source for AccountView and adapter classes.

Much of this is just AWT code to provide the graphical user interface portion of the view. The actual task of this code is just to paint the user interface. The only code relevant to this design pattern is that it implements View and paints a user interface appropriate for interacting with the Account. Note that the Account abstract class rather than the more specialized SavingsAccount is used. As mentioned earlier, using Account enables the substitution of any implementation of the Account object.

Many developers employ the MVC pattern without worrying too much about Controllers for at least two reasons. First, the benefits of the Model-View abstraction are much more clear-cut for many developers. Second, many component frameworks provided by IDEs, like JBuilder, supply plenty of Controllers, so the developer doesn't need to worry about implementing and reusing additional controllers. In fact, the implementation of the AWT classes could easily qualify as a set of prewritten controllers.

A concrete implementation of a controller for validating user input is provided by the MinBalance class, shown in Listing 13.4:

```
public abstract class InputValidator
  implements Controller
{
  public abstract void verifyInput(String s)
    throws InvalidInput;
};


public class MinBalance
  extends InputValidator
{
  public void verifyInput(String s)
    throws InsufficientMinBalance
  {
    double d = Double.valueOf(s).doubleValue();
    if (d < 0.)
      throw new InsufficientMinBalance(d);
  }
};
```

Listing 13.4 Source for MinBalance.

In this example, an abstract class called InputValidator is defined for checking any user input. The InputValidator implements Controller, and Controller extends java.io.Serializable. As a result, the MinBalance controller can be treated as a mobile object.

The AccountView makes use of this controller for reading input from the user. In the implementation of AccountView shown earlier, an instance of MinBalance is utilized to verify the amount of the balance. The MinBalance implementation of the InputValidator simply ensures that the SavingsAccount balance is not set to a negative number. An InsufficientMinBalance exception is raised if the validation fails. Note that the use of an instance of MinBalance in the AccountView is probably not the best design for this application. A better design could utilize a Chain of Responsibility of InputValidators, leaving open the possibility of easily adding new types of InputValidators to address changing requirements of the application.

These objects implement the initial models, views, and controllers for this problem. At this point, a Supplier, which acts as the source for these MVCs, is required. The Account Supplier shown in Listing 13.5 is an example of such a Supplier. AccountSupplier is an RMI server, but with fairly minor changes, it could be adapted to work with Caffeine or Voyager.

```java
import java.rmi.*;
import java.rmi.server.*;

public class AccountSupplier
  extends UnicastRemoteObject
  implements Supplier
{
  public static void main(String args[])
  {
    System.setSecurityManager(new RMISecurityManager());

    try
      {
        Supplier o = new AccountSupplier();
        Naming.rebind("AccountSupplier",o);
      }
    catch (Exception e)
      {
        System.err.println("AccountSupplier: " + e);
        e.printStackTrace();
      }
```

Continues

```
        }

    public AccountSupplier()
        throws java.rmi.RemoteException
    {
    }

    public Model getModel(String s)
        throws java.rmi.RemoteException
    {
        if (s.equals("SavingsAccount"))
            return new SavingsAccount();
        else if (s.equals("CheckingAccount"))
            return new CheckingAccount();

        return null;
    }

    public View getView(Model m, String s)
        throws java.rmi.RemoteException
    {
        // This Supplier simplistically ignores the String parameter.

        return new AccountView( (Account) m );
    }
}
```

Listing 13.5 Source for AccountSupplier.

This example implementation of AccountSupplier is somewhat contrived because the methods are called simply getModel and getView. In a more carefully architected distributed system, the Supplier should fit seamlessly into the object model. Deriving from a simplistic Supplier interface, like the one shown in this example, is definitely not necessary. This Supplier just fills the role of acting as a source for Models and Views in a simple distributed system.

The preceding example is now fully specified and ready to run in your favorite Java development environment. Try it out and verify that it works properly in its current incarnation.

What is the benefit of doing all this with mobile objects? Suppose the objects in the example were deployed in an application, implementing a SavingsAccount application. The users might happily use this application for several minutes before realizing that they also needed to support CheckingAccounts, which use business logic different from that for the SavingsAccounts already supported by the application.

Fortunately, when the Model is implemented as a mobile object, the Model for this application can be reconfigured at runtime with a new implementation of Account called CheckingAccount. The source for this is shown in Listing 13.6.

```java
public class CheckingAccount
  extends Account
{
  public double balance = 0.;

  public CheckingAccount()
  {
  }

  public double getBalance()
  {
    return balance;
  }

  public void setBalance(double d)
  {
    balance = d;
  }

  public void compound()
```

Continues

```
    {
      balance -= 15.;
    }
};
```

Listing 13.6 Source for CheckingAccount.

This implementation is still compatible with Account but provides the logic required for a bank checking account rather than a savings account. The most important difference is that rather than awarding interest to the account holder, the bank applies a $15 fee to the account. This model can now be substituted for the original SavingsAccount model with little impact on the rest of the distributed system. This is exactly the benefit of this pattern: A new model can be substituted with very little change to the rest of the system. Alternatively, a new View or Controller might also have been provided with little impact on the system. Exploring the changes required to implement this is left as an exercise for the reader.

Related Patterns

The Gang-of-Four's Observer pattern is often used to inform Views of events on Documents. The Document is the Observable, and one or more Views are the Observers. Modifications to the document provide one example of an event relevant to all Views.

Remote Proxy [GoF95]

Remote Proxy is also called Remote ProxyStub, Remote Reference, and Remote Object.

Intent

Encapsulate the location of a target object inside a mobile object that delegates to the target object, enabling location and implementation transparency at runtime when the mobile object is dynamically loaded into a new address space.

Motivation

Accessing remote objects requires a local reference to the remote object. The reference is most conveniently represented as a proxy to the remote object. For convenience, the proxy may implement the same interface as the original object.

Benefits of Mobility

Remote Proxy is a mainstay of distributed computing, but significant benefits are gained by examining it in the new light of mobile objects. Remote Proxies in historical distributed computing technologies are compiled into an application and provide little more than a transparent reference to an object located in a remote application.

By implementing a Remote Proxy as a mobile object, the implementation of the Remote Proxy may be exchanged at runtime for other implementations. In particular, this means that Remote Proxies developed for different technologies can be dynamically swapped, RMI exchanged for CORBA exchanged for Voyager ad infinitum. Since most of these tools focus on providing convenient transparency to the developer using the Remote Proxy, little work is required on the part of the developer to substitute Remote Proxies from differing technologies.

The benefits don't end with adapting different distributed technologies to one another. The Remote Proxy may include any type of implementation code. Once a request is delivered to the Remote Proxy, it may do virtually anything with it, including dynamic activation, database manipulation, or secure access. The request could be multicast, archived, queued, or authenticated. With a mobile object implementation of Remote Proxy, any of these capabilities may be added to the Remote Proxy at runtime by adding the appropriate mobile objects.

Applicability

Use the Remote Proxy pattern as follows:

♦ To dynamically load new remote object references at runtime.

♦ To encapsulate the implementation details of accessing a remote object.

♦ To implement object migration.

♦ To integrate several ORB technologies with each other.

♦ When one of several possible implementation objects are used at runtime.

Structure

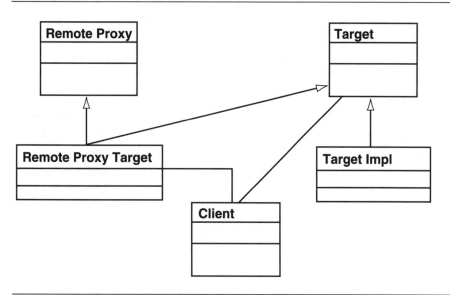

Figure 14.1 The structure of the Remote Proxy Pattern.

Participants

RemoteProxy.
A mobile object for remotely invoking a distributed resource transparently located someplace else on the network.

Target.
Specification of an interface for an object that responds to network requests.

TargetImpl.
An implementation of the Target interface.

RemoteProxyTarget.
An implementation of RemoteProxy that supports both the RemoteProxy and Target interfaces.

Client.
An application that uses a RemoteProxy to invoke a Target.

Collaborations

The Client makes all invocations using an object reference to an object implementing the Target interface. However, this implementation is not the TargetImpl. The object implementing the Target interface on the Client side is actually an instance of RemoteProxyTarget, which is a mobile object. As a mobile object, RemoteProxyTarget may be dynamically loaded by other computers. RemoteProxyTarget is implemented in terms of delegating to a remote object reference conforming to the Target interface to a TargetImpl, which may reside on yet another host. The implementation details of RemoteProxyTarget are fully encapsulated, so this implementation may be varied at runtime by substitution of other remote object references conforming to the Target interface or by the dynamic loading of other mobile object implementations of RemoteProxyTarget.

Consequences

Invoking Target in the Client is as convenient as invoking a local object. RemoteProxy may fully encapsulate the way Target is invoked remotely across the network. From a software development standpoint, this encapsulation means that the developer doesn't have to be aware of distribution details like network errors. These may be handled within the RemoteProxy or propagated in some other form.

RemoteProxy may be redirected between different implementations. The internal implementation of Client may change because it is encapsulated. An example of such a change might be to redirect the RemoteProxy toward a different Target or replace the distribution mechanism with some alternative mechanism by, for example, dynamically switching RMI for CORBA.

Implementations of the RemoteProxyTarget may be changed at runtime by the loading of the RemoteProxyTarget as a mobile object. This action enables the implementation to dynamically change between different sessions and may be useful when many different RemoteProxies are available with different implementations. These implementations can be substituted for each other by the dynamic loading of the desired implementation as a mobile object. An example of such an implementation

change might be the substitution of an RMI Remote Proxy for a
CORBA RemoteProxy, changing the protocol used on the back end of
RemoteProxyTarget. This substitution is similar to that of the RMI and
CORBA RemoteProxy mentioned earlier.

Remote Proxies can be used as forwarders. A RemoteProxy acts to
remotely access an object located someplace else on the network. The
implementation of RemoteProxyTarget enables it to delegate requests to
the new location of TargetImpl when that object migrates to a new location. If TargetImpl moves to a new location, a RemoteProxyTarget may
be left in the old location to redirect invocations to the new destination.

Implementation

The Remote Proxy pattern is already implemented by all mobile object
tools. Each tool makes its own form of remote object reference available
for use by the software developer. These remote object references follow the
Remote Proxy pattern. However, the implementations often have serious
drawbacks, including the inability of the target object to change location at
runtime, lack of location transparency, and lack of dynamic download into
the destination application. When considering the use of the Remote Proxy
pattern, decide whether the implementation of Remote Proxy supplied by
your tool of choice is sufficient or if it must be reimplemented to achieve
the desired goals. If you decide to implement Remote Proxy on your own,
consider the following issues:

♦ **Reuse. Reuse. Reuse.** Use tool-provided Remote Proxy to implement
your own, more powerful Remote Proxy. A simple way of achieving this
is to have a member variable of the type of the tool-provided Remote
Proxy that acts as a delegation target when appropriate. Doing so saves
you all the work of implementing your own ORB to handle the distribution of invocations.

♦ **Build the Remote Proxy as a mobile object.** Making RemoteProxy a
mobile object enables you to distribute instances of RemoteProxies
between distributed applications at runtime. This feature is very useful in
a dynamic system. It enables a new implementation of a RemoteProxy to
be passed into a new or different distributed application.

♦ **Don't forget: Target may be mobile, also.** In a robust system, Target may also be a mobile object. Target can be an important piece of application logic or user interface that changes locations from time to time. In this case, Target moves to a new location, leaving some Remote Proxies with invalid information about the location of Target.

♦ **Support redirection to the new location of Target.** Redirection, or forwarding requests to the new location of an object, is a very easy feature to implement with RemoteProxy. When a Target moves to a new location, rather than replacing the implementation with a null object reference and causing all references to this object to become invalid, replace it with a RemoteProxy pointing to the new location of Target. If any requests come in from other locations, the invocations can be forwarded to the new location without requiring the developer to create an exception.

Sample Code

The following code demonstrates a sample implementation of RemoteProxy that dynamically redirects requests between two different servers implemented with RMI and CORBA. The sample server for this example is a simple "Hello, World!" application. However, an operation called "transmogrify" is added to this simple server to redirect the server to a new location. The Target interface is shown in Listing 14.1.

```
/**
 * Definition of the RMI interface for Target.
 * This particular Target does something fairly trivial,
 * it just prints the Hello, World message.
 */
public interface Target
{
  public void sayHello();
  public void transmogrify();
};
```

Listing 14.1 Source for Target.

One or more implementations of Target may be available in any given system, but for this example, only one is present. The implementation of Target, called TargetImpl, is shown in Listing 14.2.

```
/**
 * TargetImpl
 *
 * An implementation of a distributed server.
 */

public class TargetImpl
  implements Target
{
  public TargetImpl()
  {
  }

  public void sayHello()
  {
    System.println("Hello, World!");
  }

  public void transmogrify()
  {
    System.println("I'm becoming something else!");
  }

};
```

Listing 14.2 Source for TargetImpl.

The implementation of RemoteProxy encapsulates the details for invoking any Target. One or more implementations of such a RemoteProxy may be present in any distributed system. The RemoteProxy interface acts as the common interface for all references, as follows:

```
/**
 * RemoteProxy can be treated as a mobile object!
```

Continues

```
    */
public interface RemoteProxy
   extends java.io.Serializable
{
};
```

An implementation of RemoteProxyTarget must be provided to support both the RemoteProxy and Target interfaces, as shown in Listing 14.2. By implementing the Target interface, RemoteProxyTarget can be cast to a Target interface. This casting enables RemoteProxyTarget to look and feel just like Target to Client. In the resulting transparency, the Client may invoke RemoteProxyTarget just as if it were an implementation of Target in the local address space. In fact, TargetImpl may reside on some other computer. RemoteProxyTarget entirely encapsulates the implementation details of the remote invocation of TargetImpl. With the full encapsulation of these implementation details, several interchangeable implementations are provided (in Listing 14.3). Two different implementations for CORBA and RMI are as follows:

```
/**
   * RemoteProxyTargetCORBA
   *
   * Pass through stub that can be redirected to RMI on demand.
   */

public class RemoteProxyTargetCORBA
   implements RemoteProxy,
              Target
{
   private Target delegate;

   public RemoteProxyTargetCORBA(Target p)
   {
     delegate = p;
   }

   public void sayHello()
   {
```

```
    delegate.sayHello();
  }

  public void transmogrify()
  {
    delegate.transmogrify();

    MyNaming naming = MyNamingLocator.resolve("Naming");
    Target t = (Target)naming.lookup("TargetRMI");
  }
};
```

Listing 14.3 Source for RemoteProxyTargetCORBA.

The implementation of the RemoteProxy for RMI is shown in Listing 14.4.

```
/**
  * RemoteProxyTargetRMI
  *
  * Pass through stub that can be redirected to CORBA on demand.
  */
public class RemoteProxyTargetRMI
  implements RemoteProxy,
            Target
{
  private Target delegate;

  public RemoteProxyTargetRMI(Target p)
  {
    delegate = p;
  }

  public void sayHello()
  {
    delegate.sayHello();
  }
```

Continues

```
public void transmogrify()
{
  delegate.transmogrify();

  MyNaming naming = MyNamingLocator.resolve("Naming");
  Target t = (Target)naming.lookup("TargetCORBA");
}
};
```

Listing 14.4 Source for RemoteProxyTargetRMI.

The implementation of both RemoteProxies includes code in the implementation of transmogrify to redirect the delegate to another reference. Implementing this redirection switches the reference back and forth between RMI and CORBA.

The sample client executes the following code:

```
Target t;
t.sayHello();
t.transmogrify();
t.sayHello();
```

In this case, the implementation of transmogrify causes the invocation to be redirected back and forth between RMI and CORBA servers. This implementation means the first invocation of sayHello occurs on one server implemented with CORBA, for example. The RemoteProxy is then redirected to a different server through the transmogrify call. Then the second invocation of sayHello occurs on the second server implemented with RMI.

Related Patterns

Remote Proxy is a specific type of the more general Proxy pattern defined by the Gang-of-Four.

Smart Proxy [Meszaros94]

Another name for Smart Proxy is Half Object.

Intent

Extend Remote Proxies to perform caching, load balancing, and local request processing in order to optimize the efficient use of system resources.

Motivation

Remote Proxies, discussed in the previous chapter, place a burden on system resources to communicate method invocations to their Target object. Under certain circumstances, more intelligent handling of invocations may be appropriate. Caching algorithms can improve the performance of the Remote Proxy by repeating known answers without hitting the network. Smart Proxies may also perform load balancing to prevent individual servers from becoming overloaded. Smart Proxies may also provide a partial implementation of the remote object. Satisfaction of some requests locally may be able to move some of the processing from the server to the client.

The Smart Proxy pattern described elsewhere, without the impact of mobile objects, is limited because the Smart Proxy must be embedded statistically in the deploy application. With the use of mobile objects, Smart Proxy becomes dynamically loadable and dynamically

Benefits of Mobility

Smart Proxy implemented without mobility provides a powerful tool for caching, performance optimization, and load balancing. However, the implementation of these must be specified at compile time.

By implementing Smart Proxy, and its weaker sibling Remote Proxy, with mobile objects different implementations of each can be exchanged dynamically at runtime. One particular benefit is that since Smart Proxy and Remote Proxy are compatible with each other, Remote Proxies may be upgraded dynamically with Smart Proxies at runtime. For Smart Proxy, this means that the implementation of the Smart Proxy can change at runtime to take into account runtime information, enabling runtime optimizations not possible in the old approach. Protocol optimization and caching algorithms are two examples of optimization techniques that may benefit from runtime information. Protocol optimization involves the trimming of a protocol based on specific usage patterns or analysis of the content of the protocol. Caching algorithms may include implementation in the Smart Proxy based on past usage patterns of the Smart Proxy. For example, initial requests may initiate a specific application process, enabling the Smart Proxy to incorporate optimizations appropriate for this specific application process.

reconfigurable at runtime. When a better implementation of SmartProxy becomes available, a Client may dynamically load the new implementation at runtime. The best Smart Proxy from a choice of alternatives may be used for a particular situation. Since the mobile form of SmartProxy and RemoteProxy implement the same interface, a SmartProxy may act as an upgrade, replacing an inefficient RemoteProxy.

Applicability

Smart Proxy is most useful in the following situations:

♦ Remote Proxy is inadequate for the system.

♦ System resources are limited.

♦ Bottlenecking is occurring on the server.

♦ Some tasks can be decoupled and moved to the client side with little effort.

♦ Custom load balancing or fault tolerance is desirable.

♦ The system is optimized in one of several possible ways.

Structure

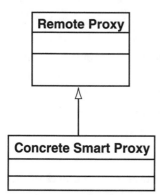

Figure 15.1 The structure of the Smart Proxy Pattern.

Participants

RemoteProxy.
The interface specifying the common behavior of all remote object references.

ConcreteSmartProxy.
An implementation of an object reference that includes additional intelligence and doesn't simply pass through all requests to a remote object.

Collaborations

ConcreteSmartProxy implements RemoteProxy.

Consequences

Smart Proxy enables the invocation of a remote object to occur in a much more efficient manner than with a Remote Proxy. The invocation may be satisfied locally rather than through the communication with a remote object. Any time the use of the network can be avoided, a substantial increase in application speed is noticeable.

By moving portions of an object to the client side to perform evaluations locally, Smart Proxy consumes those CPU resources on the client side rather than the server side. This may not be desirable for large computations that are more efficiently performed on the server because of hardware issues or other concerns. An example of such computations that are not easily moved to the client include computations on large data sets that reside on the computer, vector or parallel computations that make use of special hardware on the server, and computations using algorithms that are complex enough that moving the implementation of the computation to the server would be less efficient than simply executing the computation.

Smart Proxy may move some of the implementation of an object to the client side. This is undesirable in situations in which the implementation of the object changes rapidly at runtime. Avoid using Smart Proxy in such situations.

Implementation

Smart Proxies must be designed by hand by a developer looking at the specific Target and creating a suitable Smart Proxy. The implementation of Smart Proxy involves the following issues:

♦ **Start with a Remote Proxy.** A Remote Proxy can roughly be equated with a trivial Smart Proxy that performs no optimization or custom logic. A RemoteProxy passes all requests to a remote object. A SmartProxy may also pass most requests to a remote object, but a SmartProxy also performs some additional logic on some requests to accomplish optimization, load balancing, or fault tolerance.

♦ **Look for methods that can be executed on the client side.** A SmartProxy executes on the client side of a distributed system. Many benchmarks on distributed systems have demonstrated that local invocations are much faster than remote invocations because of the cost of network overhead. Take advantage of the speed increase that can be achieved by moving methods to the client side where possible. Static methods are often good candidates.

♦ **Replace RemoteProxy implementations with SmartProxy implementations using mobile objects.** RemoteProxy and SmartProxy implementations implement the same interfaces and are interchangeable as objects. If you develop both sets as mobile objects, you can dynamically exchange one for another at runtime to provide clients or servers with the most efficient implementation as determined at runtime.

Sample Code

The following sample code, see Listing 15.1, implements an example of a SmartProxy that performs load balancing, which is a technique for distributing tasks between multiple computers in such a way that no single computer becomes overloaded. When the tasks are divided up efficiently in this manner, all of them can be performed in a reasonably efficient manner. Bottlenecking is the opposite of load balancing. When a bottleneck occurs, one computer is performing so many tasks that the entire system is slowed down.

```
/*
 * Copyright (c) 1998 Trusted Consulting, Inc. All rights reserved.
 *
 * This software is FREE FOR COMMERCIAL AND NON-COMMERCIAL USE,
 * provided the following condition is met.
 *
 * Permission to use, copy, modify, and distribute this software and
 * its documentation for any purpose and without fee is hereby granted,
 * provided that any copy or derivative of this software or documentation
 * retaining the following disclaimer.
 *
```
Continues

```
* THIS SOFTWARE IS PROVIDED "AS IS" AND ANY EXPRESS OR IMPLIED
* WARRANTIES, INCLUDING, BUT NOT LIMITED TO, THE IMPLIED WARRANTIES OF
* MERCHANTABILITY AND FITNESS FOR A PARTICULAR PURPOSE ARE DISCLAIMED.
* IN NO EVENT SHALL THE AUTHOR OR CONTRIBUTORS BE LIABLE FOR ANY DIRECT,
* INDIRECT, INCIDENTAL, SPECIAL, EXEMPLARY, OR CONSEQUENTIAL DAMAGES
* (INCLUDING, BUT NOT LIMITED TO, PROCUREMENT OF SUBSTITUTE GOODS OR
* SERVICES; LOSS OF USE, DATA, OR PROFITS; OR BUSINESS INTERRUPTION)
* HOWEVER CAUSED AND ON ANY THEORY OF LIABILITY, WHETHER IN CONTRACT,
* STRICT LIABILITY, OR TORT (INCLUDING NEGLIGENCE OR OTHERWISE) ARISING
* IN ANY WAY OUT OF THE USE OF THIS SOFTWARE, EVEN IF ADVISED OF THE
* POSSIBILITY OF SUCH DAMAGE.
*/


/**
 * RemoteProxyTargetBalancer
 *
 * Pass through stub that can be redirected to RMI on demand.
 */

public class SmartProxyTargetBalancer
   implements RemoteProxy,
             Target
{

  private int bestDelegate;
  private RemoteProxy[] delegates;

  public SmartProxyTargetBalancer(RemoteProxy[] p)
  {
    delegates = p;
  }

  private void reevaluateBestDelegate()
  {
    // Round robin
```

```
      bestDelegate = -1 * bestDelegate + 1;
   }



   public void sayHello()
   {
      Target t = (Target)(delegates[bestDelegate]);

      t.sayHello();

      reevaluateBestDelegate();
   }

   public void transmogrify()
   {
      Target t = (Target)(delegates[bestDelegate]);

      t.transmogrify();

      reevaluateBestDelegate();
   }
};
```

Listing 15.1 Source for SmartProxyTargetBalancer.

Distributed objects rarely use load balancing because an object reference points to a specific instance of an implementation object located someplace on the network. Any requests made on that object reference always go the specific target object. If one object receives far more requests than other objects, a bottleneck may result.

This example load balancer performs a round-robin iteration through several available servers, spreading requests evenly among them. A more advanced load balancer could also be implemented. Load balancing through a round-robin invocation is not necessarily the guaranteed best load balancing policy. Often some tasks are easy and take only a second while other tasks are hard and take several minutes. In such a situation, servers performing the harder tasks may become overloaded when they receive just as many tasks as the servers processing the easier tasks. A more efficient policy might be to monitor variables such as the load of each server, the expected time to completion of already assigned tasks, and the size of new tasks. However, round-robin load balancing suffices for this simple example.

Related Patterns

Smart Proxy is a further specialization of Remote Proxy. Smart Proxies are effectively just RemoteProxies with added intelligence to perform different tasks when a distributed invocation is made.

The Gang-of-Four Strategy pattern may be useful in encapsulating the algorithms used to perform caching, load balancing, and other optimizations. However, Strategy is not always necessary and may just clutter up the code. Be careful not to overengineer your code if Strategy is not necessary.

Actor [GoF95]

Intent

Encapsulate a thread within a mobile object and move this thread with the object in order to enable the object to react to its environment without depending on other threads.

Benefits of Mobility

Multithreading is always very challenging to do correctly because of the complex issues of thread synchronization and concurrent access to resources. However, the benefits of multithreading are well understood and highly valued.

The situation may be even worse with mobile objects, because Java, like many other languages, doesn't provide a way to externalize thread state. Actors provide a natural encapsulation for threads inside of objects that prevents threads from accessing resources external to the object.

Actors provide perhaps the most effective way of integrating mobile objects with multithreading. Actors encapsulate the thread state inside the mobile object and make the externalization of the thread state explicit. With Actor, threads may be integrated inside mobile objects transparently to the applications hosting the mobile object.

Motivation

Threads are common programming constructs that enable applications to perform several operations at once. The application of threads is difficult, requiring precise code to prevent application logic errors that can result in improper results, malfunction, or deadlock of the application.

Thread behavior is difficult to control, and the state of an executing thread may be poorly defined. Many threads may access a variety of resources. The state of the thread may not even be defined well enough to make this externalization possible.

Threads are often provided for nothing more than to make up for a missing event model. A thread continuously monitors the status of a particular resource, performing a proper set of events when a change of state or other event occurs on the resources even though the resource itself is not a formal event source. In this case, the thread is acting as a stopgap solution to what may have been an original design flaw.

Threads also can be used to update a particular object without blocking the rest of an application. The operation that is performed may be as simple as recalculating a portion of a document or as complex as continuously performing background tasks derived from a queue of tasks created by the encapsulating object.

Under either of these conditions, a natural approach is to consider the thread as owned by a single object. In the case of the document that is changing, the thread might be owned by the document. In the case of the simulated event model, the thread could be owned by an event model Adapter responsible for monitoring the state of an object and throwing events when appropriate.

Applicability

Actor might come in handy under the following conditions:

♦ Implementing an event model when one is missing.

♦ Encapsulating threads.

♦ when externalization of threads is required.

Structure

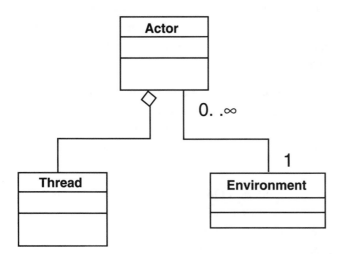

Figure 16.1 The structure of the Actor Pattern.

Participants

Actor.
An implementation of an object that encapsulates a thread.

Thread.
An object representing a runnable thread; for example, the
java.lang.Thread object.

Environment.
An abstraction for anything that the Actor might interact with or know
about.

Collaborations

Actor creates the Thread object. The flow of control of the new thread
never leaves the Actor object, and the Thread itself should be encapsulated.

Actor performs code that responds to Environment.

Consequences

Serializing an Actor requires the serialization of the state of the thread. This must be performed through use of handwritten Java externalization code, placing the burden back on the software developer to implement object serialization by hand.

Thread is entirely decoupled from Environment. Actor controls access to Environment and encapsulates access to Thread, enabling Actor to prevent extrinsic state about Thread in Environment. Any extrinsic state for Thread would make thread migration to remote hosts impossible to implement.

Actor is inefficient compared with Observer. In some cases, Actor is used to monitor a resource for changes and to update related resources. Actor periodically checks the resources for changes in state that requires some action on other objects. Spawning a great many threads to periodically poll resources like this consumes thread resources, and it wastes CPU each time an unnecessary poll occurs on the subject. Sometimes, utilizing Actor to replace an Observer can't be avoided, such as when the Subject is designed by a third party. When possible, Observer should be used to avoid wasting thread and CPU resources.

Implementation

Implementing Actor is usually a matter of building an object with an encapsulated thread. Implementing Actor with mobile objects is only slightly more complex than implementing the Actor pattern without mobile objects. The following implementation issues occur when the Actor pattern is used:

♦ **Actor should fully encapsulate Thread.** Violating the encapsulation of Thread inside Actor may enable other objects to reference Thread externally. As a result, when Actor is communicated as a mobile object to another location, all the extrinsic state of Thread may not be fully encapsulated. Thus, the full state of the thread may not be communicated when the Actor is serialized. Java doesn't provide any other mechanism for locating and serializing this extrinsic state.

♦ **Thread thrashing may result if too many Actors are created.** Each Actor contains a Thread. Threads consume a great deal of system resources. In most JVMs, Java threads map directly to operating system threads. Furthermore, some operating systems may have severe limitations on the number of threads that may be created by a single application or by all the currently running applications. Therefore, you don't want to create hundreds or thousands of Actor objects unless you devise a way to ensure that most or all of the Actors and their encapsulating threads are inactive the vast majority of the time.

♦ **Actor may contain more than one Thread.** Some problems are not easily solved with only one Thread. For example, an Actor responsible for updating several entities simultaneously may be best designed with a corresponding number of threads. You don't have to restrict all Actors to a single Thread.

♦ **Synchronization is still required inside the Actor.** Any resources that are not encapsulated within Actor could be accessed by both the Actor and other objects in the Java application. Synchronization controls must be used to protect these resources from error due to simultaneous access by different threads, such as race conditions and unpredictable behavior of calculations. In addition, resources that are encapsulated within an Actor could be accessed by multiple threads under certain circumstances. If an Actor contains multiple Threads, the Actor's own Threads might cause synchronization problems unless adequate steps are taken to prevent this. Also, Actor is often a Java object in its own right and can be invoked from other objects in the application. Outside threads could concurrently access encapsulated resources.

Sample Code

We've already looked at one example of the Actor pattern. BatteryAd from Chapter 2 is an implementation of the Actor pattern. Let's take a second look at that example.

The problem for BatteryAd was to implement an object that periodically printed out a message. The object should print, "It keeps going," pause briefly, and print " ... and going." Then it should repeat the last two steps indefinitely. A good way to attack this problem is to create a thread that loops indefinitely, printing out this message. In the BatteryAd example, this thread is called the BunnyThread, shown in Listing 16.1.

```java
import java.io.*;

public class BunnyThread
  extends Thread
  implements java.io.Externalizable
{
  public String message = "and going";   // Count number of "going" messages
  public BunnyThread() {}
  public BunnyThread(String m)
  {
    message = m;
    System.err.println( "It keeps going" );
  }

  public int counter = 1;
  public void run()
  {
    while( true )      // aka. forever()
      {
        System.err.println( message + " [" + counter + "]");
        counter++;
      }
  }

  public void writeExternal(ObjectOutput o)
    throws java.io.IOException
  {
    this.suspend();
    o.writeInt(this.counter);
    o.writeUTF(this.message);
    o.writeUTF(this.getName());
    o.writeInt(this.getPriority());
```

```
      o.writeBoolean(this.isAlive());
      o.writeBoolean(this.isDaemon());
      this.resume();
   }


   public void readExternal(ObjectInput o)
      throws java.io.IOException
   {
      this.counter = o.readInt();
      this.message = o.readUTF();
      this.setName(o.readUTF());
      this.setPriority(o.readInt());
      boolean alive = o.readBoolean();
      this.setDaemon(o.readBoolean());

      this.resume();
      this.start();



   }
};
```

Listing 16.1 Source for BunnyThread.

      BunnyThread is an Externalizable object. When BunnyThread is made externalizable, other objects that contain BunnyThread can be more easily made serializable or externalizable. The operations required to externalize BunnyThread are also bundled tightly with BunnyThread itself, which is an elegant object-oriented design. java.lang.Thread is neither externalizable nor serializable, so BunnyThread takes care of the operations required to externalize Thread as well.

      The implementation of BatteryAd follows the Actor pattern. An instance of BunnyThread is encapsulated within BatteryAd. BatteryAd also implements a mobile object, so it must be either serializable or externalizable to be compatible with mobile object tools like CORBA, RMI, and Voyager. BatteryAd, see Listing 16.2, doesn't do much other than holding an instance of BunnyThread and starting this thread when the object is instantiated.

```
public class BatteryAd
   implements java.io.Serializable
{
  public BunnyThread pink;

  public BatteryAd()
  {
  }

  public BatteryAd(String name)
  {
    pink = new BunnyThread();
    pink.setName( name );
    pink.setPriority( Thread.MIN_PRIORITY );
    pink.setDaemon( false );
    pink.start();
  }
};
```

Listing 16.2 Source for BatteryAd.

The beauty of this example is that BatteryAd may be arbitrarily moved to another host through use of mobile object techniques without concern for the Threads that are encapsulated in it. The Thread state, which is fully encapsulated by the object, can be communicated with the BatteryAd. Once an instance of BatteryAd arrives at its intended destination, encapsulated Threads are transparently restarted in the new address space. The new address space doesn't have to be aware that this object has its own thread. This transparent use of thread further decouples the implementation of a mobile object from its environment, enabling it not to depend on receiving threads from the application hosting the mobile object.

Related Patterns

Observer is often a better solution than multithreading for updating objects as a result of a changing environment.

Actor makes it easier to implement the Momento pattern because the Thread doesn't have any extrinsic state.

Object Group [Maffeis 96]

Intent

Object group defines a single abstraction around several objects that react to the same events or messages.

Benefits of Mobility

Mobile objects facilitate object groups by solving some of the challenges that have historically hampered their acceptance. Mobile objects enable participants in an object group to communicate more effectively by exchanging objects. Mobile objects can be used to create new participants by cloning participants onto new hosts. Mobile objects make state transfer, an essential part of a robust object group, much easier to implement because state is always transferred as part of a mobile object. Finally, mobile objects are flexible enough that even when group participation was not taken into the account for the design of a mobile object, such capability can be added after the fact by including an implementation for participating as a member of a group or a client-side proxy for sending messages to the group.

Motivation

Several classes of applications require objects that respond to the same set of messages. Some examples include event models, transactional systems, replication, white board collaborations, and multimedia broadcast applications. Events models require all interested participants to be notified of an event. Transactions require each member of the transaction to be notified of rollbacks and commits. Replication requires that every replicated member receive a copy of each message so that they may be kept in synchronization with each other. White board collaborations provide a shared document of which each participant maintains its own copy and view. Finally, increasingly popular multimedia broadcasts require that each audience member receive a certain set of messages from the broadcaster. Refer to Chapter 9: Clustering for a more detailed discussion of object groups.

An object group provides a convenient mechanism for implementing a communication system for a group of users that has certain guarantees regarding the communication. The implementation may guarantee that messages are received reliably by any functioning receiver, in either the order in which they were sent by a particular sender, in a causal order, or in an absolute order. The guarantee for group-based messaging is a subject of much research. The capabilities vary from product to product.

Applicability

Object Groups are useful under many contexts, including but not limited to the following:

♦ A set of objects responds to the same messages or events.

♦ The same operation is invoked simultaneously on a set of objects.

♦ Several objects must have synchronized state.

♦ Many participating applications communicate or collaborate.

♦ Messages sent to a set of objects should have certain properties, such as ordering, all-or-nothing delivery, or reliable delivery.

Structure

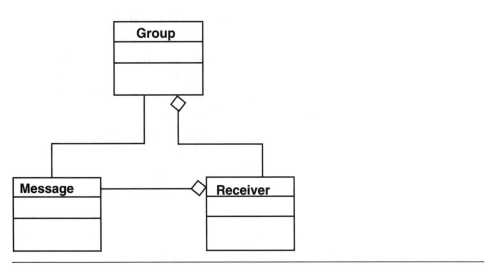

Figure 17.1 The structure of the Object Group Pattern.

Participants

Group.
An abstraction for treating many objects as a single entity.

Message.
An object encapsulating the information sent to the Group.

Receiver.
A participant in the Group.

Collaborations

The implementation of Group makes certain guarantees to Receiver regarding the delivery of Message. Any Message sent to Group is multicast to every Receiver.

Consequences

Many more configuration options than traditional client/server.
Traditional point-to-point communication is restrictive in configuration
options because one and only one entity is communicating with one
and only one other entity. The configuration options for this include
client/server or peer-to-peer. Group communication enables many more
types of interactions. A client/server group employs a client that sends
a message to a server group, which may respond with a set of replies. A
member of a peer group can send a message to its peers in the group.
A hierarchical group is a set of groups arranged hierarchically to satisfy
requests. Finally, clients may register interest in receiving messages
broadcast from a diffusion group

Failure of group survives failure of individual participants. Group communication systems are usually not dependent on the correct functioning of a single member of the group. When a single member of the
system fails, the entire group may continue to function correctly. A
group that can withstand the failure of K members is said to be K-sta-
ble where K is some number. See the Replication pattern in Chapter 18
for more information about implementing fault tolerance.

**Slower than point-to-point because of coordination overhead; quality
of service determines speed.** Group protocols often employ complex
negotiations to implement the properties of the system. The implementation of this coordination employs additional packets in the protocol
to guarantee delivery of messages, ensure correct ordering, track membership, and perform other tasks. This overhead necessarily slows
down group communication well below the theoretical limit of the
underlying network protocol. Performance is highly dependent on the
quality of service requirements placed on the protocol. The implementation of simple reliable multicast can be efficient, performing nearly at
the speed of IP Multicast. However, atomic, completely ordered reliable
multicast is much, much slower. Message delivery with these guarantees
occurs on the order of about one message per second.

Implementation

Object Groups are not easy to implement from scratch, but the benefits, such as improved system reliability, make building groups well worth the trouble. When implementing the Object Group pattern, consider the following points:

♦ **Let someone else do the real work.** Group communication is a subject of much research and several commercial products. Considerable effort is required to build a group communication system with robust support for many different levels of quality of service. Preferably the mobile object tool should provide group communication constructs, though no such products exist at the time of this writing.

♦ **Represent messages by method invocations.** The implementation of passing messages from one application to another is useful for many applications. Implementors may be tempted to represent messages in the form of raw data, such as byte arrays. A useful abstraction is to represent messages by method invocations such that each type of message has an associated method. When the message is sent, the method is invoked. This association of messages between distributed processes and method invocations was pioneered by remote procedure call technology and remains useful for the group communication abstraction. It enables the participants in the group communication system to be objects—thus the name of this pattern, Object Group.

♦ **Implement an atomic shared data segment.** One lesson learned from the history of use of group communication systems, such as HORUS, has been the utility of implementing a shared data segment among all the participants in the group. This shared data segment can be used as a white board by each of the participants to share information with the others. Research systems including Linda have pioneered ways that such white boards can be used to implement distributed systems. The new Java Spaces technology from JavaSoft follows a similar design.

♦ **Track Membership.** Tracking the membership of a replicated system can provide a useful facility over the implementation of a group that has no facility for examining its own membership. Consider the voting problem of Chapter 5: Building Mobile Objects with Voyager. This problem requires that many participants vote on a particular issue. However, when the vote is counted, how do you know whether all the participants have voted on the issue and which side won? You have to have some picture of the membership of the system. Transactional systems provide another example. When determining whether to commit a transaction, the transaction coordinator must be confident that all the members of the group have indicated their preparedness to commit.

Sample Code

Most of the examples in this book implement complete applications. Here we depart from that tradition to implement a component. This example modifies the JellyBean component to implement an object group as a drop-in replacement for the traditional PropertyChangeSupport framework used by JavaBeans. The implementation of this is based on Voyager Spaces.

PropertyChangeSupport in JavaBeans is a mechanism for notifying dependent objects of changes to the properties of a particular component. PropertyChangeSupport is a common event mechanism used within JavaBeans. A particular object registers interest in a particular property by instantiating a PropertyChangeListener with the PropertyChangeSupport object. The JavaBean interacts with this PropertyChangeSupport object to notify any registered listeners of the property change. The implementation of this interface is normally based on making invocations to local Java objects that implement the PropertyChangeListener interface. The existing interface cries out for the use of an object group because all the objects interested in the property change event implement the same interface and receive nearly simultaneous invocations. Extending this architecture using the Object Group pattern would enable the event to be simultaneously multicast to all listeners, even those distributed on other computers of the network.

The drop-in replacement for PropertyChangeSupport is called Property-ChangeGroup. The implementation is very close to PropertyChangeSupport and even extends from the default implementation of PropertyChange-Support.

The implementation of PropertyChangeGroup is in terms of Voyager Spaces. The implementations of Voyager Spaces requires that each participant register a common interface with the Space. All objects interested in receiving property change events broadcast to the Space must implement this PropertyChangeListener interface. Since they do anyway, this interface is a good choice for use with the Space. Whenever a message is sent to the Space, one of the operations on the interface is invoked to handle the message. In this case, the role played by PropertyChangeListener is a convenient interface for the common interface for the Space. When the propertyChange() operation is invoked on the Space, the propertyChange() operation of the member PropertyChangeListeners is invoked by the Voyager Space.

Implementing this is not difficult. No changes are required on the PropertyChangeListener interface. The current operations on the PropertyChangeListener interface are sufficient for exchanging the property change events. The implementation of the PropertyChangeGroup object replaces the PropertyChangeSupport object, implementing support for Voyager Spaces rather than the implementation of the local event model.

PropertyChangeGroup, which inherits from PropertyChangeSupport, has three primary methods that must be overridden. The addPropertyChange-Listener() operation is for registering interest in changes to a particular property. An instance of the PropertyChangeListener is passed to the PropertyChangeGroup, which in turn registers the PropertyChangeListener with the Voyager Space. In addition, a method is required for removing objects from the PropertyChangeGroup, enabling them to stop receiving property change events if they are no longer interested for some reason. Objects can unregister interest in receiving property change events by invoking the removePropertyChangeListener() operation. The implementation of this operation removes the listener from the Voyager Space. Finally, the firePropertyChange() operation enables a JavaBean to broadcast messages to the registered set of listeners. The implementation sends this invocation to the Voyager Space for multicasting the event to all the participants in the Space that happen to be the instances of the PropertyChangeListeners. The implementation of PropertyChangeGroup is shown in Listing 17.1.

```
/**
 * Define a distributed group for tracking changes to a Bean property.
 */                                                          Continues
```

```java
import java.beans.*;
import com.objectspace.voyager.*;
import com.objectspace.voyager.space.*;
import com.objectspace.voyager.space.multicasting.*;


public class PropertyChangeGroup
  extends PropertyChangeSupport
{
  Object source = null;
  ISubspace space = null;
  PropertyChangeListener caster = null;

  public PropertyChangeGroup(Object s)
  {
    super(s);

    source = s;

    try
      {
        space = (ISubspace)
          Namespace.lookup( "//localhost:7000/PropertyChange" );

        caster =
(PropertyChangeListener)space.getMulticastProxy("java.beans.PropertyChangeListene
r");
      }
    catch (Exception e)
      {
        System.err.println("PropertyChangeGroup: " + e);
        e.printStackTrace();
      }
  }

  public void addPropertyChangeListener(PropertyChangeListener listener)
  {
```

```
    try
      {
        PropertyChangeListener vlistener = (PropertyChangeListener)
          Proxy.of(listener);
        space.add(vlistener);


      }
    catch(Exception e)
      {
        System.err.println("PropertyChangeGroup: " + e);
        e.printStackTrace();


      }
}


public void firePropertyChange(String propertyName,
                                  Object oldValue,
                                  Object newValue)
{
  PropertyChangeEvent event = new PropertyChangeEvent(source,
                                                  propertyName,
                                                  oldValue,
                                                  newValue);


  caster.propertyChange(event);
}



public void removePropertyChangeListener(PropertyChangeListener listener)
{
  try
    {
      PropertyChangeListener vlistener = (PropertyChangeListener)
        Proxy.of(listener);

      if (space.remove(vlistener))
        System.out.println("Cleaned up after Space.");
```

Continues

```
        else
            System.out.println("Warning: Failed to cleanup properly.");
        }
    catch (Exception e)
        {
        System.err.println("PropertyChangeGroup: " + e);
        e.printStackTrace();
        }
    }
};
```

Listing 17.1 Source for PropertyChangeGroup.

The next step in implementing this example is to provide a JavaBean that implements the PropertyChangeGroup for objects that implement the PropertyChangeListener. The modifications to the JavaBean should be minimal because we want this object to be a drop-in replacement to the maximum extent possible. In particular, the goal of the implementation is to provide a mechanism that requires nothing other than replacing the existing PropertyChangeSupport objects with new instances of PropertyChangeGroup objects. The JavaBean that is chosen for this example is the JellyBean. This is appropriate because most JavaBeans developers were introduced to the JavaBean framework through this Bean. The original JavaSoft implementation for JellyBean is reused for this example. The implementation of the JellyBean for PropertyChangeGroup is shown in Listing 17.2, with modifications highlighted in bold.

```
import java.awt.*;
import java.beans.*;

/**
 * A simple bean with bound properties and one constrained property.
 * The constrained property is "priceInCents".  VetoablePropertyChange
 * listeners can reject a proposed value for this property by throwing
 * a PropertyVetoException.
 *
 * @see sunw.demo.jelly.Voter
 */
```

```
public class JellyBean extends java.awt.Component {

  /**
    * Construct a smallish JellyBean.
    */

  public JellyBean()
  {
    changes = new PropertyChangeGroup(this);
    vetos = new VetoableChangeSupport(this);

    changes.addPropertyChangeListener(new JellyBeanAdapter(this));
  }

  public void paint(Graphics g) {
      g.setColor(ourColor);
      g.fillArc(5, 5, 30, 30, 0, 360);
      g.fillArc(25, 5, 30, 30, 0, 360);
      g.fillRect(20, 5, 20, 30);
  }

  public Dimension getPreferredSize() {
      return new Dimension(60,40);
  }

  /**
    * Returns the color that the jelly bean is rendered with.
    * @see #setColor
    */
  public synchronized Color getColor() {
    return ourColor;
  }

  /**
    * Sets the color that the jelly bean is rendered with.  This is a
    * bound property.
    * @see #getColor
```

Continues

```java
      */
   public void setColor(Color newColor) {
      Color oldColor = ourColor;
     ourColor = newColor;
      changes.firePropertyChange("color", oldColor, newColor);
      repaint();
   }


   /**
      * Returns the current price.
      * @see #setPriceInCents
      */
   public synchronized int getPriceInCents() {
      return ourPriceInCents;
   }


   /**
      * Set the price in cents unless one of the VetoableChangeListeners
      * throws a PropertyVetoException.  This is a constrained property.
      *
      * @exception PropertyVetoException if the proposed price was vetoed
      */
   public void setPriceInCents(int newPriceInCents)
      throws PropertyVetoException
   {
       int oldPriceInCents = ourPriceInCents;

       // First tell the vetoers about the change.  If anyone objects, we
       // don't catch the exception but just let it pass on to our caller.
       vetos.fireVetoableChange("priceInCents",
                                   new Integer(oldPriceInCents),
                                   new Integer(newPriceInCents));
       // No-one vetoed, so go ahead and make the change.
       ourPriceInCents = newPriceInCents;
       changes.firePropertyChange("priceInCents",
                                     new Integer(oldPriceInCents),
                                     new Integer(newPriceInCents));
   }
```

```
//-------------------------------------------------------------------
// Methods for registering listeners:

/**
  * The specified PropertyChangeListeners <b>propertyChange</b> method will
  * be called each time the value of any bound property is changed.
  * The PropertyListener object is added to a list of PropertyChangeListeners
  * managed by the JellyBean, it can be removed with
  * removePropertyChangeListener.
  * Note: the JavaBeans specification does not require PropertyChangeListeners
  * to run in any particular order.
  *
  * @see #removePropertyChangeListener
  * @param l the PropertyChangeListener
  */
public void addPropertyChangeListener(PropertyChangeListener l) {
    changes.addPropertyChangeListener(l);
}


/**
  * Remove this PropertyChangeListener from the JellyBeans internal list.
  * If the PropertyChangeListener isn't on the list, silently do nothing.
  *
  * @see #addPropertyChangeListener
  * @param l the PropertyChangeListener
  */
public void removePropertyChangeListener(PropertyChangeListener l) {
    changes.removePropertyChangeListener(l);
}


/**
  * The specified VetoableChangeListeners <b>vetoableChange</b> method will
  * be called each time the value of any constrained property is changed.
  * Currently, the only constrained property is "priceInCents".
  * The VetoableChangeListener object is added to a list of
VetoableChangeListeners
```

Continues

```
    * managed by the JellyBean, it can be removed with
    * removeVetoableChangeListener.
    * Note: the JavaBeans specification does not require VetoableChangeListeners
    * to run in any particular order.
    *
    * @see #removeVetoableChangeListener
    * @param l the VetoableChangeListener
    */
public void addVetoableChangeListener(VetoableChangeListener l) {
    vetos.addVetoableChangeListener(l);
}


/**
    * Remove this VetoableChangeListener from the JellyBeans internal list.
    * If the VetoableChangeListener isn't on the list, silently do nothing.
    *
    * @see #addVetoableChangeListener
    * @param l the VetoableChangeListener
    */
public void removeVetoableChangeListener(VetoableChangeListener l) {
    vetos.removeVetoableChangeListener(l);
}


//-----------------------------------------------------------------------
// Private data fields:

private PropertyChangeGroup changes = null;
private VetoableChangeSupport vetos = null;

private Color ourColor = Color.orange;
private int ourPriceInCents = 2;
}
```

Listing 17.2 Source for JellyBean.

The original example for JellyBean included a JellyBeanBeanInfo object for providing the metadata for JellyBean. The implementation of JellyBeanBeanInfo doesn't require any changes because JellyBeanBeanInfo has nothing to do with the property change events. The two are separate concerns; PropertyChangeListeners are runtime constructs for notifying interesting objects about a property change. The BeanInfo objects are design-time constructs for examining JavaBeans during the process of linking them with other JavaBeans. For convenience, the JellyBeanBeanInfo object is quoted in Listing 17.3.

```java
/**
 * The only thing we define in the Juggler BeanInfo is a GIF icon.
 */

package sunw.demo.jelly;

import java.beans.*;

public class JellyBeanBeanInfo extends SimpleBeanInfo {

    public java.awt.Image getIcon(int iconKind) {
      if (iconKind == BeanInfo.ICON_COLOR_16x16) {
          java.awt.Image img = loadImage("JellyBeanIconColor16.gif");
          return img;
      }
      if (iconKind == BeanInfo.ICON_COLOR_32x32) {
          java.awt.Image img = loadImage("JellyBeanIconColor32.gif");
          return img;
      }
      if (iconKind == BeanInfo.ICON_MONO_16x16) {
          java.awt.Image img = loadImage("JellyBeanIconMono16.gif");
          return img;
      }
      if (iconKind == BeanInfo.ICON_MONO_32x32) {
          java.awt.Image img = loadImage("JellyBeanIconMono32.gif");
          return img;
      }
      return null;
    }
}
```

Listing 17.3 Source for JellyBeanBeanInfo.

Implementing the JavaBean event model for notifying other components of changes to a property in a JavaBean requires that an implementation of PropertyChangeListener be provided to receive the event. An instance of this PropertyChangeListener is registered to receive the events. Each object interested in receiving property change events may have a different task to perform when the event occurs. This operation is defined by the PropertyChangeListener interface. As a result, many implementations of PropertyChangeListener are possible.

For this example, an implementation of PropertyChangeListener is provided for synchronizing the properties of a set of JavaBeans. This synchronization of the state of many JavaBeans in a group is a very primitive example of a technique called virtual synchronization. This way, a distributed system can be built up with these components with the guarantee that the state of any one component is the same as that of any of the other components.

The implementation of JellyBeanAdapter, shown in Listing 17.4, listens for property change events, which contain the old and new state of the property. When these are received, the adapter causes the property of a target JavaBean to be modified to reflect the new value of the property. As a result, the state of each of the components is kept in synch with that of the others. Of course, the implementation of this on top of Voyager Spaces means that this system can't be counted on absolutely. Property change events may be accidentally lost, causing the property of a component to become accidentally out of synch with the other members of the group.

```java
import java.util.*;
import java.lang.reflect.*;
import java.beans.*;

public class JellyBeanAdapter
    implements PropertyChangeListener
{
    JellyBean target = null;

    Hashtable setters = new Hashtable();
    Hashtable getters = new Hashtable();
```

```java
public JellyBeanAdapter(JellyBean b)
{
  target = b;

  // Introspect the Bean and create two convenient hashtables
  // of its accessors and mutators

  try
    {
      BeanInfo beanInfo = Introspector.getBeanInfo(b.getClass());

      PropertyDescriptor[] descriptors = beanInfo.getPropertyDescriptors();

      Method m;
      PropertyDescriptor d;

      for (int i = 0; i < descriptors.length; i++)
        {
          d = descriptors[i];

          m = d.getReadMethod();
          getters.put(d.getName(),m);

          m = d.getWriteMethod();
          setters.put(d.getName(),m);
        }
    }
  catch (IntrospectionException e)
    {
      System.err.println("JellyBeanAdapter: " + e);
      e.printStackTrace();
    }
}

public void propertyChange(PropertyChangeEvent event)
{
```

Continues

```
        try
          {
             Method getter = (Method)getters.get(event.getPropertyName());

             if (getter.invoke(target,null).equals(event.getNewValue()))
               return;      // Value hasn't changed. Do nothing.

             Method setter = (Method)setters.get(event.getPropertyName());

             Object[] args = new Object[1];
             args[0] = event.getNewValue();

             Object o = setter.invoke(target,args);
          }
        catch (Exception e)
          {
             System.err.println("JellyBeanAdapter: " + e);
             e.printStackTrace();
          }
     }
};
```

Listing 17.4 Source for JellyBeanAdapter.

A complete JavaBean includes the implementation for the standard JellyBeanInfo and a JellyBeanAdapter for causing changes to the property to be automatically passed on to a target JellyBean. The implementation of this JellyBean and JellyBeanAdapter may be reused within any JavaBean component development environment. Try to import this Bean into your favorite development environment, then use the Bean in a couple different applications by registering JellyBeanAdapters for each instance of the JellyBean. When you do this, all instances of the JellyBean are kept in synch, even though they may be members of entirely different applications.

Related Patterns

Observer is a natural candidate for an Object Group, particularly under the conditions when every Observer should receive a message or none should receive the message.

18

Replication
[Nelson98]

Intent

Implement fault tolerance and load balancing by cloning several copies of the same mobile object.

Benefits of Mobility

Mobility solves some of the key problems of building replicated systems, including how to copy the state of an object, how to create new clones of the object on new computers, how to manage new instances of objects, and how to guarantee atomic failure of the replicated system. All mobile objects are serializable, so their state can easily be copied. New clones are created frequently in mobile object software during the process of method invocation. Byte code for new classes may be transferred between nodes of the system at runtime as part of a mobile object system, so the problem of software installation and management is all but eliminated. Mobile object applications can act as hosts for replicated services, treating them just like any other mobile object. Mobility doesn't help you address the problem of building a system that has atomic failure properties; such a system needs a carefully implemented protocol. However, mobility does address many of the challenges required to build a replicated system, and replicated systems do offer substantial benefits in the design of distributed systems.

Motivation

Large distributed systems sometimes become overly dependent on a single server to answer certain requests. The correct, efficient functioning of the entire system may eventually become dependent on the correct, efficient function of that single server. This dependency results in several serious problems.

First, because the correct functioning of the system depends on a single mission-critical server, this server is by definition a single point of failure. When it goes down, the entire system cannot proceed with its work. If a single node in a system has a 10% chance of failure per day, the current implementation of the system would have a 10% chance of total failure per day.

Second, the server can quickly become overloaded and may slow the entire system according to the Law of Minimums. For example, if 10 clients issue a request to one server, the server must satisfy 10 requests. Some of the clients may be blocked, waiting for the server to process the request and unable to perform other operations in the meantime.

The Replication pattern addresses these issues by creating multiple clones of the mission-critical server that are all capable of responding to requests. Suppose the system is deployed using the Replication pattern on 10 nodes of a distributed system and that the chance of failure of each node remains 10%, independently of whether any of the other nodes have failed. Despite the high probability that an individual node fails on any given day, the chance that all fail on the same day is just .00000001%. This equates to an average of one total failure every 10,000 years. Replication makes the complete failure of a system much less likely. Let's look at a thumbnail sketch of an example system.

The Replication pattern enables multiple copies of the server to divide the work among themselves. Rather than one server processing 10 requests, 10 servers could process one request each. This policy of dividing requests among multiple servers is called load balancing because the processing and resource consumption load is divided among all the replicated copies of the server.

Mobile objects facilitate the implementation of the Replication pattern because of the implementation details of the construction of both mobile objects and the Replication pattern. Mobile objects are, in a nutshell, objects that are cloned, copied, or moved to another computer on the network. Because one of the major tasks of implementing the Replication pattern is providing a way to clone objects to new computers across the network, it is a very natural pattern for use in conjunction with a mobile object-based system.

Applicability

Replication is most useful under the following conditions:

♦ When the system is mission critical.

♦ When the individual nodes in a system are subject to periodic failure.

♦ When the state of some of the objects in a system should be shared across multiple nodes.

♦ When load balancing is desired.

Structure

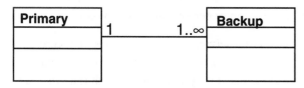

Figure 18.1 The structure of the Replication Pattern.

Participants

Primary.
The copy of application object that responds to requests.

Backup 1.
A copy of the application object that processes but does not respond to requests.

Backup 2.
A copy of the application object that processes but does not respond to requests.

Backup N.
A copy of the application object that processes but does not respond to requests.

Collaborations

Primary and all Backups receive a copy of all requests. The states of Primary and Backups are synchronized after requests are processed.

Consequences

Fault tolerance. Replication is a mechanism for providing fault tolerance to an unreliable system. Even if the individual nodes of the system are unreliable and prone to failure, the system as a whole may be made nearly 100% reliable when the service is replicated across multiple nodes. As long as only a subset of the replicated nodes fails, the system as a whole may continue without experiencing downtime.

Load balancing. Replication of a service to multiple nodes on a computer system provides a convenient platform on which to implement load balancing. The design of the replicated system may be such that all requests are not processed on every node. A dispatching technique may be used to determine which requests are sent and answered by some of the nodes. The individual requests don't have to be satisfied by every node in the system. In such a system, only a fraction of the requests are processed by any one node, dramatically decreasing the impact of many requests on the system and enabling the system to scale to a larger number of requests. In theory, a load-balancing system may scale linearly with the number of nodes on the system. This property is highly desirable for a heavily loaded distributed system.

Shared resources. Some distributed systems share resources among the nodes in the system. In a traditional system, these shared resources may represent objects of which each node in the system must have a consistent view. A typical example of this sharing is a white-board approach to collaboration in which multiple participants of a distributed system share a common view of a document. The task of coordinating these shared resources in a distributed system implementation of this sharing may require complex coordination to ensure that each participant has a consistent view. Replication often provides one of the easiest mechanisms for implementing such a system.

One detriment related to Replication is that it may slow down the system. Despite the natural inclination to think that having N copies of a server is better than having one copy of a server, the administrative overhead of Replication may negatively impact the performance of a system. This same negative impact is noticed in hardware-based forms of Replication, such as disk stripping and RAID technologies, which are often slower though more reliable than single disks. The benefits of a replicated system will generally not include the speed of the system. Considerations such as reliability, scalability, and implementation should be deciding factors rather than a belief that Replication equates directly to speed.

Implementation

Implementing a replicated system can be a difficult task depending on how many types of failures the system is required to handle. A simple replicated system without atomic failure guarantees among the participants may offer substantial benefits, while being easy to construct and maintain. However, a major financial application may require atomic failure guarantees, and the implementation requirements may increase significantly because each part of the system must be designed to handle a failure properly. Here are some issues to consider when implementing Replication:

♦ **Clone Mobile Objects onto Other Computers.** The implementation of mobile objects lends to cloning them to other computers. Every mobile object tool examined in this book provides a mechanism for cloning individual objects onto other nodes of the system. Performing this operation is as simple as making a normal method invocation. The mobile object tool then serializes the object using Java Object Serialization and sends it to the remote node. Once on the remote node, the new clone of the object may begin servicing requests as a member of a replicated group of objects.

♦ **Multicast Invocations to Each Participant.** Where possible, IP Multicast should be used to efficiently communicate each request to the replicated servers. Passing communication though point-to-point communication requires the request to be sent iteratively to each participant. This communication can be expensive when a large number of replicas are involved.

♦ **Synchronize state.** Several different approaches can be used to replicate an object on a network. One straightforward approach is to identify one replica as the master in the replicated group and each of the other replicas as backups. As a request is sent to each member of the group, only the master processes and responds to the request. Once the request is complete, the master announces its state to the rest of the replicated group so that they may update their state to the current state of the system.

An alternative approach to synchronizing the state of the system is to have every replica process every request. As long as the requests are processed in the same order and are not time dependent, this technique is often very effective at synchronizing the state of the system between the replicas. Such a system is called virtual synchronous because the individual nodes are kept in synch as they process all the same requests.

♦ **IP Multicast May Not Be Enough.** Multicast communications are not guaranteed for delivery. In a replicated system, multiple servers may fail to be maintained in a synchronous state if some messages are lost. A virtual synchronous system is particularly susceptible because the loss or misordering of a single message may result in the system's losing consistency.

Fortunately, a great deal of research has gone into the implementation of Replication and virtual synchronous systems. Some commercial products are available to address these problems, ISIS and HORUS being the best known. Lately, a Java product called iBus has been implemented to address these same issues. iBus is essentially the early stages of reimplementing HORUS in

Java. These products should be given strong consideration if absolute system confidence is required. Merging these products with a mobile object tool may require significant hand coding and design work, however.

Sample Code

The implementation of Replication in this example is based on Voyager Spaces. A Voyager Space is a fairly straightforward mapping of multicast communications onto Voyager's ORB technology. This subject was examined in more detail in Chapter 5: Building Mobile Objects with Voyager. Voyager Spaces are not reliable and may accidentally lose messages under certain conditions. In this implementation, the client is expected to reissue requests if it does not receive a response from the appropriate member of the replicated group.

This example takes another look at the HelloCaster server implemented in Chapter 3: Building Mobile Objects with Caffeine. Recall that the purpose of HelloCaster is to implement a server for storing JavaBeans that represent messages. The JavaBean moves from the client to the server for storage. Later, another client can request and introspect the JavaBean. The earlier implementation was based on CORBA-style client/server communication. This CORBA implementation is exclusively point to point. The failure of the server results in the failure of the entire system.

In this implementation, Voyager Spaces are used to replicate the server to two nodes, acting as primary and backup. The failure of the primary node does not result in the failure of the system as a whole because the backup can pick up to satisfy requests if the primary should fail. The implementation of this is examined in detail below.

In order to convert HelloCaster from CORBA to a (relatively) fault-tolerant system based on Voyager Spaces, we simply have to convert the server and modify each client to use the new server. First, the original specification for HelloCaster is not compatible with Voyager Spaces. In particular, Spaces don't allow a return value to come back from a method invocation; any method invocations on a Space must return void. The return parameter of the pop() method causes trouble. Here is the original interface:

```
public interface HelloCaster
   extends org.omg.CORBA.Object
{
   public void push(Hello h);
   public Hello pop();
};
```

The most straightforward technique for rearchitecting this system to avoid passing the return parameter is to provide a callback. A new interface called HelloListener is introduced to provide this callback mechanism. The implementation is shown here:

```
public interface HelloListener
   extends UnaryFunction
{
   public Object execute( Object o );
};
```

HelloListener provides the callback. When the pop() operation is completed, the execute method on the HelloListener method is invoked, passing the Hello object as the first parameter. HelloListener is implemented as a UnaryFunction for no particularly strong reason other than that it leaves open the door of using HelloListener objects as part of a Function object framework at some future time.

With this modification, the implementation of HelloCaster is modified to accept a HelloListener object. However, instead of passing in a HelloListener object directly, it adds a layer of abstraction to the system. HelloListener is bundled into an object, called Current, that represents the current execution context for the invocation on the Voyager Space. Current just contains the appropriate HelloListener and a number uniquely identifying the request. A request identification parameter is useful for connecting request-reply pairs with one another. Without a unique request identification number, participants in the distributed system may not be able to determine whether a request has been answered. For now, suffice it to say that the ability to determine this is important for a fault-tolerant system. The new specification for the HelloCaster interface is shown here:

```
public interface HelloCaster
   extends java.io.Serializable
```

```
{
  public void push(Current c, Hello h);
  public void pop(Current c);
  public void done(Current c);
};
```

You might notice one other new feature of the HelloCaster interface: the addition of a done() method. This method is used to indicate when a particular invocation has been completed by the primary server. The implementation of the client instantiates an object of this type and passes it along with the invocation. Any actions that the client would like to perform on the return parameter should be performed or triggered by the execute() method. This way, they can be automatically started when the server invokes this callback method.

The implementation of the server in this fault-tolerant example is shown in Listing 18.1. The implementation creates a primary and backup server to respond to requests from clients. The client broadcasts each request to the primary and backup servers using Voyager Spaces. Both the primary and backup process the requests, but only the primary responds to the request. The backup doesn't respond to a request until it determines the primary has failed.

```
import com.objectspace.voyager.*;
import com.objectspace.voyager.space.*;

public class Server
{
  public static void main(String args[])
  {
    try
      {
        Voyager.startup();

        ISubspace space = (ISubspace)
          Factory.create( "com.objectspace.voyager.space.Subspace",
                          "//localhost:7000/Hello" );            Continues
```

```
        HelloCaster self = (HelloCaster)
          Factory.create("HelloCasterImpl",
                              new Object[]{ space,
                                                new Boolean(HelloCasterImpl.PRIMARY)
        },
                              "//localhost:8000" );


        space.add(self);


        HelloCaster secondary = (HelloCaster)
          Factory.create("HelloCasterImpl",
                              new Object[]{ space,
                                                new Boolean(HelloCasterImpl.BACKUP)
        },
                              "//localhost:7000" );
        space.add(secondary);
        }
    catch( Exception e )
      {
        System.err.println("Voter: " + e);
        e.printStackTrace();
      }


    Voyager.shutdown();


  }


}
```

Listing 18.1 Source for Server.

The implementation of the clients also must be changed to communicate with the Voyager Space rather than have a CORBA object reference invoked. If this change were a requirement, the different possible invocations could be encapsulated inside the Interpreter pattern. This example doesn't worry about these aesthetic considerations. The implementation of a client that opens a Voyager spaces and pushes new messages onto the server is given in Listing 18.2.

```java
import com.objectspace.voyager.*;
import com.objectspace.voyager.space.*;

public class PushClient
{
  public static void main(String args[])
  {
    try
      {
        Voyager.startup();

        ISubspace space = (ISubspace)Namespace.lookup( "//localhost:7000/Hello"
);

        HelloCaster greeter = (HelloCaster)space.getMulticastProxy(
"HelloCaster" );

        HelloListener self = new HelloListenerImpl();
        HelloListener vself =
          (HelloListener) Proxy.of( self );

        Current current = new CurrentImpl( vself );

        // Push a message specified by the command line.
        Class c = Class.forName( args[0] );

        Hello h = (Hello)c.newInstance();
        h.setMessage( args[1] );

        greeter.push( current, h );

        System.out.println("Pushed \"" + args[0] + "\"." );

        // Can't shutdown, have to wait for reply.
        Voyager.shutdown();
    }
```

Continues

```
    catch (Exception e)
      {
        System.err.println("PushClient: " + e);
        e.printStackTrace();

      }

    Voyager.shutdown();

  }

}
```

Listing 18.2 Source for PushClient.

This example is implemented in full on the CD. Starting the example requires the same steps as in the other Voyager Spaces examples we have examined, such as the Vote application shown in Chapter 5. First, the Voyager place processes should be started with commands that look something like the following, depending on your operating system. You'll need quite a few windows to run this example!

```
Window 1
Prompt> voyager 7000
voyager™ 2.0 beta 1, copyright objectspace 1997
address = localhost:7000


Window 2
Prompt> voyager 8000
voyager™ 2.0 beta 1, copyright objectspace 1997
address = localhost:8000


Window 3
Prompt> java Server
voyager™ 2.0 beta 1, copyright objectspace 1997
address = localhost:1031


Window 4
```

```
Prompt> java PushClient Hello "Still kicking!"
voyager™ 2.0 beta 1, copyright objectspace 1997
address = localhost:1039
Pushed "Still kicking!".
```

```
Window 5
Prompt> java PushClient Hello "Hello, World!"
voyager™ 2.0 beta 1, copyright objectspace 1997
address = localhost:1039
Pushed "Hello, World!".
```

```
Window 6
Prompt> java PopClient Hello
voyager™ 2.0 beta 1, copyright objectspace 1997
address = localhost:1039
Popped "Hello, World!"
```

At this point, try closing the Voyager place process in Window 2, which hosts the primary server, by pressing CONTROL + C, closing the window or doing whatever it takes to stop a process in your operating system. Once the primary server process has stopped executing, try to run the PopClient again to pop another message.

```
Window 7
Prompt> java PopClient Hello
voyager™ 2.0 beta 1, copyright objectspace 1997
address = localhost:1039
Popped "Still kicking!"
```

In a nonreplicated system, this invocation would fail. However, the replicated system that we have designed here has support for fault tolerance. Rather than failure, the backup server responds to the request after a five-second delay. This delay gives the primary server a chance to respond to requests if it is still functional. This example has been adapted from the earlier HelloCaster example to support fault tolerance by using replication.

Does this rough implementation of fault tolerance on top of Voyager Spaces have any weaknesses? Don't fool yourself. The example is an interesting demonstration of a concept, but the actual example has significant implementation weaknesses. One weakness can be found in Voyager Spaces; they are not reliable. They can lose messages and never inform you that the message was lost. As a result, a correct primary server can fail to receive a message and consequently fail to respond. In addition, the backup may fail to receive a message. In this situation, the backup may fail to respond even if the primary if faulty. A backup may also incorrectly respond to a message that the primary server has already responded to if the backup fails to receive the message containing the done() invocation, indicating that the request has been processed correctly by the primary server. Finally, lost messages result in the primary and backup becoming out of synchronization. Some of these issues might be fixed if a reliable multicast implementation of Voyager Spaces were available for use with this example.

Related Patterns

Replication is an implementation of a type of Object Group. The objects in this group all respond to the same requests to maintain the current state of the system in each node.

Command [GoF95]

Intent

Build a mobile object representing a Command that can be sent to other nodes.

Benefits of Mobility

The Command pattern provides a powerful tool for encapsulating small bits of functionality of an application and enable them to be chained, swapped, or added in different ways. However, Commands are restricted to the scope of the application in which they were original coded and compiled.

With mobile objects, Commands can migrate dynamically across the network at runtime. The implementation of a new Command can be added or substituted for older versions of the same Command. Command provides an excellent abstraction for separating application logic and enabling alternative application logic to be added at runtime since Commands are often atomic and loosely coupled to their environment.

When a Command is migrated to a new application, the implementation of the Command, whatever that may entail, becomes available to the new application. This may include displaying new user interfaces, providing database access, or alternative implementations for old Commands.

Motivation

A complex distributed system may encompass the solution to a number of problems and span many hosts. The implementation of the code that performs the required tasks often spans multiple running applications across multiple hosts. The nature of this architecture leads to interdependencies in which the correct functioning of the system is dependent on the correct functioning of many interrelated applications. These interdependencies may be simplified when one host in enabled to send a Command directly to another. The sending application may have a specific requirement of which the other application is unaware. When a Command is sent as a mobile object to the remote host, arbitrary Commands may be evaluated without compile time limitations on the content of either application.

Commands may perform virtually any code. They can draw new windows, process a computation then return the results, or access static objects resident in another application. Under an appropriately loose security model, they can even write files and execute system processes.

Applicability

Use the Command pattern as follows:

♦ To enable two different applications to invoke each other in arbitrary ways.

♦ To share resources across hosts by sharing Commands.

♦ To create new windows or processes on another host.

Participants

Command.
The common parent of all commands.

ConcreteCommand.
An implementation of a specific Command object to evaluate.

Consumer.
An application capable of receiving and evaluating Commands.

Environment.
A singleton defining the environment accessible by Commands.

Source.
An application that distributes Commands.

Structure

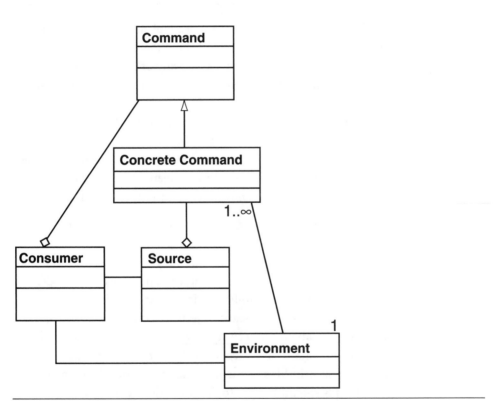

Figure 19.1 The structure of the Command Pattern.

Collaborations

ConcreteCommand is a specific mobile object that supports the interface defined by Command. A Source application obtains a Remote Proxy to a Consumer application and utilizes the Remote Proxy to submit Commands to the Consumer. Consumer should provide a concrete implementation of an Environment singleton.

Consequences

ConcreteCommand and Consumer are decoupled. The implementation of ConcreteCommand is encapsulated behind the Command interface. As a result, Consumer is not dependent on any of the implementation details of each individual Command. However, this decoupling is often unidirectional since ConcreteCommand may utilize some of the resources of Consumer. In other words, the Command may modify some of the application data, where the Consumer is an abstraction for the application in this context. A natural way to restore as much decoupling as possible is to introduce the Environment object as the sole point of access that ConcreteCommands have with the application data.

The arbitrary operations that can be performed on Consumer are limited only by the Java SecurityManager. The implementation of ConcreteCommand may contain any legal Java byte code, including file I/O, graphical user interface, database access, and networking code. This flexibility gives you the ability to do almost anything within a Command. Has access to any static objects in Consumer however, if you are concerned about the security of your computer, you may not want every Command to have access to all your files and other resources. The SecurityManager can be used to restrict the scope of what Commands should be able to do under these conditions.

The pattern has access to any static objects in Consumer Concrete-Command objects can access any static variables in the Java application that is currently hosting them. As a result, a bad implementation of a ConcreteCommand may be closely coupled to any static variables in the application.

Resources of Consumer can be overutilized accidentally or maliciously. Each Command may perform actions like starting threads, utilizing CPU, painting user interfaces, and accessing disk files. All of these operations consume significant system resources. The number and type of Commands should be controlled to prevent overconsumption of resources.

The pattern encourages collaboration between applications and end users because new and original Commands can easily be shared across the network. Commands implemented as mobile objects can be sent to other computers with little effort. The Command can be used as a tool for collaboration, performing some particular task required to implement the collaborative system. Each participant can arbitrarily share and examine the set of Commands as part of the collaboration. For example, a Command pattern implementation of a gesture based whiteboard could share gestures across the network. In this example, the Command pattern is virtually all that is required to implement robust collaboration between the participants in the whiteboard.

Implementation

The benefits realized by the use of the Command pattern are strongly dependent on how completely the Command pattern is embraced in application design. Embracing the Command pattern completely often results in an application with a rich set of Commands that can be dynamically substituted for each other. When implementing the Command pattern, keep the following points in mind:

♦ **Command can and should be as simple as an interface implementing Serializable and Runnable.** Each ConcreteCommand should simply be evaluated upon receipt by a Consumer who invokes some operation on the Command. The standard void run() operation on Runnable is a perfectly reasonable choice for such an operation. Making Commands implement Runnable enables Command to be compatible with Java multithreading as well. Command implements Serializable only because most mobile object toolkits require that a mobile object implement the serializable interface in order to support Object Serialization.

♦ **Anything can be in a Command.** Any legal Java code can be placed inside a Command, as with many other mobile objects. A Command can draw graphical user interfaces, access a database, execute operating system commands, or start additional threads. The only restriction is when a SecurityManager is present to regulate the types of operations conducted by a Command.

♦ **Merge Commands implemented as mobile objects and non-mobile objects.** If you are using the Gang-of-Four's Command pattern, implement an architecture that enables any Command to be used as a mobile object Command and vice versa. The Command pattern is general enough to enable Commands to be implemented as mobile objects, making them mobile object Commands. There are two huge benefits that result. First, all those Commands written as mobile objects and not written as mobile objects can be used interchangeably, even those that are mobile objects, simplifying the application development process. Second, following the Command pattern is a very effective way of exposing the capabilities of a program for invocation by Commands (otherwise, the Command pattern would not be possible). An application that has already exposed such invocation capabilities for the Command pattern without mobile objects can often be slightly modified to enable all the same capabilities to be invoked by the Command pattern with mobile objects. The tighter you embrace the Command pattern in your application, the better the results from the merging of these two patterns. An example of this is shown in the Sample Code section.

♦ **Decouple Environment from Consumer and Command.** The Environment portion of this pattern enables a Command to interact with its Consumer. However, if Environment is too specific to a single Command, adding Commands may require substantial rewriting of the Environment variable. Experience has shown that the most effective way to use Environment is to adopt a framework-like approach of enabling Environment to provide access to general portions of the Consumer application but not make Environment's operations too specific to a single Consumer or Command. This approach enables the same Command to be reused across multiple Consumers that support their own implementation of Environment. As a general rule, Commands should not be directly coupled to classes in the application; rather, they should operate on resources provided by Environment.

♦ **Use prototyping.** Prototyping is a technique for object creation in which an instance of an object is cloned to create a new instance of the object. Prototyping can be a convenient way to create new objects. The logic required to create new instances is bundled with each object, resulting in a very natural factoring of objects with code that constructs those objects. In particular, an large-scale environment heavily oriented toward the Command pattern might have hundreds of types of Command classes. Even a relatively small implementation of the Command pattern often has dozens of Commands. If any part of the application needs to construct these Commands, it might need to know the class name and ways to invoke the constructor. In addition, in a mobile object environment, issues regarding the appropriate host that is the source of the classes for the Command may be a concern. Prototyping eliminates all of these concerns by enabling one object to easily construct a copy of itself for the system to use without knowing its name or how to invoke its constructors.

In order to implement prototyping, each object defines a clone() method that creates a duplicate copy of this object, with identical implementation and state. In Java, cloning objects is convenient because the Java environment can automatically create a shallow copy of any object implementing the java.lang.Clonable interface. If you want more than a shallow copy, a customized clone() method can be provided by the developer.

Sample Code

Implementing the Command pattern is remarkably simple, yet powerful. The following code is a reasonable implementation of the common behavior of all commands. In practice, you may find it convenient to place additional behavior in Command to accomplish tasks like maintaining metadata about each Command.

```
public interface Command
    extends Runnable,
```

Continues

```
        java.io.Serializable,
        java.lang.Clonable
{
};
```

Command implements the java.lang.Clonable interface in order to enable easy creation of copies of this Command through prototyping as discussed earlier in the Implementation section. A host application can then create new copies of this Command by invoking the clone() method.

Listing 19.1 is an implementation of a ConcreteCommand for printing a message specified during the construction of the instance of the command. The implementation of the PrintCommand includes a string message representing the message that should be printed when a particular instance of the PrintCommand is invoked.

```
public class PrintCommand
    implements Command
{
  private String msg;

  public PrintCommand(String m)
  {
    msg = m;
  }

  public void run()
  {
    System.out.println(msg);
  }
};
```

Listing 19.1 Source for PrintCommand.

Listing 19.2 is another example of a ConcreteCommand that implements a command for drawing a line. An instance of this LineCommand acts just like a line gesture in a paint program. Each instance of LineCommand is a unique line. The implementation of this is as follows:

```
public class LineCommand
   implements Command
{
   private long x, y, x2, y2;

   public LineCommand(long x, long y, long x2, long y2)
   {
      this.x = x;
      this.y = y;
      this.x2 = x2;
      this.y2 = y2;
   }

   public void run()
   {
      System.out.println("Line from (" + x + "," + y
                     + ") to (" + x2 + "," + y2 + ")");
   }
};
```

Listing 19.2 Source for LineCommand.

This example prints out a diagnostic message when the line is drawn, but it's not hard to extend this to implement a gesture in a real user interface. One way to do this is to store a buffer as part of the Document, which is accessible through the Environment. As each gesture is executed, it can update the buffer with its implementation. Building on this architecture, Command becomes a very effective way of implementing a paint program. In addition, with the power of mobile objects, new gestures can move into the paint application at runtime.

PrintCommand and LineCommand can be reused in the following simple RMI application. The implementation of this program is meant only to simulate a simple paint program. Rather than providing all the user interface code required to implement a full user interface, the gestures are displayed through diagnostic text messages.

The Document for this application acts as a host for the gestures. Document stores all the gestures in a Stack. Two important helper methods

are also provided: addGesture() enables the paint application to push additional gestures to the top of the Command stack, and showGestures()
invokes each of the gestures in turn, giving them a chance to perform their
specific action on the Environment. In the case of LineCommand and
PrintCommand, these actions are simply to print some text messages. The
implementation for the Document is shown in Listing 19.3.

```java
import java.awt.*;

/**
 * This is sort of an empty document framework right now,
 * because it doesn't do anything other than host Gestures.
 * Use your imagination about what you could use this for.
 * Gestures can be ANYTHING.
 */

public class Document
   implements java.io.Serializable
{

   /**
    * This array of Commands is intended to represent Gestures
    * on a document, but this is very primitive right now.
    * A real Gesture framework would be much more gesture-like,
    * just like the implementation of a paint program.
    */

   public Stack Gestures = new Stack();

   public Document()
   {

   }


   Object junk;
```

```java
/**
 * We could just as easily call these Annotations to some
 * other document model.  Since this Document is empty,
 * I prefer Gestures because they represent the entire content
 * of the document.
 */
public void addGesture(Command c)
{
    junk = Gestures.push( c );
}


// Implement some simple document semantics.
private Stack undoStack = new Stack();

public void undo()
{
    if ( gestures.empty() )
        return;

    junk =  undoStack.push( gestures.pop() );
}

public void redo()
{
    if ( undoStack.empty() )
        return;

    junk = gestures.push( undoStack.pop() );
}



/**
 * In this framework, Gestures are coupled with the Document.
 * Some approaches make Gestures on Views rather than Documents.
 */

public void printGestures()
```

Continues

```
    {
      Command annote = null;

      for (Enumeration e = Gestures.elements();
           e.hasMoreElements();
           gesture = e.nextElement())
        {
          // Apply this Gesture to the Document.
          // What the Gesture does is entirely dependent
          // on the Command's implementation.

          gesture.run();
        }
    }
};
```

Listing 19.3 Source for Document.

The Source is responsible for distributing copies of the Document to clients on request. In a robust enterprise application, Source could be the point in the distributed system responsible for document management and versioning. Here, Source produces a new clone of the document on request.

This example uses RMI because it's fairly straightforward and widely available in most development environments. RMI requires that an interface be specified for the distributed server. The Source interface, shown here, is such an interface.

```
import java.rmi.*;

/**
 * Source just acts as a means to obtain the Document,
 * which contains a set of Commands.
 */

public class Source
  implements Remote
{
```

```
  public Document getDocument()
    throws RemoteException;
};
```

The Source interface represents the interface used by the client to access the server. The server is implemented in the class SourceImpl. This class just instantiates a Document, initializes it with a few Commands, then distributes this Document to any clients that request it. The implementation of this is shown in Listing 19.4.

```
import java.rmi.*;
import java.rmi.server.*;


public class SourceImpl
  extends UnicastRemoteObject
  implements Source
{
  private Document theDocument = new Document();

  public static void main(String args[])
  {
    System.setSecurityManager(new RMISecurityManager());

    try
      {
        SourceImpl o = new SourceImpl();

        // This is intended to implement something like a document with
        // annotations.
        o.theDocument.addGesture( new LineCommand( 0,0,1,1 ));
        o.theDocument.addGesture( new LineCommand( 1,1,2,0 ));
        o.theDocument.addGesture( new LineCommand( 2,0,0,0 ));
        o.theDocument.addGesture( new PrintCommand( "Vincent" ) );

        Naming.rebind("Source",o);
      }
```
Continues

```
    catch (Exception e)
      {
        System.err.println("SourceImpl: " + e);
        e.printStackTrace();
      }
  }


  public SourceImpl()
    throws java.rmi.RemoteException
  {
  }


  public Document getDocument()
    throws RemoteException
  {
    return theDocument;
  }
}
```

Listing 19.4 Source for SourceImpl.

Environment supplies the reference that enables Commands to access the Document (Listing 19.5). Each Command uses the Environment Singleton to access the Document resident in the application and apply its gestures to the Document.

```
/**
  * Environment
  *
  * For our purposes, Environment is a Singleton.  This makes sense
  * because only one Environment should be present in an application.
  * The implementation should locate the Document and add the
  * document to the Environment before examining the annotations.
  * This gives the Annotations the entry point into the Document
  * or rest of the application without having to be coupled to
  * the Consumer.
  *
```

```
     * Notice that Environment does not implement a mobile object.
     * Its purpose is to provide the coupling logic between Commands
     * and the Consumer.
     */

public class Environment
{

  private Environment()
  {
  }


  /**
     * Environment is a singleton.
     */

  public static Environment theEnvironment = null;

  public static Environment instance()
  {
    if (theEnvironment == null)
      theEnvironment = new Environment();

    return theEnvironment;
  }


  /**
     * Only one instance of a Document lives in this Environment,
     * resulting in a single document model for this application.
     * You could nearly as easily store a Hashtable of documents
     * to implement a multiple document model.
     */

  public Document theDocument = null;
```

Continues

```
public Document getDocument()
{
  // Automatically construct an empty document if requested before
  // a default document is set.
  if (theDocument == null)
    theDocument = new Document();

  return theDocument;
}

public void setDocument(Document d)
{
  theDocument = d;
}
};
```

Listing 19.5 Source for Environment.

This Environment follows the single document framework, supplying only one Document per application. However, it's not hard to generalize this for a multiple-document framework. Just store a hashtable of documents indexed by the name of each document.

The implementation of the Consumer acts as the RMI client. This application utilizes the RMI registry to locate the RMI object reference for the Source (Listing 19.6). With this object reference, the Consumer requests the Document from the Source. Finally, the Consumer prints the contents of the document, causing each of the gestures to display its messages to standard output.

```
import java.rmi.*;

public class Consumer
{
  public static void main(String args[])
  {
    try
      {
```

```
        Source theSource =
          (Source)Naming.lookup("//localhost/Source");

        Document d = theSource.getDocument();

        // Bind the Document to the Environment.
        Environment.instance().setDocument(d);

        d.printGestures();

      }
    catch (Exception e)
      {
        System.out.println("Consumer: " + e);
        e.printStackTrace();
      }

  };
};
```

Listing 19.6 Source for Consumer.

In this simple example, only two types of Commands were provided, LineCommand and PrintCommand. These can easily be extended to include a host of other gestures. The beauty of the mobile object implementation of the Command pattern is that new Commands, which means new gestures for this simulated paint application, can be obtained at runtime.

Related Patterns

Sources may employ the Federation pattern to find Commands that are not available locally. Singleton may be used to implement Environment.

Predicate [GoF95]

Predicate is also known as Strategy or Function Object.

Intent

To perform a test on a remote node, define a mobile object representing that test, and send it to the appropriate destination for execution.

Benefits of Mobility

Predicates have always a beautifully simple abstraction for implementing tests in applications, but mobility enables predicates to reach a new height. In a nutshell, predicates without mobility are interchangeable within a single application. Add mobility, and predicates are interchangeable across multiple applications on different computers. Predicates were a tool for implementing applications that could be flexibly reconfigured at compile time. With mobile objects, predicate becomes a tool for implementing distributed systems that can be flexibly reconfigured at runtime.

Motivation

Predicates are actually among the oldest programming constructs in existence. They were introduced with the Lisp language almost 40 years ago. A predicate is an object that performs some test and returns some result.

In the following text, the term "Predicate" refers to any one of the UnaryPredicates, BinaryPredicates, UnaryFunctions, or BinaryFunctions, unless otherwise noted.

Applicability

The Predicate pattern is useful when one is doing the following:

♦ Searching.

♦ Sorting.

♦ Testing.

♦ Selecting.

♦ Updating.

Structure

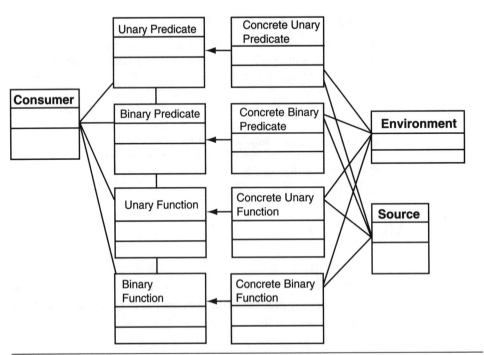

Figure 20.1 The structure of the Predicate Pattern.

Participants

UnaryPredicate.

An interface that accepts a single object as a parameter and returns a boolean result.

BinaryPredicate.

An interface that accepts two objects as parameters and returns a boolean result.

UnaryFunction.

An interface that accepts a single object as a parameter and returns an object result.

BinaryFunction.

An interface that accepts two objects as parameters and returns an object result.

ConcreteUnaryPredicate.

An implementation of the UnaryPredicate. Many such implementations may exist in a single application.

ConcreteBinaryPredicate.

An implementation of the Binary Predicate. Many such implementations may exist in a single application.

ConcreteUnaryFunction.

An implementation of the UnaryFunction. Many such implementations may exist in a single application.

ConcreteBinaryFunction.

An implementation of the Binary Function. Many such implementations may exist in a single application.

Consumer.

An application capable of receiving and evaluating Predicates.

Environment.

A singleton defining the environment accessible by Predicates.

Source.

An application that distributes Predicates.

Collaborations

Concrete objects implement their respective interfaces; that is, ConcreteUnary-Predicate implements UnaryPredicate, and so forth. The test or action performed by the Predicate is entirely encapsulated within the Predicate. Instances of Predicates may be nested if the return type of one Predicate matches an input parameter of another. A Source application obtains a Remote Proxy of a Consumer application and utilizes the Remote Proxy to submit Predicates to the Consumer. Consumer may provide a concrete implementation of an Environment.

Consequences

Encapsulates tests or actions on objects. Each Predicate is identified only by name and matches a specific interface common to many classes of Predicates. As a result, one Predicate looks very much like another, no matter what the Predicate does. The implementation of the test on the Object or Objects passed into the Predicate is entirely encapsulated.

Changes applications easily by rearranging Predicates. Predicates all implement one of a small set of Java interfaces, making them interchangeable at runtime. Putting a great deal of the functionality of an application in Predicates enables this application logic to be varied widely at runtime by the addition of new Predicates. For example, if a certain Predicate is used to test whether an object meets a set of criteria, "logical and" Predicates can be used to make sure that the object meets all the criteria simultaneously. In another example, if a user interface is heavily based on Predicates, you may rearrange the user interface by rearranging a few Predicates.

Conveniently reuses Predicates between applications. Predicates are very self-contained, often performing fairly generic operations. Some Predicates are application specific, but experience has shown that users of the Predicate pattern often implement large collections of reusable Predicates. The Java Generic Libraries (JGL) from Object Spaces is an example of an incredibly successful prewritten library of Predicates.

Implementation

Implementing Predicates with mobile objects is not unlike implementing them in traditional, monolithic applications. The following points should be addressed when you are implementing the Predicate pattern:

♦ **Identify tests or actions that can be decoupled from the application.** Obviously, you have to have something in mind when you start implementing your Predicate. This pattern wraps some part of your application, a part that implements a test or some action. Consider using this pattern only if you identify tests or actions that can be easily encapsulated in this manner. Another qualifier is that the test or action should be easily decoupled from the rest of the application. Tests that are operating on many variables in the local stack, state variables of several objects, or otherwise are closely coupled to a specific piece of the application are poor candidates for Predicates. The most effective Predicates are those that are general enough to apply to a large class of objects and situations.

♦ **Choose the appropriate interface to implement according to how many objects are being tested and the type of their return value.** For tests or actions on a single Object that return a boolean, implement the UnaryPredicate interface. For tests or actions on two Objects that return a boolean, implement the UnaryPredicate interface. For tests or actions on a single Object that returns an Object, implement the UnaryFunction interface. For tests or actions on two Objects that return an Object, implement the BinaryFunction interface. Ignore the type of test or action that is being performed when making this determination. The type of test or action is encapsulated inside the interface. The important point is that the return and parameter values for the Predicate are appropriate.

♦ **Nested Predicates—that is, Predicates that take other Predicates as arguments—may be especially useful.** You don't have to limit your use of the Predicate pattern to a single layer of testing on the objects inside your application. The Predicate pattern can be used to create elaborate nested structures that perform multiple complex steps. The utility of this is dependent on several factors. The implementation of the Predicates that are nested must take the same variables as both input and return. The result enables you to easily build structures of Predicates because the output of one can be the input of another. A simple example of a nested Predicate is the "logical and" Predicate. A BinaryPredicate, it accepts two other Predicates for input and returns true if both are true; otherwise, it returns false.

♦ **Don't be afraid to embed graphical user interfaces in Predicates.** One example of a useful application of Predicates is to perform pop-up dialog box queries of the user. A Predicate may paint a Yes/No dialog box to ask the user to respond to a question. The implementation could depend on the particular user interface details of a specific application. This application of Predicates has proven extremely useful in the experience of the author.

♦ **Don't limit yourself to user interfaces.** Predicates can do anything! The implementation of a user interface is just one application of the type of implementation you can encapsulate in a Predicate to accomplish the specific tests or actions that you have in mind. The implementation can also include database queries, invocations of distributed objects, file access, or virtually anything else you can dream up to include in the implementation of your Predicate. The entire framework for an application can be built on top of a Predicate architecture. This proves remarkably flexible in the long run, when you can efficiently restructure the application by changing a few Predicates.

Sample Code

The four generic Predicate types shown in Listing 20.1 were popularized by the Java Generic Library (JGL) toolkit from ObjectSpace and are widely accepted.

```
public interface UnaryPredicate
  extends java.io.Serializable
{
  public boolean execute( Object object );
};

public interface BinaryPredicate
  extends java.io.Serializable
```

```
{
  public boolean execute( Object first,
                          Object second );
};

public interface UnaryFunction
  extends java.io.Serializable
{
  public Object execute( Object object );
};

public interface BinaryFunction
  extends java.io.Serializable
{
  public Object execute( Object first,
                         Object second );
};
```

Listing 20.1 Interface for Predicates and Functions.

Many different generic implementations of these Predicates are available as part of the JGL toolkit. Examples of the Predicates provided by the JGL toolkit include GreaterThan, LessThan, NotEqual, PositiveNumber, NotEqualTo, and InstanceOf, as well as many others.

The generic Predicates are often extremely useful, but application development can benefit if you implement application-specific Predicates as well. The code in Listing 20.2 is an example of a custom Predicate designed to perform a specific task for an application. In this example, a dialog box is displayed to query for user input. This use of Predicates in the design of user interface makes it very easy for you to redesign and extend the user interface by simply moving around a few Predicates.

```
import java.awt.*;
import java.awt.event.*;
public class YesNoDialogPredicate
  implements UnaryPredicate
{
  public YesNoDialogPredicate()
  {                                                  Continues
```

```
    }

    /**
      * Instantiate a Yes/No Dialog box and ask the user for his feedback.
      */

    public boolean execute( Object object )
    {
        // This is perhaps the world's ugliest Yes/No confirmation dialog box.
        // I don't have a layout utility on hand at this moment.

        if (! (object instanceof String))
          {
            // Woops
            System.err.println("YesNoDialog should takes a String argument.");
            return false;
          }

        // Instantiate a Yes/No dialog with the appropriate query.

        Frame parent = new Frame();

        YesNoDialog d = new YesNoDialog( (String)object, parent );
        d.show();

        return d.value;
    }
};
```

Listing 20.2 YesNoDialogPredicate.

The dialog box that is displayed by this code simply asks the user a yes-or-no question. The user responds to this question by choosing either the Yes button or No button, and the result is returned as a boolean value from the predicate. The dialog box is implemented by the YesNoDialog class shown in Listing 20.3.

```
cclass YesNoDialog
  extends Dialog
{
  public boolean value = false;

  Panel p = new Panel();
  Label label1 = new Label();
  Button button1 = new Button("Yes");
  Button button2 = new Button("No");
  // Cancel is not a very good use of a Predicate.
  // In past implementations I've made Cancel throw an exception.

  GridLayout layout1 = new GridLayout(3,1);

  public YesNoDialog(String query, Frame parent)
  {
    super(parent,true);

    setSize(200,100);

    label1.setText(query);

    try {
      jbInit();
    }
    catch (Exception e) {
      System.err.println("YesNoDialogPredicate: " + e);
      e.printStackTrace();
    }
  }
  public void jbInit() throws Exception{
    p.setLayout(layout1);
    p.add(label1);
    p.add(button1);
    button1.addActionListener(new YesNoDialog_button1_actionAdapter(this));
    p.add(button2);                                          Continues
```

```
        button1.addActionListener(new YesNoDialog_button2_actionAdapter(this));
        this.add(p);
    }


    /*
    public void update( java.util.Observable o,
                                Object arg )
    {
      p.repaint();
    }
    */


    public void button1_actionPerformed( ActionEvent e )
    {
        // Request that the document perform the calculation.

        value = true;
        dispose();
    }


    public void button2_actionPerformed( ActionEvent e )
    {
        // Request that the document perform the calculation.

        value = false;
        dispose();
    }
};
```

Listing 20.3 Source for YesNoDialog.

The dialog box makes use of two adapter classes specifically for user interface purposes. These adapter classes don't have much impact on how mobile objects affect this application, but they are shown here, see Listing 20.4, for completeness. Adapter classes such as these are common elements of Java user interfaces to convert user interface events into specific method invocations on a target class. In this case, the JBuilder tool was used to assist us in the construction of these user interfaces, and JBuilder automatically generated these adapter classes in order to handle events from the buttons in the dialog box.

```
class YesNoDialog_button1_actionAdapter implements java.awt.event.ActionListener
{
  YesNoDialog adaptee;

  YesNoDialog_button1_actionAdapter(YesNoDialog adaptee) {
    this.adaptee = adaptee;
  }

  public void actionPerformed(ActionEvent e)
  {
    System.err.println("action");

    adaptee.button1_actionPerformed(e);
  }
}


class YesNoDialog_button2_actionAdapter implements java.awt.event.ActionListener
{
  YesNoDialog adaptee;

  YesNoDialog_button2_actionAdapter(YesNoDialog adaptee) {
    this.adaptee = adaptee;
  }

  public void actionPerformed(ActionEvent e)
  {
    System.err.println("action");

    adaptee.button2_actionPerformed(e);
  }
}
```

Listing 20.4 Source for YesNoDialog adapters.

The user interface for this YesNoDialog, is admittedly primitive, but that's not related to the programming technique that this Predicate demonstrates. Here you see a UnaryPredicate object that moves from the Source to the

Consumer application and displays a dialog box to query the user for input. This type of technique is powerful for developing applications that are extended at runtime through interaction with other network servers.

```
public interface Source
  extends java.rmi.Remote
{
  public UnaryPredicate askDude()
    throws java.rmi.RemoteException;

};
```

The implementation of the Source, called SourceImpl, shown in Listing 20.5, is a fairly straightforward implementation of an RMI server. This example Source simply instantiates the appropriate Predicate and supplies it to the Consumer through a remote invocation.

```
import java.rmi.*;
import java.rmi.server.*;

public class SourceImpl
  extends UnicastRemoteObject
  implements Source
{
  UnaryPredicate predicate = null;

  public static void main(String args[])
  {
    System.setSecurityManager(new RMISecurityManager());

    try
      {

        UnaryPredicate p = new YesNoDialogPredicate();
        SourceImpl o = new SourceImpl(p);

        Naming.rebind("Source",o);
      }
```

```
    catch (Exception e)
      {
        System.err.println("SourceImpl: " + e);
        e.printStackTrace();
      }
  }


public SourceImpl(UnaryPredicate predicate )
  throws java.rmi.RemoteException
{
  this.predicate = predicate;
}



public UnaryPredicate askDude()
  throws RemoteException
{
  return predicate;
}
}
```

Listing 20.5 Source for SourceImpl.

The implementation of the Consumer is equally obvious as an RMI client. The implementation contacts the Source, obtains a UnaryPredicate, and executes the Predicate with its desired question. The implementation of the Consumer is given in Listing 20.6.

```
import java.rmi.*;

public class Consumer
{
  public static void main(String args[])
  {
    try
      {
        Source theSource =
          (Source)Naming.lookup("//localhost/Source");          Continues
```

```
        UnaryPredicate p = theSource.askDude();

        // Ask the user a question.  Note that in this implementation
        // the question lives on the client side, but you could always
        // make a Predicate implementation in which the server stored
        // the question in the predicate.  Then you could use the
        // Predicate argument for something else.
        boolean answer = p.execute("Would you like to play a game?");
        System.err.println("The user answered " + answer + ".");
      }
    catch (Exception e)
      {
        System.out.println("Consumer: " + e);
        e.printStackTrace();
      }
  };
};
```

Listing 20.6 Source for Consumer.

This implementation of the Predicate pattern enables the Source to supply any desired implementation of UnaryPredicate to the Consumer. In this application, it allows the Source to specify how a question is asked of the end user at runtime by instantiating a dialog box. Other implementations might perform other types of actions to ask the user this question, or they might derive their answer by examining the subject passed into the Predicate. The Predicate might have also been used to establish a criterion for selecting a group of remote objects that pass the Predicate.

Related Patterns

Command can be viewed as a trivial form of Predicate that doesn't return a value. However, this view underemphasizes the importance of the Command pattern itself.

Predicates may be organized in a Chain of Responsibility to solve certain problems that involve a series of tests.

Composable Views [Krasner88]

Intent

Implement the view for each object as a composite of many views of member objects implemented as mobile objects.

Motivation

User interface code is subject to four key technical challenges, often overlooked by novice developers. First, user interface code is frequently coupled to application logic. Second, user interfaces are not easily adapted to meet new requirements. Third, user interface code, often constructed from the ground up with low-level AWT components, doesn't benefit from code reuse. Finally, user interfaces implemented in a large distributed system become scattered throughout the applications of the distributed system in a way that makes it difficult to migrate the user interfaces without redeploying many of the applications in the distributed system.

A developer can decouple application logic from the user interface by applying the MVC pattern. Recall that Views are user interfaces for Models in the MVC pattern. A single Model may have many different Views, but a View should observe only a single Model. The View of the MVC pattern addresses ways to avoid a tight coupling between the application logic and the user interface. The decoupled architecture of the MVC pattern enables the View to reference and use the Model, but the Model should not directly access its Views.

Benefits of Mobility

Composable Views provides a useful implementation of View reuse for implementing user interfaces during application design and construction, but it doesn't achieve its true potential until Composable Views are implemented as mobile objects. A Composable View can, by definition, be embedded in another Composable View. In an application development context, this means that Views of some objects in the system can be reused to implement Views for other parts of the system. In a mobile object context, a View for a mobile object can move from application to application on demand. Because any Composable View can be embedded in any other Composable View, the implementation of a Composable View as a mobile object enables the Composable View to be sent to new applications and dynamically embedded within that application's Composable Views. Mobile object normally can include user interfaces, but by implementing Composable Views the implementation can achieve a whole new level of interoperability in which any mobile object View can be embedded in the application no matter what its content, providing a useful way for interoperability of mobile object applications in a very flexible manner. Any of the Composable Views provided by any of the mobile object applications anywhere on the network can be composed to create new user interfaces at runtime. The result is a very fluid and flexible framework for interacting with any mobile object application on the network with the dynamic construction of new user interfaces.

MVC is very good at decoupling the user interface from the application logic by making the View depend on the Model, but not the reverse. As a result, the Model and View can evolve much more easily and independently from each other, establishing the value of Views as an architectural element in user interface design.

One limitation of Views is that some implementations require each View to be individually constructed from a core set of user interface components. This requirement does not allow Views to be reused when additional Views are constructed. Often this design is elegant because the Subject of a View may contain members that are Subjects of other Views. For example, in the implementation of a BankAccount object that represents the bank activity of an account holder, the BankAccount object might naturally contain at least one Person object representing the owner of the account. The implementation of the View for the BankAccount could naturally benefit from reusing the View of the contained Person object. Indeed, the BankAccount object might simply reuse the entire View of the Person object.

A benefit of embedding the Person View inside the BankAccount View is that the Person View implementation can be migrated to accommodate new requirements, reflecting the modifications each time the Person View is reused, including in the BankAccount View. As a result, Composable Views, Views in which individual views are composed among each other, is a powerful abstraction. Individual Views can be reused again in the construction of additional Views for higher-level objects.

In addition, the best models for reuse of user interfaces enable user interface elements to be shared among many distributed applications. When user interface application code is isolated to a single computer in a distributed system, any modification to the user interface of a single element in the system requires that a large fraction of the applications be upgraded or replaced. This can be an expensive operation. Implementing user interface elements as mobile objects enables the user interface elements to be shared across the network in such a way that the individual participants can share the appropriate user interface elements without modifying their own code each time the user interface elements change. Mobile objects enable them to change dynamically at runtime. Thus, implementation of a user interface through the composition of Views implemented as mobile objects provides a strong foundation for building a user interface.

Composable Views is often lumped together with Model, View, Controller. However, many of the implementations of MVC do not support Composable Views. The features of the Composable Views pattern are unique and provide benefits separate from those typically associated with MVC, so I have chosen to document the MVC and Composable View pattern independently of each other.

Applicability

Composable Views can help you do the following:

♦ Build complex user interfaces out of smaller elements.

♦ Reuse user interface elements in several places.

♦ Plan for the migration of user interfaces.

- Distribute user interface elements among multiple participants.
- Reuse user interface elements among the members of a distributed system.
- Assist in the application of object-oriented design concepts to user interface.

Structure

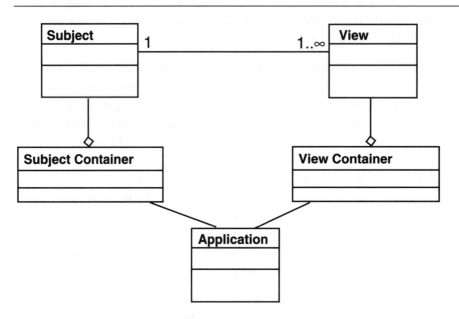

Figure 21.1 The structure of the Composable Views Pattern.

Participants

Subject.
An object implementing some application logic.

View.
An implementation of some user interface for a particular Subject. A single Subject may have multiple Views.

SubjectContainer.
A composite object that contains several Subject objects.

ViewContainer.
A composite user interface for a composite object. A user interface that reuses the user interface for several other Subjects.

Application.
An application with composite objects.

Collaborations

Application interacts with composite objects that follow some guidelines defined by SubjectContainer. SubjectContainer paints a user interface by using ViewContainer. The user interfaces of any contained Subject objects are painted through use of one or more of their corresponding Views.

Consequences

User interface reuse can be maximized. The implementation of user interfaces in terms of a composite view enables the reuse of views already defined for other objects. A new user interface does not have to be created from the ground up for the composite object.

New View objects may be dynamically introduced into a distributed system. As the requirements for an application change over time, the user interface must change to implement the new functionality. The implementation of these user interface changes can be made to the appropriate View. The changes are then reflected to any CompositeViews that reuse the View.

User interfaces may change when contents of composite objects change. As each CompositeView provides a user interface for a CompositeSubject, changes made to CompositeSubject are reflected in the CompositeView. Such changes may include the evolution of the contents of Composite-Subject and the addition of new or different objects to CompositeSubject.

Flexibility of architecture is governed by the design of ViewContainer. ViewContainer implements user interfaces using each of the View objects corresponding to the Subjects in the target SubjectContainer. As new Subject elements are added to the SubjectContainer, the

ViewContainer must detect and incorporate their Views if appropriate. This may mean that ViewContainers are not forward compatible with new SubjectContainers, forcing the updating of ViewContainers to reflect changes to SubjectContainers. The migration of updated Views should usually be an automatic result of the download of the new implementation of View objects in the form of mobile objects.

Implementation

Implementing Composable Views follows naturally from an implementation of MVC and the object-oriented model of building large things out of many small things. Consider the following when implementing Composable Views:

- **Follow MVC. Live MVC. Be MVC.** The proper implementation of this pattern requires the use of the MVC to decouple Views from their Subjects. If View and Subject remained coupled, implementing composite views based on the Views of elements of a composite object becomes complex and impractical.

- **Two approaches: Generic or specific.** Two very different approaches can be used for implementing Composable Views. First, the implementation can be based on designing a generic SubjectContainer and ViewContainer that act as containers for any Subjects or Views. The benefit of this approach is that it maximizes decoupling between the containers and their members. As a result, any member implementing the appropriate Subject or View interface can be added to the container. The disadvantage of this approach is the same as the advantage. The decoupling of the container from the members limits the container's ability to coordinate interaction between the members of the containers. All the implementation details of the member objects are hidden behind the Subject or View interface. The second approach is the opposite. A specific container may be implemented for a specific set of member elements. In this approach, the SubjectContainer and ViewContainer may have many different implementations rather than a single generic implementation. One implementation of the specific approach is discussed in the following point.

- **Build the View of an object from its members.** When you are implementing your objects out of many different members, the most natural way to build a user interface for the object is by reusing the views of the member objects to the greatest extent possible. This approach to reusing Views is at the heart of the Composable Views pattern.

♦ **The implementation of ViewContainer couples with the implementation of SubjectContainer.** When you are constructing the ViewContainer, it's difficult or impossible to avoid a close coupling of the implementation of ViewContainer with the implementation of SubjectContainer. ViewContainer is responsible for looking at the contents of SubjectContainer and paints the appropriate user interface by reusing Views of the Subject elements in the SubjectContainer. The implementation of ViewContainer may even be hard-coded to perform specific operations to paint this user interface. In this situation, when any changes are made to an implementation of SubjectContainer, any ViewContainers must be updated to reflect the changes. When implementing ViewContainers, strive to make as few assumptions about SubjectContainer as possible in order to make ViewContainer robust to handle as many changes to SubjectContainer as possible.

Sample Code

Almost any application that displays a user interface could benefit from this pattern and serve as an example. We've chosen to implement a contact management system, similar to the class of application used by presales organizations to track sales progress and manage prospects.

The implementation of this type of contact management system should clearly be able to display the set of contacts for the end user. Many types of contacts are possible, including companies and individuals. Each should have its own user interface. However, each type of contact is composed of similar elements such as name, address, and incident reports.

The first incarnation of this application should simply track the name and address of each contact. Each Contact is a composite of a Name and an Address object, as shown in Listing 21.1. The implementation of the ContactView is in terms of NameView and AddressView, pursuant to the Composable Views pattern. We'll examine the benefits of this approach as this example proceeds.

```
public class Contact
  implements Subject
{
  public Contact(Name name, Address address)
  {
    this.name = name;
    this.address = address;
  }

  public View getView()
  {
    // This should be constructed quickly as a composite of
    // the element views.

    return new ContactView(this);
  }

  public Name name;
  public Address address;
};
```

Listing 21.1 Source for Contact.

The implementation of the ContactView provides the user interface for an instance of the Contact object. The implementation of the Contact object provides a method called ettView that is capable of constructing a default implementation of a View object for an instance of a Contact (see Listing 21.2).

```
import java.awt.*;

public class ContactView
  extends View
{
  public ContactView(Contact contact)
  {
    // Notice, no coupling here except that the subelement
    // can produce a view.
```

```
    View nameView = contact.name.getView();
    View panelView = contact.address.getView();

    GridBagLayout layout = new GridBagLayout();

    setLayout(layout);

    GridBagConstraints c = new GridBagConstraints();
    c.gridwidth = GridBagConstraints.REMAINDER;
    c.weightx = 1.0;

    layout.setConstraints( nameView, c );
    this.add(nameView);

    layout.setConstraints( panelView, c );
    this.add(panelView);
  };
};
```

Listing 21.2 Source for ContactView.

The Contact object is an implementation of a Subject in this pattern. This is demonstrated in the source code listing by the inheritance of the Contact Java object from the Subject parent class. The implementation of this Subject class is shown in Listing 21.3.

```
public interface Subject
  extends java.io.Serializable
{
  public View getView();

};
```

Listing 21.3 Source for Subject.

With the implementation of the Subject with a default View provided, anyone who accesses any Subject can automatically construct a View for the Subject without any additional information about the type or value of the instance of the Subject. Specifying the Subject interface mandates that every Subject have this capability, regardless of the type of the Subject. In addition, the construction is performed through the use of the Factory Method pattern documented by the Gang of Four. This pattern enables the construction process of the View object to be encapsulated in such a way that a caller doesn't have to know the process or even the type of the View under construction.

Similarly, the implementation of the ContactView object is a View. The implementation inherits from the View parent class. The View object depends on the Subject object. The implementation of the View is shown in Listing 21.4.

```
import java.awt.*;

public class View
   extends Panel
{
};
```

Listing 21.4 Source for View.

The implementation of the Contact has two member objects: the Name and Address of the Contact. Whether the Contact refers to a company or a person, the Name object contains the name of the entity. The Address object contains the Address of the object. The implementation of the object in this example doesn't require us to differentiate the Contact and ContactView objects for different types of contacts, such as persons or companies. This differentiation can occur in this example through the assignment of names and addresses with customized behavior. The Name object provides an example of this. The base Name class is shown in Listing 21.5.

```
public interface Name
   extends Subject
{
};
```

Listing 21.5 Source for Name.

The implementation of Name provides the base behavior shared by derived Name objects that are specialized for individual types of contacts. The implementation of the Person object includes a customized type of Name that incorporates the behavior expected by the name of an individual. This includes the standard name components, such as the first name and last name. The implementation of the PersonName is implemented to as shown in Listing 21.6.

```java
public class PersonName
  implements Name
{
  public PersonName(String first, String last)
  {
    this.first = first;
    this.last = last;
  }

  public View getView()
  {
    return new PersonNameViewPnl(this);
  }

  public String first;
  public String last;
};
```

Listing 21.6 Source for PersonName.

The implementation of the CompanyName is even simpler than that of the PersonName. The CompanyName includes only one string, the name of the company. No additional information is required in the naming of a company. The implementation of CompanyName is shown in Listing 21.7.

```java
public class CompanyName
  implements Name
{
  public CompanyName(String name)
```

Continues

```
   {
      this.name = name;

   }

   public View getView()
   {
      return new CompanyNameViewPnl(this);
   }

   public String name;
};
```

Listing 21.7 Source for CompanyName.

The implementations of both CompanyName and PersonName inherit from the Name object in order to enable them to polymorphically behave as names when appropriate in the object model. One place this occurs is in the Contact object.

The implementation of the Address is homogenous across people and companies. In this example, the two different types of addresses are not differentiated. The implementation of the Address contains information such as the street, city, state, and ZIP code. The Address object constructs a AddressView when the getView method is invoked. As a result, any holder of an instance of the Address class can automatically construct an AddressView. The implementation of the Address is shown in Listing 21.8.

```
public class Address
   implements Subject
{
   String street1 = null;
   String street2 = null;
   String city = null;
   String state = null;
   String zipCode = null;

   public View getView()
```

```
  {
     return new AddressViewPnl(this);
  }

  public Address()
  {
  }

  public Address(String street1,
                 String street2,
                 String city,
                 String state,
                 String zipCode)
  {
     this.street1 = street1;
     this.street2 = street2;
     this.city = city;
     this.state = state;
     this.zipCode = zipCode;
  }
};
```

Listing 21.8 Source for Address.

The implementations of Name, PersonName, CompanyName, and Address are Subjects. Following the MVC pattern, a View should be provided for each of these Subjects. The implementation of these Views provides the user interface for each Subject.

The base class of all names, Name, is abstract. No instances of this Name parent class are ever created because we expect that instances of the PersonName and CompanyName classes should be created directly. The implementation of the NameViewPnl can itself be declared abstract to enforce the rule that only child classes of NameViewPnl should be instantiated, paralleling the structure of the Subjects. NameViewPnl implements the View for the base Name class, painting nothing but an empty rectangle. The implementation, trivial as it is, is shown in Listing 21.9.

```java
/**
 * Class NameView
 *
 * This Java source was generated by
 * the Java AWT Dialog Editor version 3.0
 *
 * on 29-Jun-98 8:44:47 PM
 */
import java.awt.*;
import java.awt.event.*;


abstract class NameViewPnl
  extends View
  implements
    java.awt.event.ActionListener,
    java.awt.event.AdjustmentListener,
    java.awt.event.ItemListener
{

  // Fields

  NameViewPnl(Name n)
  {
    this();
  }

  // Constructor
  NameViewPnl ()
  {

    setLayout (null);

  }

  /**
     * Overrides method in java.awt.Container
```

```
 *    Get preferred size.
 */
public java.awt.Dimension getPreferredSize ()
{
  return new java.awt.Dimension (270, 62);
}


/**
   * Implements java.awt.event.ActionListener interface.
   *    Handle ActionEvents fired by Components.
   */
public void actionPerformed (java.awt.event.ActionEvent evt)
{
}


/**
   * Implements java.awt.event.AdjustmentListener interface.
   *    Handle AdjustmentEvents fired by Components.
   */
public void adjustmentValueChanged (java.awt.event.AdjustmentEvent evt)
{
}


/**
   * Implements java.awt.event.ItemListener interface.
   *    Handle ItemEvents fired by Components.
   */
public void itemStateChanged (java.awt.event.ItemEvent evt)
{
}


} // End of class NameViewPnl
```

Listing 21.9 Source for NameViewPnl.

The implementation of the NameViewPnl as an abstract class mandates the creation of derived classes to implement the behavior for specific types of names. The NameViewPnl base class cannot be instantiated.

The first derived class provided to extend NameViewPnl is PersonName-ViewPnl, an implementation of a NameViewPnl that displays the name of a contact object, which is a person. The PersonNameViewPnl expects that the person's name is composed of two elements: the first name and last name. The View should present these elements in a reasonable manner in the implementation of the PersonNameViewPnl. In this example implementation of PersonNameViewPnl, the elements of the name are even labeled appropriately as "First" and "Last." The ContactView, already shown, reused this PersonNameViewPnl to display a Name object as part of the user interface for the Contact. The implementation of PersonNameViewPnl is shown in Listing 21.10.

```java
/**
 *  Class PersonNameViewPnl
 *
 *  This Java source was generated by
 *  the Java AWT Dialog Editor version 3.0
 *
 *  on 29-Jun-98 6:23:35 PM
 */
import java.awt.*;
import java.awt.event.*;


class  PersonNameViewPnl
   extends NameViewPnl
   implements
      java.awt.event.ActionListener,
      java.awt.event.AdjustmentListener,
      java.awt.event.ItemListener
{

   // Fields
   java.awt.TextField
      FIRSTNAME;
   java.awt.TextField
      LASTNAME;
```

```java
java.awt.Label
  LABEL1;
java.awt.Label
  LABEL2;

// Constructor
PersonNameViewPnl ()
{
  this(new PersonName("John","Doe"));
};

public PersonName name;

PersonNameViewPnl (Name n)
{
  if (!(n instanceof PersonName))
    {
      System.err.println("PersonNameView requires PersonName");
      return;
    }

  name = (PersonName)n;

  setLayout (null);

  FIRSTNAME = new java.awt.TextField (name.first);
  FIRSTNAME.addActionListener (this);
  FIRSTNAME.setBounds (6, 6, 122, 23);
  add (FIRSTNAME);

  LASTNAME = new java.awt.TextField (name.last);
  LASTNAME.addActionListener (this);
  LASTNAME.setBounds (140, 5, 117, 23);
  add (LASTNAME);

  LABEL1 = new java.awt.Label ("First");
  LABEL1.setBounds (7, 31, 38, 23);
```

Continues

```
    add (LABEL1);

  LABEL2 = new java.awt.Label ("Last");
  LABEL2.setBounds (141, 31, 38, 23);
  add (LABEL2);
}


/**
  *  Overrides method in java.awt.Container
  *     Get preferred size.
  */
public java.awt.Dimension getPreferredSize ()
{
  return new java.awt.Dimension (262, 54);
}


/**
  *  Implements java.awt.event.ActionListener interface.
  *     Handle ActionEvents fired by Components.
  */
public void  actionPerformed (java.awt.event.ActionEvent evt) {

  if (evt.getSource () == FIRSTNAME) {
    /****
        *     Insert own code to handle event
        ***/
    return;
  }
  if (evt.getSource () == LASTNAME) {
    /****
        *     Insert own code to handle event
        ***/
    return;
  }
}


/**
  *  Implements java.awt.event.AdjustmentListener interface.
```

```
   *    Handle AdjustmentEvents fired by Components.
   */
  public void  adjustmentValueChanged (java.awt.event.AdjustmentEvent evt)
  {
  }


  /**
   *   Implements java.awt.event.ItemListener interface.
   *    Handle ItemEvents fired by Components.
   */
  public void  itemStateChanged (java.awt.event.ItemEvent evt)
  {
  }
} // End of class PersonNameViewPnl
```

Listing 21.10 Source for PersonNameViewPnl.

This example uses two types of Contacts: persons and companies. The PersonNameViewPnl, shown in Listing 21.10, is an appropriate user interface for a person with a first and last name. However, a company is not identified by a first and last name. The implementation of this user interface is not appropriate for companies and must be customized to provide a way of displaying the name of a company.

Following object-oriented design concepts, another implementation of a child of NameViewPnl is provided that includes the desired behavior of painting the name for a company. The company name is simpler with only a single component and no need to label the name with "First" and "Last." This class is called the CompanyNameViewPnl, shown in Listing 21.11.

```
/**
 *  Class CompanyNameViewPnl
 *
 *  This Java source was generated by
 *  the Java AWT Dialog Editor version 3.0
 *
 *  on 29-Jun-98 6:23:35 PM
 */
```

Continues

```java
import java.awt.*;
import java.awt.event.*;


class   CompanyNameViewPnl
  extends NameViewPnl
  implements
    java.awt.event.ActionListener,
    java.awt.event.AdjustmentListener,
    java.awt.event.ItemListener
{

  //   Fields
  java.awt.TextField
    COMPANYNAME;
  java.awt.Label
    LABEL1;

  //   Constructor
  CompanyNameViewPnl ()
  {
    this(new CompanyName("Doe and Sons, Ltd."));
  };

  public CompanyName name;

  CompanyNameViewPnl (Name n)
  {

    if (!(n instanceof CompanyName))
      {
        System.err.println("CompanyNameView requires CompanyName");
        return;
      }

    name = (CompanyName)n;
```

```
    setLayout (null);

    COMPANYNAME = new java.awt.TextField (name.name);
    COMPANYNAME.addActionListener (this);
    COMPANYNAME.setBounds (6, 6, 250, 23);
    add (COMPANYNAME);

    LABEL1 = new java.awt.Label ("Company");
    LABEL1.setBounds (7, 31, 200, 23);
    add (LABEL1);
}


/**
  *  Overrides method in java.awt.Container
  *     Get preferred size.
  */
public java.awt.Dimension getPreferredSize ()
{
    return new java.awt.Dimension (262, 54);
}


/**
  *  Implements java.awt.event.ActionListener interface.
  *     Handle ActionEvents fired by Components.
  */
public void  actionPerformed (java.awt.event.ActionEvent evt)
{

  if (evt.getSource () == COMPANYNAME) {
    /****
         *      Insert own code to handle event
         ***/
    return;
  }

}
```

Continues

```
/**
 *   Implements java.awt.event.AdjustmentListener interface.
 *     Handle AdjustmentEvents fired by Components.
 */
public void  adjustmentValueChanged (java.awt.event.AdjustmentEvent evt)
{
}


/**
 *   Implements java.awt.event.ItemListener interface.
 *     Handle ItemEvents fired by Components.
 */
public void  itemStateChanged (java.awt.event.ItemEvent evt)
{
}
} // End of class CompanyNameViewPnl
```

Listing 21.11 Source for CompanyNameViewPnl.

A View corresponding to the Address object also must be provided to enable objects that make use of the Address object to display a user interface for it. The Contact object is an example of such an object that includes an Address displayed as part of the user interface. The implementation of the AddressView, shown in Listing 21.12, provides the user interface for an Address object.

```
/**
 *   Class AddressView
 *
 *   This Java source was generated by
 *   the Java AWT Dialog Editor version 3.0
 *
 *   on 29-Jun-98 7:21:55 PM
 */
import java.awt.*;
import java.awt.event.*;

class  AddressViewPnl
```

```
  extends View
  implements
    java.awt.event.ActionListener,
    java.awt.event.AdjustmentListener,
    java.awt.event.ItemListener
{

  // Fields
  java.awt.TextField
    STREET1;
  java.awt.TextField
    STREET2;
  java.awt.Label
    LABEL1;
  java.awt.Label
    LABEL2;
  java.awt.TextField
    CITY;
  java.awt.TextField
    STATE;
  java.awt.Label
    LABEL3;
  java.awt.Label
    LABEL4;
  java.awt.TextField
    ZIPCODE;
  java.awt.Label
    LABEL5;

AddressViewPnl()
{
  this(new Address());
}

// Constructor
AddressViewPnl (Address address)
{
```

Continues

```
setLayout (null);

STREET1 = new java.awt.TextField (address.street1);
STREET1.addActionListener (this);
STREET1.setBounds (7, 6, 288, 23);
add (STREET1);

STREET2 = new java.awt.TextField (address.street2);
STREET2.addActionListener (this);
STREET2.setBounds (8, 59, 286, 23);
add (STREET2);

LABEL1 = new java.awt.Label ("Street");
LABEL1.setBounds (7, 30, 46, 23);
add (LABEL1);

LABEL2 = new java.awt.Label ("Street");
LABEL2.setBounds (10, 82, 46, 23);
add (LABEL2);

CITY = new java.awt.TextField (address.city);
CITY.addActionListener (this);
CITY.setBounds (9, 108, 96, 25);
add (CITY);

STATE = new java.awt.TextField (address.state);
STATE.addActionListener (this);
STATE.setBounds (115, 109, 34, 23);
add (STATE);

LABEL3 = new java.awt.Label ("City");
LABEL3.setBounds (9, 133, 36, 23);
add (LABEL3);

LABEL4 = new java.awt.Label ("State");
LABEL4.setBounds (114, 133, 42, 23);
add (LABEL4);
```

```
    ZIPCODE = new java.awt.TextField (address.zipCode);
    ZIPCODE.addActionListener (this);
    ZIPCODE.setBounds (157, 109, 59, 23);
    add (ZIPCODE);

    LABEL5 = new java.awt.Label ("Zip Code");
    LABEL5.setBounds (159, 134, 64, 23);
    add (LABEL5);
}


/**
  *  Overrides method in java.awt.Container
  *     Get preferred size.
  */
public java.awt.Dimension getPreferredSize ()
{
  return new java.awt.Dimension (302, 252);
}


/**
  *  Implements java.awt.event.ActionListener interface.
  *     Handle ActionEvents fired by Components.
  */
public void  actionPerformed (java.awt.event.ActionEvent evt)
{
  if (evt.getSource () == STREET1) {
    /****
        *     Insert own code to handle event
        ***/
    return;
  }
  if (evt.getSource () == STREET2) {
    /****
        *     Insert own code to handle event
        ***/
    return;
  }
```

Continues

```
    if (evt.getSource () == CITY) {
      /****
            *      Insert own code to handle event
            ***/
      return;
    }
    if (evt.getSource () == STATE) {
      /****
            *      Insert own code to handle event
            ***/
      return;
    }
    if (evt.getSource () == ZIPCODE) {
      /****
            *      Insert own code to handle event
            ***/
      return;
    }
  }


  /**
    *   Implements java.awt.event.AdjustmentListener interface.
    *      Handle AdjustmentEvents fired by Components.
    */
  public void  adjustmentValueChanged ( java.awt.event.AdjustmentEvent evt )
  {
  }


  /**
    *   Implements java.awt.event.ItemListener interface.
    *      Handle ItemEvents fired by Components.
    */
  public void  itemStateChanged (java.awt.event.ItemEvent evt)
  {
  }
} // End of class AddressViewPnl
```

Listing 21.12 Source for AddressViewPnl.

Finally, an implementation of a Server must be provided to keep track of and distribute Contact objects when clients make requests for them. The simple Server provided as part of this example simply instantiates a short list of two Contacts, then sends these Contacts to Clients that make requests for them. One of the two Contacts is a Person, the other is a Company (see Listing 21.13).

```java
import java.rmi.*;

public class Server
  extends java.rmi.server.UnicastRemoteObject
  implements ContactRepository
{
  ContactList list;

  public Server()
    throws java.rmi.RemoteException
  {
    list = new ContactListImpl();

    CompanyName wileyName = new CompanyName("Wiley, Inc.");
    Address wileyAddress = new Address("200 W. Java Way",
                                       "",
                                       "New York",
                                       "NY",
                                       "10001");
    Contact wiley = new Contact(wileyName, wileyAddress);

    list.push(wiley);

    PersonName jeffName = new PersonName("Jeff","Nelson");
    Address jeffAddress = new Address("1150 W Addison",
                                      "",
                                      "Chicago",
                                      "IL",
                                      "00001");
    Contact jeff = new Contact(jeffName, jeffAddress);
```

Continues

```
    list.push(jeff);

}


public ContactList getList()
   throws java.rmi.RemoteException
{
   return list;
}


public static void main(String[] args)
{

       System.setSecurityManager(new RMISecurityManager());

   try
     {
       Server o = new Server();

       Naming.rebind("Contacts",o);
     }
   catch (Exception e)
     {
       System.err.println("SourceImpl: " + e);
       e.printStackTrace();
     }
 }
};
```

Listing 21.13 Source for Server.

> The implementation of the Client connects to the Server and requests the current list of Contacts. The Client automatically displays the first element of the Contact list. A button bar is shown that enables the end user to iterate through the Contact list, displaying each of the Contacts in turn by pushing either Next or Back. The OK and CANCEL buttons shown as part of the user interface are not currently implemented in this example. Note

that the code for interacting with these buttons follows the Command pattern for mobile objects, discussed earlier.

The implementation of the Client is somewhat limited. It does not attempt to modify the values of the Contact list at all; it simply displays the View we implemented earlier in this example. Creating the code to enable the values of Contact objects to be modified is just a matter of adding the appropriate user interface code to the Client, but this additional user interface code has little to do with the pattern demonstrated by this example, other than showing the further reuse of this code when elements of the user interface are composed together (see Listing 21.14).

```java
import java.rmi.*;
import java.util.*;
import java.awt.*;
import java.awt.event.*;

public class Client
{
  public static void main(String[] args)
  {
    try
      {
        ContactRepository repository =
          (ContactRepository)Naming.lookup("//localhost/Contacts");

        // We obtain all the Contacts in one lump sum.  Kind of lame,
        // but this is only an example.
        ContactList list = repository.getList();

        DisplayContact doDisplay = new DisplayContact(list);
        doDisplay.run();
      }
    catch (Exception e)
      {
        System.out.println("Consumer: " + e);
        e.printStackTrace();                            Continues
```

```
        }
    }
};
```

Listing 21.14 Source for Client.

All the pieces of this example application are now in place, and we are ready to try running it. The application is a straightforward client/server. You can start the distributed system, using the same process you use in starting any other RMI application. First, start the rmiregistry.

```
% rmiregistry
```

The server application, Server, distributes the ContactList on demand when Client requests a copy of it. Therefore, Server must be started before Client to allow Server to initialize itself in preparation to respond to requests from Client. If you use the JDK, execute the server with the command line shown in the following command line. If you're not using the JDK, execute the server with the mechanism provided by your favorite Java development environment.

```
% java Server
```

The client application, Client, contacts the server and uses it to obtain the ContactList and the implementation for all the Views as mobile objects. Client displays each Contact individually by composing the views of many different types of objects. You can execute the Client following the same procedures as for Server. For the JDK, the following command line should suffice:

```
% java Client
```

The Client displays a window, similar to that created by Listing 21.2, that displays the first Contact. The user interface for the Contact object, as implemented by the ContactView class, is downloaded over the network as part of the Contact mobile object with the same RMI ClassLoader that was used to load the byte code for the Contact class. The ContactView is built up from the views of the subobjects of Contact, including the NameView and AddressView. Both classes are also downloaded from the server as part of the ContactView mobile object.

The first Contact is a person, so the NameView for this first Contact shows the customizations characteristic of the PersonNameView. The PersonNameView is reused by the ContactView to display the content of the Name element contained in the Contact object. The particular implementation of the NameView class is specified by the Server, not the Client. The Server is free to specify which implementation of NameView is passed to the Client and embedded within the composable view for the Contact.

An example of such an extension is the CompanyNameView. The CompanyNameView paints the user interface appropriate for a company contact. To view the Company contact, press the "Next" button shown on the bottom of the Contact window. The Client then moves forward to the second contact in the ContactList. The second contact is still an object of type Contact. However, the view for the Company contact makes use of the CompanyNameView object rather than the PersonNameView. When the Contact is displayed, the CompanyNameView is displayed inside the ContactView and shows the customizations appropriate for a Company contact. The implementation of the CompanyNameView is downloaded along with the Contact mobile object. Thus, the Server is free to specify any desired implementation for this embedded view.

The PersonNameView is polymorphically embedded in the ContactView. The ContactView itself does not have to know about the differences in the implementation of the different available NameView and AddressView classes. It therefore enables dynamic runtime extensibility of the user interface by enabling the server to specify new implementations of the NameView or AddressView objects embedded in the ContactView. This dynamic extensibility of the user interface as well as the benefits of the object view reuse make up the characteristic benefits of this pattern.

Related Patterns

The Composable views pattern utilizes the Gang-of-Four Composite pattern in its nesting of Views. Composite may also be useful in nesting Subjects.

Chain of Responsibility is often useful in implementing composite views by giving each member of the composite an opportunity to handle a request.

Extension [Nelson98]

Intent

Create a set of associated mobile objects that adds functionality to a mobile object, then distribute these mobile objects to appropriate hosts.

Benefits of Mobility

One of the clearest benefits of mobility is the ability to move new objects, with their state and implementation, into an application at runtime without any complex software installation process or recompilation. The Extension pattern captures the essence of this capability by defining a mechanism for adding new features into an application by implementing a common Extension interface. Once this Extension interface is defined, new features can be added to the application by implementing the interface and moving into the target application through a remote method invocation. The capabilities of the new Extension are limited only by the SecurityManager registered inside of the target application and may include painting new user interfaces, implementing file access, accessing or modifying static variables, communicating with new network services, or any other capability of a Java object.

Motivation

Applications necessarily have limited capability. A single application can perform only the limited number of tasks for which it was designed. Memory, performance, and the size of the deployed applications are considerations that may limit the features bundled into an application.

In addition, some applications require that certain capabilities be available to some individuals but not to others, as defined by the job functions of a particular group of users. For example, members of the support staff should be able to add or modify entries to the Help Desk. Members of the engineering team should be able to annotate a problem with proposed solutions. Members of the management team should be able to track the schedules of staff members. All of these application details may be embodied in a security policy that defines what each user can and can't do. In the best case, the applications deployed to each of these end users would parallel their capabilities.

A mobile object approach to application development enables an innovative new approach to this problem. The capabilities of this system can be broken up into many different mobile objects and distributed only to the end users allowed to possess their capabilities. As a result, not only does the security policy enforce what a user can and can't do, the actual application code never reaches end users who are not allowed to perform certain actions.

Objects require specific functionality during the course of their lives. Depending on the situation, breaking up functionality that is required only under certain conditions into separate objects may offer an opportunity to remove or eliminate capabilities that should not be available under most conditions. Configurators and Editors for components in development environments are examples of this type of object. Configurators enable developers to conveniently modify the properties of a specific component at design time. Configurators should be distributed to only a limited audience of developers, but they should not be deployed in the end product. The same argument applies to Editors, which are similar to Configurators in that they enable developers to edit a specific type of property used by many different components.

The implementation of software is inherently a multiple-stage process. As new functionality is added to a system, observations are made regarding desires for additional functionality. Extension enables additional functionality to be added after the fact to a system that may already be deployed. The original implementation of objects may be replaced by extension objects to provide greater functionality.

Applicability

Use Extension in the following situations:

♦ Requirements change rapidly.

♦ Applications should be extensible at runtime.

♦ Many different behaviors are expressed by an application under a variety of conditions.

Structure

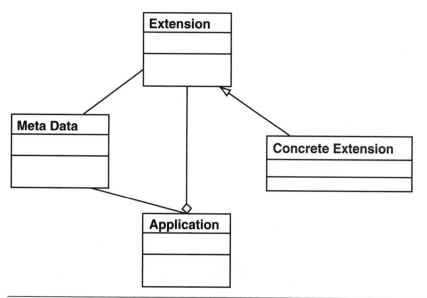

Figure 22.1 The structure of the Extension Pattern.

Participants

Extension.
An abstract interface common to all extensions.

ConcreteExtension.
An implementation of a specific extension.

MetaData.
One or more objects documenting a specific extension.

Application.
An application that can host extensions.

Collaborations

ConcreteExtension is an implementation of Extension that includes some new functionality. Many different implementations of ConcreteExtensions may be available for an Extension. MetaData describes the capability of ConcreteExtension. Applications may contain many or few Extensions.

Consequences

Application flexibility is improved. Any implementation of a ConcreteExtension conforming to Extension can be added to the application at runtime. As the application requirements evolve and change, new Extensions can be produced to encompass these new requirements.

Obtaining feature enhancements as mobile objects at runtime may impact performance if the implementation, and therefore the class files, for these mobile objects is large. Clearly, a difference exists between loading a couple of classes that paint a new type of checkbox and loading the hottest new Web browser as an extension to your application. The sizes of the implementation of these two extensions are quite different. Whenever they are loaded from across the network, their implementation must be loaded in the form of a set of Java classes and serialized objects. This requirement can and will impact system performance for large extensions.

Copying many Extensions into the application incurs a performance hit. Each Extension must be loaded from across the network as a mobile object. This loading process incurs the same overhead as any other mobile object operation, which is a slight network overhead for loading the state and class files for the mobile object. This overhead should be slight except when many Extensions are involved.

Success depends on the design of the Extension interface. All ConcreteExtensions must implement Extension. Application interacts with every Extension through the Extension interface. As a result, the design of the Extension interface is critical to the value of the Extension pattern.

Implementation

The Extension pattern is relatively simple to implement, particularly when you have a good idea about the type of Extensions that should be possible within the system. Consider the following points:

- **Keep Extension as general as possible.** Since each ConcreteExtension must implement Extension, building a complex Extension interface complicates the construction of additional Extensions.

- **Use MetaData in place of the Extension interface.** An abstract interface such as Extension defines the operations that each Extension must implement. Effectively, this Extension interface becomes a contract between each ConcreteExtension and the rest of the application. The operations on the Extension interface define how the application can invoke each ConcreteExtension. These operations must fully declare the capabilities of the ConcreteExtension for the application because no additional specification about the ConcreteExtension is available. An alternative to mandating a specific Extension interface for each ConcreteExtension is to provide some source of MetaData for ConcreteExtensions to document their capabilities. Using MetaData is a totally different approach that can totally eliminate the need for a root Extension interface. MetaData describes the capabilities of a ConcreteExtension. Applications use this description to determine how to interact with specific ConcreteExtensions and to make choices on how to use each ConcreteExtension. Extension is generally easier to implement but less flexible than MetaData. Extension is easier to implement because it is simply a matter of defining and implementing a base interface. MetaData requires additional overhead, including the examination of the MetaData object whenever a new ConcreteExtension is added to an application. However, MetaData enables an object to become an Extension without having to implement a base interface. The resulting system can be more flexible because no intrusive modifications are required to make an object into a ConcreteExtension.

♦ **Consider an architecture based on Chain of Responsibility or Decorator.** An application that follows the Extension pattern should enable many Extensions to be added arbitrarily to the application. Chain of Responsibility enables an application to query a list of extensions, giving each an opportunity to handle a given request. This architecture places the logic required to handle requests squarely in the individual Extensions, decoupling it from the application itself. Decorator enables an Extension to be layered on top of another feature. Each Decorator may be independent from the other Decorators and implement the appropriate features.

♦ **Enable extension removal.** The implementation of the Smorgasbord pattern should enable Consumers to easily obtain numerous Extensions. The selection of Extensions is generally going to be based on documentation contained in a set of MetaData objects. This information may be incomplete, even misleading, resulting in users' selecting Extensions that they later regret. For this reason, some mechanism should be provided for removing extensions from an application after the fact. The process for removing an Extension as well as the determination of whether such removal is even possible will vary depending on how the Extension pattern is implemented. This may be as simple as removing the extension from a Chain of Responsibility or throwing away a particular Decorator.

♦ **Piggyback on a component framework if possible.** Component frameworks, such as JavaBeans, parallel the goals of the Extension pattern. JavaBeans, in particular, may often be treated as mobile objects, already have MetaData, and be an already widely adopted standard for building additional functionality for Java applications. Since many components now follow specific contracts regarding their functionality, components may not be immediately useful as Extensions without some additional effort. However, the benefits of having access to adding any available component as an Extension into your application may outweigh the difficulty in mapping the components to Extensions.

Sample Code

The following example demonstrates an implementation of the Extension pattern through the use of Mobile Beans. Unfortunately, this example, based on Sun's BeanBox, is fairly extensive and cannot be quoted in its entirety here. Please refer to the CD for the complete example.

In this example, the client application starts running without any Beans compiled into it. The first action it takes is contacting a network service called Antenna to download a set of Beans. These Beans are Extensions that are now available for consumption by the client application. Because this example is based closely on the BeanBox demonstration container provided by JavaSoft, the Bean Extensions are just components that can be reused within the BeanBox. In another application, the mobile Beans could be used in any number of other ways. Beans might implement database access, new user interfaces, spell-checking features, or any number of other features the original application lacked. The important point is that the Beans are now available in the client application and can implement functionality previously unavailable.

Caffeine is used for this application to provide the mechanism for communication in the distributed system. However, the JavaBeans in this application are communicated in a very straightforward manner, as prepackaged Jar files that the JarLoader built into the BeanBox is capable of reading. The Jars are communicated as raw byte arrays. This application doesn't take advantage of the mobile object features built into Caffeine, preferring a low-level solution to the high-level functionality provided free by Caffeine. Although this solution might not sound pretty, it's very effective when used with the JarLoader because all the class, resources, and serialized objects, which are members of the Bean, can be communicated as one unit in the Jar. This architecture is still mobile object based, because the state and implementation of the Beans are moving as part of the Jar file. However, in this case, the application itself contains most of the logic for interpreting and loading these objects through the JarLoader.

The implementation of the CORBA interface for communicating the Extensions is then provided in Listing 22.1.

```
module sun
{
  module beancaster
  {
    interface Iterator
    {
      typedef sequence<octet> ByteArray;
      exception NoMoreElements {};
      ByteArray getNext() raises (NoMoreElements);
    };

    interface Antenna
    {
      Iterator getBeans();
    };
  };
};
```

Listing 22.1 Interface for Antenna.

In the sample IDL, ByteArray represents a bytecode encapsulation of the contents of a complete Jar file. This Jar file is the implementation of the Extension to this application. Multiple Extensions can be downloaded during the initial phase of communication. All the Extensions available from the Server are downloaded every time the client connects to the server.

The implementation depends on having a CORBA server capable of providing the Extensions. For no good reason, this server is called Antenna for this application. Antenna is responsible for keeping track of all the Extensions and sending them to the client on demand. The implementation of Antenna is therefore a CORBA server as shown in Listing 22.2.

```
// Server.java

import java.util.*;
import sun.beancaster.IteratorPackage.*;
import java.io.*;

// Auxiliary class
```

```
class JarIterator extends sun.beancaster._sk_Iterator
{
  int i;
  byte[][] jars;

  public JarIterator(byte[][] j)
    {

      jars = j;
      i = 0;

    }

  public byte[] getNext() throws NoMoreElements
    {

      if ( jars == null)
        throw new NoMoreElements();
      else if ( i >= jars.length )
        throw new NoMoreElements();

      return jars[i++];

    }

}

public class Server extends sun.beancaster._sk_Antenna
{
  byte[][] jars = null;

  public Server( String s )
    {
      super( s );
```

Continues

```
    // read in Jars and build hashtable

    Vector jarNames = getJarNames();

    jars = new byte[jarNames.size()][];

    try
      {

        for (int i = 0; i < jarNames.size(); i++)
          {

            String name = (String)jarNames.elementAt(i);
            System.err.println("Reading: " + name);

            FileInputStream is = new FileInputStream(name);
            jars[i] = new byte[is.available()];
            is.read(jars[i]);

          }

      }
    catch (Exception e)
      {

        System.err.println("Server: File not found " + e);
        System.exit(1);

      }


  }

private static Vector getJarNames() {
    File cwd = new File(System.getProperty("user.dir"));
    System.err.println("cwd: " + cwd);
```

```
    File pwd = new File(cwd.getParent());
    System.err.println("pwd: " + pwd);

     File jars = new File(pwd, "jars");
    System.err.println("jars: " + jars);


    if (! jars.isDirectory()) {
      System.err.println(jars+" is not a directory!!");
      }


     Vector result = new Vector(0);
String names[];
names = jars.list(new sun.beancaster.FileExtension(".jar"));
for (int i=0; i<names.length; i++) {
result.addElement(jars.getPath() + File.separatorChar + names[i]);
}


return result;
  }


  public static void main(String[] args) {
    try {
      // Initialize the ORB.
      org.omg.CORBA.ORB orb = org.omg.CORBA.ORB.init();
      // Initialize the BOA.
      org.omg.CORBA.BOA boa = orb.BOA_init();

      Server s = new Server( "BeanCaster" );

      // Export self.
      boa.obj_is_ready( s );
      System.out.println( s + " is ready." );
      // Wait for incoming requests
      boa.impl_is_ready();
```

Continues

```
    }
    catch(org.omg.CORBA.SystemException e) {
      System.err.println(e);
    }
  }


  public sun.beancaster.Iterator getBeans()
    {
      return new JarIterator(jars);
    }
}
```

Listing 22.2 Implementation of the Server.

The relevant code responsible for loading the Extensions is shown in Listing 22.3. This code first initializes the CORBA ORB, connects to the Antenna, downloads all the Jars from the Antenna, and finally loads them into the BeanBox using the JarLoader.

```
org.omg.CORBA.ORB orb = org.omg.CORBA.ORB.init();

// Locate BeanCaster
sun.beancaster.Antenna receiver =
  sun.beancaster.AntennaHelper.bind(orb, "BeanCaster");
sun.beancaster.Iterator iter = receiver.getBeans();

try
  {
    while (true)
      {
        byte[] buf = iter.getNext();
        ByteArrayInputStream is = new ByteArrayInputStream(buf);
        JarLoader.loadJarDoOnBean("", is, helper);
        doLayout();
      }
  }
catch (sun.beancaster.IteratorPackage.NoMoreElements e)
```

```
{

    System.err.println("Done reading beans.");

}
```

Listing 22.3 Source for loading JAR files.

To run this example, start Visigenic and the Smart Agent. Next, run the Server in the top-level directory of the BDK. The server was designed to try to load any file stored in a subdirectory called "jars" if they end with a file extension *.jar. Any files matching these criteria are loaded and sent to the client as Extensions. Finally, start the modified BeanBox itself, called bean-caster. As each Bean is loaded from the server and added to the client, a new icon appears in the ToolBox portion of the BeanBox application.

Related Patterns

The implementation of Extension can be assisted through the use of some of the core Gang-of-Four patterns. Decorator is an effective way of augmenting the base behavior of an object by adding additional implementation to the object. An application implemented with Chain of Responsibility may provide a convenient and easy-to-use mechanism for adding new functionality by simply adding the Extension to the chain.

Smorgasbord
[Mowbray97]

Intent

Provide a pick list of available mobile objects representing additional or optional capabilities that may be added to an application at runtime.

Benefits of Mobility

The Smorgasbord pattern has success in a number of areas of building and configuring applications to meet user requirements. However, one limitation of the traditional approach is that all the extensions available in the Smorgasbord must be pre-installed and must be present in the client whether or not the Extension is used. Mobile objects enable the Smorgasbord pattern to selectively include or exclude Extensions based on user preferences. Unused Extensions don't have to be present in the application or even installed on the computer. As a result, unused Extensions don't impact application performance or the size of the application. The Smorgasbord pattern can be viewed as the front end for selecting from potentially thousands or millions of Extensions available throughout a host network.

Motivation

Different users have different preferences and requirements for the functionality of an application. If extensions above and beyond the core functionality of an application are proved to be mobile objects at run-time, users may choose among the features they desire. The appropriate mobile objects implementing the preferences of the user are then obtained to provide the desired functionality.

The cost of feature enhancement is often spread across all users with little regard for whether they will use all features. Many applications quickly become bloated when many extensions are added into the application. Application bloat results in greater consumption of system resources such as disk space and processing power. Some systems may have performance requirements that dictate which combinations of features are possible and still enable the system to achieve the mandated performance.

Mobile objects encapsulate portions of the functionality of an application. However, application bloat inevitably results if all possible extensions are added into every application. The functional requirements or preferences of users may differ considerably from individual to individual. By providing the user with a choice between available extensions, all requirements can be met while maintaining the desired level of performance.

Applicability

Use the Smorgasbord pattern under the following conditions:

♦ Performance requirements prevent the simultaneous use of all possible features.

♦ Numerous enhancement options are made available on a continuous basis.

♦ End users are being charged for premium features.

♦ Users must be made aware of new features.

♦ New features should be available to users as soon as possible after delivery.

Participants

Extension.
The specification for the interface that each Extension must implement. This may be a trivial interface.

ConcreteExtension.
The implementation of each extension as a mobile object.

MetaData.
Objects that describe and document the extensions.

Consumer.
An application developed by a user.

Directory.
A directory containing information about available extensions and how to obtain them.

Structure

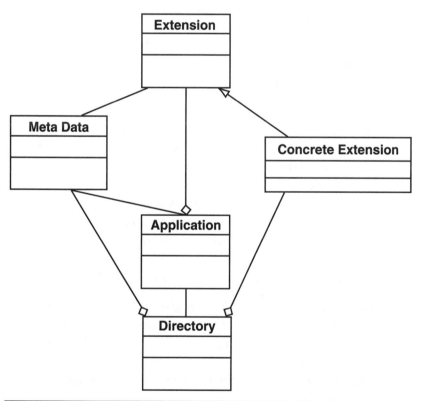

Figure 23.1 The structure of the Smorgasbord Pattern.

Collaborations

Application obtains MetaData and offers a presentation to users, enabling them to select their preferences. ConcreteExtension for the selected extensions should be obtained from the appropriate sources. MetaData may be stored in Directory.

Consequences

MetaData loading is cheaper than Extension loading. MetaData is normally a collection of one or more small Java objects. An extension may be a large, complex component composed of an extensive set of Java objects. A complex system may have thousands of possible extensions. Importing of all of them may significantly impact the system performance. Performance may be degraded to such a great extent that loading all extensions is unrealistic. Loading the MetaData for each extension to give the client a choice of extensions to load is often a cheaper, more realistic path to implementing an application.

Users can be made aware of new product features and try them out immediately as they become available. Implementing Smorgasbord, sending MetaData about the functionality of each component to the client to give the client an opportunity to choose which components to consume, provides the perfect opportunity to learn about new product features as they become available. Implementing Smorgasbord may provide a user interface for displaying this information to the user. New features, like old features, are displayed in this list of alternatives. In addition, a mechanism could certainly be implemented for highlighting new or alternative features as they become available.

Users can select desired product features given their personal preferences for functionality and performance of an application. Application bloat is always a problem as applications acquire new features and follow a growth path toward the large and complex. In the mobile object arena, the impact of network overhead is also a consideration. Extensions may be expensive to load; therefore, this impact must be minimized. Extensions may additionally impact the performance of an application as they increase the number of tasks that the client application must perform. When the possible feature set is displayed and the user can choose features, only the desired features are loaded, eliminating the impact of undesirable features on the application.

A costing model for individual enhancements can be made. Smorgasbord enables the individual extensions of an application to be singled out and selected for their individual merit. Considerations may include performance, cost, size, and any other factors important to the user. Smorgasbord can be implemented alongside an electronic commerce framework to enable individual extensions to be purchased and added to the application, providing an interesting alternative to always selling an application as an indivisible product.

If the number of extensions is large, accessing a completely new copy of the extension MetaData with every session may not be realistic. Even though loading MetaData is generally cheaper than loading extensions, the number of extensions may imply that the set of MetaData is itself quite considerable. Loading all the MetaData may significantly impact system performance, particularly if the MetaData is stored in an inefficient manner or loaded from a network source every time. As a result, application developers should consider implementing a local cache for MetaData, possibly by storing MetaData objects in a local database or implementing an efficient flat-file representation of the required MetaData.

Implementation

Smorgasbord adds to the capabilities of the Extension pattern by providing a mechanism for enabling endusers to select desired Extensions. As a result, the first task of implementing the Smorgasbord pattern is to implement the Extension pattern. In addition, the following are some issues of Smorgasbord implementations:

♦ **Obtain and display ExtensionMetaData.** ExtensionMetaData informs users about the capabilities of the available extensions. The implementation of the ExtensionMetaData should include appropriate documentation for describing the Extension to the user. Since ExtensionMetaData objects are mobile objects, ExtensionMetaData may implement the appropriate user interfaces to display options to inform the user regarding the available extensions.

- ◆ **Use an Extension Directory Service.** ExtensionMetaData may be stored in a manner similar to that for a directory service. The central service or a group of federated directory services acts as a repository for the MetaData for any possible extensions. Extensions don't necessarily need to be stored in the directory service—just information regarding how to obtain each extension.

- ◆ **Obtain and use selected ExtensionImplementations.** The extension implementations are mobile objects. You may obtain them by invoking an appropriate operation to construct the Extension and return it to the consumer. A simple mechanism for obtaining these Extensions is to make them mobile objects that are return parameters for remote invocations. Once the operation is invoked, the Extension is returned to the Consumer as a mobile object.

- ◆ **Cache MetaData and Extension objects between sessions.** The loading of large numbers of MetaData and Extension objects between Sessions may negatively impact performance. Since MetaData and Extension objects should often be implemented as mobile objects, communication of each object incurs some state and class copying overhead. Although this overhead is small enough to be ignored for low-volume situations, significant overhead occurs when hundreds and thousands of objects are available. Caching the state and class files for MetaData and Extension objects between sessions eliminates the overhead of loading these across the network. Voyager has an integrated caching mechanism. Other mobile object tools may require considerable handcoding to cache extensions.

- ◆ **Use Surrogates.** Scaling to many hundreds or thousands of extensions in an application requires that the application be properly designed to avoid significant performance hits for each extension. One method for enhancing such performance is the use of Surrogate objects. A Surrogate is a place-holder object that doesn't incur the initialization and resource consumption of the original object. Surrogates can be used with Smorgasbord in at least two ways. First, the MetaData objects may be Surrogates to avoid the loading and construction of complete MetaData objects. This method saves the performance cost of this initialization phase when many Extensions are available with thousands of MetaData objects. An application can benefit from using

Surrogates in place of Extensions initially. Doing so ensures that an application with many thousands of installed Extensions may not suffer from a performance loss for Extensions that are not employed with every session.

♦ **Build a generic container for Extensions rather than shrink-wrapped applications.** A shrink-wrapped application is a static product that is frozen, packaged, and shipped to a customer base. Changing or improving the shrink-wrapped application requires the shipment of a new, updated product to the customer. Instead of this approach to software, consider the merits of building a generic container application for Extensions following the Smorgasbord pattern. A generic container could implement no useful capabilities of its own, but the container application may host any number of Extensions. The Extensions may implement any number of application functions including application windows, menus, database access, and application logic. The implementation of an application in terms of Extensions enables very flexible construction of the product and migration of the functionality of the product over time. Shipping an end product to a user involves shipping a generic container application with a set of default Extensions.

♦ **Enable any client or consumer to select alternatives without a user interface.** Smorgasbord may often be a mechanism for enabling an end user to choose a desired feature set. This implies that a user interface is used to display the possible alternatives to the user. However, Smorgasbord can also be used to enable any client or consumer to select from a range of possible alternatives. The client may make these decisions with little or no user input based on its own criteria.

Sample Code

Because of the relationship between Extension and Smorgasbord, implementing Smorgasbord often builds on Extension. This example continues from where the Extension example left off, with the implementation of a pick list for choosing components that are to be included in the application. The goal is to enable the user of the BeanBox application to choose the components to include in the application rather than including all of them.

To implement this choice, an implementation of BeanInfo is provided to represent the MetaData for each of the beans. However, this implementation of BeanInfo is very limited. Only the name of the bean is displayed as part of the application. The default implementation of BeanInfo utilizes a class called BeanDescriptor to describe all the information about the Bean. Sadly, the way this BeanDescriptor object was designed, the Bean and its customizer must be loaded into the application to construct the BeanDescriptor object. This requirement represents a significant weakness because it means that the Bean object must be loaded into the JVM before a consumer can even look at its MetaData. In a setting that includes potentially thousands of components, loading each component to determine its MetaData is impractical. Rather than depending on this default implementation, a BeanInfoLite class, shown in Listing 23.1, is implemented that provides a light-weight representation of a Bean's MetaData and does not suffer from the limitation that the Bean must be loaded before it can be examined.

```
public class BeanInfoLite
   implements NullBeanInfo
{
   public String beanName;

   public BeanInfoLite(String beanName)
   {
      this.beanName = beanName;
   }

   public BeanDescriptor getBeanDescriptor()
   {
      return new BeanDescriptorLite(beanName);
   }

   /**
    * A more robust implementation of this might instantiate the correct
    * BeanInfo and return the actual EventSetDescriptor.  However, in this
    * case, we just return null.
    */
```

```
   public EventSetDescriptor[] getEventSetDescriptors()
   {
     return null;
   }


   // ÷
};
```

Listing 23.1 Source for BeanInfoLite.

The goal of this BeanInfoLite class is to represent the core portions of the bean MetaData while avoiding the instantiation of the bean or loading of its classes. For the purposes of this prototype, only the name of the Bean is present in the BeanInfoLite object. Not much MetaData is there, but additional MetaData could be added with additional effort. A fabricated value is returned for the more advanced MetaData for the bean. For example, the EventSetDescriptor set is null. The BeanDescriptorLite class is implemented as shown in Listing 23.2.

```
/**
  * BeanDescriptorLite
  *
  * Implementation of a BeanDescriptor that can be ported across
  * the network as a mobile object.
  */

public class BeanDescriptorLite
   extends BeanDescriptor
   implements java.io.Serializable
{
   public BeanDescriptorLite(String beanName)
   {
     super(null);
     setName(beanName);
   }


   // Need a way to get access to the class on demand÷
   public Class getBeanClass()
```

Continues

```
      {
        return null;
      }
  };
```

Listing 23.2 Source for BeanDescriptorLite.

This implementation of BeanDescriptor keeps track of only the name of the Bean. Other information is derived from the default implementation of FeatureDescriptor.

In a more robust implementation, the bean could be loaded if some MetaData is required that isn't present in the BeanInfoLite implementation. This loading is lazy and performed only on demand, so this implementation is still far less efficient than the default implementation of BeanInfo. The following BeanFactory class is suggested to accomplish the goal of loading the bean on demand, although it is not part of this example application. The getBeanClass method would be a good place to use this BeanFactory, see Listing 23.3.

```
public class BeanFactory
{
  public Helper helper;

  public BeanFactory(Helper helper)
  {
    this.helper = helper;
  }

  public void loadBean(String beanName)
  {
    /* Load network beans */

    org.omg.CORBA.ORB orb = org.omg.CORBA.ORB.init();

    // Locate BeanCaster
    sun.beancaster.Antenna receiver =
      sun.beancaster.AntennaHelper.bind(orb, "BeanCaster");
```

```
    byte[] buf = receiver.getBean(beanName);
    ByteArrayInputStream is = new ByteArrayInputStream(buf);

    JarLoader.loadJarDoOnBean("", is, helper);
    doLayout();
  }
};
```

Listing 23.3 Source for BeanFactory.

The specification of the Antenna interface must be changed to accommodate the new requirements of the server. Now only the MetaData for all the beans is sent to a client initially. Following that, a client requests the desired beans from the server. The MetaData is sent as an array of BeanInfoLite objects. Finally, each desired bean is requested individually by name and returned in the form of a byte array as follows:

```
package sun.beancaster;
public interface Antenna extends org.omg.CORBA.Object
{
  public BeanInfoLite[] getBeanMetaData();
  public byte[] getBean(String beanName);
}
```

The implementation of the Server for this interface is left as an exercise for the reader.

The client is predominately unchanged from the modified form of the BeanBox presented for the Extension pattern. The differences focus on the new tasks of obtaining the MetaData from the Server, displaying it for the application user to choose desired beans and loading the desired beans. The task of obtaining the MetaData is shown in the following code.

```
    /* Load network beans */
    org.omg.CORBA.ORB orb = org.omg.CORBA.ORB.init();

    // Locate BeanCaster
    sun.beancaster.Antenna receiver =
      sun.beancaster.AntennaHelper.bind(orb, "BeanCaster");
    sun.beancaster.BeanInfoLite[] infos = receiver.getBeanMetaData();
```

The following code, shown in Listing 23.4, performs the task of displaying this MetaData for the user and implements a user interface. It uses the tried-and-true approach of building a simple user interface in Java with the AWT and GridLayout. The implementation simply places checkboxes in the user interface for each of the possible components that can be imported into the application. The user selects those components that are desired and then clicks an "OK" button to perform the actual loading.

```java
// Display a modal dialog box to enable the user to choose
// desired Bean set. Just a pick list layout. Only the
// chosen set of Beans is loaded rather than the full set.
// In the true spirit of a Java GUI...

frame1 = new Frame("Smorgasbord");

Panel panel1 = new Panel();
frame1.add(panel1);
frame1.show();
frame1.pack();

GridLayout layout1 = new GridLayout(infos.length + 1,1);
panel1.setLayout(layout1);

Label label1 = new Label();
label1.setText("Which extensions do you want?");
panel1.add(label1);

checkboxes = new Checkbox[infos.length];
for (int i = 0; i < infos.length; i++)
    {
        // Unravel the name of the Bean from the BeanInfo object.
        String beanName = infos[i].getBeanDescriptor().getName();

        Checkbox checkboxes[i] = new Checkbox(beanName, false);
        panel1.add(checkboxes[i]);
    }
```

```
    Button button1 = new Button("OK");
    button1.setLabel("OK");
    this.add(button1);

        insertThread = new Thread(this);
        insertThread.start();
}


Frame frame1 = null;
public Checkbox[] checkboxes = null;
public org.omg.CORBA.ORB orb = null;
public sun.beancaster.Antenna receiver = null;

public void button1_actionPerformed(ActionEvent e)
{
  // the user hit the "OK" button, load all the desired beans.
  if (orb == null || receiver == null)
    {
        org.omg.CORBA.ORB orb = org.omg.CORBA.ORB.init();

        // Locate BeanCaster
        sun.beancaster.Antenna receiver =
          sun.beancaster.AntennaHelper.bind(orb, "BeanCaster");
    }

  byte[] buf;
  ByteArrayInputStream is;

  for (int i = 0; i < checkboxes.length; i++)
    {
        // Test whether bean is selected.
        if (checkboxes[i].getState())
          {

            buf = receiver.getBean(checkboxes[i].getLabel());
            is = new ByteArrayInputStream(buf);
            JarLoader.loadJarDoOnBean("", is, helper);      Continues
```

```
            }
        }
     frame1.dispose();

     doLayout();
  }


  class ToolBox_button1_actionAdapter
     implements java.awt.event.ActionListener
  {
     ToolBoxPanel adaptee;

     ToolBoxPanel_button1_actionAdapter(ToolBoxPanel adaptee) {
        this.adaptee = adaptee;
     }

     public void actionPerformed(ActionEvent e)
     {
        System.err.println("action");

        adaptee.button1_actionPerformed(e);
     }
  }
```

Listing 23.4 Source for user interface.

Only those components that are selected are actually loaded; the other components are not imported. As a result, the BeanBox is not overloaded with undesirable components. Classes for undesirable components don't have to be loaded into the JVM. The ToolBox displays only those components that are appropriately loaded.

Related Patterns

Extensions follow the Extension pattern. The implementation of the process for obtaining and constructing new extensions might benefit from the Gang-of-Four's Factory Method pattern.

Interpreter [GoF95]

Intent

Implement network protocols and other interpreters as mobile objects in order to dynamically replace and extend these at runtime.

Benefits of Mobility

Interpreters perform the basic task of converting data streams into something more meaningful. The implementation of interpreters uses constructs such as syntax trees and other elements to parse the data stream. Implementing the interpreter using mobile objects may provide the significant benefit of being able to move new interpreters from computer to computer and application to application. When a new application receives an interpreter as a mobile object, it can immediately begin interpreting new data streams that would otherwise be meaningless. This abstract feature becomes more powerful when you consider specific instances of how interpreters are used in practical software design. One example is network protocols. Every network protocol, including those in distributed object toolkits, is interpreted in order to determine the content of each message. Tools such as DCE and CORBA have traditionally been incompatible at the network protocol level, because they didn't have an appropriate interpreter for each others protocols. Implementing a mobile object solution to these interpreters could enable the appropriate interpreter to be loaded by the distributed object application at runtime in order to make entirely different applications compatible with each other. Another example, file formats are read by interpreters. A mobile object interpreter implementation could enable an application to load the appropriate interpreter to read a new file format on demand.

Motivation

The lack of extensible network protocols poses a significant problem to the traditional software development approach. Network protocols, once implemented in static code, cannot be changed dynamically. As a result, once a product is shipped with a specific set of protocols, it is difficult to extend the product with additional protocols as they are developed.

An example of the problems resulting from this limitation is the conflict between CORBA- and DCOM-based systems. CORBA and DCOM both use their own, static protocol. These protocols are not compatible with each other. If one application was designed to work with CORBA and another to work with DCOM, the two would never be able to work together. Making two incompatible applications communicate in this situation requires intrusive source code modification to one of the applications to make it speak the protocol of the other application. Note that CORBA does provide ways of creating DCOM-compatible objects at development time, but CORBA objects are incompatible with DCOM unless code is specifically provided at development time. With the flexibility of a pluggable protocol, this compatibility could be achieved dynamically at runtime. A pluggable protocol enables the two applications to share a common protocol and communicate with each other, even if one or both of the applications were not specifically written with this common protocol in mind. Two applications can negotiate a common protocol at runtime, then share the common protocol as a mobile object between themselves and other applications.

The problem in interpreting a stream of data flowing across the network is inherently similar to that for interpreting other types of data streams. For example, when an application saves some data, the application is implicitly following a convention for how to write the data. The reader of the data must be able to interpret the data and make some sense of it. As a result, the same problem of incompatible applications may occur. The application writing the data may have different formatting conventions from those of the application reading the data. The two applications then can't read and write each other's data.

This problem is solved by an interpreter. When the first application saves a particular data format, the application can also provide a compatible interpreter. The interpreter can be read and used by the reader of a specific file to interpret the content of the file, even though it may not have originally known the data format.

Other types of interpreters can also benefit from this pattern (see Figure 24.1). A programming language compiler could potentially even use this pattern to dynamically acquire support via interpreters for additional programming languages at runtime.

Applicability

Use Interpreters to do the following:

♦ Revise data formats or network protocols.

♦ Handle changing requirements for data format.

♦ Add support for new network protocols to an application.

♦ Change network protocols at runtime.

♦ Optimize communication between two applications based on context.

Structure

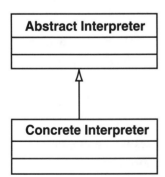

Figure 24.1 The structure of the Interpreter Pattern.

Participants

AbstractInterpreter.
The interface supported by all interpreters.

ConcreteInterpreter.
A specific implementation of an interpreter as a mobile object.

Collaborations

ConcreteInterpreter implements AbstractInterpreter.

Consequences

An application may support many interpreters and acquire support for new interpreters over time. Since ConcreteInterpreter implements AbstractInterpreter, many interpreters may be used interchangeably. As a result, an application may act as a host for many different interpreters. In addition, since interpreters are implemented as mobile objects, you may obtain additional interpreters by sending them to the target through a remote invocation. This can be a powerful tool for adding interpreters to an application on demand. Examples of uses could be interpreters for graphical formats, network protocols, programming languages, compression algorithms, or file formats.

The pattern may be expensive to start because of the need to dynamically load the interpreter. As a mobile object, the implementation for the interpreter must be loaded at runtime. For complex interpreters, this overhead may be quite significant. A caching mechanism may greatly reduce the impact of this disadvantage.

The pattern is tunable to arbitrary efficiency because a nonoptimal interpreter can be replaced at runtime with a more efficient interpreter. Because each ConcreteInterpreter implements the AbstractInterpreter interface, interpreters are interchangeable. If two interpreters are both capable of parsing the same input, the more efficient or better interpreter can be used according to the criteria for what makes the best interpreter. The preferred interpreter can then be loaded dynamically at runtime.

Interpreter implementation is decoupled from the application.
ConcreteInterpreter must implement AbstractInterpreter, but it can otherwise be entirely decoupled from the application. When this decoupling is
achieved, diverse interpreters can be reused in different applications
because no application dependencies exist in the interpreter.

**Versioning can be implemented if an interpreter is provided for a
stream of data along with the data.** Traditional application development requires that an interpreter for a particular stream of data be
compiled into an application before deployment. This requirement can
be very inconvenient, particularly in light of the fact that the format for
a stream of data changes with the release of new versions of an application. The static implementation of traditional applications makes it
very difficult for applications to be forward compatible with new versions of file formats. When interpreters are mobile objects, the interpreter for a particular stream of data may be flexibly loaded at runtime.

Implementation

Interpreter implementation is a complex issue because interpreters may take
many different forms. The basic problem is to convert a data stream into
something more meaningful. In a mobile object context, the more meaningful element is often an object invocation. The following issues must be
addressed when you are implementing the Interpreter pattern:

♦ **Decouple the interpreter.** For the implementation of this pattern to suc-
ceed, the interpreter must be decoupled from the application sufficiently to
enable new interpreters to be swapped in with few code changes. The best
interpreter is one that doesn't depend on the application at all. Often
decoupling is not a realistic goal because the interpreter must return something useful to the host application, such as the result of the parsed data.

♦ **Make AbstractInterpreter goal oriented.** The operations supported by
AbstractInterpreter should return the results that the application expects
from the interpreter. If a specific interpreter is responsible for reading
an Account object from a data file, the interpreter should return such an
Account object. For the sake of maximizing code reuse, AbstractInterpreter
should not contain details that are specific to any one implementation of
an interpreter. For example, when the first ConcreteInterpreter is expected

to operate by reading from a TCP/IP socket, adding host name and port number to part of the AbstractInterpreter might be tempting, but this is a mistake that adds unnecessarily specific data to the generic interface.

♦ **Use Proxies or Adapters to Proxies.** A natural place to start for implementing pluggable protocols with toolkits that support both distributed and mobile objects is to reuse remote proxies, also known as the stubs, that are automatically generated by the toolkit. Because most toolkits use stubs that are very similar, they can often be substituted one for another. This practice can enable the implementation of pluggable protocol objects by substituting remote object references from different toolkits for each other. If some of the operation signatures in the remote object references are incompatible because of the conventions used by the different toolkits, an Adapter object must be implemented to make the full compatibility. Creating this adapter is generally very straightforward.

♦ **Assign an appropriate level of responsibility.** A fine-grained interpreter may be little more than the implementation of a specific grammar. A large-grained interpreter may include network protocols, file access, and other functionality. Adding this responsibility to your interpreter enables application features such as network protocols or file access to be replaced along with the format of the data stream. An application that initially uses TCP/IP could be extended to support UDP or IP Multicast. The application becomes more flexible when the Interpreter has as much responsibility as possible; however, the added responsibility places a greater burden on the implementor of a ConcreteInterpreter because it must support all the required functionality.

Sample Code

This example implementation of the Interpreter pattern is for parsing a stream of user input that is multicast to a group of participants in an Object Group. Sound like a boring example? Not when you think about all the different types of applications that react to input sent to a group of users. One such example is a Multi-User Dungeon (MUD) application, which enables a group of users to chat with each other in a simulated text environment.

Implementing a MUD in terms of a series of mobile object interpreters is surprisingly easy and flexible. In the simple example, only a few interpreters are implemented to print messages sent between users and perform even more trivial tasks. However, this mobile object framework for interpreters enables any participant in the MUD to dynamically create and multicast a new interpreter to other participants at runtime. You can surprise your friends by implementing a clever new interpreter that performs a unique operation based on user input.

This example is implemented on top of Voyager because, at the time of this writing, Voyager is the mobile object tool with the best support for Object Groups. The disadvantage of this is that Voyager Spaces are not reliable and may occasionally lose messages or Interpreters.

The interpreter in this example is acting on a stream of data multicast to the Voyager Space. Each participant communicates with the other members of the MUD by multicasting raw messages to everyone. The reader of these messages utilizes a sequence of known Interpreters in order to act on these messages. This behavior enables the Interpreter complete freedom to define both the data format and the implementation of what happens when a message is received.

The basic interface for each Interpreter is shown in Listing 24.1.

```
/**
 * Interpreter
 *
 * Parses and executes the contents of a StringTokenizer.
 * Invokes subinterpreters on any portion of the contents
 * of StringTokenizer that must be parsed by child interpreters.
 * Returns any portion of the StringTokenizer that does not apply
 * to this interpreter.  The parent of this interpreter should
 * then perform whatever action is desired.
 */
import java.util.*;

public interface Interpreter
   extends java.io.Serializable
{
   public String getTrigger();
   public void setTrigger( String s );
```

Continues

```
public String usage();

public StringTokenizer parse( StringTokenizer st );
};
```

Listing 24.1 Source for Interpreter.

The operations defined on Interpreter make it more convenient for the client to employ an instance of an Interpreter. The main operation is parse(), which reads a sequence of String tokens and does something defined by the implementation of the mobile object. The implementation of this mobile object may do something reasonably trivial, provide a user interface, or even conduct enterprise tasks such as update a database based on the content of the parsed stream. Other operations on the Interpreter are getTrigger() and setTrigger(). Each of these operations provides feedback to the environment regarding which token should trigger this interpreter. The trigger token is a specific token, a word with no spaces, that is associated with this interpreter. For example, the name "Rumpelstiltskin" might send off a Rumpelstiltskin-Interpreter, causing the parse() method to be invoked on this interpreter. This makes it easy to implement a parser architecture. A hashtable of triggers that stores the Interpreters may be maintained. As a token is encountered, the hashtable may be consulted to look up the appropriate Interpreter. An alternative implementation of an interpreter framework like this one might use Chain of Responsibility to give each interpreter a chance to respond to the String-Tokenizer, but this implementation, while more elegant, is necessarily not as efficient as a hashtable lookup.

Of course, the interface in Listing 24.1 doesn't actually do anything; it's just a Java interface. A set of derived classes must be provided that implement interpreters. The first example interpreter, called PrintInterpreter in Listing 24.2, shows an interpreter that simply prints a message to standard output based on the content of the stream.

```
import java.util.*;

public class PrintInterpreter
    extends TrivialInterpreter
{
```

```
   public PrintInterpreter(String s)
   {
     super(s);
   }

   public String usage()
   {
     return "print";
   }

   public StringTokenizer parse( StringTokenizer st )
   {
     if (st.hasMoreTokens())
       {
         String msg = st.nextToken();
         System.out.println(msg);
       }

     return st;
   }
};
```

Listing 24.2 Source for PrintInterpreter.

The PrintInterpreter is a derived class of another interpreter called TrivialInterpreter. This parent class implements some reasonable default behavior for interpreters, and it's convenient to reuse this implementation for PrintInterpreter. The implementation of TrivialInterpreter is shown in Listing 24.3.

```
import java.util.*;

public class TrivialInterpreter
  implements Interpreter
{
  public TrivialInterpreter(String trigger)
  {
    this.trigger = trigger;
  }
```

Continues

```java
public String trigger;

public String getTrigger()
{
  return trigger;
}

public void setTrigger(String t)
{
  trigger = t;
}

public String usage()
{
  return "Usage:\n" + trigger
        + " *\nThis command echoes its input to its output.\n";
}

public StringTokenizer parse( StringTokenizer st )
{
  return st;
}
};
```

Listing 24.3 Source for TrivialInterpreter.

The TrivialInterpreter implements a String to store the trigger and provides a parser that does absolutely nothing to the StringTokenizer. Interpreters that do something can override this parse() method to provide the desired behavior.

This server part of the example is easy: there is no server. The implementation of this example is peer-to-peer as opposed to client/server, which means the clients communicate directly with each other through the Voyager Space rather than contacting a server process. An application must be provided to initialize the Space, but no active server is required to maintain the communication among participants, aside from that provided by Voyager. In order to facilitate the communication among the different participants, the Voyager Space must simply be initialized, and then Voyager takes care of the rest. The application that initializes the Voyager Space is called MUD, shown in Listing 24.4.

```java
/**
  * MUD
  *
  * Initialize the MUD space.
  */

import com.objectspace.voyager.*;
import com.objectspace.voyager.space.*;

public class MUD
{
  public static void main(String args[])
  {
    try
      {
        Voyager.startup();

        ISubspace space = (ISubspace)
          Factory.create( "com.objectspace.voyager.space.Subspace",
                          "//localhost:7000/MobsMud" );

        Thread.sleep(2000);

      }
    catch( Exception e )
      {
        System.err.println("Voter: " + e);
        e.printStackTrace();
      }

    Voyager.shutdown();
  }
}
```

Listing 24.4 Source for MUD.

The client portion of this application is responsible for providing the user interface for a participant in the collaboration. The Client, shown in Listing 24.5, can be remarkably simple because the set of interpreters does all the real work.

```java
/**
 * Avatar
 *
 * A client.
 */

import java.io.*;
import java.util.*;
import com.objectspace.voyager.*;
import com.objectspace.voyager.space.*;

public class Client
{
  private LineInterpreter lineInterpreter = new LineInterpreter("eval");

  public static void main(String args[])
  {

    try
      {
        Voyager.startup();

        ISubspace space = (ISubspace)
          Namespace.lookup( "//localhost:7000/MobsMud" );

        AvatarImpl self = new AvatarImpl();

        // This enables Space messages to be delivered to self
        Avatar vself = (Avatar)Proxy.of(self);
        space.add(vself);
```

```
        // This creates a handle to broadcast to the space.
        Avatar room = (Avatar)
           space.getMulticastProxy( "Avatar" );


        // Start interpreting any input provided in standard input
        BufferedReader in
           = new BufferedReader(new InputStreamReader(System.in));

        String str = in.readLine();
        while (str != null)
           {
              room.interpret( str );
              str = in.readLine();
           }
     }
  catch (Exception e)
     {
        System.err.println("Avatar: " + e);
        e.printStackTrace();
     }

  Voyager.shutdown();
  }
}
```

Listing 24.5 Source for Client.

The client includes only one interpreter by default, the LineInterpreter, shown in Listing 24.6. The LineInterpreter performs the dispatching of a command to a set of known interpreters. The LineInterpreter is responsible for knowing how to interpret any line of text multicast to the group by using the set of known interpreters. Like PrintInterpreter, LineInterpreter inherits the default behavior of TrivialInterpreter. When the LineInterpreter parses its input, it looks for tokens matching triggers for the known interpreters. Then it invokes the appropriate interpreter to parse the remaining input from StringTokenizer. This example shows how interpreters may be nested, with one interpreter calling another to parse additional text.

```
import java.util.*;

public class LineInterpreter
  extends TrivialInterpreter
{
  public LineInterpreter(String s)
  {
    super(s);
  }

  public static Hashtable interpreters = new Hashtable();

  public StringTokenizer parse( StringTokenizer st )
  {
    if (st.hasMoreTokens())
      {
        String cmd = st.nextToken();
        Interpreter interpreter = (Interpreter)interpreters.get(cmd);
        st = interpreter.parse(st);
      }

    return st;
  }

  public void addAction( Interpreter action )
  {
    interpreters.put( action.getTrigger(), action );
  }
};
```

Listing 24.6 Source for LineInterpreter.

LineInterpreter adds an action to the default behavior of Interpreter, the addAction() method. This method is for adding new Interpreters to the set of known Interpreters maintained by LineInterpreter. The interpreters are called actions in this context because in the MUD environment, each trigger word is associated with a particular action, such as speaking, shouting, or moving. The Interpreter then implements the behavior required of the specific action using information gleaned by parsing the input from the StringTokenizer.

All the messages are multicast to a Voyager Space to communicate with each of the clients. The implementation of Voyager Spaces requires that each Space define a particular interface to be implemented by each participant in the Space. Messages sent to the Space are wrapped within an RPC style invocation of the appropriate method implemented by the participant in the Space.

The implementation of the interface for this example is called Avatar, a word commonly used for the electronic identity of a person in a virtual reality environment. The specification of this Avatar interface, shown in Listing 24.7, declares a way for each participant to receive new messages and new interpreters.

```
/**
  * Avatar
  *
  * A specification for a participant in a MUD environment.
  */

public interface Avatar
   extends java.io.Serializable
{
  public void interpret( String s );
  public void addAction( Interpreter s );
};
```

Listing 24.7 Source for Avatar.

The implementation for this interface is uncreatively called AvatarImpl, shown in Listing 24.8. An instance of AvatarImpl is maintained inside the client to handle the input multicast to the Voyager Space. As a message is sent to the Voyager Space, one of the methods on AvatarImpl is invoked to handle the incoming message.

```
/**
  * AvatarImpl
  *
  * The object that resides on the client side to perform actions    Continues
```

```
   * on behalf of the client when an invocation is made on the space.
   * This is the thingie that executes the grammar rules.
   *
   * Exercise for the reader: Implement a good mechanism for
   * tracking personal information.
   */
import java.util.*;

public class AvatarImpl
   implements Avatar,
              java.io.Serializable
{
   private LineInterpreter lineInterpreter = null;

   public AvatarImpl()
   {
      lineInterpreter = new LineInterpreter("eval");
   }

   public void interpret( String s )
   {
      StringTokenizer st = new StringTokenizer( s );
      // Only parse the first command and its arguments, ignore everything else.
      if ( st.hasMoreTokens() )
         st = lineInterpreter.parse( st );
   }

   public void addAction( Interpreter action )
   {
      lineInterpreter.addAction(action);
   }
};
```

Listing 24.8 Source for AvatarImpl.

So far, we have seen two different interpreters used by this example: one
for doing the brute-force work of keeping track of other interpreters and
one for printing text. The next interpreter, Listing 24.9, is an example of

adding an Interpreter not to perform any specific action, but to be a programming construct. This Interpreter implements a loop mechanism called for each. It reads input from the StringTokenizer and parses the input by sending it to a nested Interpreter as long as more input is available.

```
import j
ava.util.*;

// This is starting to look a great deal like a function object

public class ForeachInterpreter
  extends TrivialInterpreter
{
  public Interpreter interpreter = null;

  public ForeachInterpreter(String s, Interpreter interpreter)
  {
    super(s);

    this.interpreter = interpreter;
  }

  public StringTokenizer parse( StringTokenizer st )
  {
    while ( st.hasMoreTokens() )
      st = interpreter.parse( st );

    return st;
  }
};
```

Listing 24.9 Source for ForeachInterpreter.

Other types of programming interpreters that could also be implemented include conditional tests, ways to define symbols, and even ways to define simple functions. In fact, the structure of this interpreter architecture is accidentally quite similar to the Lisp programming language.

Finally, a tool is needed for multicasting new Interpreters to the Voyager Space. This capability could be added into the Client, but here the message interaction of the Client is separated from the addition of new interpreters to the participants of the Space. You can add new interpreters to the participants in the Space by invoking this NewInterpreter application, shown in Listing 24.10, and passing in the name of the Interpreter class. The specified Interpreter, a mobile object, is then instantiated and multicast to all the participants.

```java
import com.objectspace.voyager.*;
import com.objectspace.voyager.space.*;
import java.lang.reflect.*;


public class NewInterpreter
{
  public static void main(String args[])
  {
    try
      {
        Voyager.startup();

        ISubspace space =
          (ISubspace) Namespace.lookup( "//localhost:7000/MobsMud" );

        Avatar room = (Avatar)
          space.getMulticastProxy( "Avatar" );

        // Push a message specified by the command line.
        java.lang.Class c = java.lang.Class.forName( args[1] );

        Interpreter i = (Interpreter)(c.newInstance());
        i.setTrigger( args[0] );

        room.addAction( i );

        System.out.println("Added \"" + args[0] + "\"." );
```

```
        Thread.sleep(2000);

        // Can't shutdown, have to wait for reply.
        // Voyager.shutdown();
      }
    catch (Exception e)
      {
        System.err.println("NewInterpreter: " + e);
        e.printStackTrace();

      }

    Voyager.shutdown();
  }
}
```

Listing 24.10 Source for NewInterpreter.

To run this example, first start a Voyager place process to host the Space as shown in the following code:

```
Window 1
Prompt> voyager 7000
voyager™ 2.0 beta 1, copyright objectspace 1997
address = localhost:7000
```

Next, start up a few participants, as many as you like.

```
Window 2
Prompt> java Client
voyager™ 2.0 beta 1, copyright objectspace 1997
address = localhost:1031
```

```
Window 3
Prompt> java Client
voyager™ 2.0 beta 1, copyright objectspace 1997
address = localhost:1037
```

```
Window 4
Prompt> java Client
```

```
voyager™ 2.0 beta 1, copyright objectspace 1997
address = localhost:1039
```

Note that the host name specified in the source code for this example, as with many examples in this book, is localhost. If you want to run the example on multiple computers, the source code must be modified to specify the name of the host computer that is used as the host of the Space in all cases where localhost appears in this example.

Then, add some interpreters to the group. The NewInterpreter command enables you to perform this task by specifying the name of the interpreter to add on the command line.

```
Window 5
Prompt> java NewInterpreter say PrintInterpreter
voyager™ 2.0 beta 1, copyright objectspace 1997
address = localhost:1041
```

In this invocation of NewInterpeter, we are associating the word *say* with the PrintInterpreter. Whenever anyone multicasts a message that starts with the word *say* to the group, the parse() method on the PrintInterpreter object is invoked with a StringTokenizer object containing the rest of the message. The PrintInterpreter just prints the message to standard output. As a result, whenever any participant uses *say,* a message is printed for all the other participants to read! Given the MUD style implementation of this example, *say* is called an action that any participant in the MUD can invoke.

You can try to use the *say* action in one of your clients. Type *say Hello* into the first Client window as follows:

```
Window 2
Prompt> java Client
voyager™ 2.0 beta 1, copyright objectspace 1997
address = localhost:1031
say Hello from Jeff!
```

Once you type this message into one of the Clients, the message is multicast to all the clients in the group. The PrintInterpreter is invoked to handle the message for each of the Clients. As a result, the other Client windows should display the message as shown:

```
Window 3
Prompt> java Client
voyager™ 2.0 beta 1, copyright objectspace 1997
address = localhost:1037
```
Hello from Jeff!

```
Window 4
Prompt> java Client
voyager™ 2.0 beta 1, copyright objectspace 1997
address = localhost:1039
```
Hello from Jeff!

We've provided only a couple of interpreters for this brief example. Interpreters are full mobile objects in their own right and can do virtually anything, including implement a user interface, file access, or anything else that can be done within the confines of the current SecurityManager. If you are interested in experimenting with this example, here are a few ideas for other interpreters you could use:

♦ **PeopleInterpreter**. Displays a physical representation of a particular participant in the group. Nice for establishing an identity for each participant in the group. Each message could represent the description of a particular user in the collaboration.

♦ **GeographyInterpreter**. Tracks coordinants on a map. The interpreter might display a user interface including a map in the window. Messages for this interpreter could simply be (x,y) coordinates.

♦ **FileInterpreter**. Transfers files to participants in the collaboration. Entire files might be encoded as the messages for this interpreter.

♦ **StockTickerInterpreter**. Implements a real-time stock ticker. The user interface for this interpreter might be as simple as printing messages to standard output or as complex as a side-scrolling real-time chart. The Messages for this interpreter could include the symbols for stocks and the current share price.

♦ **ObjectInterpreter**. This example was designed to pass Strings and parse individual strings, but with a few changes, you can embed serialized objects in the messages to the participants.

Related Patterns

The Interpreter pattern from the Gang-of-Four describes how to build an interpreter using object-oriented concepts. This approach is also useful, but not required, in the implementation of an Interpreter.

Federation [Nelson98]

Intent

When a large task is too much for a single server, share the work across objects on multiple servers according to some mutual relationship between the servers.

Motivation

Suppose that you are handed the impossible task: implement a document management facility capable of indexing terabytes worth of documents across thousands of computers in a manner that allows documents matching a certain set of programmatic constraints to be located on demand. The catch is that simple key word searching is not enough. The constraints appropriate for each search cannot be foreseen at design time and must be entirely flexible. An example of a search might be to find the document with less than 1500 bytes in size with three occurrences of the word "ruckus" wherein the second occurrence is capitalized. One way to tackle this problem is to utilize the Predicate pattern to express the search criteria, distributing a Predicate mobile object that returns true when the appropriate document is evaluated. Even so, the problem is far too large for any one computer.

The solution is to use many computers. In this case, the best condition would be to have each computer participate by searching its own documents. However, the end user should not have to connect to each computer individually and search each of the computers. The

Benefits of Mobility

Federation provides a convenient way to share the resources of multiple computers to attack large problems. However, a fundamental problem with large Federated systems is that the problems are statically implemented as part of applications that must be installed on the host systems. In the existing Federated systems, these static systems collaborate by communicating using traditional TCP/IP protocols, but software management issues must be addressed with other tools. Mobility brings a significant benefit of enabling the algorithms to move to the resources at runtime. When a particular task is required to execute on a target system, the task may be passed as a mobile object and executed immediately without an additional effort. Because mobile objects must simply conform to a specific interface, compatibility of a particular implementation is defined only in terms of whether the Federated system can handle the specific interface. Any implementation may be passed to the server as long as it conforms to the interface.

In addition, mobile objects are already set up to move between different computers, so it's easy to move them to other destinations according to the requirements of the federated system. In a large problem implemented as a large collection of mobile objects, a subset of the objects may be moved among multiple computers. This provides an easy path to Federation, enabling a traditional monolithic system to be partitioned into a distributed system with relative ease.

implementation should enable the end user to connect to a single server and have the server transparently coordinate with other servers to contribute to the solution to the problem.

Applicability

Federation is appropriate under the following conditions:

♦ Multiple servers are explicitly invoked individually.

♦ The information required to solve a problem is spread across many computers.

♦ Any single computer doesn't have enough resources to solve the entire problem.

♦ Multiple servers perform the same tasks.

Structure

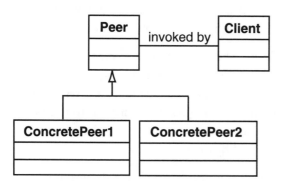

Figure 25.1 The structure of the Federation Pattern.

Participants

Peer.
The core interface of a server that contributed to the solution to a specific problem.

ConcretePeer1.
An entity with partial information to fulfill a request.

ConcretePeer2.
An entity with partial information to fulfill a request.

Client.
An entity making a request.

Collaborations

Client makes a request on ConcretePeer1. ConcretePeer1 coordinates with ConcretePeer2 to obtain additional information required to satisfy the request.

Consequences

Peers can contribute resources and share information to solve a particular problem. Once a request is made of a particular Peer, it may obtain resources directly from other Peers and share information required to solve the problem. The Peer may perform any particular coordination required to appropriately address a particular problem. The Peer accomplishes this task without the intervention of the Client.

Federation simplifies the Client. The Federation pattern enables a transparent view of the coordination that goes on in the background to solve a particular problem for the Client. A single request is sent by the Client to a specific Peer, and then the request is farmed out to one or more other Peers. The potentially complex coordination that happens on the Client side is encapsulated by the initial Peer.

Federation adds interactions to the protocol. In a simple client/server system, a simple request and response are exchanged in the following stages:

1. The client issues a request to the server.

2. The server sends back a response.

Such a protocol has only two interactions. Many implementations of Federation require additional coordination among the Peers once the request is received by the initial Peer. Further, although requests are satisfied immediately by the server in the traditional client/server model, the Federation model may involve communication among several peers. As a result, additional stages must be added to the protocol for responding to a particular request by the Client. The Client sends the request to an initial Peer, then the request may be delegated to one or more other Peers. An example of such an interaction is the following:

1. The Client issues a request to ConcretePeer1.

2. ConcretePeer1 determines that ConcretePeerX has sufficient information to find a peer to solve this particular problem and delegates the request to ConcretePeerX.

3. ConcretePeerX determines that ConcretePeerY can solve this problem and delegates the request to ConcretePeerY.

4. ConcretePeerY sends a response back to ConcretePeerX.

5. ConcretePeerX sends a response back to ConcretePeer1.

6. ConcretePeer1 sends a response back to Client.

The pattern is equivalent to forcing the client to contact multiple servers to solve a problem. In a normal distributed system in which the information required to solve a particular problem is spread across multiple nodes, the client can make initial requests on some servers to determine who has the information to solve it. Using this additional information, the Client can eventually track down the solution to that problem. Effectively, such a client-driven system is equivalent to Federation in which all the logic of how the resources on different servers interact resides on the Client. Federation enables you to push this logic to an appropriate location on one or more of the servers, but Federation is not inherently solving problems that might be impossible otherwise.

Implementation

Many different types of communication between multiple applications fit the mold for the Federation pattern. Let's briefly consider different types of communication between federated applications.

Federation can be separated into two different categories, pass through invocation and problem partitioning. Federated applications in both categories share one property: the client should not be aware of any additional levels of interaction required to satisfy the request on the federated system. From the perspective of the client making the invocation, the distributed system should look like a simple client/server, like that shown in Figure 25.1.

Pass through invocation describes a set of applications in a distributed system that are federated through a combination of sending invocations to federated applications, then returning the response back to the requesting application. Federated applications, clients and servers, in this type of federated environment should have little or no code proprietary to the federated system.

Three different configurations of pass through invocation are used in Federated systems. The first is familiar to us, a proxy. Proxies are one of the most useful software constructs, and it proves useful for Federation

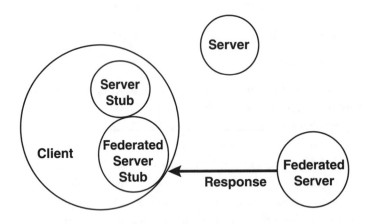

Figure 25.2 Simple client/server system.

also. However, this type of proxy is not altogether identical to the type of proxy we have already examined in the Proxy pattern back in Chapter 14, Remote Proxy. In the simple client/server system of Figure 25.2, a Proxy can reside on the server side of the distributed system to send any incoming requests to a different destination than the Primary server, called FederatedServer. The result of this proxy invocation is returned to the PrimaryServer and then sent back to the Client. In such a scenario, the Client is unaware that the request was delegated to a different server, but the PrimaryServer receives significant benefits from delegating the request to a system that may be in some way more suitable to respond to the request. This process is shown in Figure 25.3.

Request forwarding is a second way of implementing pass through invocation. Request forward is close to the implementation of proxy. Considering a simple client/server invocation as shown in Figure 25.2 again. The request is submitted by the Client to the PrimaryServer, but the request is then forwarded to the FederatedServer. Request forwarding differs in that once the request is forwarded to another server, the PrimaryServer is no longer involved. The response is sent directly from the FederatedServer to the Client. On the Client side, a customized stub can be used to preserve the transparency that only a single server was invoked in processing the request, see Figure 25.4

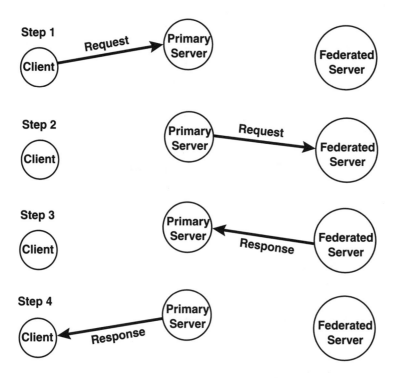

Figure 25.3 Proxy Federation.

Transparent reference sharing is the final type of pass through invocation. This type of federation is based on one of the excellent properties of distributed object systems. Each reference to a distributed object matches some kind of interface specification. References that match the same interface may be used interchangeably. As a result, whenever an object reference is returned as a result of a distributed object invocation, any compatible object reference may be substituted for the original distributed object. During an invocation, an object reference to a FederatedServer may be substituted for an object reference to the PrimaryServer. Following this, whenever an invocation is made on the object reference, the invocation goes directly to the FederatedServer without ever communicating with PrimaryServer, as shown in Figure 25.5. This solution can completely eliminate bottlenecking on the PrimaryServer.

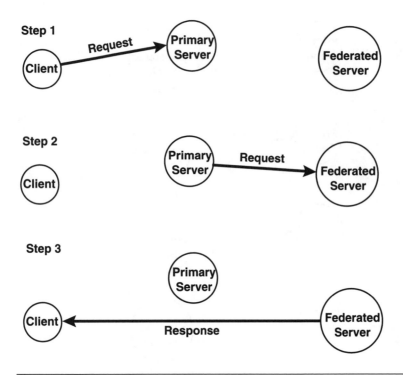

Figure 25.4 Request forwarding Federation.

Problem partitioning can require much more work on the part of the server application. Problem partitioning divides a problem into smaller parts for easier manageability. Smaller parts may be more easily handled by each system participating in the federated system.

Two different forms of problem partitioning can be identified, responsibility partitioning and resource partitioning. Responsibility partitioning occurs when multiple servers establish some agreement regarding the division of labor for how a problem should be solved. In this scenario, the rules for how responsibility is partitioned in the federated system are used to determine which server should process a request. An example of this is the Internet DNS system. In this system, multiple hosts are federated to resolve the host names of different computers on the Internet into raw IP addresses. This task is accomplished primarily by clearly partitioning the responsibility of which servers are responsible for which set of host names (see Figure 25.6).

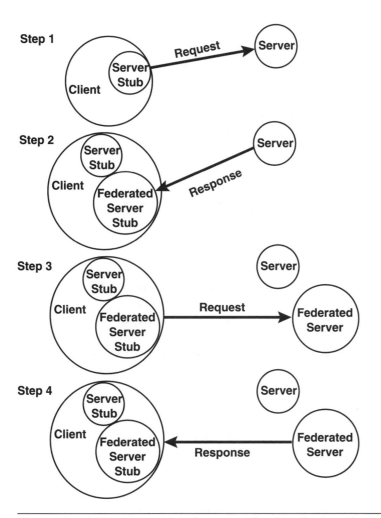

Figure 25.5 Transparent reference sharing Federation.

Resource partitioning is more simplistic. Resource partitioning occurs when many computers share certain system resources in order to accomplish a particular computational task. Nearly any computational resource may be involved, including CPU, files, memory, databases, and network bandwidth. A resource sharing federated system divides the resources required to attack a problem between multiple participants. The resources which are divided may include CPU, disk space, database, user interaction, bandwidth,

Programming Mobile Objects with Java

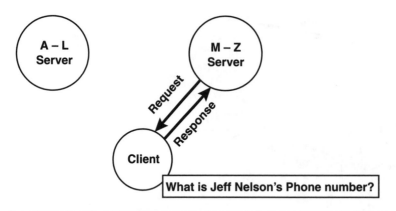

Figure 25.6 Responsibility partitioning.

and others, as shown in Figure 25.7. Resource partitioning differs from responsibility partitioning in that tasks are not shared between hosts, instead the resources required to solve the problem are shared between hosts.

Given these possible designs for the Federation pattern, a software designer must decide which is the most appropriate for a particular problem. The following additional issues point out some other decisions to make when implementing the Federation pattern.

♦ **Don't add too many levels of Federation.** Federation is not without cost. The stages added to the protocol can substantially slow down the solution to a problem. As a general rule, solve a problem locally if possible. Delegate when necessary. Try to ensure that only one or two additional stages of the protocol are required in a particular Federation.

♦ **Delegate requests to the appropriate server(s).** One very straightforward implementation of the Federation pattern is to build Peers that support identical interfaces. Simple request delegation can be used in this case to coordinate the different servers. A Peer may retain a set of federated peers. When a request comes in that cannot be satisfied locally, the request is delegated to each of the alternative Peers until the request can be satisfied.

♦ **Restrict the Client to a specific entry point into the Federation.** The Federation pattern does not mandate that all Peers should be capable of answering requests from a Client. A more effective architecture might

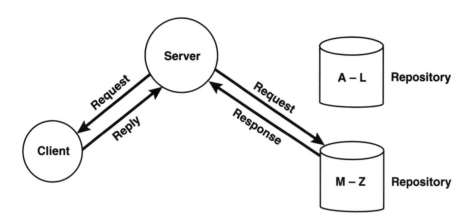

Figure 25.7 Resource partitioning.

make only some of the Peers respond to Client requests while most are responsible for a small portion of the information related to the problem. Peers do not have to be identical to each other, and many systems benefit from placing different responsibilities on different Peers.

♦ **Specify an explicit mechanism for partitioning the problem among the participants in the Federation and routing a specific request to a Peer capable of satisfying a request.** Federation works best when it can be partitioned into several subproblems. Unfortunately, not every problem can be easily partitioned. One way to partition a problem easily is to split the different resources required to solve the problem among several computers. For example, if you are using the Federation pattern to implement a telephone directory, it is appropriate to partition the archive of all telephone numbers along geographic lines. Given this rule for partitioning the telephone directory problem, a request by a Client for the phone number of "John Doe living in Tulsa, Oklahoma" can be immediately dispatched to a Peer responsible for tracking the telephone directory of Tulsa, called the Tulsa Peer. Further, we can have reasonable confidence that the Tulsa Peer can satisfy this request for the obvious reason that Tulsa was part of the search criteria. Partitioning the problem is often a very effective means of implementing the Federation pattern.

Sample Code

Implementing Federation is often highly dependent on the specific problem and the way it can effectively be solved by multiple participants. The following example demonstrates how to add Federation to the Interpreter example shown earlier.

In the previous chapter, the Interpreter pattern was used to implement a simple MUD environment. Mobile objects were used to create new interpreters that were multicast to each of the participants. One limitation of this pattern concerns participants that join after a particular Interpreter is announced to the group. Only the participants that were already members of the group when an interpreter is announced know about the interpreter. If a particular trigger is encountered for an interpreter that is missed, new members won't know about any of the interpreters that were announced before they joined the group. In order to work around this weakness, every participant in the Interpreter example had to join in at the beginning of the session, before any interpreters were announced to the group.

Federation is the perfect solution to this problem. With Federation, a participant that is missing a particular interpreter can transparently ask another participant for the interpreter. Since at least some other participants should have been present when the desired interpreter was announced, some participant should be capable of supplying the desired interpreter. From there, the interpreter can be sent as a return parameter and added to the list of known interpreters.

This architecture has several advantages. First, it enables new members that don't know about any interpreters at all to continue processing messages, even for interpreters that are unknown. Second, it requires only that the members of the group be able to look up interpreters known by other participants. Finally, you can locate interpreters on demand rather than transfer the set of all interpreters at initialization. This ability minimizes the overhead of transferring the potentially large number of interpreters in use by all the participants in the group.

The architecture for making requests on other participants could be implemented in many possible ways. One approach might be to have a participant that doesn't know about an interpreter to multicast a message to the entire group requesting the Interpreter. Such a group broadcast has the disadvantage that it doesn't scale well to very large numbers of participants. Whenever a single participant can't locate a single interpreter, it multicasts a message to everyone! The processing required by every participant to look at the request and consider responding with the appropriate interpreter could significantly impact system performance.

Instead, a point-to-point invocation is used to look up an interpreter from a single federated participant. This design has several ramifications. First, a point-to-point protocol must be implemented in parallel to the Voyager Space. Second, each participant must have a way of directly accessing every other participant. This may seem like a trivial detail to point out, but group-based systems don't always provide a way of accessing members individually. Those that do should implement a feature called a "membership layer," a way of performing operations appropriate for the individual members of the group.

Voyager doesn't implement a membership layer at the time of this writing. Voyager Spaces don't provide a way for you to access the members individually. As a result, we must roll our own membership layer on top of Voyager Spaces. Building membership layers for group-based protocols is a subject of much research. It is quite difficult to build a robust membership layer, as discussed in Chapter 9: Clustering. However, this example already isn't 100% reliable because it's built on top of Voyager Spaces, which don't implement reliable multicast messaging. Let's suffice to implement an unreliable membership layer for Voyager.

This membership layer is unreliable in that when certain combinations of actions happen at exactly the same time, unpredictable behavior can result. For example, when a new participant joins the group, a small window of time exists in which the new participant doesn't know about all the other participants in the group. Under this condition, the new participant may not be able to find enough federated participants to locate an interpreter to parse messages that it receives from the group. This problem is a result of a weakness in our membership layer: membership is not atomic. During the process of a new member's joining the group and finding out about other members of the group, other events may occur. As stated, we'll ignore this lack of robustness for this example.

Finally, the following mechanism used to track membership formally shouldn't be called a membership layer. As discussed earlier, a membership layer in a group-based protocol is a layer on top of the existing API for tracking group membership. Here, we are implementing the membership tracking system as an API on the individual participants of the Voyager Space, not formally on a layer. A layer would be more elegant than our solution because our solution requires intrusive modifications to the participants. However, a layer is more difficult to implement and should be integrated with the mobile object tool. In the sample code, the membership capabilities implemented are referred to as a "membership system" rather than a membership layer.

The modifications we make to the Avatar object are focused mostly on implementing this membership system, including the enter() and welcome() operations. If Voyager provided its own membership layer, these code modifications would not be necessary. The other new operation is lookup(). This operation enables a client to look up interpreters by name from a federated participant. The new specification for the Avatar interface is shown in Listing 25.1 with the changes in bold.

```
/**
  * Avatar
  *
  * A specification for a participant in a MUD environment.
  */

public interface Avatar
   extends java.io.Serializable
{
   public Interpreter lookup( String cmd );
   public void enter( Avatar s );
   public void welcome( Avatar s );
   public void interpret( String s );
   public void addAction( Interpreter s );
};
```

Listing 25.1 Source for Avatar.

The AvatarImpl object is still responsible for providing the implementation of the Avatar interface. The appropriate operations on AvatarImpl are invoked when a new message is multicast to the Voyager Space. Implementations must be provided for the new operations introduced into the Avatar interface. These modifications are shown in bold in Listing 25.2.

```
/**
 * AvatarImpl
 *
 * The object that resides on the client side to perform actions
 * on behalf of the client when an invocation is made on the space.
 * This is the thingie that executes the grammar rules.
 *
 * Exercise for the reader: Implement a good mechanism for
 * tracking personae information.
 */
import java.util.*;
import com.objectspace.voyager.*;
import com.objectspace.voyager.space.*;

public class AvatarImpl
   implements Avatar,
              java.io.Serializable
{
   private LineInterpreter lineInterpreter = null;

   public AvatarImpl()
   {
      lineInterpreter = new LineInterpreter("eval");
   }

   public void interpret( String s )
   {
      StringTokenizer st = new StringTokenizer( s );

      // Only parse the first command and its arguments, ignore everything else.
```

Continues

```
    if ( st.hasMoreTokens() )
      st = lineInterpreter.parse( st );
}


public void addAction( Interpreter action )
{
  lineInterpreter.addAction(action);
}


// Invoked when a new Avatar enters a Room.
// Right now there is no way to leave, just to enter.
// Leaving is left as an exercise for the reader. :-)
// This might look like a membership layer, but it really
// isn't.  It's just a very informal way for each new node
// to join into the system.
// Interpreters that are broadcast before any participants
// join the system are still lost.  If an interpreter parses
// in the forest...

public void enter( Avatar s )
{
  try
    {

        // Someone just broadcast an enter message to the group.
        // Welcome them.

        Avatar vself = (Avatar)Proxy.of( this );
        s.welcome( vself );
        lineInterpreter.addParticipant( s );
    }
  catch (Exception e)
    {
        System.out.println("Error: AvatarImpl: " + e);
        e.printStackTrace();
    }
}
```

```
  // This method was designed for point-to-point invocation,
  // but can be invoked through Spaces.
  public void welcome( Avatar s )
  {
    lineInterpreter.addParticipant( s );
  }


  // This method should be invoked synchronously on a VObject
  // reference.  It can't be invoked through the space due to
  // the return value.
  public Interpreter lookup( String cmd )
  {
    return lineInterpreter.lookup(cmd);
  }
};
```

Listing 25.2 Source for AvatarImpl.

The implementation for the Client almost doesn't require modification. Unfortunately, one additional line of code is required to enable the Client to interact with the membership system. This line of code is to invoke the enter() method on behalf of the Client when it is joining the group. Listing 25.3 shows the final version of the Client with changes in bold. Note the striking similarity between the add() operation on the Voyager Space and the enter() operation used by our objects to track membership. This similarity makes it obvious how the Space itself would provide the most natural place to implement membership.

```
/**
 * Avatar
 *
 * A client.
 */

import java.io.*;
import java.util.*;
import com.objectspace.voyager.*;
import com.objectspace.voyager.space.*;                    Continues
```

```java
public class Client
{
  private LineInterpreter lineInterpreter = new LineInterpreter("eval");

  public static void main(String args[])
  {

    try
      {
        Voyager.startup();

        ISubspace space = (ISubspace)
          Namespace.lookup( "//localhost:7000/MobsMud" );

        AvatarImpl self = new AvatarImpl();

        // This enables Space messages to be delivered to self
        Avatar vself = (Avatar)Proxy.of(self);
        space.add(vself);

        // This creates a handle to broadcast to the space.
        Avatar room = (Avatar)
          space.getMulticastProxy( "Avatar" );

        room.enter(vself);

        // Start interpreting any input provided in standard input
        BufferedReader in
          = new BufferedReader(new InputStreamReader(System.in));

        String str = in.readLine();
        while (str != null)
          {
            room.interpret( str );
            str = in.readLine();
          }
      }
    catch (Exception e)
```

```
        {
            System.err.println("Avatar: " + e);
            e.printStackTrace();
        }


    Voyager.shutdown();


  }


}
```

Listing 25.3 Source for Client.

Most of the changes we've seen so far have to do with implementing the membership system. The modifications required to implement Federation are mostly isolated inside LineInterpreter, a sign that our design was reasonably effective at encapsulating changes to the system.

The implementation for Federation used by LineInterpreter detects when an interpreter is unknown to the Client, then attempts to contact federated participants to obtain the missing interpreter. It does this primarily by iterating through the set of participants and asking each in turn whether it has the missing interpreter. This process continues until either one of the participants is able to supply the desired interpreter or all the participants have been asked. If no participants know about the interpreter, an error message is displayed. The implementation of this federated LineInterpreter is shown in Listing 25.4, with changes in bold.

```
import java.util.*;

public class LineInterpreter
   extends TrivialInterpreter
{
  public LineInterpreter(String s)
  {
    super(s);
  }

  public static Hashtable interpreters = new Hashtable();
```

Continues

```
public static Vector participants = new Vector();

public StringTokenizer parse( StringTokenizer st )
{
  if (st.hasMoreTokens())
    {
      String cmd = st.nextToken();
      Interpreter interpreter = (Interpreter)interpreters.get(cmd);
      if (interpreter != null)
        st = interpreter.parse(st);
      else
        {
          // Can't find the interpreter for this command!
          // Federate with other Clients to interpret command.

          Enumeration e = participants.elements();

          boolean found = false;
          while (!found && e.hasMoreElements())
            {
              Avatar a = (Avatar)e.nextElement();

              // Attempt to locate interpreter in other participants.
              // Bundling this code to locate the interpreter in
              // something called FederatedInterpreter might provide a
              // nice additional transparency.

              interpreter = a.lookup(cmd);
              if (interpreter != null)
                {
                  st = interpreter.parse(st);
                  found = true;
                }
            }

          if (!found)
            System.out.println("Unknown Command: " + cmd);
```

```
        }
      }

   return st;
}


public void addAction( Interpreter action )
{
   interpreters.put( action.getTrigger(), action );
}


public Interpreter lookup( String cmd )
{
   return (Interpreter)interpreters.get(cmd);
}


public void addParticipant( Avatar s )
{
   participants.addElement( s );
}
};
```

Listing 25.4 Source for LineInterpreter.

This example is run in exactly the same way it was in Chapter 24: Interpreter, with one exception: you can start new participants at any time without concern for whether the new member has access to the full set of interpreters. The new participant transparently uses Federation in LineInterpreter to locate any missing interpreters!

Related Patterns

Composition can often be used to build Federation. The leaves in a composite distributed system may be polymorphically substituted between local and remote objects, enabling a transparent view of many servers.

Bibliography

Gamma, Erich, et al. *Design Patterns*. Addison-Wesley: Reading, Massachusetts, 1995.

Krasner, G.E., and Pope, S.T. "A cookbook for using the Model-View-Controller user interface paradigm in Smalltalk-80," *Journal of Object-Oriented Programming* 1(3), pp. 26–49, August/September 1988, SIGS Publications: New York, NY, USA, 1988.

Maffeis, Silvano. "The Object Group Design Pattern," *Proceedings of the 1996 USENIX Conference on Object-Oriented Technologies*. The USENIX Association: Toronto, Canada, June 1996.

Meszardos, G. "Pattern: Half Object + Protocol (HOPP)," *Proceedings of PLOP '94*, pp. 129–132.

Mowbray, Tom. *Corba Design Patterns*. John Wiley & Sons: New York, NY, 1997.

Appendix

What's on the CD-ROM?

The companion CD-ROM contain tons of great stuff designed to make your exploration of mobile object more exciting.

Examples. Nearly every chapter in this book contains a substantial example to demonstrate the concepts under discussion. By running these examples, exploring their source code, and even modifying and extending them to suit your own needs, you will get much more out of this book.

Design Patterns. The second hald of this book is dedicated to documenting some design patterns for mobile objects. Every single design pattern includes a running example of the design pattern implemented in Java. These examples can teach you how to implement the design patterns in source code.

Trial Edition of VisiBroker For Java, version 3.2. The leading Java distributed object tool also supports mobile objects. VisiBroker, a product of Inprise, is an implementation of the CORBA standard developed by the OMG. One of the VisiBroker tools, Caffeine, makes writing CORBA applications extremely easy and also has the essential support for mobile objects that is critical to it's use in this book. Many of the examples of this book are written with VisiBroker.

Voyager versions 1.01 and 2.0.0. An innovative pure Java distributed object product by the makers of the Java Generic Libraries. Object Space continues to produce winners with this ORB toolkit. In addition to supporting mobile objects, Voyager has support for CORBA, transactions, and basic security.

JDK version 1.1.7. The Java Developer's Kit is the standard for Java development. In order to insure maximum interoperability across multiple platforms and development environments, the JDK was used to build all of the examples in this book. However, you can also import these examples into another development environment of your choice with ease.

BDK version 1.2. JavaBeans are the component standard for Java development. The Bean Developer's Kit, while not absolutely required to develop Beans, contains a useful set of examples and tools for testing your JavaBeans.

mpEDIT version 1.13. A great text editor put together by a group of software developers collaborating over the Internet. While mpEDIT has roughly the same functionality as Notepad, but mpEDIT excells at the source code level. The elegant design of mpEDIT makes it an excellent starting point for use as an example of mobile objects in this book.

OROMatcher. A toolkit for performing text matches created by ORO. This toolkit is required by the mpEDIT text editor for performing string matches, but you can also use it with other applications.

TogetherJ/Whiteboard Edition version 2.0. TogetherJ is one of the leading object oriented analysis and design tools with support for UML. Each of the design patterns used in this book are diagrammed with UML. Diagramming your work like this can help you organize your thoughts and spot elements of your design that you might otherwise miss without a formal design. This tool can help you create and analysize the designs of your own projects.

iBus Java Software Bus version 0.5. iBus is a unique toolkit from Softwired AG of Zurich for writing robust group-based distributed systems using objects. It may be an invaluable tool to you if you decide to further explore the use of object groups and replication in your own software.

Trial Edition of JBuilder 2. Inprise, the developer of one of the best development environments in the market, now owns one of the best Java ORBs. Both products come together in the latest version of JBuilder. The trial copy on this product can be used to run the examples throughout the book.

What is Freeware?

Freeware is software that is distributed by disk, through BBS systems and the Internet free. There is no charge for using it, and can be distributed freely as long as the use it is put to follows the license agreement included with it.

Hardware Requirements

All of the examples in this book are written with pure Java, so all you need is the following system requirements to use these examples:

♦ Any computer with a JVM

♦ Any development environment that supports JDK 1.1 or better

♦ TCP/IP Networking

Installing the Software

To install any of the products contained on the CD-ROM, please follow the manufacturers installation instructions found with the product.

To install the example projects used throughout this book, follow these simple steps:

For Windows:

1. Start Windows on your computer.

2. Place the CD-ROM into your CD-ROM drive.

3. From Program Manager, Select File,Run, and type **X:\SETUP** (where **X** is the correct letter of your CD-ROM drive)

4. Follow the screen prompts to complete the installation.

For Unix:

1. Place the CD-ROM into your CD-ROM drive.

2. Open a shell.

3. Type **cp /cdrom/pmoj ~/pmoj** (where **/cdrom** is the directory of your CD-ROM drive)

Using the Software

For the products enclosed on the CD-ROM, please see the manufacturer's instructions on how to use the software.

Any of the example projects can be run by following these simple steps:

1. Change to the appropriate directory of the example.

2. Type **doit**.

3. Follow the screen prompts to complete running the example.

User Assistance and Information

Please send comments about this book to **jnelson@DistributedObjects.com** or visit the Web site of this book at **www.DistributedObjects.com**. Additional samples and mobile object software will be posted on this site as it becomes available.

The software accompanying this book is being provided as is without warranty or support of any kind. Should you require basic installation assistance, or if your media is defective, please call our product support number at (212) 850-6194 weekdays between 9 A.M. and 4 P.M. Eastern Standard Time. Or, we can be reached via e-mail at: **wprtusw@wiley.com**.

To place additional orders or to request information about other Wiley products, please call (800) 879-4539.

A

AbstractInterpreter, 542–544
AbstractMpAction, 254, 257, 264, 266
AccountSupplier, 384, 386
AccountView, 380
ACID test. *See* Atomic Consistent
    Isolated Durable test.
Action, 250, 251, 257, 286, 288, 301
ActionResourceBundle, 268, 275
Active Channels (Microsoft), 360
ActiveX, 114
ActiveXControls, 116–118
  object, 115
Actor [GoF95], 407
  applicability, 408
  collaborations, 409
  consequences, 410
  implementation, 410–411
  intent, 407
  motivation, 408
  participants, 409
  structure, 409
Actors, 58, 61, 407, 409, 410
ADA, 344
Adapter classes, 474
addAction() method, 552
addToDict, 282, 284
Agent API, 71, 72, 76
Agent-enhanced, definition, 139–141
Agent-enhanced ORB, 139, 140
Agents, 140. *See also* Mobile agents.
  software, 72–75
Aggregation, 368, 369
All-or-nothing delivery, 416
Antenna, 518, 522
  interface, 535
Antipatterns, 365–366
API, 22, 27, 38, 55, 76, 83, 85, 89, 114,
    144, 156, 218, 347, 348, 362, 574.
    See also Agent API;
    SecurityManager; Standardized API.
Applet objects, 238

APPLET tag, 238
AppletClassLoader, 32, 48
Applets, 54, 210, 227, 243, 349
AppletTask, 233–236, 238. *See also*
    SerializableAppletTask.
Appletviewer, 206
Application, 376, 483, 514
  flexibility, 514
Application logic, 479
Association, 368, 369
Atomic case/ordering.
    See First in first out.
Atomic Consistent Isolated Durable
    (ACID) test, 130
Avatar interface, 574, 575
Avatar object, 574
AvatarImpl, 553
  object, 575
AWT, 536
AWT code, 383
AWT components, 172, 173, 479
AWT event, 330
AWTEvents, 330

B

Bable. *See* Tower of Babel.
Backup, 435, 436
  servers, 441, 445
Ballot object, 166, 167, 181
Ballots, 1767
Base type, choice. *See* Common base type.
Basic Object Adapter (BOA), 17
BatteryAd, 61–63, 65, 66, 412–414
BDK, 523
BeanBox, 523, 531, 535, 538
BeanDescriptor, 534
  object, 532
BeanInfo, 98, 99
BeanInfoLite
  class, 533
  implementation, 534

Beans. *See* Hello Bean; JavaBeans;
    Mobile beans.
BinaryFunction, 466, 467
    interface, 469
BinaryPredicate, 466, 467
BOA. *See* Basic Object Adapter.
Borland, 80, 109. *See also* JBuilder.
Bottlenecking, 401, 403
Broadcast, 25–26
Broken encapsulation, 26–27
BunnyThread, 60, 61, 65–67, 412, 413
Business patterns, 365
Byte array, 535
ByteArrayOutputStream, 214
Byte-code, 49, 67
    implementation, 33

C

Cache MetaData, 530
Caesar cipher, 324
Caffeine, 33, 79–88, 96, 144, 378, 384,
    439. *See also* Common Object Request
    Broker Architecture.
    class library, 83
    future, 80
    usage. *See* Mobile objects.
Callback, 440
Castanet (Marimba), 360
Causal ordering, 312
Chain of Responsibility. *See* Responsibility
    chain.
Chat application, 160
checkAccept(String, int), 328–329
checkAccess(Thread), 329
checkAccess(ThreadGroup), 330
checkAwtEventQueueAccess(), 330–331
checkConnect(Sting, int, Object), 331
checkConnect(String, int), 331
checkCreateClassLoader(), 331–332
checkDelete(String), 332
checkExec(String), 332–333
checkExit(int), 333
checkLink(String), 333–334
checkListen(int), 334
checkMemberAccess(Class, int), 334
checkMulticast(InetAddress, byte), 335
checkMulticast(InetAddress), 334–335
checkPackageAccess(String), 335
checkPackageDefinition(String), 335–336

checkPrintJobAccess(), 336
checkPropertiesAccess(), 336–337
checkPropertyAccess(String), 337
checkRead method, 55
checkRead(FileDescriptor), 337
checkRead(String, Object), 338
checkRead(String), 337
checkSecurityAccess(String), 338
checkSetFactory(), 338–339
checkSystemClipboardAccess(), 339
checkTopLevelWindow(Object), 339–340
checkWrite(FileDescriptor), 340
checkWrite(String), 341
ChoiceVote, 167, 171–173, 175, 180, 181
    object, 186
Ciphers, 323–324. *See also* Caesar cipher.
Class
    conflict comparison, 205
    files, 54
    loading, 47–51, 85, 144–147, 211–212
    variables, 44
ClassDescriptor, 211
    object, 50
Classes, 367–368
ClassLoader, 32, 48–50, 81, 145, 332. *See
    also* Java ClassLoader;
    Network-enabled ClassLoader.
CLASSPATH, 145, 146, 205, 208, 209,
    212, 235, 250, 354
Client, 7, 8, 136, 391, 396, 400, 505, 506,
    550, 558, 563, 564, 570, 571, 577.
    See also Generic client.
    applet, 235
    application, 164, 301
    machine, 236
    writing, 201–203
Client/Server, 6–9, 262, 418, 565
    architecture, 222, 263, 312
    comparison. *See* Peers.
    models, 114, 162
    software, 161
    system, 55, 348
Client-side installation, 25
Client-side software, 25
Clustering, 305, 573
    fundamentals, 306–319
COBOL, 1, 20, 23
Code. *See* Sample code.
CODEBASE, 145, 146
Collaboration group, 219

Collaborations, 356, 370. *See also* Actor
 [GoF95]; Command [GoF95];
 Composable Views [Krasner88];
 Extension [Nelson98]; Federation
 [Nelson98]; Interpreter [GoF95];
 MVC [Krasner88]; Object Group
 [Maffeis 96]; Predicate [GoF95];
 Remote Proxy [GoF95]; Replication
 [Nelson98]; Smart Proxy
 [Meszaros94]; Smorgasbord
 [Mowbray97].
COM, 109–122
 acronym choice, 113–114
 building, Java usage, 119–122
 components usage,
  DCOM interaction, 122–125
 enhancements, 128–138
 usage. *See* Java.
COM/DCOM, 109
Command [GoF95], 447
 applicability, 448
 collaborations, 450
 consequences, 450–451
 implementation, 451–453
 intent, 447
 motivation, 448
 participants, 448–449
 structure, 449
Common base type, choice, 220–221
Common Object Request Broker
  Architecture (CORBA), 14–28, 96,
  107, 127, 156, 157, 344, 345, 349,
  365, 392–394, 396, 398, 413, 439, 539
 applications, 79
 CORBA-based distributed system, 83
 CORBA-based system, 156, 540
 CORBA-compatible Caffeine, 76
 CORBA-compliant ORBs, 191
 CORBA-style client/server
  communication, 439
 integration, 141, 156–157
 interface, 517
 limitations, 22–28
 ORB, 522
 server, 518
Common packet format, 19
Common protocol, 19–20
Compilation, 205
Complexity, hiding, 4–5
Component framework, 516

Component integration framework, 89
Component-based software
  applications, 90
Component-based system, 91
Components, 27, 38.
  See also Distributed components;
  Mobile components.
 argument, 89–90
Composable Views [Krasner88], 479
 applicability, 481–482
 collaborations, 483
 consequences, 483–484
 implementation, 484–485
 intent, 479
 motivation, 479–481
 participants, 482–483
 structure, 482
Composite objects, 483
ComputationTask, 242–244
ConcreteBinaryFunction, 467
ConcreteBinaryPredicate, 467
ConcreteCommand, 448, 450, 454
ConcreteController, 376
ConcreteExtension, 513–515, 527
ConcreteInterpreter, 542
ConcreteModel, 375
ConcretePeer, 563–565
ConcreteSmartProxy, 401
ConcreteUnaryFunction, 467
ConcreteUnaryPredicate, 467
ConcreteView, 375
Concurrency, 58–69, 88, 154–155, 214
Confidentiality, 326
Configuration options, 418
Configurators, 512
Conflict, comparison. *See* Class.
Connection Machines, 242
Consequences, 370, 372. *See also* Actor
 [GoF95]; Command [GoF95];
 Composable Views [Krasner88];
 Extension [Nelson98]; Federation
 [Nelson98]; Interpreter [GoF95];
 MVC [Krasner88]; Object Group
 [Maffeis 96]; Predicate [GoF95];
 Remote Proxy [GoF95]; Replication
 [Nelson98]; Smart Proxy
 [Meszaros94]; Smorgasbord
 [Mowbray97].
Consumer, 449, 450, 467, 476, 477, 527
 resources, 451

Contact, 494, 497, 505
  list, 506, 507
  object, 486, 487, 500
ContactView, 35, 486, 488
Controller, 376, 377
Coordination overhead, 418
CORBA. *See* Common Object Request
    Broker Architecture.
Counter, 154
CoWorker object, 187
Cryptography, 323–327
  tools, 325–327
Customer support, 75

D

DACM. *See* Decoupling And Coupling
    Management.
Daemon thread, 63
Data formats, 541
Database access, 450
Database queries, 470
Data-oriented applications, 159
Date object, 167
DateVote, 182
DCE, 539
DCOM, 91, 107, 122–125, 540.
    See also COM/DCOM.
  integration, 156–157
  interaction. *See* COM.
  mixing. *See* Remote
      Method Invocation.
  Unix, choice, 124
  usage. *See* Mobile objects.
DCOM-compatible tools, 344
Decorator, 516, 523
Decoupling And Complexity
    Management (DACM), 365
Delphi, 349
Design patterns
  definition/explanation, 364–366
  overview, 363
Directory, 527
Distributed applications,
    RMI usage, 192–206
  example, running, 204
  kinks, resolving, 205–206
  problem, identification, 192
Distributed components, 90–92
  programming, 90

Distributed objects, 1, 31, 89, 190, 203, 404
  computing, 9–14
  development, 189
  extinction, 28
  interface, 345
Distributed server, 458
Distributed system, 327, 433
Distributing computing, 51
DNS, 6
Dynamic linked library, 333, 334

E

E-commerce environment, 331
Editors, 512
EJB. *See* Enterprise JavaBeans.
Elements/meaning, 2–4
E-mail client, 322
E-mail message, 292
E-mail server, 291, 303
Encapsulation, 4–5, 13. *See also* Broken
    encapsulation.
Enterprise JavaBeans (EJB), 344
Environment, 409, 410, 449, 452, 455,
    456, 467, 468
EventQueue, 330, 331
EventSetDescriptor, 533
Extensibility, plan, 377
Extension Directory Service, 530
Extension [Nelson98], 511
  applicability, 513
  collaborations, 514
  consequences, 514–515
  implementation, 515–516
  intent, 511
  motivation, 511–512
  objects, 530
  participants, 513–514
  structure, 513
Extension pattern, 516
ExtensionDirectory, 279, 284
ExtensionDirectoryImpl, 279–281, 284
ExtensionImplementations, 530
ExtensionMetaData, 529
Extensions, 278, 290, 513–515, 526, 531
  interface, 515–516
  loading, 528
  object, 275
  objects, 530
  removal, 516

ExternalizableImage object, 43
Externalization, 7, 42–44, 61

F

Failover, 306
Fault tolerance, 261, 433, 436, 440, 445
Fbcast, 310
Feature enhancements, 514   ·
Federation
    levels addition, 569–570
    pattern, 463
Federation [Nelson98], 561
    applicability, 562–563
    collaborations, 563
    consequences, 564
    implementation, 565–571
    intent, 561
    motivation, 561–562
    participants, 563
    structure, 563
FIFO. *See* First in first out.
File based access, 355
FileDescriptor, 337, 340
FileInterpreter, 559
Files, saving/sharing, 218
First in first out (FIFO), 310, 311
    atomic case, 311
    atomic ordering, 312
Forwarder object, 152
Forwarders, 393
Frame, 172, 177, 237
FTP, 218, 352
FTP protocol, 149

G

Gang of Four, 488
Gang-of-Four
    Composite pattern, 509
    Factory Method, 538
    observer pattern, 388
    patterms, 523
    strategy, 405
Garbage collection, 153
General Interoperable Protocol (GIOP), 19
Generic client, 227–228
Generic server, 222–227
GeographyInterpreter, 559
GIOP. *See* General Interoperability Protocol.

Globally unique identifier (GUID),
    114, 115, 118
Gossip, 50, 51
Graphical user interfaces (GUIs), 26, 313,
    352, 450, 470
GridLayout, 536
    object, 171
Group, 417
    building, mobile objects usage, 314–319
    communication, 419
    failure, 418
    messaging, 314
Group-based approach, 262
Group-based communication, 222
    protocols, 354
Groups of objects. *See* Object groups.
Groupware, 217
    approach, 217–219
    building. *See* Mobile groupware building.
GUID. *See* Globally unique identifier.
GUIs. *See* Graphical user interfaces.

H

Hardware independence, 20
hashCode, 224
Hashtable, 80, 82, 177, 223
Hello Bean, 97–105
HelloCaster, 439–441, 445
HelpAboutDialog, 269, 270, 272, 280
HORB, 36, 41, 45–47
HORUS, 317, 419, 438
    implementation algorithms, 58
Host, 199
Host computer, 199
Host name, 202, 558
HTML documents, 329
HTML file, 238
HTML pages, 361
HTML-based Internet, 361
HTTP, 32, 86
    protocol, 38, 149
    request, 145, 329

I

iBus, 438
IDispatch interface, 125, 126
IDL. *See* Interface Definition Language.
IIOP, 80, 86, 191

Image object, 43
Implementation, 370, 372. *See also* Actor
[GoF95]; Command [GoF95];
Composable Views [Krasner88];
Extension [Nelson98]; Federation
[Nelson98]; Interfaces; Interpreter
[GoF95]; Mobile stream; MVC
[Krasner88]; Object Group [Maffeis
96]; Object groups; Objects;
RemoteProxyTarget; Replicated
system; Root interface; Smart Proxy
[Meszaros94]; Smorgasbord
[Mowbray97]; Tasks.
  interoperability, 346–348
  object, 404
  usage. *See* Remote Proxy [GoF95].
InetAddress, 335
Information sharing, 217
Inheritance, 5–6, 105–106, 368–369
  tree, 6
InputValidator, 384
Inter Process Communication (IPC), 365
Interface Definition Language (IDL),
    12, 14, 23, 24, 79, 518. *See also*
    Standardized IDL.
  files, 22, 156
InterfaceDef object, 17
Interfaces, 469. *See also* Extensions; Java.
  definition/implementation, 12–13
  hiding, 377
  implementation. *See* Root interface.
Internet, 53, 135, 158, 213, 343
  IP address, 202
Internet Explorer (Microsoft), 209–210
Interoperability, 14–28. *See also*
    Implementation; Protocol; Remote
    Method Invocation.
Interoperable object reference (IOR), 156
Interpreter [GoF95], 539
  applicability, 541
  collaborations, 542
  consequences, 542–543
  intent, 539
  motivation, 540–541
  participants, 542
  structure, 541
Interpreters, 542, 572. *See also*
    Nonoptimal interpreter.
  decoupling, 543
  implementation, 543

IOR. *See* Interoperable object reference.
IP Multicast, 51, 154, 159, 334, 335,
    438, 544
IPC. *See* Inter Process Communication.
IPX, 19
ISIS, 438
ISubspace interface, 160

J
JAR files, 86, 95, 96, 258, 517
JarLoader, 517, 522
Java, 6, 22–24, 39, 45, 47, 51, 56, 59,
    109, 111, 113, 127, 196, 328–341,
    410. *See also* Pure Java.
  applets, 114, 145, 201
  applications, 58, 148, 191, 200, 201,
    328, 354, 516
  AWT, 164
  Class, 124
  classes, 48
  code, 452
  component models, 96
  Date object, 116
  Dates, 164
  developers, 21, 51, 113, 117, 351
  events, 120
  garbage collector, 87
  integration, 135
  interface, 79, 80
  interpreter, 288, 328
  I/O, 197
  language, 67, 353
  mail libraries, 337
  Native interface, 208
  Object Serialization, 81, 83, 191
  ORB, 80
  program, 63, 131
  programming, 313
  run-time environment, 331, 336
  SDK, 111, 126
  software, 110
  source files, 205
  threads, 68, 154, 155
  tools, 206–208
  usage. *See* COM.
  windows, 180
Java, COM usage, 110–119
  limitations, 111–119
Java ClassLoader, 32

Java Development Kit (JDK), 79, 104, 126, 184, 188, 189, 195, 206–207, 235, 353
Java Generic Library (JGL), 139, 468, 470, 471
Java objects, 13, 33, 41, 47, 59, 80, 81, 111, 121, 137, 152, 195, 221, 411, 528
    reference, 190
Java Remote Method Protocol, 191
Java SecurityManager, 450
Java Stack, 223
Java Virtual Machine (JVM), 7, 37, 44, 46, 51, 60, 67, 81, 86, 87, 117, 121, 126, 242, 532, 538
JavaBean-based component model, 258
JavaBeans, 89, 94–106, 115, 116, 121, 122, 128, 248, 258, 420, 430, 432, 439. *See also* Enterprise JavaBeans.
    developers, 424
JAVAC compiler, 198
JavaSoft, 44, 80, 191, 206–207
    implementation, 424
Java-specific data types, 15
JBuilder (Borland), 207, 383, 474
JCE, 151
JDK. *See* Java Development Kit.
JellyBean, 424, 428, 432
    Adapter, 430
JellyBeanAdapter, 432
JellyBeanBeanInfo, 429
JGL. *See* Java Generic Library.
JMS, 93
JNI, 15, 208
JVM. *See* Java Virtual Machine.

K

KIF, 346
KQML, 346

L

Label object, 172
LAN, 136, 242, 343
Language independence, 20–21
LCD. *See* Least Common Denominator.
Least Common Denominator (LCD), 22–24
LineCommand, 454–456, 463
LineInterpreter, 551, 579, 581

LinePrinter, 192, 194, 201, 202
LinePrinterImpl, 198
LISP, 344
Lisp language, 465
Lisp programming language, 555
LISP-like languages, 346, 347
ListResourceBundle, 268
Load balancing, 436
Location transparency, 13
Lotus Notes, 218

M

MagicCap, 71, 72
main() method, 199, 226
MakeWork, 228, 230, 232, 235
Marimba. *See* Castanet.
Member variables, 45, 46
Membership layer, 573
Messaging, 134–136; 357–359
    approach, 262
MetaData, 279, 514–516, 527–529, 532–536
    loading, 528
    object, 270, 271, 275, 278, 516
Metadata file, 95
Method invocation, 16, 68
Methods, 2, 5
Microsoft. *See* Internet Explorer; Visual J++.
    RMI usage, 208
Microsoft Interface Definition Language (MIDL), 122
Microsoft Message Queue Server (MSMQ), 135, 136
Microsoft Transaction Server (MTS), 131, 133, 134
MIDL. *See* Microsoft Interface Definition Language.
Mobile agents
    comparison. *See* Mobile object.
    contrast. *See* Mobile objects.
    definition, 70–72
    patent, 71
Mobile beans, 92, 96
Mobile code, 24–25
Mobile components, 88–106
    building, mobile object tools usage, 97
    comparison. *See* Mobile objects.
Mobile groupware building, RMI usage, 221–231

Mobile objects, 40, 58, 68, 161, 220, 221,
    249, 259, 314, 315, 317, 322, 327,
    335, 336, 339–341, 354, 362, 378,
    415, 433, 447, 452, 481, 543, 562.
    See also Vote mobile objects.
  actions, 293
  cloning, 437–438
  collaboration, 219–221
  definition, 31–36
  development, 210–215
  feasibility, DCOM usage, 125–128
  mobile agents, comparison, 70–77
  mobile agents, contrast, 75–77
  mobile components, comparison, 92–94
  operation, 514
  ramifications, 36–69
  support, 260–263
  taxonomy, 31
  tools, usage. *See* Mobile components.
  trends, 343
  usage. *See* Group; Mobs.
  utility, 84
  voting, 165–188
Mobile objects, building, 378
  Caffeine usage, 79
  Voyager usage, 139
Mobile objects, securing, 321
  risks, 321–323
  technology, 323–341
Mobile stream
  building, 214
  implementation, 214–215
MobileByteArrayOutputStream, 214, 215
Mobility. *See* Target.
  benefits, 373, 390, 400, 407, 415, 433,
    447, 465, 480, 511, 525, 539, 562
  choice, 220
  features, 84–88, 141–158, 211–214
  reason, 371–372
  role, 312–313
Mobs, mobile objects usage, 158–188
  approaches, 161–165
  problem, 161
Model, 375, 377–379, 479
Model View Controller (MVC),
    371, 480, 484
  pattern, 373–375, 377, 383, 479, 491
Model-View-Controller pattern, 35
Momento pattern, 414
Monolithic systems, 69

mpEDIT
  application, 247–263, 282
  application, mobilization, 263–290
  architecture, 249–258
  considerations, 291–303
  stumbling blocks, 259–260
MSMQ. *See* Microsoft Message Queue
    Server.
MTS. *See* Microsoft Transaction Server.
MUD. *See* Multi-User Dungeon.
Multicast approach, 262
Multicast invocations, 438
Multicast UDP, 25
Multihomed hosts, 329
Multiplicity, 369–370
Multithreading, 69
Multi-User Dungeon (MUD), 544, 545,
    549, 552, 558
MVC. *See* Model View Controller.
MVC [Krasner88], 373
  applicability, 375
  collaborations, 376
  consequences, 376–377
  implementation, 377–378
  intent, 373
  motivation, 374–375
  participants, 375–376
  structure, 374

N

Name, 489. *See also* Host name; Patterns.
  object, 488
NameViewPnl, 493, 494
Naming object, 200, 202
Nasty activities, 323
Navigator (Netscape), 209
Nested Predicates, 469–470
NETBEUI, 19
Netcaster (Netscape), 360
Network protocols, 541
NetworkClassLoader, 49
Network-enabled ClassLoader, 32
New View objects, 483
Non-mobile objects, 452
Non-object-oriented programming
    languages, 1
Nonoptimal interpreter, 542
Non-static member variable static, 196
Non-transient member variable
    transient, 196

O

Object Group [Maffeis 96], 415
  applicability, 416
  collaborations, 417
  consequences, 418
  implementation, 419–420
  intent, 415
  motivation, 416
  participants, 417
  structure, 417
Object groups, 308, 354–355, 419
  communication, spaces usage, 159–161
  implementation, 308–312
Object Management Group (OMG), 14,
    23–25, 28, 79, 156, 344, 347, 348, 351
Object Request Brokers (ORBs), 13–16,
    20, 23, 44, 82, 88, 139, 189, 198,
    211, 393. *See also* Agent-enhanced
    ORB; Common Object Request Broker
    Architecture; Java.
  environment, 159
  technologies, 390
  usage, 10–12
Object Serialization, 32, 36, 41–48, 53, 57,
    60, 80, 85, 86, 144, 150, 211, 231,
    236–238, 269. *See also* Java.
Object Spaces, 348, 468
Object Web, 350
ObjectInputStream, 48–50
ObjectInterpreter, 559
Object-oriented application, 36
Object-oriented design, 370, 482
Object-oriented developers, 35
Object-oriented model, 484
Object-oriented program, 259
Object-oriented programming
    languages, 1, 16
Object-oriented relationships, 368
Object-oriented software, 13, 45, 90
  development, 12, 31
Object-oriented system, 45
Object-oriented user interface, 26
ObjectOutputStream, 50
Objects. *See* Composite objects; Java; New
    View objects.
  adapters, 17
  bus, 21–22
  choice, 192–196
  cloning, 453
  computing. *See* Distributed object
    computing.

  definition, 1–6
  identity, 51–53, 86–88, 151–153, 213
  implementation, 196–198
  interaction, limits, 9
  mobility, 88
  sea, 360–362
  sharing, 57–58, 153–154, 213
  state, 40–47
  taxonomy. *See* Mobile objects.
  tests/actions, 468
  web, 348–350
Objects-by-Value, 24
ObjectSpace, 139, 140, 148, 153, 344, 470
Observer, 410
OLE components, 113
OLE2, 114
OMG. *See* Object Management Group.
Operating systems, 37, 123, 209, 333
Operation invocations, 58
ORBs. *See* Object Request Brokers.
Ordering, 416
Organizational patterns, 365
OutputStream, 82, 84

P

Packets, 7–9, 18. *See also* Standardized
    packets.
  format. *See* Common packet format.
Parallel computing, 241–245
Participant objects, 161
Participants, 370. *See also* Actor [GoF95];
    Command [GoF95]; Composable Views
    [Krasner88]; Extension [Nelson98];
    Federation [Nelson98]; Interpreter
    [GoF95]; MVC [Krasner88]; Object
    Group [Maffeis 96]; Predicate [GoF95];
    Remote Proxy [GoF95]; Replication
    [Nelson98]; Smart Proxy [Meszaros94];
    Smorgasbord [Mowbray97].
Partitioning, 571
Pass-By-Value, 350–354
  feature, 100
Patterns
  applicability, 367
  format, 366–371
  intent, 367
  motivation, 367
  name, 202, 366
  structure, 367–371
  usage, 366

Peers, 563, 570, 571, 574
    Client/Server comparison, 162
Peer-to-peer, 262, 548
PeopleInterpreter, 559
Performance, 418
    hit, 514
Perl, 344, 349
Piggybacking, 516
Pluggable software, 22
POA. *See* Portable Object Adapter.
Point-of-sale system, 75, 76
Point-to-point approach, 262
Point-to-point communication, 418
Point-to-point connection, 136
Point-to-point protocol, 26
PoisonPill object, 212
Polymorphism, 6
pop() method, 102
POP3 mail host, 302
POP3 protocol, 38
PopClient, 101, 102, 104, 196
popTask, 225
Port number, 202
Portable Object Adapter (POA), 17
PowerBuilder, 119, 344, 365
Predicate [GoF95], 465
    applicability, 466
    collaborations, 468
    consequences, 468
    implementation, 469–470
    intent, 465
    motivation, 465–466
    participants, 467
    structure, 466
Predicates, 468–471. *See also* Nested
        Predicates.
    rearranging, 468
    reuse, 468
Prefix, 202
Primary, 435
Primary servers, 441, 446, 566
PrimaryServer, 566, 567
PrintClient, 204
PrintCommand, 455, 456, 463
PrintInterpreter, 546, 547, 551, 558
PrintServer, 201, 204
Private keys, 325
Private/secure, definition comparison, 46
Problem partitioning, 568
Procedures, 2

Process group, 308
Process scope, 44
PropertyChangeGroup, 421, 424
PropertyChangeListener, 420, 421, 424,
        429, 430
PropertyChangeSupport, 420, 424
Protected, 45
Protocol. *See* Common protocol.
    interoperability, 344–346
Prototyping, 453
Proxies, 565
    usage, 544
Public, 45
Public key cryptography, 324–325
Pure Java, 128
Push environment, 355
Push-based technologies, 360
PushClient, 101, 102, 106, 194
Pushdown stack, 223
pushTask, 224
Python, 344

Q
Queuing, 358

R
RAID technologies, 437
Rapport Bean, 104
readObject, 196
Receiver, 417
Relationships, 368
Remote construction, 158
Remote invocation, 16, 80, 137, 157
Remote Method Inference,
        object reference, 462
Remote Method Invocation (RMI), 33, 41,
        56, 76, 96, 115, 122, 144, 189, 193,
        205–210, 263, 335, 344, 349, 378,
        392, 394, 397, 398, 413, 458
    applications, 145, 194, 201, 281, 455
    classes, 201
    client, 462, 477
    compilation, 206
    DCOM mixture, 126–127
    interface, 194
    interoperability, 191
    introduction, 189–191
    Naming service, 226, 227, 232, 235

server, 192, 384
usage. *See* Distributed applications;
      Microsoft; Mobile groupware
      building.
Remote Object, 389
Remote Proxy [GoF95], 389
   applicability, 390
   building, 393
   collaborations, 392
   consequences, 392–393
   implementation, 393–394
   intent, 389
   motivation, 389–390
   participants, 391
   redirection, implementation usage, 392
   structure, 391
Remote ProxyStub, 389
Remote Reference, 389
RemoteException, 193, 194
RemoteProxy, 391, 393–395, 397, 398,
      400–403
RemoteProxyTarget, 391, 396
   implementation, 392–393
Replacability concepts, 37
Replicated system, implementation, 314
Replication, 307–319, 356–357, 416,
      437, 445
   pattern, 434, 435
Replication [Nelson98], 433
   applicability, 435
   collaborations, 436
   consequences, 436–437
   implementation, 437–439
   intent, 433
   motivation, 434–435
   participants, 435–436
   structure, 435
Request for proposal (RFP), 25, 348
Request forwarding, 566
Resource management, 37
Resource partitioning, 568
ResourceBundle, 250, 268, 275, 288, 302
ResourceLoaders, 145, 146
Responsibility chain, 478, 509, 516,
      523, 546
Restarting, 306–307
Return value, 469
Reusability, 5–6
Reuse, 393
RFP. *See* Request for proposal.

RMI. *See* Remote Method Invocation.
RMIC compiler, 198, 203
RMIClassLoader, 212
RMISecurityManager, 213, 226
Root interface, 222
Root interface, implementation, 221–222
RPC, 91, 343
RPC/DCE systems, 114
run() operation, 231
Runnable, 220, 451
Run-time additions/deletions, 376
Run-time environment, 55, 104.
      See also Java.
Run-time introspection, 91, 94
Run-time processing, 46

S

Sample code, 370–371, 378–388, 393–398,
      403–405, 411–414, 420–432,
      439–446, 453–463, 470–478,
      485–509, 517–523, 531–538,
      544–559, 572–581
Sand-box security, 148
Sandbox security model, 328
Scheme, 60
SDK. *See* Java.
Sea of objects. *See* Objects.
Secure, definition comparison.
      See Private/secure.
Secure Socket Layer (SSL), 151, 213
   protocol, 86
      SSL-protected TCP/IP socket
         communication, 151
Security, 40, 53–57, 86, 136–138,
      148–151, 212–213
Security API, 338
SecurityException, 150
SecurityManager, 34, 55, 56, 146, 147,
      150, 207, 328, 332, 336, 511
   API, 340
SendTo action, addition, 291–303
SendToBundle, 302
SendToDialog, 293, 300
Serializable, 451
Serializable object, 144
SerializableAppletTask, 236–241
SerializableStringMan, 267, 268
Serialization, 42–44, 210
   approaches, 44–47

Servant, 199
Server, 7, 8, 101, 136, 199, 228, 235, 280,
    288, 291, 306, 307, 318, 357, 581.
    See also Client/Server; E-mail server;
    Generic server; Remote Method
    Invocation.
  object, 84, 281
  request delegation, 570
  writing, 198–201
Service quality, 418
Service-providing applications, 309
Shared resources, 436–437
Shippable places, 359–360
Skeletons, 17–18, 18, 83–85, 122
SlaveApplet, 232, 233, 240, 243
Smalltalk, 22, 23, 353
Smart Proxy [Meszaros94], 399
  applicability, 400–401
  collaborations, 401
  consequences, 402
  implementation, 402–403
  intent, 399
  motivation, 399–400
  participants, 401
  structure, 401
Smorgasbord [Mowbray97], 525
  applicability, 526
  collaborations, 528
  consequences, 528–529
  implementation, 529–531
  intent, 525
  motivation, 525–526
  participants, 526–527
  structure, 527
SMTP e-mail server, 328
SMTP protocol, 38
SocketFactory, 338
Software. *See* Mobile agents; Pluggable
    software.
  design patterns, 364
  execution, 219
  objects, 2–5
Source, 449, 458, 467, 475, 476
Source code, 39, 98, 369
  manipulation, 89
SourceImpl, 459, 476
Spaces, 154, 175, 421, 553, 555, 557, 577.
    See also Voyager.
  usage. *See* Object groups.
SSL. *See* Secure Socket Layer.
Stack-based storage, 100
Standardized API, 15–16

Standardized IDL, 15
Standardized packets, 19–20
Standardized streams, 19–20
State preservation, 85, 143–144, 211
Stateful server, 318
States, synchronization, 438
Static systems, 27–28
Status code, 333
StockTickerInterpreter, 559
Streams. *See* Mobile stream;
    Standardized streams.
StringBallot, 178
StringTokenizer, 546, 551, 555
Stubs, 16, 26, 81–83, 85, 122, 156, 190
Subject, 482, 487
SubjectContainer, 482, 484, 485
Subspace, 178
Supplier, 376, 384
Surrogates, 530–531
Symantec. *See* Visual Cafe.
Synchronization, 309, 407, 411, 416.
    See also States.
  approaches, 438
Synchronous system, 314
System Properties, 337

T

Target, 391, 395, 396, 399
  class, 474
  interface, 392
  mobility, 394
TargetImpl, 391
Targetinvocation, 392
Task objects, 222, 223, 227, 230–232,
    242, 243, 245
Tasks, 225
  implementation, 231–241
  origin, 226–231
TCL, 344
TCP/IP, 19, 20, 25, 34, 343
  connection, 134
  library, 205
  protocol, 562
  settings, 205
TCP/IP network, 191
  connection, 49
TCP/IP socket, 52, 80, 81, 83, 85, 190,
    191, 193, 358, 544
  communication. *See* SSL-protected
      TCP/IP socket communication.
Tengah, 344

Text Editor, 247, 336, 346
TextCanvas, 266, 299
   object, 269, 283
TextCanvasMpAction, 264–266, 268, 272, 284, 293
textFrame member variable, 269
Threads, 59, 321, 329, 407–411, 414
   class, 62
   encapsulation, 410
   fixed-sized pools, 68
   object, 59
   thrashing, 411
toString, 224
Totally ordered message delivery, 311
Tower of Babel, 14
Transactions, 128–134
Transient variables, 44
Trial-and-error method, 363
TrivialTask, 231–233
Trust models, 327–328
type() operation, 196, 197

U

UDP, 544
UDP/IP, 19
UML, 367
UnaryFunction, 466, 467
UnaryPredicate, 466, 467, 477, 478
   interface, 469
   object, 475
UnicastRemoteObject, 197, 224
Unix, 124, 150, 179, 349
   choice. *See* DCOM.
Unix-based Web servers, 20
User interaction, 569
User interfaces, 34, 35, 37, 91, 94, 110, 163, 247, 293, 300, 301, 373, 455, 470, 475, 483, 485, 497, 517, 531
   code, 479, 507
   elements, 481, 482

V

VBX controls, 113
Vector, 261
Versioning, 195–196, 351–354, 543
View, 375, 377–380, 480–482, 484–485, 491, 500
ViewContainer, 483–485
VisiBroker, 101
Visigenic, 80

Visual Basic, 109, 119, 120, 127, 128, 349
Visual Cafe (Symantec), 207
Visual J++, 208
Visual J++ (Microsoft), 208
Vote application, 444
Vote mobile objects, 181
Vote object, 165, 166, 175, 177, 178, 313
VoteListeners, 175, 184
Voter object, 174, 175, 181
Voting. *See* Mobile objects.
Voyager, 33, 41, 56, 96, 115, 139–141, 313, 317, 358, 378, 384, 413, 419, 445, 557
   applications, 155
   goodies, 156–158
   processes, 179
   threading model, 155
   usage. *See* Mobile objects.
Voyager Spaces, 162, 420, 439–442, 444, 446, 545, 548, 549, 553, 556, 573, 575, 577
VoyagerClassLoader, 145, 146
VoyagerSecurityManager, 148, 150

W

Weak references, 153
Web browsers, 54, 55, 93, 192, 208–210, 291
Web browsing, 361
Web document, 93
Web pages, 10, 35, 134, 145, 222, 240, 349
Web server, 27, 50, 81, 85, 134, 149, 218
Web site, 70, 73, 74
Windows Registry, 112
Workflow environment, 359
Wrapper object, 87, 88
Write Once, Run Anywhere, 137
writeObject, 196

X

XA relational databases, 133
XA standard, 131, 132
XA-compliant systems, 131, 132

Z

ZIP archive, 95

Inprise Corporation
TRIAL EDITION SOFTWARE

License Statement

YOUR USE OF THE TRIAL EDITION SOFTWARE DISTRIBUTED WITH THIS LICENSE IS SUBJECT TO ALL OF THE TERMS AND CONDITIONS OF THIS LICENSE STATEMENT. IF YOU DO NOT AGREE TO ALL OF THE TERMS AND CONDITIONS OF THIS STATEMENT, DO NOT USE THE SOFTWARE

1. This software is protected by copyright law and international copyright treaty. Therefore, you must treat this Software just like a book, except that you may copy it onto a computer to be used and you may make archive copies of the Software for the sole purpose of backing up out Software and protecting you investment from loss. Your use of this software is limited to evaluation and trial use purposes only.

   FURTHER, THIS SOFTWARE CONTAINS A TIME-OUT FEATURE THAT DISABLES ITS OPERATION AFTER A CERTAIN PERIOD OF TIME. A TEXT FILE DELIVERED WITH THE SOFTWARE WILL STATE THE TIME PERIOD AND/OR SPECIFIC DATE ("EVALUATION PERIOD") ON WHICH THE SOFTWARE WILL EXPIRE. Though Inprise does not offer technical support for the software, we welcome you feedback

   If the Software is an Inprise development tool, you can write and compile applications for your own personal use on the computer on which you have installed the Software, but you do not have a right to distribute or otherwise share those applications or any files of the Software which may be required to support those applications. APPLICATIONS THAT YOU CREATE MAY REQUIRE THE SOFTWARE IN ORDER TO RUN. UPON EXPIRATION OF THE EVALUATION PERIOD, THOSE APPLICATIONS WILL NO LONGER RUN. You should therefore take precautions to avoid any loss of data that might result.

2. INPRISE MAKES NO REPRESENTATIONS ABOUT THE SUITABILITY OF THIS SOFTWARE OR ABOUT ANY CONTENT OR INFORMATION MADE ACCESSIBLE BY THE SOFTWARE, FOR ANY PURPOSE. THE SOFTWARE IS PROVIDED 'AS IS' WITHOUT EXPRESS OR IMPLIED WARRANTIES, INCLUDING WARRANTIES OR MERCHANTABILITY AND FITNESS FOR A PARTICULAR PURPOSE OR NONINFRINGEMENT. THIS SOFTWARE IS PROVIDED GRATUITOUSLY AND, ACCORDINGLY, INPRISE SHALL NOT BE LIABLE UNDER ANY THEORY FOR ANY DAMAGES SUFFERED BY YOU OR ANY USER OF THE SOFTWARE. INPRISE WILL NOT SUPPORT THIS SOFTWARE AND IS UNDER NO OBLIGATION TO ISSUE UPDATES TO THIS SOFTWARE.

3. While Inprise intends to distribute (or may have already distributed) a commercial release of the Software, Inprise reserves the right at any time to not release a commercial release of the Software or, if released, to alter prices, features, specifications, capabilities, functions, licensing terms, release dates, general availability, or other characteristics of the commercial release.

4. Title, ownership rights, and intellectual property rights in and to the Software shall remain in Inprise and/or its suppliers. You agree to abide by the copyright law and all

other applicable laws of the United States, including, but not limited to, export control laws. You acknowledge that the Software in source code form remains a confidential trade secret or Inprise and/or its suppliers and therefore you agree not to modify the Software or attempt to decipher, decompile, disassemble or reverse engineer the Software, except to the extent applicable laws specifically prohibit such restriction.

5. Upon expiration of the Evaluation Period, you agree to destroy or erase the Software, and to not re-install a new copy of the Software. This statement shall be governed by and construed in accordance with the laws of the State of California and, as to matters affecting copyrights, trademarks and patents, by U.S. federal law. This statement sets forth the entire agreement between you and Inprise.

6. Use, duplication or disclosure by the Government is subject to restrictions set forth in subparagraphs (a) through (d) of the Commercial Computer-Restricted Rights clause at FAR 52.227-19 when applicable, or in subparagraph (c)(1)(ii) or the Rights in Technical Data and Computer Software clause at DFARS 252.227-7013, and in similar clauses in the NASA AR Supplement. Contractor/manufacturer is Inprise Corporation, 100 Enterprise Way, Scotts Valley, CA 95066.

7. You may not download or otherwise export or reexport the Software or any underlying information or technology except in full compliance with all United States and other applicable laws and regulations. In particular, but without limitation, none of the Software or underlying information or technology may be downloaded or otherwise exported or reexported (i) into (or to a national or resident of) Cuba, Haiti, Iraq, Libya, Yugoslavia, North Korea, Iran, or Syria or (ii) to anyone on the US Treasury Department's list of Specially Designated Nationals or the US Commerce Department's Table of Deny Orders. By downloading the Software, you are agreeing to the foregoing and you are representing and warranting that you are not located in, under control of, or a national or resident of any such country or on any such list.

8. INPRISE OR ITS SUPPLIERS SHALL NOT BE LIABLE FOR (a) INCIDENTAL, CONSEQUENTIAL, SPECIAL OR INDIRECT DAMAGES OF ANY SORT, WHETHER ARISING IN TORT, CONTRACT OR OTHERWISE, EVEN IF INPRISE HAS BEEN INFORMED OF THE POSSIBILITY OF SUCH DAMAGES, OR (b) FOR ANY CLAIM BY ANY OTHER PARTY. THIS LIMITATION OF LIABILITY SHALL NOT APPLY TO LIABILITY FOR DEATH OR PERSONAL INJURY TO THE EXTENT APPLICABLE LAW PROHIBITS SUCH LIMITATION OR INCIDENTAL OR CONSEQUENTIAL DAMAGES, SO THIS LIMITATION AND EXCLUSION MAY NOT APPLY TO YOU.

9. HIGH RISK ACTIVITIES. The Software is not fault-tolerant and is not designed, manufactured or intended for use or resale as on-line control equipment in hazardous environments requiring fail-safe performance, such as in the operation of nuclear facilities, aircraft navigation or communication systems, air traffic control, direct life support machines, or weapons systems, in which the failure of the Software could lead directly to death, personal injury, or severe physical or environmental damage ("High Risk Activities"). Inprise and its suppliers specifically disclaim any express or implied warranty of fitness for High Risk Activities.

Java™ Development Kit Version 1.1.7 and BDK Version 1.2 Combined Binary Code License

This binary code license ("License") contains rights and restrictions associated with use of the accompanying software and documentation ("Software"). Read the License carefully before installing the Software. By installing the Software you agree to the terms and conditions of this License.

1. **Limited License Grant.** Sun grants to you ("Licensee") a non-exclusive, non-transferable limited license to use the Software without fee for evaluation of the Software and for development of Java™ compatible applets and applications. Licensee may make one archival copy of the Software. Except for the foregoing, Licensee may not re-distribute the Software in whole or in part, either separately or included with a product. Refer to the Java Runtime Environment Version 1.1 binary code license(http://java.sun.com/products/JDK/1.1/index.html) for the availability of runtime code which may be distributed with Java compatible applets and applications.

2. **Redistribution of Demonstration Files.** Sung grants Licensee the right to use, modify and redistribute the Beans example and demonstration code, including the Bean Box("Demos"), in both source and binary code form provided that (i) Licensee does not utilize the Demos in a manner which is disparaging to Sun; and (ii) Licensee indemnifies and holds Sun harmless from all claims relating to any such use or distribution of the Demos. Such distribution is limited to the source and binary code of the Demos and specifically excludes any rights to modify or distribute any graphical images contained in the Demos.

3. **Java Platform Interface.** Licensee may not modify the Java Platform Interface("JPI", identified as classes contained within the "java" package or any subpackages of the "java" package), by creating additional classes within the JPI or otherwise causing the addition to or modification of the classes in the JPI. In the event that Licensee creates any Java-related API and distributes such API to others for applet or application development, Licensee must promptly publish an accurate specification for such API for free use by all developers of Java-based software.

4. **Restrictions.** Software is confidential copyrighted information of Sun and title to all copies is retained by Sun and/or its licensors. Licensee shall not modify, decompile, disassemble, decrypt, extract, or otherwise reverse engineer Software. Software may not be leased, assigned, or sublicensed, in whole or in part. Software is not designed or intended for use in on-line control of aircraft, air traffic, aircraft navigation or aircraft communications; or in the design, construction, operation or maintenance of any nuclear facility. Licensee warrants that it will not use or redistribute the Software for such purposes.

5. **Trademarks and Logos.** This License does not authorize Licensee to use any Sun name, trademark or logo. Licensee acknowledges that Sun owns the Java trademarks and all Java-related trademarks, logos and icons including the Coffee Cup and Duke ("Java Marks") and agrees to: (i)comply with the Java Trademark Guidelines at http://www.java.sun.com/trademarks.html; (ii) not do anything harmful to or inconsistent

with Sun's rights in the Java Marks; and (iii) assist Sun in protecting those rights, including assigning to Sun any rights acquired by Licensee in any Java Mark.

6. Disclaimer of Warranty. Software is provided "AS IS," without a warranty of any kind. ALL EXPRESS OR IMPLIED REPRESENTATIONS AND WARRANTIES, INCLUDING ANY IMPLIED WARRANTY OF MERCHANTABILITY, FITNESS FOR A PARTICULAR PURPOSE OR NON-INFRINGEMENT, ARE HEREBY EXCLUDED.

7. Limitation of Liability. SUN AND ITS LICENSORS SHALL NOT BE LIABLE FOR ANY DAMAGES SUFFERED BY LICENSEE OR ANY OR ANY THIRD PARTY AS A RESULT OF USING OR DISTRIBUTING SOFTWARE. IN NO EVENT WILL SUN OR ITS LICENSORS BE LIABLE FOR ANY LOST REVENUE, PROFIT OR DATA, OR FOR DIRECT, INDIRECT SPECIAL, CONSEQUENTIAL, INCIDENTAL OR PUNITIVE DAMAGES, HOWEVER CAUSED AND REGARDLESS OF THE THEORY OF LIABILITY, ARISING OUT OF THE USE OR INABILITY TO USE SOFTWARE, EVEN IF SUN HAS BEEN ADVISED OF THE POSSIBILITY OF SUCH DAMAGES.

8. Termination. Licensee may terminate this License at any time by destroying all copies of Software. This license will terminate immediately without notice from Sun if Licensee fails to comply with any provision of this License. Upon such termination, Licensee must destroy all copies of Software.

9. Export Regulations. Software, including technical data, is subject to U.S. export control laws, including the U.S. Export Administration Act and its associated regulations, and may be subject to export or import regulations in other countries. Licensee agrees to comply strictly with all such regulations and acknowledges that is has the responsibility to obtain licenses to export, re-export, or import Software. Software may not be downloaded, or otherwise exported or re-exported (i) into, or to a national or resident of Cuba, Iraq, Iran, North Korea, Libya, Sudan, Syria or any country to which the U.S. has embargoed goods; or (ii) to anyone on the U.S. Treasury Department's list of Specially Designated Nations or the U.S. Commerce Department's Table of Denial Orders.

10. Restricted Rights. Use, duplication or disclosure by the United States government is subject to the restrictions as set forth in the Rights in Technical Data and Computer Software Clauses in DFARS 252.227-7013(c) (1) (ii)and FAR 52.227-19(c) (2) as applicable.

11. Governing Law. Any action related to this License will be governed by California law and controlling U.S. federal law. No choice of law rules of any jurisdiction will apply.

12. Severability. If any of the above provisions are held to be in violation of applicable law, void, or unenforceable in any jurisdiction, then such provisions are herewith waived to the extent necessary for the License to be otherwise enforceable in such jurisdiction. However, if in Sun's opinion deletion of any provisions of the License by operation of this paragraph unreasonable compromises the rights or increases the liabilities of Sun or its licensors, Sun reserves the right to terminate the License and refund the fee paid by Licensee, if any, as Licensee's sole and exclusive remedy.

ObjectSpace Voyager™; Core Technology Version 2.0.0 License Agreement

ObjectSpace Voyager™ Core Technology Version 2.0.0 End User License Agreement

WHEREAS, ObjectSpace, Inc. is the owner of valuable intellectual property rights relating to the ObjectSpace Voyager™ Version 2.0.0 Software ("Voyager™") and wishes to license Voyager™ subject to the terms and conditions set forth below; and WHEREAS, you ("Licensee") acknowledge that ObjectSpace, Inc. has the right to grant licenses to the intellectual property rights relating to Voyager™, and that you desire to obtain a license to use Voyager™ subject to the terms and conditions set forth below;

ObjectSpace, Inc. grants Licensee a non-exclusive, non-transferable, non-assignable, royalty-free license to use Voyager™ and related materials without charge provided the Licensee adheres to all of the terms and conditions of this Agreement.

By downloading, using, or copying Voyager™ or any portion thereof, Licensee agrees to abide by the intellectual property laws and all other applicable laws of the United States of America, and to all of the terms and conditions of this Agreement, and agrees to take all necessary steps to ensure that the terms and conditions of this Agreement are not violated by any person or entity under the Licensee's control or in the Licensee's service.

Licensee shall maintain the copyright and trademark notices on the materials within or otherwise related to Voyager™, and not alter, erase, deface or overprint any such notice. Except as specifically provided in this Agreement, Licensee is expressly prohibited from copying, modifying, merging, selling, leasing, assigning, reverse engineering, or transferring in any manner, Voyager™ or any portion thereof.

Licensee may copy materials within or otherwise related to Voyager™ that bear the ObjectSpace copyright only as required for backup purposes or for use solely by the Licensee.

Licensee may not distribute in any form of electronic or printed communication the materials within or otherwise related to Voyager™ that bear the ObjectSpace copyright, including but not limited to the source code, documentation, help files, examples, and benchmarks, without prior written consent from ObjectSpace, Inc. Licensee may not distribute to any third party in any form the results of benchmark or other performance tests run on Voyager™ without the prior written consent of ObjectSpace.

Licensee may use Voyager™ internally for any purposes and in any systems provided that any distribution, sale or license of systems including Voyager™ or developed using Voyager™ to third parties are restricted as stated in this agreement. Licensee may develop and distribute to third parties applications using Voyager™ that execute on general purpose computing platforms except as restricted below. Specifically, Licensee may distribute binaries (.class files) derived from or contained within Voyager™ ("Binaries") provided that:

The Binaries are not distributed as part of any competing class library.

The Binaries are not distributed as part of or publicly associated with in any manner any software technology generally considered any of the following: object request brokers, databases, compilers, development environments, or other middleware products.

The Binaries are not packaged with, or embedded in, hardware.

The Binaries are not documented in any material distributed by Licensee.

The Binaries are not packaged with, embedded in, distributed as part of, or publicly associated with any software that is marketed or sold.

OBJECTSPACE, INC. DISCLAIMS AND MAKES NO REPRESENTATIONS OR WARRANTIES ABOUT THE SUITABILITY OF VOYAGER™, EITHER EXPRESSED OR IMPLIED, INCLUDING BUT NOT LIMITED TO THE IMPLIED WARRANTIES OF MERCHANTABILITY, FITNESS FOR A PARTICULAR PURPOSE, OR NON-INFRINGEMENT. OBJECTSPACE, INC. SHALL NOT BE LIABLE FOR ANY DIRECT OR CONSEQUENTIAL DAMAGES SUFFERED BY LICENSEE AS A RESULT OF USING, MODIFYING, OR DISTRIBUTING VOYAGER™ OR ITS DERIVATIVES.

This agreement shall be construed and enforced in accordance with the laws of the United States of America and the State of Texas (excluding its choice of law rules).

To redeem this offer, mail this original coupon (no photocopies, please) along with payment and shipping information to:

Inprise Corporation
Order Processing
P.O. Box 660005
Scotts Valley, CA 95067-0005

Or call 1-800-932-9994, offer code 1583.

Name _____

Address _____

City _____

State/Province _____ Zip/Postal Code _____

Phone (_____) _____ Fax (_____) _____

Select one:

❏ JBuilder 2 Standard for Windows 95 & Windows NT		CD-ROM	$99.95
❏ JBuilder 2 Professional for Windows 95 & Windows NT (Reg. $799)		CD-ROM	$249.95
❏ JBuilder 2 Client/Server Suite for Windows 95 & Windows NT (Reg. $2,499)		CD-ROM	$1,999.00

Subtotal $ _____

State sales tax* $ _____

Method of payment:

❏ Check enclosed (Make checks payable to Inprise Corporation)

Freight ($10.00 per item) $ _____

❏ VISA ❏ MasterCard ❏ American Express

Total order $ _____

Card number: __ __ __ __ - __ __ __ __ - __ __ __ __ - __ __ __ __

Expiration date: __ __ / __ __

Offer Code 1583

Offer expires November 30, 1999.

This offer good in the U.S.A. and Canada only. International customers, please contact your local Inprise office for the offer in your country. Corporate Headquarters: 100 Enterprise Way, Scotts Valley, California 95066-3249; 831-431-1000. **Internet: http://www.inprise.com** Offices in Australia (61-2-9248-0900), Canada (905-477-4344), Chile (56-2-233-7113), France (33-1-55-23-55-00), Germany (49-6103-9790), Hong Kong (852-2572-3238), Japan (81-3-5350-9380), Latin American Headquarters in U.S.A. (831-431-1126), Mexico (525-543-1413), The Netherlands (+31 [0] 20-503-5100), Taiwan (886-2-718-6627), and United Kingdom ([0800] 454065)

INPRISE™
Integrating the Enterprise